From Tiny To to Toddler 2009

Practical guide for parents from pregnancy to age two

Nicole Doré and **Danielle Le Hénaff**
Authors of the original text

Update
Chantale Audet
Amélie Bourret
Nicole April

Communication and Distribution
Pascale Turcotte

Technical and Administrative Support
Igor Baluczynski

Direction
Johanne Laverdure
Réal Morin

Institut national de santé publique
Québec

First edition: 1988. Revised, expanded editions:
1995, 2003 and 2008.

How to refer this book:
Doré, Nicole; Le Hénaff, Danielle.
From Tiny Tot to Toddler, Practical guide for parents from pregnancy to age two.
Québec, Institut national de santé publique du Québec, 2009. 656 pages.

Legal Deposit 1st quarter 2009
Bibliothèque et archives nationales du Québec
Library and archives Canada

ISSN: 1711-411X (printed version)
ISSN: 1911-6004 (pdf version)
ISBN: 978-2-550-54524-8 (printed version)
ISBN: 978-2-550-54525-5 (pdf version)

2009 Edition

Authors of the original text
Nicole Doré, Danielle Le Hénaff

Writers
Christiane Auray-Blais, Lucie Baribeau, Claude Bégin, Céline Belhumeur, France Bilodeau, Julie Boissoneault, Marie-Andrée Bossé, Nicole Boulianne, Lise Brassard, Marie-Ève Caty, Brigitte Chaput, Isabelle Charbonneau, Aurore Coté, Dominique Cousineau, Rosanne Couture, Marie-Paule Duquette, Luc Ferland, Cécile Fortin, Suzanne Goyette, Édith Guilbert, Julie Guimond, Ginette Lamarre, Richard Larocque, André Lavallière, Johanne Laverdure, Michel Lavoie, Céline Lemay, Linda Lemire, Brigitte Lépine, Suzanne Lépine, Anne Letarte, Patrick Levallois, Chantal Lévesque, Marie-Joëlle Lévesque, Michel Lévy, Sylviane Manseau, Jean-Claude Mercier, Langis Michaud, Christina Morin, Julie Poissant, Marie-Claude Quintal, Marie-Josée Santerre, Diane Sergerie, Isabel Thibault, Lucie Thibodeau, Josée Trahan, Roch Tremblay, Jean-Jacques Turcotte, Mylène Turcotte, Pascale Turcotte, Hélène Valentini, Ginette Veilleux.

Secretarial work
Chantal Forest, Ludmila Moulaoui

Revision of the French version and proofreading of the English version
Services d'édition Guy Connolly

Translation
Stevenson & Writers Inc.

Graphic design and computer graphics
Luz design+communications

Illustrations
Maurice Gervais

Cover photos
Veer and iStockphoto.com

Printing
Transcontinental Impression

Publicity
Catherine Brochu

New sections on pregnancy and delivery

Writers

Nicole April, physician; Chantale Audet, anthropologist; Hélène Rousseau, family physician; Céline Lemay, midwife; Linda Lemire, nurse; Julie Lauzière, nutritionist; Amélie Bourret, anthropologist; Pascale Turcotte, responsible for the development and distribution; François Beaudoin, obstetrician gynecologist; Amélie Blanchet-Garneau, nurse; Marie-Andrée Bossé, sex therapist; Catherine Chouinard, chargée de projet en périnatalité; Cécile Fortin, lactation consultant; Anne Harvey, physiatrist; Josée Laroche, agente de recherche; Johanne Laverdure, psychologist; Lyse Lefebvre, pharmacist; Michel Lévy, dentist; Jean-Claude Mercier, pediatrician; Marie-Josée Santerre, lactation consultant.

Writing coordination team

Nicole April, Chantale Audet, Hélène Rousseau, Céline Lemay, Linda Lemire, Julie Lauzière, Amélie Bourret, Pascale Turcotte.

Scientific committee

Manon Allard, Ordre des infirmières et infirmiers du Québec, Marc Billard, Collège des médecins du Québec, Lise Brassard, Info-santé, Catherine Chouinard, Association pour la santé publique du Québec, Pierre Desjardins, Ordre des psychologues du Québec, Emmanuelle Hébert, Ordre des sages-femmes du Québec, Caroline Morin, Ordre des pharmaciens du Québec, Mélanie Savard-Côté, Association des omnipraticiens en périnatalité du Québec, Louise Sirard, Ordre professionnel des diététistes du Québec, François Beaudoin and Julie Guimond, Association des obstétriciens et gynécologues du Québec, Marc Simard and Isabelle Théberge, Parents, Jeannine Auger and France Laverdière, ministère de la Santé et des Services sociaux, Violaine Bélanger, Diane Blain-Lamoureux, Julie Brousseau and Julie Goulet, Fondation Lucie et André Chagnon

Individuals and groups consulted

Marjorie Aunos, CRDI Lisette-Dupras; Lise Benoît-Gosselin, CSSS Haute-Yamaska; Danielle Boulard, Direction de santé publique de la Capitale Nationale; Emmanuel Bujold, Centre de recherche du CHUL; Christiane Charest, CH Brome-Missisquoi; Isabelle Clerc, Université Laval; Cécile Cloutier, Efficom; Maria De Koninck, Université Laval; Catherine Denis, SOS Grossesse; Martin Duclos, CLSC Lamater; Éric Dewailly, Centre de recherche CHUL; Réjean Dion, INSPQ; Sylvie Dodin, Université Laval; Adrienne Einarson, Motherisk; Jeff Farber, Santé Canada; Lorraine Fontaine, Regroupement Naissance-Renaissance; Stéphane Fortier, CLSC Basse-Ville; Annie Gunner, CH Pierre-Legardeur; Bouchra Kaache, Centre International des Femmes de Québec; France Lebrun, CH St-Eustache; Isabelle Marc, Université Laval; Andrée-Anne Morin, CH Saint-François d'Assises; Denis Ouellet, Ministère de la Santé et des Services sociaux; Renée Proulx, CRDI Lisette-Dupras; Hélène Senay, Centre hospitalier de l'Université Laval; Johanne Tessier, Collectif Les Accompagnantes; Alice Tofan, Alliance des communautés culturelles pour l'égalité dans la santé et les services sociaux; Hélène Vadeboncoeur, researcher.

Comité national d'orientation et de mobilisation en périnatalité de l'ASPQ; Regroupement des diététistes en périnatalité de la Capitale nationale; First Nations of Quebec and Labrador Health and Social Services Commission; Groupe de travail sur l'implantation d'un programme québécois de dépistage prénatal du syndrome de Down; Comité des pères de Cible Famille Brandon; Montreal Diet Dispensary.

Plain language and revision of the French version

Danielle Bergeron

Journalist advisors

Christian Benoit-Lapointe, Andrée-Anne Guénette

Fondation Lucie et André Chagnon

The new sections on pregnancy and delivery were made possible by the financial support of the Fondation Lucie et André Chagnon.

Acknowledgements

For more than 30 years now, many professionals have added their expertise and support to each issue of this guide. Our special thanks go to everyone involved in updating the 2009 edition. If your name was omitted during the challenging task of listing all our contributors, please accept our double thanks.

Establishments in the health and social services network and organizations

ACEF de l'Est de Montréal, Association pour la santé publique du Québec, Centre antipoison, Centre de médecine génétique du Québec, Comité québécois en allaitement, CSSS du Lac-des-deux-Montagnes, Direction de santé publique de Québec, de Lanaudière, de la Montérégie et de Montréal, Dispensaire diététique de Montréal, Hôpital Sainte-Justine, Les Publications du Québec, Centre de santé et de services sociaux de la Vieille-Capitale: Équipe de rédaction des protocoles infirmiers Info-Santé, Société de l'assurance automobile du Québec, Réseau des centres de ressources périnatales du Québec.

Individuals

Denis G. Allard, Suzanne Atkinson, Colette Beauregard, Daniel Beauregard, Éric Bédard, Claude Bégin, Sadja Bekal, Martine Bienvenue, Linda Blais, Sarah Blunden, Madeleine Boudreau, Isabelle Brabant, Selma Buckett, Jérôme Comeau, Lise Comtois, Louise Condrain, François Côté, Suzanne Dionne, Louise Dumas, Nathalie Faucher, Suzanne Forgues, David Fortier, Colette Gaulin, Denis Gauvin, Sophie Gravel, Louise Guyon, Jennifer Houston, Gloria Jeliu, Véronique Laberge-Gaudin, Gideon Koren, Danielle Landry, Monique Landry, Mélanie Lavoie, Michel Lavoie, France Lebrun, Éric Leclerc, Stéphanie Ledoux, Marie-Hélène Legault, Luc Legris, Maire-Claire Lepage, Nathalie Lévesque, Pierre Lévesque, Diane Major, Micheline Maltais, Jocelyne Martel, Louise Mathers, Yves Michaud, Morton Miller, Sylvie Muller, Josée Nadeau, Isabelle Pageot, France Paradis, Ginette Paquet, Véronique Pelchat, Marie-Claude Pigeon, Lise Primeau, Caroline Quach, Marie-Claude Quintal, Danielle Ramsay, Sylvie Renaud, France Richard, Elizabeth Robinson, Daniel Roy, Guy Sanfaçon, Monique Séguin, Paule Simard, Monik St-Pierre, Lucie St-Onge, Chantal Théberge, Lucie Tremblay, Michèle Tremblay, Roch Tremblay, Julie Trudel as well as many volunteers working win breast-feeding support groups.

Photographers

A sincere thank you to all photographers-parents, professionals and amateurs who allowed us to illustrate this 2009 edition. It's a great contribution.

We would also like to thank all those whose comments and questions have helped make this a better guide over the years. Your contributions are invaluable to our annual updates to the guide's contents.

Many thanks also to the parents who use this guide and return the feedback survey to us (questionnaire at the end of the booklet).

The 2009 edition of *From Tiny Tot to Toddler, Practical guide for parents from pregnancy to age two* and *Mieux vivre avec notre enfant de la grossesse à deux ans* are offered free of charge to the following people to support Québec parents:

- Prenatal workers at CLSCs
- Physicians and midwives providing health care to pregnant women and newborns
- Health care workers in community organizations serving young families
- Lactation consultants and volunteers supporting new mothers through breast-feeding support groups

Foreword

The Institut national de santé publique du Québec is proud to present the 2009 edition of *From Tiny Tot to Toddler*, which, for the second year, focuses on the period from pregnancy until the child reaches the age of two. The new sections on pregnancy and delivery have been received with a great deal of enthusiasm by mothers, fathers, and health professionals who use this guide regularly in dealing with pregnant women. The guide is still distributed free of charge to future parents. It is now given out to pregnant women during pregnancy checkups. Making sure that all pregnant women and adoptive parents receive the guide is a colossal challenge. With support from health institutions, doctors, nurses, midwives and public health regional managers, we are making every effort to ensure that the people for whom this guide is intended get a personal copy.

The 2009 edition, like its predecessors, is the product of the cooperation of many experts in the fields of pregnancy, delivery, child development, nutrition, prevention, child care and parental support. This update focuses on a few issues that have been in the news over the past year, in particular, ensuring that your baby sleeps safely, prevention of food borne infections such as listeriosis, and the safe use of baby carriers. The guide now includes the Government of Québec publication *Becoming a parent*, which is an important source of practical information for future parents.

In order to continue the practice of providing a guide that is scientifically rigorous and easy to use, we are calling on you as users of *From Tiny Tot to Toddler* to provide your comments and suggestions for future editions. A short questionnaire is printed on page 654; we encourage you to complete it and return it to the address indicated.

Happy reading!

Luc Boileau, MD
President and Chief Executive Officer

From Tiny Tot to Toddler 2009

Pregnancy

Delivery

Family

Being a father

Being a mother

Growing as a family

Your baby

Talking with your baby

© sonia jam.com

© sonia jam.com

© sonia jam.com

Pregnancy

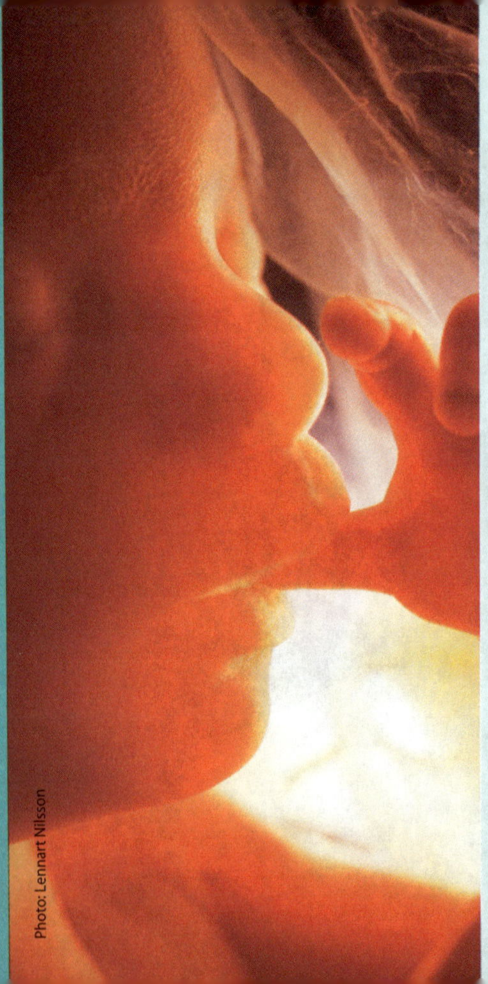

Photo: Lennart Nilsson

The fetus

Fertilization

Most women take a pregnancy test when they notice that their period is late. If your test is positive, the **embryo** is already growing, because **fertilization** took place around the 14th day of your cycle based on a 28-day **menstrual cycle**. Three weeks after the first day of your last menstrual period, which is also 7 days after fertilization, the fertilized egg is already beginning to implant in the uterus.

▶ **Embryo:** The early stage of new human life, growing in the mother's belly, up to 10 complete weeks of pregnancy.
▶ **Fertilization:** Penetration of the male sperm cell into the female egg cell (ovum), which together creates the first human embryo cell.
▶ **Menstrual cycle:** The time between two menstrual periods, lasting an average of 28 days but which can be longer or shorter.

Length of pregnancy

As soon as you learn that you're pregnant, you'll want to know how many weeks along you are and when you can expect to give birth. The length of pregnancy and the expected delivery date are calculated based on the first day of your last period, because the exact moment of fertilization is not known. This means that the number of weeks of pregnancy also includes the first two weeks after your last period, even if you weren't pregnant at that time. For example, "20 weeks pregnant" means 20 complete weeks have occurred since the first day of your last menstrual period.

When will the big day be? A full-term pregnancy is between 37 and 42 weeks and it is assumed that the baby will be born at 40 weeks. But in truth, he'll be born when he's ready! The expected delivery date is therefore an approximate date. To calculate it, we count 40 complete weeks beginning from the first day of your last period, assuming that you have a regular 28-day cycle. If you have an irregular cycle or you don't know the date of your last period, an **ultrasound** performed before you are 20 weeks pregnant will give a good idea of the expected delivery date, accurate to within a 7- to 10-day range.

Health professionals usually talk about your pregnancy in terms of the number of weeks you are pregnant. The reason for this is simple: it is more accurate to speak in terms of weeks than in calendar months. The 42 weeks of pregnancy (maximum length) are also divided into three trimesters of 14 weeks each.

▶ **Ultrasound:** A medical examination using an ultrasound device that can see the embryo or fetus in the mother's belly.

Fetus's environment

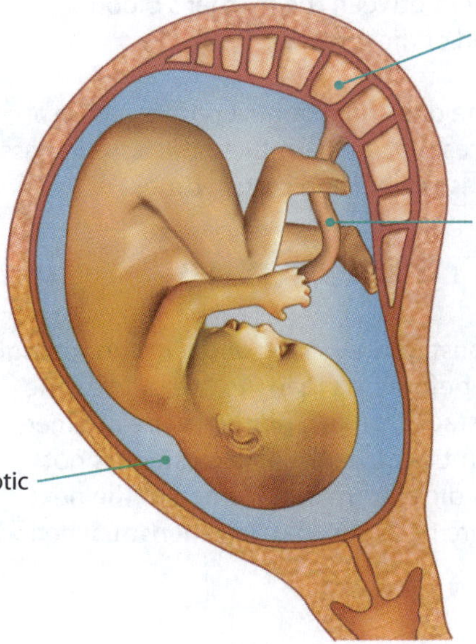

Illustration: Maurice Gervais

Amniotic fluid

The amniotic fluid surrounding your baby is needed for his growth and development. The amniotic fluid:

- Helps keep the baby at the right temperature;
- Protects the baby against shocks;
- Allows the baby to move and to develop his muscles and lungs.

This liquid is contained in a kind of pouch that surrounds the baby called the amniotic sac. The sac will break just before or during **labour**, causing amniotic fluid to run out (when your "water breaks").

▶ **Labour:** The process by which a baby passes from the uterus to the outside world, mainly through contractions of the uterus.

Umbilical cord

The umbilical cord connects the fetus to the placenta. The blood circulation between you and your fetus develops when you are 4 weeks pregnant. The umbilical cord brings your baby oxygen and the nutrients needed to grow. The waste produced by the **fetus** returns into your system through the umbilical cord and the placenta, and then is eliminated by your body.

Placenta

The placenta starts to grow as soon as the fertilized egg is implanted in the uterus. The placenta does the following:

- Feeds the baby;
- Brings the baby the oxygen he needs;
- Eliminates the baby's waste by disposing of it in the mother's blood;
- Secretes into the mother's blood the necessary hormones to maintain the pregnancy and help the fetus grow;
- Act as a barrier between the mother's blood and the blood of the fetus.

But the placenta does not filter everything. It can allow some substances that are harmful to the fetus to pass through, such as alcohol and certain drugs.

Growth of the fetus

Your baby is constantly evolving and must go through several stages before he's ready to live outside the uterus. These stages, or key moments, are outlined below. The number of weeks of each stage is not exact and may differ from one woman to the next. The numbers are based on your last menstrual period.

▶ **Fetus:** The early stage of a human being, growing in the mother's belly, from the start of the 11th week of pregnancy to birth.

First trimester: from fertilization to 14 weeks

The embryo's heart begins to beat 22 days after conception – when you are **5 weeks** pregnant – but the heartbeat cannot yet be heard during a medical exam. At 6 weeks, the embryo measures 5 mm.

When you are **7 weeks** pregnant, the embryo's head is much bigger than the rest of the body. Its arms begin to form with elbows and hands appearing. Fingers haven't yet separated from each other, but its eyes are quite visible.

Embryo at 40 days of gestation (7 weeks after the first day of the last menstrual period).

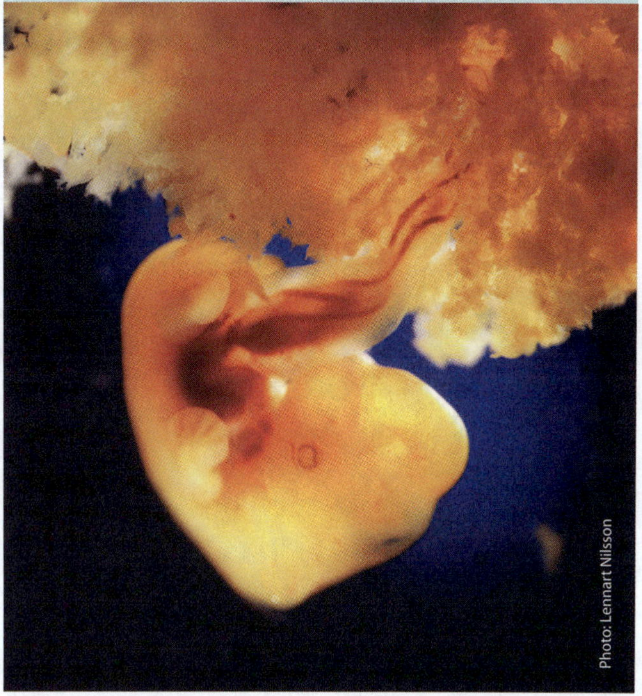

Photo: Lennart Nilsson

At **10 weeks**, the embryo already has a human appearance: its eyes, nose and mouth are recognizable. Its eyelids are closed. The fingers are now separated and toes begin to form. Your baby begins to move his limbs, but you won't feel it yet. **He goes from the embryonic stage to the fetal stage:** all his body parts are in place, but are not yet completely formed. They will continue to grow and develop throughout the pregnancy.

At the end of the 1st trimester, **between 10 and 14 weeks**, the fetus grows and the skeletal bones begin to form. His waste goes into the mother's blood through the placenta.

The fetus at the end of the 1st trimester.

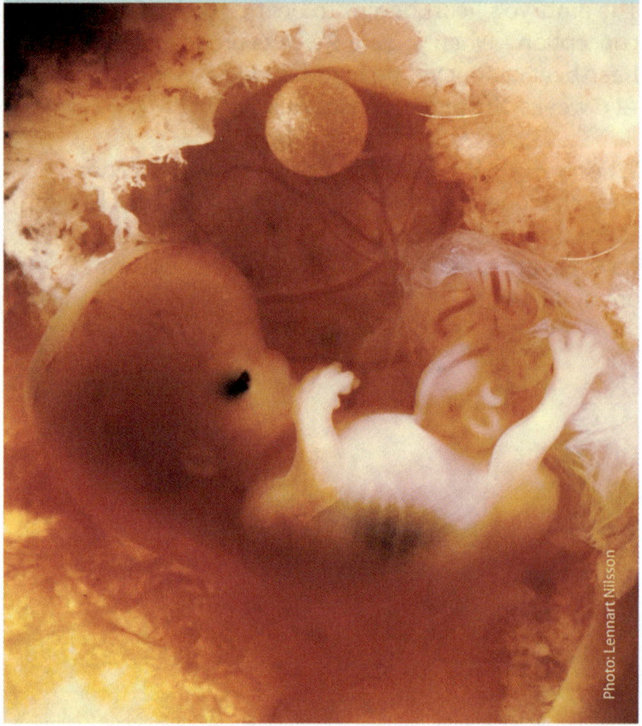

Second trimester: 15 to 28 weeks

Boy or girl? At **14 weeks**, your baby's genitals are developed enough to know whether it will be a boy or girl, but they aren't completely formed yet. Your baby's ultrasound will normally reveal the big secret between l6 and 18 weeks. At 16 weeks, his head will still be disproportionately large compared to the rest of his body, but his trunk, arms and legs begin to lengthen.

The fetus at the beginning of the 2nd trimester.

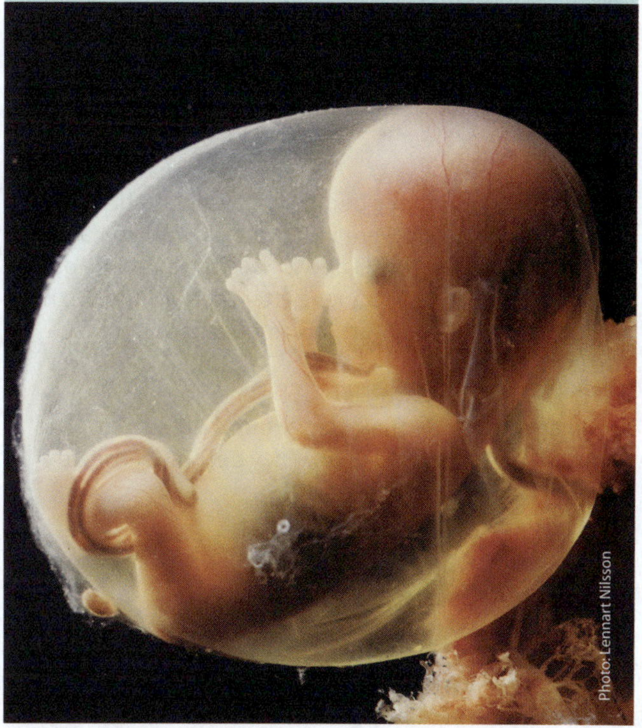

Around 20 weeks, your uterus will have reached the level of your belly button. Your baby's movements are more distinct and strong enough that you can feel them. Some women will feel these movements either a little earlier or a little later in their pregnancy. The vernix caseosa, which looks like a white cream, covers your baby's skin to protect it.

At 22 weeks, your baby begins to have eyelashes and hair and his body is covered with soft down-like hair called lanugo. Between 23 and 27 weeks, your baby gains weight and his head becomes better proportioned to his body. At 24 weeks, he hears low frequency sounds from outside the uterus.

At the end of the 2nd trimester, **around 28 weeks**, the baby's eyes begin to open. They become sensitive to light later on, around 32 weeks.

Fetus at the end of the 2nd trimester.

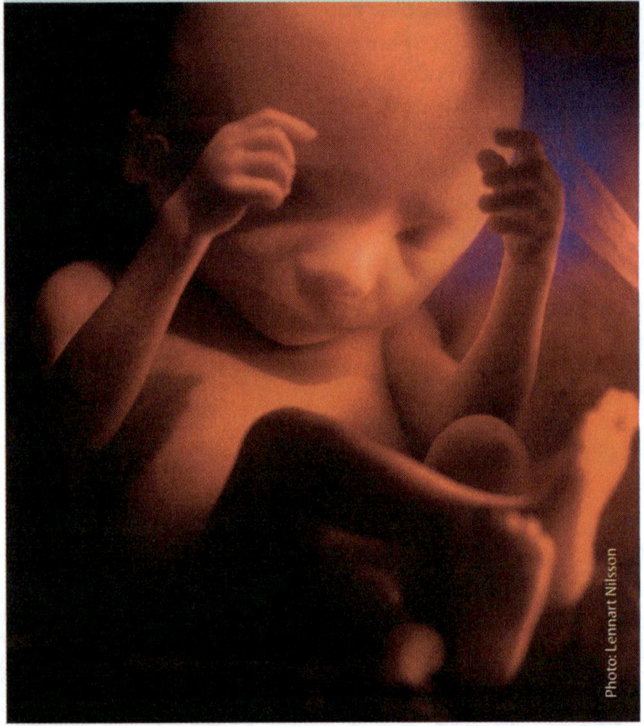

Photo: Lennart Nilsson

Third trimester: from 29 weeks to birth

At 32 weeks, the uterus reaches the level of your stomach, also called the epigastric fossa. Your intestines, liver and lungs are pushed upwards. As the pregnancy advances and the baby gains weight, the uterus expands towards the front, stretching the muscles and skin of your abdomen.

At 36 weeks, the baby's skin is dewy and the downy hair begins to disappear, although it can remain until after your baby is born. The baby is bigger because of the fat reserves he is building up. Between 38 and 41 weeks, his skin is soft and dewy, he has good muscle tone, and he can make sustained movements. He's ready for the big day!

Fetus at the end of the 3rd trimester.

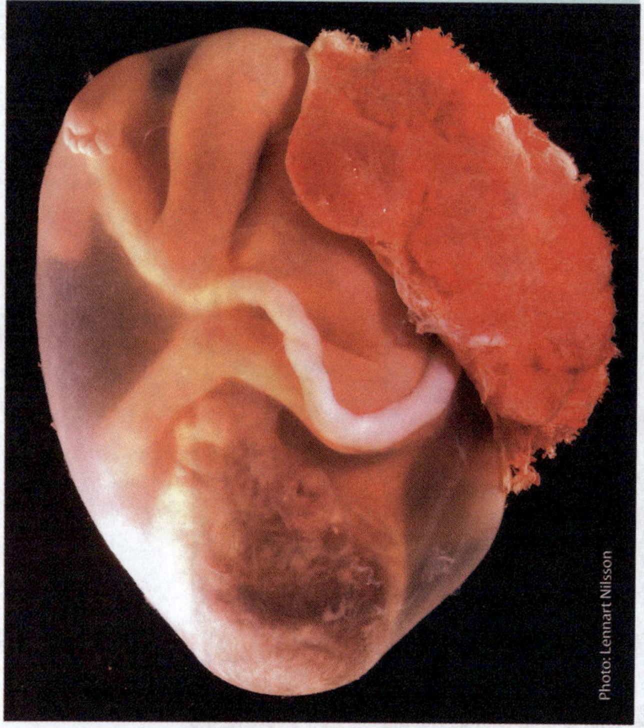

Photo: Lennart Nilsson

Pregnancy day to day

Physical changes

Your body goes through a lot of changes during pregnancy. Many of these changes take place without you even being aware of them, while others may be more difficult to deal with.

Heart

During pregnancy, your heart rate can increase by up to 10 beats a minute, and the volume of your blood increases from 40% to 45% to meet the needs of the fetus. Your heart is shifted a bit within your rib cage as your uterus expands.

Lungs

Many pregnant women are more aware of their breathing and may have difficulty doing so at the end of their pregnancy, even at rest.

Kidneys

You will probably have to urinate more frequently at night. During the day, your body tends to accumulate water in your tissues, but when you sleep these water reserves are sent to your kidneys and – once again! – you feel the need to urinate.

Bladder

At the beginning of pregnancy, the bladder is more sensitive and you may feel the need to urinate more urgently or more often. These sensations can reappear later in pregnancy when the uterus expands and the baby's head puts pressure on the bladder.

Breasts

Your breasts may become more sensitive and increase in size. The blue veins that crisscross the surface of your skin may become more visible. Your nipples and areolas (the part that surrounds the tips of your breasts) prepare for breast-feeding by growing slightly and may also become darker. Little raised bumps form on your areolas: they are glands that produce oil that will help keep your skin moisturized and protected during breast-feeding. Beginning at 16 weeks, the mammary glands start producing the first food your baby will have after he is born: colostrum. Some women leak colostrum during pregnancy.

Uterus

Before pregnancy, the uterus is the size of a small pear. As pregnancy advances, the uterus expands to meet the needs of the fetus. It changes shape and position in your abdomen.

Gait

The increasing weight of the uterus causes your posture to change and moves your centre of gravity further forward. That's why some pregnant women appear to waddle when they walk.

GROWTH OF THE FETUS IN THE MOTHER'S UTERUS

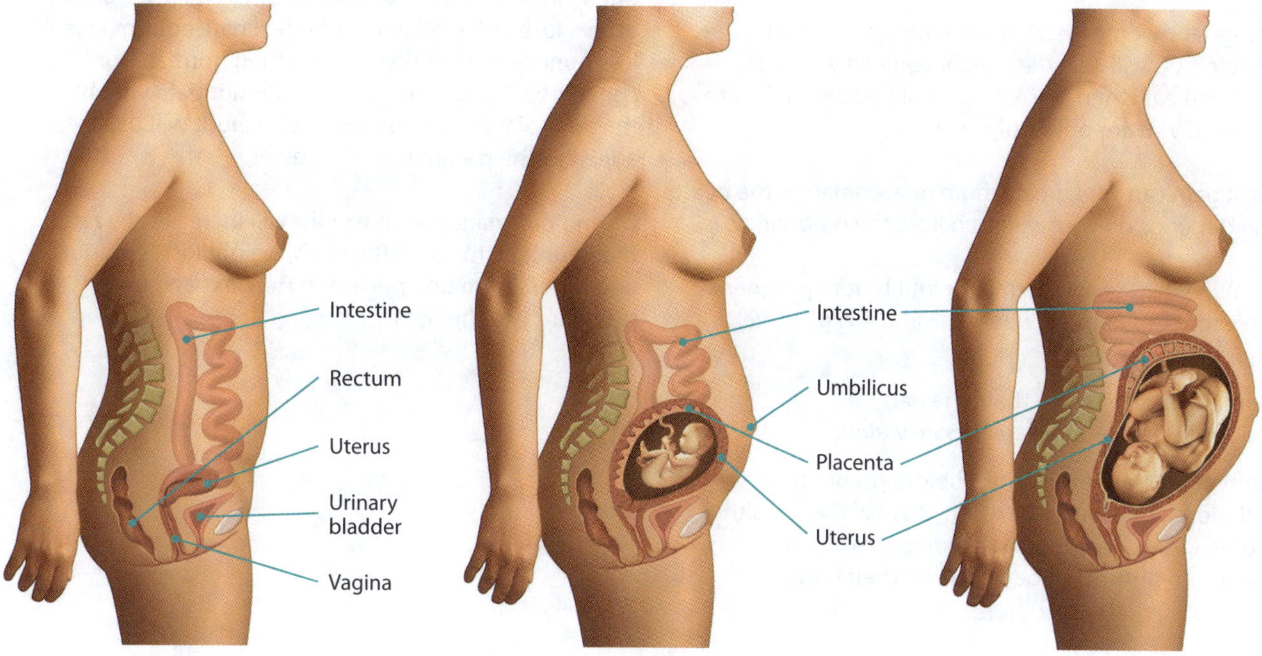

Before pregnancy

Around 20 weeks

Around 32 weeks

Illustrations: Maurice Gervais

Weight gain

All pregnant women gain weight; it's normal and desirable. You will gain the weight you and your baby need if you eat when you're hungry, if you have a healthy diet, and if you are physically active.

Weight gain can vary greatly from one woman to the next. It also depends on your weight before the pregnancy.

- Women who are at a normal weight before pregnancy can expect to gain between 11.5 and 16 kg, or 25 to 35 pounds.
- Women carrying more than one baby (e.g., twins, triplets) will gain more weight.
- Women who are overweight before pregnancy and those who are underweight can ask their health professional or a dietitian for advice to get the maximum nutritional benefit from their food.

At the beginning of pregnancy, weight gain varies from one woman to the next. Some women gain weight while others lose some. Women who feel nauseous may feel less hungry, or may be hungrier than normal. Don't be concerned if you gain weight or do not gain weight at the start of your pregnancy. Your weight will usually adjust as the pregnancy progresses.

During pregnancy, your weight will increase at a rate that is unique to you. After birth, weight loss is gradual and differs from one person to the next and one pregnancy to the next.

DISTRIBUTION OF WEIGHT GAIN DURING PREGNANCY, AT 40 WEEKS, FOR A WOMAN WHO GAINED 12.5 KG, AROUND 28 POUNDS (27½ POUNDS)

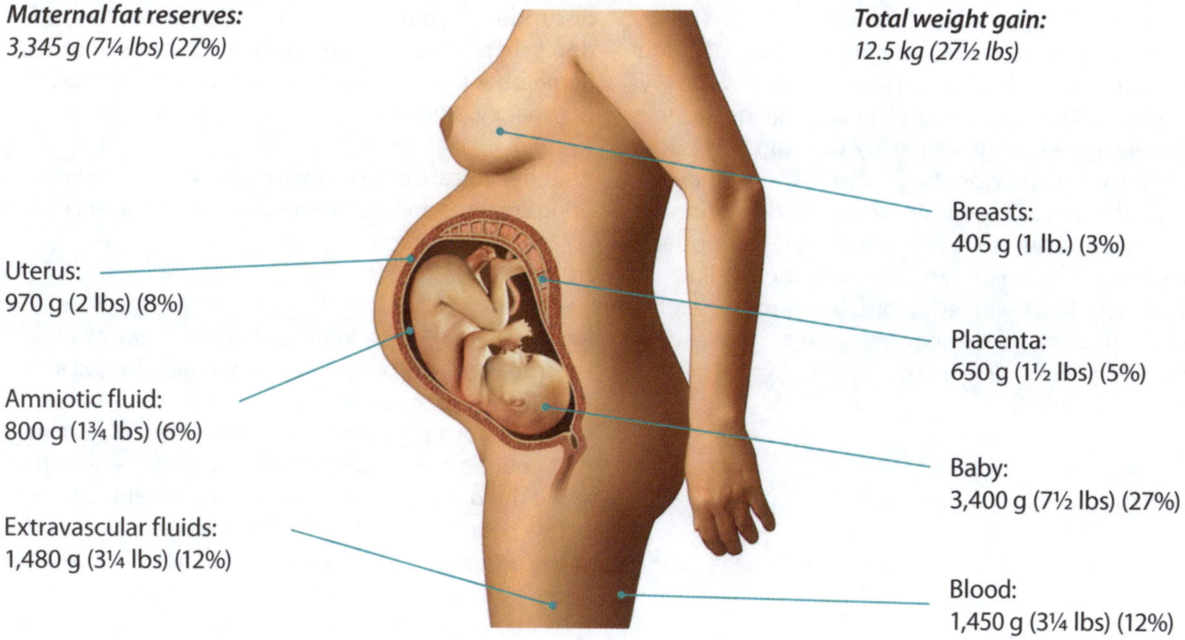

Illustration: Maurice Gervais

Emotional changes

For the mother

Many women experience what may seem to be conflicting emotions during pregnancy, even some women who very much desired a baby. The arrival of a baby changes your life and while these changes bring joy, they can also lead to many questions and worries. Or, you may find that your life goes along as normal with daily, hardly noticed adjustments to the demands of a new baby. It is important not to ignore your emotions and to accept them. Allow yourself to experience your emotions, try to understand them and, especially, share them with your partner and those close to you. You'll feel less alone and you'll get the support you need.

Talk to other pregnant women or those who were pregnant in the recent past. Sharing with them will help you see that you aren't alone in experiencing disruption in your life. You may also notice that you don't share the same emotions or concerns as others. Remember that every woman is different and that each pregnancy is unique.

Whether you are on your own or in a couple, pregnancy brings many emotional, psychological and social changes.

For the father

Since you aren't carrying the child, you may not feel the impact of the pregnancy on your life as quickly as your partner does. You may feel the reality of the coming baby only later on. The simple fact of knowing that your partner is pregnant is not always enough to make the pregnancy feel real to you. Listening to the baby's heartbeat, feeling the first movements or being at the ultrasound are events that can help you develop a sense of fatherhood. For some men, it's only when the baby is born that they become conscious of their new role as a father.

Men who are waiting for the birth of their child with their partner are also drawn into the whirlwind of changes. Some are concerned about their partner's reaction to their involvement with the child, and wonder if they will meet her expectations. Remember that pregnancy is a good time to begin your relationship with your baby. Even if the baby isn't born yet, this relationship starts in your head and heart, and will become more real if you talk to and touch your baby through his mother's belly and participate in prenatal sessions.

For the couple

Going from a two-person relationship to one that involves three people, or expanding an existing family, brings its share of changes and adjustments. This is also true for parents who plan to adopt a child.

You and your partner both have concerns but they won't necessarily be the same and may not come at the same time. You may wonder how your partner will react if you talk about your fears or share your questions. Regardless of what you're feeling, it's important to communicate because it will allow you to express your different emotions and to understand the other person's point of view. You should learn to accept your partner's differences and to respect his or her rhythm. Your relationship as a couple is important because it forms the basis of your family.

For the family

If you already have children, you may have the impression that you are neglecting the older ones because the discomfort of your pregnancy and fatigue prevent you from looking after them in the way you did before. You may feel guilty or ask yourself how you'll be able to love all your children and give each one the attention they deserve. These are normal reactions and the father may also share these concerns. Talk to him or to someone close to you.

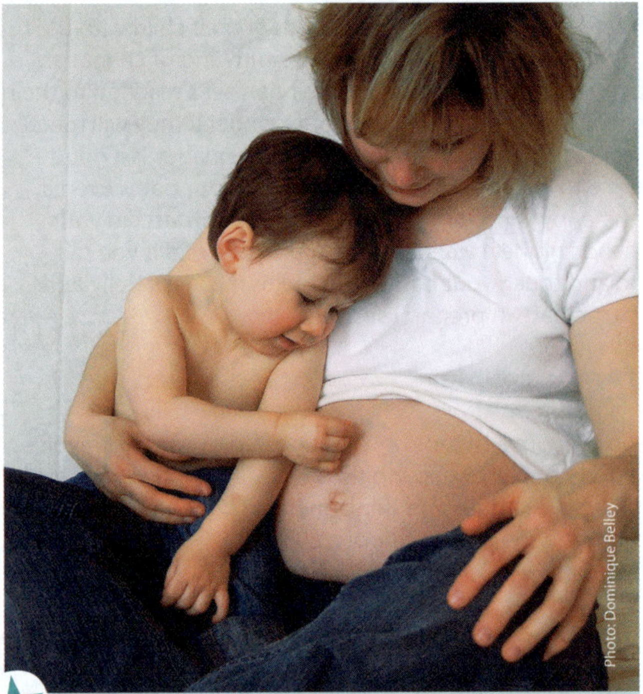
Photo: Dominique Belley

Have your children touch your belly when the baby's moving.

Your other children, regardless of age, may feel jealous at the idea of welcoming a new member into the family. They may be worried about where they will fit in during the pregnancy and after the birth of their brother or sister. Reassure them and help them accept the baby's arrival more easily by talking to them about it and having them make contact with the baby by touching your belly when the baby is moving. You can help them feel included by trying to involve them and get them to help; for example, in decorating the baby's room or drawing the baby a picture. It's a good idea to tell them that you'll always love them and to prove this by showing your affection. Your family and friends can also help by giving your children individual attention.

Sexuality

Pregnancy can have an impact on a couple's sexual life. Sexual desire and the frequency of sexual relations may increase, decrease or vary during the pregnancy. For example, the changes taking place to the woman's body and the new perception of yourself and your partner as parents and not lovers can create feelings that may increase or decrease sexual desire.

Various reasons, including a big belly, medical advice against it, discomfort, personal limitations or a desire for increased tenderness, may lead you to set aside certain sexual practices. But you may choose to try new ones. Pleasure, whether physical (the ability to have an orgasm or enjoy touch) or psychological (for example, increased feelings of closeness or womanliness), is sometimes experienced differently by each partner.

You may have some fears about sexual activities. You can make love without worrying: vaginal penetration and orgasm will not cause a **miscarriage** and will not lead to premature labour or hurt your baby. The baby is well protected in the amniotic sac and uterus.

In some situations you may be advised not to have sexual intercourse; for example, if you have bleeding, abdominal pain or problems with the placenta, or if there is concern about a premature labour or a rupture of the amniotic sac. Your health professional will tell you if this is the case.

If you have high-risk sex, you should use some form of protection, like a condom. During pregnancy, it is of utmost importance to protect yourself against sexually transmitted infections (STIs) to prevent the infection from being transmitted and to help avoid complications it may cause to a mother and her baby.

▶ **Miscarriage:** An involuntary end to the pregnancy, for a variety of possible reasons, such as deformity or disease.

★ Sexual intercourse can continue throughout pregnancy without any problem, as long as you respect each other's needs, discomforts and limits.

Personal care

Cosmetics and sunscreen

Most cosmetics (creams, makeup) can be used during pregnancy. Face cream and hand and body lotions that do not contain any medicinal ingredients can be used safely. If you use a medicated cream, your doctor or pharmacist can check to see if you can continue doing so while pregnant.

You should use sunscreen when you are exposed to the sun. This is especially important during pregnancy because the sun can increase hyperpigmentation (dark spots on the skin) and the **pregnancy mask**. Use a cream or lotion with an SPF (sun protection factor) of at least 30 and protects against both UVA and UVB rays. Be especially sure to protect your face.

Hair products

Hair products and treatments including dyes, colouring shampoos, highlights and perms are not dangerous to the pregnant woman or baby. However, if you use these products as part of your work (hairdresser), speak to your health professional.

Laser hair removal and electrolysis

There are no scientific studies on the risks of electrolysis and laser hair removal to pregnant women and fetuses. Given the lack of scientific knowledge, you should avoid these hair removal methods until after the pregnancy.

Tanning salons

It is recommended that you not go to the tanning salon during your pregnancy even if the ultraviolet rays don't reach the fetus. The extreme heat an individual is exposed to during a tanning session can increase body temperature significantly and harm the baby. Many tanning salons will not allow pregnant women to have tanning sessions unless they have written medical permission.

▶ **Pregnancy mask (chloasma):** Brownish marks that appear on the face of some pregnant women.

Nutrition during pregnancy

The following general advice may not fit your individual situation if, for example:

- You are a young mother less than 20 years old;
- You have an illness which requires a certain diet;
- You systematically avoid one or more of the food groups;
- You have other particular needs.

Talk about it with your health professional, who can evaluate your situation, give you advice or refer you to a nutritionist.

The physical changes brought on by pregnancy increase your nutritional and energy needs. You will eat a bit more than you are used to, especially starting in the second trimester (15 weeks or more). But eating should be pleasant as well as healthy, so eat a variety of foods cooked in different ways. Have fun with flavours, colours, and different ingredients. Having a baby is a good way to improve your diet for you and your family.

Eating well while pregnant will contribute to:

- A smooth pregnancy;
- The health, growth and development of your baby;
- Maintaining and improving your health.

Eat regularly – it's important!

Your baby needs you to feed it. Don't go for long periods without eating.

Eating regularly means three meals a day, with snacks as needed between meals. This allows you to:

Get all the nutrients you need during pregnancy;

Avoid low-energy periods during the day.

On the menu: variety, colours and flavours

Eating well during pregnancy is not complicated. Eat regularly from a wide choice of tasty and colourful foods. Eat something every day from each of the **4 food groups in *Canada's Food Guide*: fruits and vegetables, grain products, milk and substitutes, and meat and substitutes**. Refer to *Canada's Food Guide* on the following Web site: www.hc-sc.gc.ca/fn-an/food-guide-aliment/index_e.html for an illustration of the number and sizes of recommended portions.

Tasty and colourful, fruits and vegetables should be included in all meals and snacks!

Fruits and vegetables

Tasty and colourful, fruits and vegetables should be included in all meals and snacks! Don't skip them. Among other things, fruits and vegetables contain:

- Folic acid, which contributes to the formation of the placenta, the baby's growth and the development of its brain and nervous system;
- Vitamin C, which helps you absorb iron;
- Fibre, which helps the intestines work properly and helps control sugar in the blood.

Where to start?

- Load up on colourful fruits and vegetables because they are rich in important nutrients. Try to eat at least one dark green vegetable and one orange-coloured daily. Examples are broccoli, spinach, romaine lettuce, carrots, sweet potatoes and winter squash.
- Add other fruits and vegetables to enhance your meals and snacks.

Some advice

- Eat fruits and vegetables in different ways – fresh, frozen, preserved, dried, in stews and sauces, in soups, in cooked dishes and as 100% pure juice.
- If you eat fruits and vegetables raw, be sure to wash or peel them first to remove soil, dirt and pesticide residues. Also wash prepared salads and spinach packed in bags. Don't drink non-pasteurized juice.

Essential elements – Folic acid

Folic acid is an important vitamin for all pregnant women, especially early in their term. Folic acid reduces the chance of the baby suffering from birth defects. Many foods contain folic acid, but during pregnancy it is recommended to take a supplement that contains folic acid (see page 151).

What foods contain folic acid?

- Legumes: red, romaine and white beans, soy beans, chick peas, lentils.
- Dark green vegetables: asparagus, broccoli, romaine lettuce, spinach, Brussels sprouts.
- Enriched pasta and flour.
- Orange-coloured fruits: oranges and orange juice, tangerines, mandarin oranges, cantaloupe.
- Sunflower seeds.

Grain or cereal products include bread, rice, pasta and much more.

Grain products

Grain or cereal products include bread, rice, pasta and much more. You can add variety to your menu with grains like oats, barley, buckwheat, rye, millet, quinoa and others. Among other things, grain products contain:

- Starch and sugar, which help produce energy;
- Group B vitamins, iron, zinc, magnesium, vitamin E and fibre, which help the baby's nervous system, cardiovascular system and digestive system to develop and work.

Contrary to popular belief, pasta, bread and rice do not cause weight gain. Just don't add lots of fatty foods like butter and rich sauces.

Where to start?

- Add whole grain cereal products to your diet. Try to have them make up at least half of your daily servings of grain products. Some examples are whole-wheat bread, oatmeal porridge, barley, multigrain spaghetti, brown rice, wild rice, high-fibre breakfast cereals and bran muffins.

Some advice

- Choose mainly bread, cereal, pasta and rice because they have less fat and sugar than other baked goods and pastries such as biscuits, croissants, cakes and muffins.
- Don't rely on colour when choosing whole-grain foods. Read the list of ingredients – the first one on the list must be a whole grain.

Milk and milk substitutes

Dairy products and enriched soy drinks have much to offer, and not just to children! Among other things, they contain:

- Calcium and phosphorus, which help the baby's bones and teeth to form and stay healthy;
- Protein, which helps the organs and muscles to form.

Where to start?

- Drink the equivalent of two glasses of milk or an enriched soy beverage daily. If you don't want to drink it, you can add it to your recipes.
- Add yogurt or cheese to your meal or snack.

★ Dairy products and enriched soy drinks have much to offer, and not just to children!

Photo: iStockphoto

Some advice

- Use pasteurized milk and dairy products.
- If you don't like the taste of milk or soy drinks, you can:

  - Add them to your cereal for breakfast or a snack, or use them to replace water in hot cereals like porridge and cream of wheat;

  - Flavour them with vanilla or almond extract, spices, fruits, chocolate, etc.;

  - Include them in your recipes for cream soups, blanc-mange, pudding, custard, tapioca, milkshakes, etc.

- Do you suffer from lactose intolerance? You can find lactose-free milks and enriched soy drinks at the grocery store. There are also pills and drops at the drug store to help digest milk products.

Essential elements – Calcium and vitamin D

Bones and teeth cannot be formed without calcium. It is essential to your baby. Vitamin D's role is to help the body absorb and use the calcium. That's why we think of them together.

What foods contain calcium and vitamin D?

Calcium

- Dairy products – milk, yogurt and cheese made from pasteurized milk.
- Enriched soy drinks, tofu (with calcium sulphate).
- Canned fish containing edible bones (salmon, sardines).
- Calcium-enriched products such as some orange juice, for example.

Vitamin D

- Milk
- Soy-enriched drinks
- Fatty fish such as salmon
- Margarine

Most legumes, dark-green vegetables, grains, almonds and other nuts also contain small amounts of calcium. Think of them as a bonus.

> Meat and meat substitutes are nourishing foods that provide lots of energy.

Meat and meat substitutes

Meat and meat substitutes are nourishing foods that provide lots of energy which add variety to your daily diet. Among other things, meat and meat substitutes contain:

- Protein, which helps organs and muscles develop and repair themselves;
- Iron, needed for blood to form;
- Omega-3 and omega-6 fatty-acids, which help your baby's brain, eyes and skin develop.

Where to start?

- Choose every day from a variety of meats, poultry, fish, legumes and other substitutes, such as eggs, nuts and grains. Some examples of legumes are lentils, red and other beans, dried peas, peanut butter and tofu.
- Try to eat fish at least twice a week. You can eat most of the species of fish and seafood sold on the market.

Advice

- Cook meat, poultry, eggs, fish and seafood thoroughly. The same goes for all dishes containing them. The flesh must be cooked through and should drip clear liquid. When cooking eggs, both the white and yolk must be firm.
- You can eat as much as you want of salmon, trout, canned light tuna, sardines, sole, cod and tilapia, for example.

Some precautions

- However, some fish must be eaten more moderately, while other species should not be eaten during pregnancy.
- Here are a few ways to benefit from fish regularly while reducing the risk of exposure to toxins such as mercury:
  - Choose light canned tuna over white canned tuna, which contains more mercury. Read the labels to tell them apart.
  - Do not eat more than one portion a month of the following fresh or frozen fish: shark, swordfish, marlin and tuna (except canned tuna).
  - Only eat bass, pike, wall-eyed pike, muskellunge or lake trout (grey trout) occasionally. If you eat game fish regularly, you should find out about the contamination level of the fish based on where they were fished as well as the recommended frequency for eating them. Consult the Guide de consommation du poisson de pêche sportive en eau douce (www.mddep.gouv.qc.ca/eau/guide) or call the ministère du Développement durable, de l'Environnement et des Parcs at 418 521-3830 or 1 800 561-1616.

Essential elements – Iron

Iron is needed for the growth of both the baby and placenta.
That's why you need more iron during pregnancy than at any other time in your life.

What foods contain iron?

Animal-based foods

- Meat – beef, lamb, pork and ham, veal, game
- Poultry – chicken, turkey
- Seafood – clams, cooked oysters

Vegetable-based foods

- Legumes – red and white beans, lentils, chick peas, tofu
- Iron-fortified breakfast cereals, enriched pasta
- Pumpkin, sesame, squash and sunflower seeds
- Nuts – pecans, pistachios, almonds and cashews
- Dried fruits – apricots, raisins

As a general rule the body absorbs iron more easily from meats than from vegetable-based foods.
To help the body absorb iron from vegetables, eat foods rich in vitamin C, such as citrus fruit and tomatoes.

Every food group is valuable

No food contains all the nutrients needed for good health. That's why it's important to eat a variety of foods every day from each of the food groups in *Canada's Food Guide*. A helpful idea is to include foods from at least three food groups in every meal and from at least two groups in every snack.

Some ideas for healthy snacks:

- A fruit or vegetable with a piece of cheese
- Some nuts and yogurt
- One or two slices of bread with peanut butter
- A half pita with hummus (chickpea spread)
- A muffin and a glass of milk or enriched soy drink
- Fresh-cut vegetables with cream cheese
- A handful of mixed nuts and dried fruits
- A fruit milkshake
- A boiled egg with melba toasts

Are oils and fats good for your baby?

Some fats, such as the omega-3 and omega-6 families, are healthy and important during pregnancy. Our bodies can't produce all of them so it's important to consume a small amount every day.

Omega-6 is common, so it is easy to eat enough of it. However, omega-3 is only found in certain types of food.

Omega-3 fats

Omega-3 fats help the baby's brain and eyes develop.

What foods contain omega-3?

- Fatty fish – salmon, trout, mackerel, sardines, herring.
- Linseed, canola and soy oil, and soft (non-hydrogenated) vinaigrettes and margarines made from them.
- Sunflower seed, ground linseed, pumpkin seed, walnuts.
- Products enriched with omega-3 (some milk and eggs, for example).

Artificial sweeteners

Some people prefer to use substitutes instead of sugar, or choose yogurt, drinks, jams, chewing gum and other products containing artificial sweeteners. Are they safe during pregnancy?

- Three sugar substitutes are considered safe today: aspartame, acesulfame K (potassium acesulfame) and sucralose. These are the ones found in prepared foods.
- Don't use saccharine and the cyclamates because their effects are not known. They are only sold powdered, in pouches and tablets.

Drinks

Drink often to stay well hydrated. Drinking water and eating dietary fibre help the intestines do their work and reduce the risk of constipation. You can also drink milk, 100% pure fruits and vegetable juice and broth.

Caffeine

Coffee, tea, cola soft drinks, chocolate and some medications contain caffeine. Consuming a small amount of caffeine will not harm the baby, so if you limit your consumption of other sources of caffeine you can safely drink about two 8-ounce/250-ml cups of coffee a day. Energy drinks can contain as much caffeine as coffee does. Drinking them during pregnancy is not recommended anyway. Decaffeinated drinks are fine during pregnancy.

Herbal teas

We know that some plant-based products can interfere with pregnancy, for example by triggering contractions. Science knows too little about herbal teas to be able to make recommendations for pregnancy. If you are a tea drinker you should know that Health Canada considers tea made from citrus-fruit skins, ginger, balm and wild rose to be harmless if taken in moderation: no more than 2 to 3 cups a day. Choose different teas instead of the same one every day. Another interesting option is lemon juice or ginger slices in hot water.

Preventing food-borne infections

Whether we like it or not, germs are part of life. Water and food can contain germs in the form of viruses, bacteria and parasites. Germs are also found in animals, meat, fertilizers and gardens. In fact, micro-organisms are everywhere but your digestive and immune systems will protect you from most food-borne infections caused by these invaders.

But there are two exceptions: listeriosis and toxoplasmosis, which are rare food-related infections that can sometimes be dangerous during pregnancy. Listeriosis is caused by bacteria and can be very serious for the fetus and the newborn, even if it doesn't cause a birth defect. Toxoplasmosis, caused by a parasite, can bring problems for the baby.

General advice

The following tips will help you reduce the risk of food-related infection, whichever micro-organisms are involved, including listeriosis and toxoplasmosis.

Cleanliness

- Wash your hands well with soap before and after handling food.
- Clean the refrigerator regularly.

Choosing and preparing food

- Cook meat, poultry, eggs, fish and seafood completely.
- Choose milk, cheeses and other dairy products that have been pasteurized.
- Wash all fruits and vegetables under a stream of water, whether they are to be eaten cooked or raw and with or without the peel.
- Choose pasteurized fruit and vegetable juice (most juice is pasteurized).

- Don't use raw sprouts, in particular alfalfa sprouts.
- Don't eat food after the best-before date on the package.

Storing and handling food

- Keep raw meat, fish and poultry away from other foods.
- Make sure your refrigerator temperature is 4°C (40°F) or colder and the freezer temperature is -18°C (0°F).
- Don't leave foods that should be kept cold or hot at room temperature for more than 2 hours.
- Avoid having raw foods like meat and fish touch cooked foods or those that are ready to serve. For example, don't put food that is ready to serve on a platter or plate that had raw meat on it, unless the dish has been washed well.
- Use hot, soapy water to wash plates, utensils, cutting boards and other surfaces that have been used to prepare raw foods (to disinfect them, mix 10 ml [2 teaspoons] of bleach with 1,000 ml [4 cups] of water and rinse well).
- Keep leftovers for a maximum of 2 to 3 days. Completely reheat foods that should be served hot. Soups, sauces or foods in a sauce, like stews, should be brought to a boil before being served.
- Defrost foods in the refrigerator and not at room temperature. You can also defrost them in the microwave and then cook them as soon as they're defrosted.

Listeriosis prevention: Advice for pregnant women

The bacterium that causes listeriosis is present in the environment and may contaminate some already cooked foods. It can survive and develop even in cold temperatures. This is why pregnant women are warned not to eat:

- Smoked sausages (hot dogs) that have not been heated
  - To be extra safe: heat hot dogs well before eating them.
- Non-dried deli meats (e.g., sliced cold meats)
  - To be extra safe: cook meat at home; heat non-dried deli meats well before eating them.
- Refrigerated pâtés and meat spreads
  - To be extra safe: choose canned spreadable pâtés or ones that can be stored for an extended period of time (e.g., in a jar, can or vacuum-sealed package, and that can be stored at room temperature).
- Refrigerated or frozen smoked fish and seafood
  - To be extra safe: cook smoked fish or seafood; choose canned smoked fish or seafood or products that can be stored for an extended period of time (e.g., in a jar, can or vacuum-sealed package, and that can be stored at room temperature).
- Unpasteurized milk, unpasteurized dairy products (butter, yogurt) and cheeses made from unpasteurized milk.
  - Note: soft and semi-soft cheeses (e.g., brie, camembert and blue) made from pasteurized milk can present a risk for listeriosis, because contamination may occur after the pasteurization. This risk is currently difficult to measure.

Other precautions

Is there a cat in your house? No problem – except that your four-legged friend could be carrying toxoplasmosis. To reduce the risk of catching it, don't clean the cat's litter box. If no one else will clean it, wear rubber gloves and wash your hands well afterward.

Are you a gardener? A cat or another animal may have done its business in your garden. As a precaution, wear gloves while gardening or handling earth or sand. Wash your hands well afterward, and wash any fruits or vegetables you harvest if they have touched the ground.

Preventing allergies

Food restrictions are not recommended during pregnancy in an effort to reduce the risk of food allergies in the newborn. By not eating certain foods, you are likely to miss some of the nutrients you and your baby need. If you're worried about allergies, talk about them with your health professional.

Vitamin and mineral supplements

Even during pregnancy food is by far the best source of nutrients. **Vitamin and mineral supplements will never replace good nutrition and a varied diet.** If your health professional recommends supplements, they are intended only to add to your food intake, as a way to ensure that you are getting all the nutrients you need for a good pregnancy.

Folic acid

Taking a folic acid supplement will reduce the risk of your baby suffering from an anomaly of the **neural tube**, such as **spina bifida** or other **birth defects**. Supplements usually have 0.4 to 1 mg of folic acid, but your health professional may advise you to take a supplement that contains more than that. It is recommended to start taking a folic acid supplement two or three months before becoming pregnant and continue taking it through the entire first trimester (first three months). If you are already taking a multi-vitamin supplement, be sure it contains enough folic acid.

▶ **Neural tube:** Part of the embryo that becomes the brain and spinal cord.

▶ **Spina bifida:** Birth defect of the spine.

▶ **Birth defects:** Deformity present at birth that started in the mother's belly.

Other supplements

In general, Health Canada recommends that pregnant women take a multi-vitamin supplement that contains iron as well as folic acid.

Advice

! Follow the product instructions for the number of tablets to take daily. Taking too much of certain elements such as vitamin A can hamper your baby's development.

- Talk with your health professional before taking a different vitamin or mineral supplement than the one recommended to you. The same rule applies to all other natural health products.
- Always keep your supplements out of reach of children, especially those containing iron.
- Taking supplements with iron may cause constipation or digestive problems in some people. If this is your case, see page 82 for advice on relieving this discomfort. You can also take your supplement while eating.

To learn more about nutrition:

Eating Well With Canada's Food Guide. Health Canada, 2007.

- The *Guide* shows you the number and size of recommended portions. You can get a copy at your CLSC, or order it from Health Canada at www.hc-sc.gc.ca/fn-an/food-guide-aliment/index_e.html.
- There is a version of the *Guide* for First Nations, Inuit and Métis people.
- On the Health Canada Web site, you can print yourself a personalized copy of *Canada's Food Guide* in English, French, Arabic, Chinese (traditional or simplified), Farsi, Korean, Russian, Punjabi, Spanish, Tagalog, Tamil or Urdu.

The *Votre guide du consommateur.* MAPAQ, 2005 (A French-language consumer guide from the ministère de l'Agriculture, des Pêcheries et de l'Alimentation du Québec)

- This French-language guide shows correct cooking temperatures and provides general advice on preventing food-related infections. You can obtain a copy from the Québec food and animal health inspection centre, (the Centre québécois d'inspection des aliments et de santé animale), or on the Web site of the ministère de l'Agriculture, des Pêcheries et de l'Alimentation du Québec at www.mapaq.gouv.qc.ca/Fr/Consommation, in the section *"La sécurité des aliments et vous"* (food safety and you).

Centre québécois d'inspection des aliments et de santé animale
1 800 463-5023
dga@mapaq.gouv.qc.ca

Staying active

Physical activity during pregnancy will add to your physical and mental well-being. Exercise will help you feel more energetic and improve your breathing.

If you are already active, the best thing is to continue. If you are the sedentary type, a person who doesn't move around very much, start being more active gently and gradually. Choose activities suitable for your physical condition and your stage of pregnancy. Don't be afraid – physical exercise does not increase the risk of miscarriage or problems with the baby. And women who are active while pregnant adapt better to the physical changes caused by pregnancy. They also recover better after birth.

Women who are active while pregnant adapt better to the physical changes caused by pregnancy and recover better after delivery.

Photo: Anouk Jolin

If your pregnancy has no complications, you can stay in good physical shape by doing moderate regular exercise such as walking, swimming, aquafitness, cycling, stationary cycling, cross-country skiing and snowshoeing. You can also add stretching, posture and muscle-strengthening movements to your exercise routine. Relaxation exercises will help you control your breathing and increase the baby's oxygen supply.

Don't practice extreme sports, underwater diving or any activity that might cause you to fall or be hurt. Athletes who want to continue training while pregnant should be supervised by a doctor.

Your health professional can give you advice if you develop any health problem related to pregnancy, or if you don't feel capable of staying active.

For more information and some examples of physical activity during pregnancy, look for the Kino-Québec pamphlet *Active pour la vie* at your CLSC or medical clinic, or visit the Web site www.kino-quebec.qc.ca.

Tobacco, alcohol and drugs

Throughout your pregnancy your health professional will ask you about your cigarette smoking and alcohol and drug use. You may feel guilty or uncomfortable by saying that you use one of these products, but be assured that they are asking the questions:

- To inform you;
- To talk about your worries over what effect using tobacco, alcohol or drugs might have on you and your baby;
- To provide help if you want to stop;
- To refer you to specialists if you need more help.

> ★ It is not always easy to stop tobacco, alcohol or drug.
>
> Ask a health professional for advice or help.

Tobacco

Don't smoke tobacco or expose yourself to other people's smoke while pregnant. The dangers to both mother and child are real and well known.

Smoking harms the growth of the fetus and may disturb your pregnancy:

- It increases the risk of detachment of the placenta, premature rupture of the membranes and premature childbirth;

- It may slow the growth of the fetus and thus reduce the baby's birth weight;
- It increases the risk of having a stillborn baby or a baby who dies in the days after delivery;
- It increases the risk of **sudden infant death syndrome**.

Pregnancy is an excellent time to quit smoking. Those around you who smoke can help by not exposing you to their smoke. It's also a good time for the father to quit as well!

It's never too late to quit smoking. It's a decision that will help the baby at any stage of your pregnancy.

Most smokers are addicted to tobacco and have a hard time quitting. There is a telephone help line, a Web site and the network of more than 160 stop-smoking centres, the Centres d'abandon du tabagisme, which offers free service to everyone. Here is their contact information:

- 1 866 jarrête (1 866 527-7383)
- www.jarrete.qc.ca
- Centre d'abandon du tabagisme: To find out where stop-smoking centres are located, call 1 866 jarrête or visit www.jarrete.qc.ca

---

▶ **Sudden infant death syndrome:** An unexplained and sudden death of an apparently healthy baby under 1 year of age.

Alcohol

Don't drink alcohol when you're pregnant.

The more alcohol you drink, the greater the risks of harm to the baby. Drinking regularly and drinking a large amount at once are particularly harmful. We are not sure of the effects of having an occasional and small amount.

All types of alcohol – beer, wine and liquor – have the same effect on the baby.

Alcohol can harm your baby in many ways. It can cause a miscarriage, stillbirth or premature birth. Alcohol increases the chance that your baby will suffer from slow growth or birth defects.

! The placenta does not filter alcohol.

Alcohol goes directly through the placenta from the mother's blood to the baby's.

Fetal alcohol syndrome

Drinking alcohol while pregnant can cause various problems. We sometimes talk about Fetal Alcohol Spectrum Disorder (FASD). Fetal Alcohol Syndrome, part of the spectrum, is especially severe. How much the baby is affected depends on several factors, such as the amount consumed and the amount of alcohol in the mother's blood at a given moment.

Children suffering from fetal alcohol syndrome:

- Are smaller and weigh less than normal;
- Have facial deformities;
- Have brain damage.

Being pregnant is a good time to learn about non-alcoholic cocktails and drinks that are just as pleasant!

Photo: iStockphoto

The brain is the organ most sensitive to alcohol and it is growing throughout your pregnancy. Alcohol can damage the baby's brain so the child will have learning and memory problems, attention deficit, difficulty solving problems, and behaviour problems.

Like other women, you may have consumed alcohol in early pregnancy before you learned you were going to have a baby. If you are worried, you can discuss it with your health professional or call the Motherisk telephone help line for advice.
Motherisk: 1 877 327-4636

Advice

Being pregnant is a good time to learn about non-alcoholic cocktails and drinks that are just as pleasant!

- Sparkling fruit juice (apple, peach or other)
- Exotic fruit juice diluted with sparkling mineral water, ginger ale or lemon-lime soft drinks
- Fresh or frozen fruit juice

- A slice of lemon, orange or melon as a decoration. Frozen strawberries, raspberries or blueberries as ice cubes…

Cannabis and other drugs

Do not take drugs or expose yourself to second-hand smoke of any kind while pregnant.

The effects of drugs on your baby depend on three factors: the type of drug used, the amount consumed and the time it was consumed.

In general, babies born to mothers who take drugs while pregnant can suffer from withdrawal at birth. Since the drugs available are illegal, exactly what they contain is unknown and cannot be evaluated accurately. This increases the danger of using them.

The effects of using cannabis (marijuana and other cannabis derivatives) while pregnant are little known but worrisome. Cannabis may harm your baby's growth, and since it is smoked, it may have the same effect on the fetus as tobacco. We recommend you not smoke cannabis while pregnant.

Using cocaine while pregnant can cause bleeding and separation of the placenta, which in turn may cause the death of the fetus or a premature birth.

Questions, concerns and help

Do you have questions or concerns about using alcohol or drugs? Do you need help to quit?

- Talk about it with a health professional.
- Call the toll-free telephone help line *Drogue: aide et référence*, open 24/7, at 514 527-2626 or 1 800 265-2626 www.drogue-aidereference.qc.ca.
- Call the toll-free telephone help line of Motherisk, a group that answers questions about the effects of drug and alcohol use during pregnancy and breast-feeding.

  Motherisk: 1 877 327-4636
  www.motherisk.org

For information about fetal alcohol syndrome, contact:

SAFERA
A group dedicated to preventing fetal alcohol syndrome
418 882-2488
info@safera.qc.ca
www.safera.qc.ca

Chemicals and X-rays

Insect repellent

You can protect yourself from insects by wearing long sleeves and pants. If you must use insect repellent, choose one containing DEET (the most commonly used chemical in repellents), because it is effective. There is no proof that using DEET is harmful to the unborn baby. Using a repellent containing 20% to 30% DEET on the skin or clothing will prevent 90% of mosquito and tick bites. This is the best protection if you can't avoid mosquitoes or ticks.

You can also reduce your exposure to DEET by applying it to your clothing instead of your skin. Apply it only to exposed areas and wash carefully afterward to remove any excess.

Using citronella oil while pregnant is not recommended. It only lasts about half an hour and it is not known if it is safe during pregnancy. As well, many citronella products also contain other products such as eucalyptus, camphor and other oils, which should be avoided during pregnancy.

Cleaning products

Ordinary cleaning products such as dish and laundry detergents, window cleaner and all-purpose cleaner are not dangerous during pregnancy. Corrosive products such as javel water and oven cleaner may irritate or burn your airways but inhaling small amounts will not harm your baby.

Stronger cleaners and air fresheners containing solvents release toxic vapours that can stay in your home for many hours. Pregnant women should be careful to use these products only when really necessary.

Always read and follow the instructions for all products.

Paint and paint removers

Most indoor paints are latex based and thinned with water. Latex paints are considered to be safe if used occasionally during pregnancy.

Don't use oil-based paints. They contain solvents that are toxic to your unborn child. A few hours in a newly painted room is not likely to be harmful though, especially if it has been well aired.

Don't do any sanding or use paint remover. You might expose yourself to old lead-based paint and the toxic chemicals used in all paint removers.

X-rays

X-rays may be needed while you're pregnant. Warn your doctor or dentist if you are or suspect you may be pregnant. He or she will be able to help you decide if the x-ray is worth the risk to you and your fetus. Some examinations can be delayed or replaced by other tests. In other cases, it is safer to have the x-ray than not to.

On your first pregnancy follow-up appointment, tell your health professional if you had any x-rays before knowing that you were pregnant at the time. If you must have an x-ray, tell the technician that you are pregnant. He or she can then take all the extra precautions possible, such as using a lead apron.

Travel and trips

Safety in the car

The Highway Safety Code requires everyone in an automobile to wear seat belts. When worn correctly, the belt can prevent injuries during an accident. This picture shows how to wear your seat belt throughout your pregnancy.

Travelling abroad

Before leaving the country, you could discuss with your health professional where you are going, the duration of your trip, what vaccinations you need and what route you will take. Your health professional may then make some adjustments to your follow-up.

Before leaving, check whether you have an insurance policy covering medical costs if you must be hospitalized or give birth outside Canada, and also whether your baby will also be insured. This coverage is even more important for premature births, because a stay in intensive care can be very expensive. The provincial health insurance board,

★ You must wear your seatbelt throughout pregnancy. The lower part of the belt should be tightened comfortably on your pelvis, below your belly.

Photo: BSIP

the *Régie de l'assurance maladie du Québec*, will refund the amount your care would have cost in Québec. Since health care can be more expensive elsewhere, you (if you and your baby are not insured) or your insurance company might have to pay out a large amount.

By air

Pregnant women may travel by air. There is no international regulation on the subject, but each airline has its own rules. To be on the safe side, check your carrier's regulations before buying your tickets.

Bring with you a note from your health professional, stating the expected date of birth, your health status and the progress of your pregnancy. The airline may require such a statement.

If you have any worries or questions about everyday life during pregnancy, contact:

Info-Santé
Across Québec, except for one region: 811
The far north (Terres-Cries-de-la-Baie-James and Nunavik): Look in the phone book under the heading "Centre de santé et de services sociaux."

S.O.S. Grossesse
1 877 662-9666
www.sosgrossesse.ca

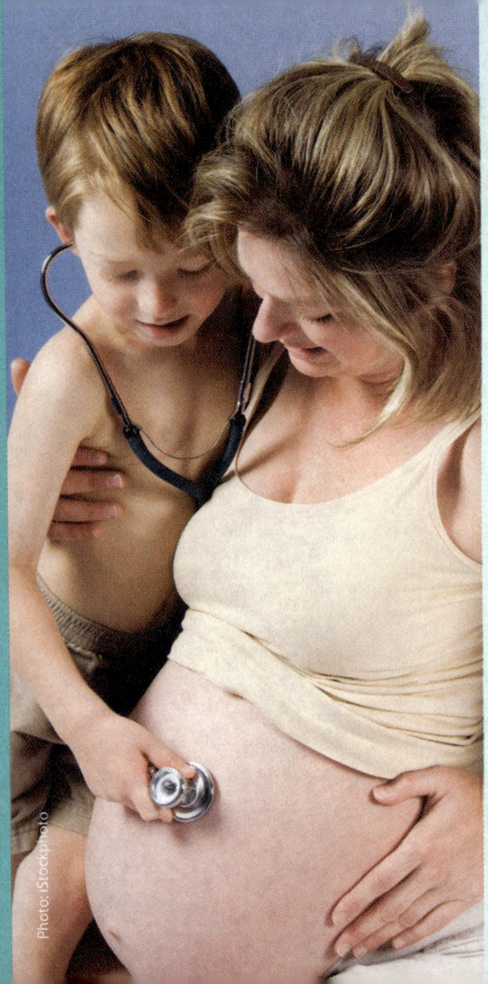

Health during pregnancy

Professionals and services

During your pregnancy, you will be busy helping a little being grow and develop. You need support from others during this time. In addition to the father as well as extended family and friends to support you, a large number of professionals can contribute to your health and your baby's (nurses, midwives, doctors and birth companions). A wide range of services is also available to help you through this important time in a woman's life. This section describes resources that can help you make the most of your pregnancy, labour and the birth of your new baby.

Health professionals responsible for pregnancy and delivery

You'll meet nurses throughout your pregnancy, whether at prenatal classes, the CLSC, a medical clinic or the high-risk pregnancy clinic (GARE) of a hospital. Nurses will also help you in the obstetrics department of the hospital; they offer the support and care you need during labour and delivery. Their experience with women in labour will be of great benefit to you.

In Québec, family doctors, midwives and obstetrician-gynecologists are the health professionals that follow pregnancy and delivery. As of 2007, "nurse practitioners specializing in primary care" have been added to this list. These nurses can follow low-risk, complication-free pregnancies for up to 32 weeks and work with the doctor who delivers the baby. The doctor will take over from 32 weeks until delivery. Nurse practitioners can also follow up with you and your newborn after you leave the hospital.

Many health professionals work as a team, in a group practice. You can ask your health professional how his or her team works and who will be there during your delivery. It's important for you to have confidence in your health professional and feel supported. Don't hesitate to ask questions no matter how trivial they seem. You can also switch to another health professional at any stage of your pregnancy, but be sure to have your file transferred so you and your baby are followed in a safe and satisfying way.

The following table lists health professionals and their roles in monitoring your pregnancy and delivery. **This information is meant as a guideline only; there are many exceptions and specific situations depending on individual professionals, their setting, and the region.** If you need tests, care or treatment that is not offered by your health professional, he or she can request a consultation or refer you to the proper professional. Some health professionals do not follow pregnancies but have specific expertise that may be of benefit to you, depending on your situation. These include dietitians, pharmacists, psychologists, social workers, sex therapists and others.

Following a pregnancy	Pregnancy without complications
	High-risk pregnancy
Planned place of delivery	Hospital
	Birthing centre
	Home
At the time of delivery	Vaginal delivery with **no foreseeable complications** and no pain medication or epidural
	Delivery under **epidural**
	Delivery by **caesarean**
After birth	Gynecological follow-up for the mother
	Follow-up of the mother and baby during the first 6 weeks (with home visits)
	Long-term medical follow-up of the mother and baby

* In cooperation with a doctor who delivers (since 2007)

Health professionals responsible for pregnancy and delivery

Nurse practitioners specializing in primary health care*	Family doctors	Midwives	Obstetricians/Gynecologists
✔ Up to 32 weeks	✔	✔	Some of them do
	Consultation, shared-care or referral to an obstetrician/gynecologist	Consultation, shared-care or referral to a doctor	✔
	✔	In some hospitals	✔
		✔	
		✔	
	✔	✔	✔
	✔	Referral to a doctor	✔
	Referral to an obstetrician/gynecologist (or a surgeon)	Referral to an obstetrician/gynecologist	✔
	✔		✔
		✔	
✔	✔		

Don't hesitate to ask your health professional questions! He or she is the best person to provide answers.

Photo: BSIP

Birth companions

Birth companions, or doulas, are not health professionals in the true sense but they provide support and information that adds to the medical care you will receive. They offer services to parents during pregnancy, delivery and after your baby is born.

It is better to tell your health professional that you will have a doula with you when you give birth. Doula services are often at a cost. The costs may differ from one organization to the next and are sometimes based on your financial situation.

If you want a doula to help, choose someone you trust. Talk about your specific needs during the pregnancy and delivery. Remember that she will be with you during an important moment in your life.

Prenatal information

Prenatal information is available to answer your questions about topics like pregnancy, labour, delivery, breast-feeding and caring for a newborn. The information may be given to groups, women or couples. Prenatal information is usually offered at meetings commonly referred to as prenatal classes. These sessions also give you a chance to meet and talk to other people living the same experience as you. And, they help get fathers ready for their new role – and ready to participate in the delivery.

Many CLSCs, community organizations and private companies offer prenatal information and activities, including prenatal yoga and aqua fit. The philosophy, timing, length of the class, number of participants and costs vary between organizations.

CLSC services

"My CLSC is for life!" is a slogan (translated) that summarizes the mission of the local community service centres we've come to know as CLSCs. The services offered to parents differ from one region to the next but one thing stays the same: all CLSCs have a mandate with young families.

★ You can go to the CLSC as soon as you find out that you're pregnant. Many CLSCs organize prenatal classes or can refer you to organizations that do.

If you have financial problems, you may be eligible for a program (OLO) providing: 1 egg, 1 litre of milk, 1 glass of orange juice and a vitamin and mineral supplement daily at no cost to pregnant women in precarious social or economic circumstances. The program also provides personalized follow-up by a nurse or dietician.

A few days after your baby is born, a CLSC nurse can come to your home to make sure that everything is going well for both you and your baby.

When your baby arrives on the scene, your CLSC will also be there! Your CLSC can help you adapt to motherhood or fatherhood by giving you access to various services such as home visits, respite care, support for parents and parent-child stimulation groups. If needed, you can also meet with a social worker.

CLSCs work with government-funded child-care centres to help you, as needed. They also work with community groups that support young families. Your CLSC will guide you to the resources available in your community, if necessary.

You can always contact a CLSC Info-Santé nurse. It doesn't matter what time of day or night you call. There is always someone on the other end of the phone to answer your questions.

To find the phone number for your CLSC, look in the phone book under Centre de santé et de services sociaux.

Services in your area

Access to health professionals, birthing centres, doulas, prenatal meetings and activities is different from one region to the next. The following people can help you find information about the services available in your area:

- Parents who already have children. Ask them about their experiences and what services they appreciated.
- Health professionals in hospitals, clinics or your CLSC, to find out:
  - the names of doctors who deliver babies and midwives who practice in your region;
  - services offered by your CLSC;
  - prenatal classes and activities offered in your region;
  - community groups that can help you.

Helpful resources

Regroupement Naissance-Renaissance
Breast-feeding, parental support and other activities.
514 392-0308
info@naissance-renaissance.qc.ca
www.naissance-renaissance.qc.ca

Fédération québécoises des organismes communautaires famille
This Web site lists community groups in your region that offer support to families.
450 466-2538
www.fqocf.org

Réseau des centres de ressources périnatales
A network to help you find resources in your region focusing on pregnancy and new parenthood
418 603-3762
www.reseaudescrp.org

Médecins de famille accoucheurs de l'Association des omnipraticiens en périnatalité du Québec
info@aopq.org
Directory of family doctors who deliver babies.
www.aopq.org

Association of obstetricians and gynecologists of Quebec
514 849-4969
www.gynecoquebec.com
info@gynecoquebec.com

Ordre des sages-femmes du Québec
1 877 711-1313 / 514 286-1313
ordresagesfemmes@osfq.org
www.osfq.org

Regroupement les Sages-femmes du Québec
514 738-8090
sages.femmes.qc@bellnet.ca

Ordre des infirmiers et infirmières du Québec
1 800 363-6048 / 514 935-2501 / 514 935-2505
www.oiiq.org

Health care

Drugs and natural health products

! During pregnancy, you should think carefully about using medication, whether prescribed or not, and natural health products. Some of them may be ineffective, harmful to the pregnancy or dangerous for your baby.

If you have discomfort, pain or health problems, find the treatment that is best suited to the problem and your stage of pregnancy. Many people think that taking medication during pregnancy is dangerous. Thanks to research and experience, in most cases pregnant women can be treated safely.

Natural health products (plants, supplements or vitamins) should be used with the same caution as drugs. Plants used in cooking, like parsley, basil and garlic generally don't cause problems. But when they come in the form of capsules, tablets, tinctures or extracts, these plants may be stronger and may be dangerous during pregnancy. The effect of natural health products is not always known and their exact contents are not always clearly marked on the packaging. Some ingredients may be toxic during pregnancy. You should stop taking natural health products before becoming pregnant or as soon as you learn you're pregnant. A health professional can give you more information and answer questions such as: "Is this product helpful for me?" "Is this a controlled product, and do we know the exact composition?" "Is this a product I can take safely during my pregnancy?"

Here are some situations involving medication and general tips to guide you in using them.

Situation	What to do?
You want to get pregnant and you're taking medication for a specific problem such as: • anxiety • epilepsy • high blood pressure • depression • asthma • diabetes	Consult your doctor when you are planning to get pregnant or as soon as you find out you're pregnant.
You're pregnant and taking medication that you need to continue taking.	See your doctor quickly to have him or her check your treatment.
You took medication before you knew you were pregnant, but you've stopped taking it now.	At your first appointment, tell your doctor the name of the medication(s) that you took.
You have a health problem during your pregnancy.	See a health professional quickly to be examined.
Two health professionals have different opinions about your treatment.	Ask the two individuals to talk to each other to agree on your treatment.

You should know

- Some adjustments may be made to your medication.

- In general, stopping your treatment may lead to more complications for you and your baby than problems from the medication itself.
- It is very important not to stop ongoing treatment because you are afraid of harming the baby or concerned about the effect on your pregnancy.
- Your pharmacist can let you know whether you need to adjust your medication.

- As a general rule, few medications will have an effect on the baby so early in the pregnancy.
- Talk to your doctor or a pharmacist to find out more about the effects of this medication.

- Most infections and chronic problems can be treated with safe drugs.
- Pain can be relieved.
- Fear of taking medication should not mean that you have to let your health condition get worse.

During your pregnancy, always ask a health professional before taking any prescribed drug, over-the-counter medication or natural health product.

Common discomforts of pregnancy

Your body will change throughout your pregnancy. These changes sometimes lead to discomfort and ailments that are not usually dangerous, but some can be difficult to deal with. The following charts describe some common types of discomfort and offer tips to provide relief.

Some over-the-counter drugs can occasionally be taken for short periods of time. Check with a health professional before taking any such medication. He or she may:

- Suggest ways to relieve your discomfort without taking drugs;
- Provide advice about the drugs that can be helpful to you during pregnancy;
- Check to see whether you are taking other products that should not be taken at the same time as these medications (drug interactions);
- Explain the best way to take these drugs;
- Tell you the maximum quantity you can take;
- Tell you about the maximum length of time you can take the drugs.

If these tips don't help you feel better, if your health problem worsens or if you are worried, do not hesitate to contact a health professional quickly.

Nausea and vomiting

Description	What should I do?	Not feeling any better?
• Most likely due to: hormone changes. • Frequency: – nausea: affects 70 to 85% of pregnant women – vomiting: affects 50% of pregnant women • When: – Generally starts between the 4th and 8th week after the start of the last menstrual period – Usually the worst around the 9th week of pregnancy – Rare after the 20th week	• Try to rest. • Eat foods that you feel like eating. • Avoid being hungry (going for too long without eating). • See what works best for you: – Eat smaller quantities and eat more often (light meals and snacks). – Avoid strong smells and food textures that bother you. – Do not drink while eating or when you feel nauseous. It's better to drink between meals. – Eat something light before you get up in the morning. Crackers or toast are often suggested. – Take your time getting out of bed. • Acupuncture or acupressure can be effective for some people: pressure is exerted on the P6 or Neiguan point, located on the wrist. Acupressure bracelets are also available.	See your health professional if: • The nausea or vomiting interferes with your activities. Your health professional may recommend that you take an over-the-counter drug or prescribe a drug that can relieve your symptoms and is safe for you and the baby (e.g., Diclectin™). • You are losing weight. You should see a doctor quickly to treat these problems: • If you show signs of dehydration: dry mucous membranes (mouth, nose) and dark-coloured urine. • If you are vomiting a lot and often.

Leg cramps

Description	What should I do?
• Cause: an accumulation of acids (lactic and pyruvic) in the leg muscles. This accumulation leads to very painful but harmless involuntary cramps. They occur especially at night. • Frequency: more than 50% of pregnant women experience leg cramps. • When: during the second half of the pregnancy.	When you have a cramp you can: • Stretch your leg by pointing your toes upward • Massage the painful muscles • Get out of bed • Walk around. Don't worry if you feel some pain the next day, it's not serious. **Not feeling any better?** • See your health professional.

Heartburn and gastric reflux

Description	What should I do?
• Possible cause: hormonal changes during pregnancy slow down digestion, which leads to reflux of the stomach liquids in the **esophagus**. • When: from the start of the pregnancy. It may increase as your pregnancy progresses.	You can: • Avoid lying down after a meal • Sleep with your head raised • Wear loose clothing • Change your diet: – Eat smaller quantities and eat more often (light meals and snacks). – Eat fewer fatty foods. – Avoid things that irritate the stomach like caffeine and spices. – Avoid drinking or eating large amounts before going to bed. **Not feeling any better?** • You can take an antacid temporarily, such as those with calcium carbonate (e.g., Tums™). • See your health professional if: – You get only temporary relief – Your symptoms continue even after taking antacids – You need to take antacids regularly for several days – Your symptoms are accompanied by fever, nausea and vomiting or severe headaches.

▶ **Esophagus:** The tube that carries food from the mouth to the stomach.

Constipation and hemorrhoids

Description	What should I do?
• Cause of constipation: hormonal changes during pregnancy that slow down digestion; iron supplements; hemorrhoids. • Cause of hemorrhoids: as the uterus gets bigger it puts pressure on the veins and causes them to swell. • When: these problems occur particularly during the 2nd and 3rd trimesters.	• Eat foods that are rich in fibre: bran or whole-grain cereals have a lot of fibre. • Eat dried fruits, fresh fruits and vegetables and drink prune juice. • Drink lots of liquids. • If you have hemorrhoids, you can take sitz baths (container filled with warm water that fits in a toilet bowl). You can sometimes ease the pain by applying zinc cream or witch hazel compresses. **Not feeling any better?** • Your health professional may prescribe a more effective ointment or suggest that you: – Take dietary fibre supplements or psyllium (e.g., Metamucil™ or Prodiem™); drink lots of liquids so that you don't worsen the constipation; – Take a stool softener (e.g., docusate).

Numbness and pain in the hands

Description	What should I do?
• Most likely caused by: the fluid retention in the body (edema), which causes swelling that compresses the median nerve in the wrist. • Frequency: 25% of pregnant women experience this problem. • When: especially during the 3rd trimester and particularly at night. • Often affects both hands.	• These problems aren't dangerous and disappear after the baby is born. • If the symptoms bother you or cause you pain, you can wear a brace or wrist protector like those used for roller skating. Wear them while you are feeling pain or numbness. They are effective when worn for a few hours a day or during the night. **Not feeling any better?** • See a doctor if: – Your hands feel weak – The problems continue after your baby is born.

Backache

Description	What should I do?
• Most likely due to: – Sway back: curving your back towards the rear to compensate for the weight in your abdomen. – Increased looseness of the ligaments: the ligaments in the whole body are looser during pregnancy. This allows the pelvis to open to allow the baby to pass through it during delivery. • Frequency: approximately 75% of pregnant women have backaches.	• By doing the following exercises regularly you can prevent or relieve backaches during pregnancy. You can: – exercise in a pool, such as aqua fit or swimming; – exercise at home or during your daily activities: tilt the pelvis while lying down or standing; round your back. **Not feeling any better?** • You may take acetaminophen over a few days to relieve the pain. • If the pain continues, increases or runs down your legs, speak to your health professional during your next follow-up visit. • If you are at the end of your pregnancy and feel back pain that spreads to the stomach or that comes and goes regularly, you could be experiencing your first contractions (see Recognizing the start of labour, page 129).

ROUND BACK

PELVIC TILT

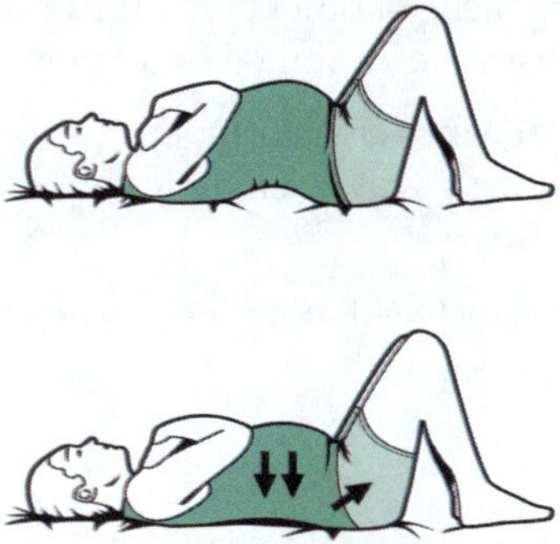

Acetaminophen (Tylenol™, Atasol™) is safe during pregnancy.

Do not confuse acetaminophen with aspirin or ibuprofen (Motrin™, Advil™). Aspirin and ibuprofen should not be taken at any time during pregnancy. Don't take them unless your health professional recommends it.

Treating minor health problems

While you're pregnant you may experience other discomforts that are unrelated to the pregnancy. Some of them may happen more often or be worse when you're pregnant.

Problem	Possible solutions	See your health professional if:
Cold and stuffed up nose	• Use a saline nasal solution (e.g., Salinex™). • If this doesn't provide relief, use a decongestant that comes in the form of nose drops (e.g., xylometazoline or oxymetazoline) for a maximum of 3 days. Prolonged use of this product can make your stuffed up nose worse.	• You have a fever: – temperature of 38-38.4°C (by mouth) that lasts 24 hours or more – temperature of 38.5°C or more (by mouth), twice in a row • if you have been in contact with someone who has scarlet fever or streptococcus • your cough or sore throat lasts more than 3 days • the recommended doses of medication do not help you feel better • your headache or other pain lasts longer than 3 days even if you take acetaminophen • your headaches are accompanied by other symptoms, such as fever, confusion, vision problems or drowsiness • your general health is getting worse • you're worried.
Sore throat	• Try gargling with salt water. • If there is a lot of pain, you may take acetaminophen for a few days.	
Headache, muscular or other pain	• Rest. • You may take acetaminophen for a few days.	

Problem	When should you see your health professional?
Symptoms of a urinary tract infection	Many pregnant women feel the need to urinate more often and in smaller quantities than before they were pregnant. See your health professional to find out if you have a urinary tract infection if: • You have difficulty starting to urinate • You feel burning when you urinate • Only a few drops come out when you feel the need to urinate • You feel the need to urinate again just after you went • You feel pain in your lower abdomen, especially after you urinate • You see blood in your urine. You could have a urinary tract infection even if you don't have these symptoms. It can be diagnosed through urine tests done during routine exams.
Symptoms of vaginitis (inflammation of the vagina)	Pregnant women often experience more vaginal discharge than before they were pregnant. See your health professional to see if you have vaginitis and to be treated if: • You feel a burning sensation in your vulva when you urinate or during sex • You have itchiness around your vulva • You notice changes in the colour or smell of your discharge.

Contact with children who have infectious diseases

Pregnant women often worry more about infections, especially those causing skin rashes (spots and small pimples) and those more common in children. Several diseases may be involved.

Fifth disease or slapped cheek syndrome (also known as erythema infectiosum, or parvovirus B19)

This generally harmless disease is seen mainly in school-age children, who may show some discomfort and particularly reddening of the cheeks (as if they have been slapped or like when they are coming back from outside in winter time), the trunk, arms and legs.

If a pregnant woman becomes infected with Fifth disease before the 20th week of pregnancy, there is a small chance of the fetus becoming infected. In that case, the fetus might become seriously anemic and the mother might have a miscarriage. After 20 weeks, there is little or no chance of this. Fifth disease does not cause birth defects.

Women who have previously had Fifth disease are safe, along with their babies. A blood test is the only way to confirm whether a mother is protected.

If you come in contact with a child who has Fifth disease, see your health professional to evaluate your situation. If you become sick while pregnant, he or she will follow you more closely to be sure your baby is doing well.

Chicken pox

Chicken pox is usually not serious in children but it can cause problems for pregnant women and their babies. The new chicken pox vaccine should reduce the number of cases.

Here's what to do if you are in contact with chicken pox:

- If you have already had chicken pox you just relax because your baby is safe.
- If you don't know whether you have had chicken pox and haven't received the vaccine, see a doctor within 48 hours so your blood can be tested for immunity. If you were born in North America, there is a 90% chance that you are immune to chicken pox. If you haven't had chicken pox, you will be given immunoglobulin to help you avoid the disease or to reduce its effect. You should then plan to be vaccinated after giving birth.

Other contagious diseases

Vaccination has made rubella or German measles very rare in Québec and Canada. Tests during early pregnancy determine whether a mother is immune to rubella. Women not immune should be vaccinated after they give birth.

There is no special danger to the fetus from the mother being in contact with a person who has one or more of the following diseases: roseola, hand-foot-and-mouth disease, measles, mumps, whooping cough or scarlet fever.

But if you're sick with symptoms possibly caused by one of these contagious diseases, see your doctor for a precise diagnosis, advice and possibly treatment.

Dental health

Life goes on during pregnancy and you may need dental care. Your changing hormones make your gums more sensitive. They may swell or bleed more easily. This makes good dental hygiene more important than ever. Brush your teeth regularly and use dental floss every day. This should soon stop gums from bleeding.

Go for your annual dental check-up and cleaning even though you are pregnant. Tell the dentist your condition and he or she might delay non-essential treatment until after the birth. You can go ahead with treatment for decay, an abscess or other urgent problem. If needed, the dentist can x-ray your teeth while shielding your belly with a lead apron to protect the baby. When treatment requires it, your dentist can also use a local anesthetic (freezing) and prescribe antibiotics for infections. He or she can ask your doctor or pharmacist whether these treatments are safe.

Prenatal appointments

Prenatal care during pregnancy also means seeing your health professional, having blood and urine tests, one or more ultrasounds, and in some cases, screening tests. The father is welcome to attend doctor's appointments, to ask his own questions, show support for the mother and start taking his place as a father.

Your health professional uses your regular visits to see whether your pregnancy is progressing as it should and to detect any problems that may arise. These appointments are also a chance to ask questions.

> When you wonder about something, write it down so you remember to ask at your next appointment.

If you feel the need at any time, you can:

- Ask for explanations about the tests and examinations you are offered;
- Ask for the opinion of a second health professional on a question that worries you;
- Have access to your file.

Frequency of checkup appointments

The timing of pregnancy checkups depends on certain factors. Visits may be more frequent if you have a particular health problem, but in general the schedule goes as follows:

- A first visit before the 12th week of pregnancy;
- From 12 to 30 weeks, a visit every 4 to 6 weeks;
- From 31 to 36 weeks, a visit every 2 or 3 weeks;
- From 37 weeks on, a visit every week.

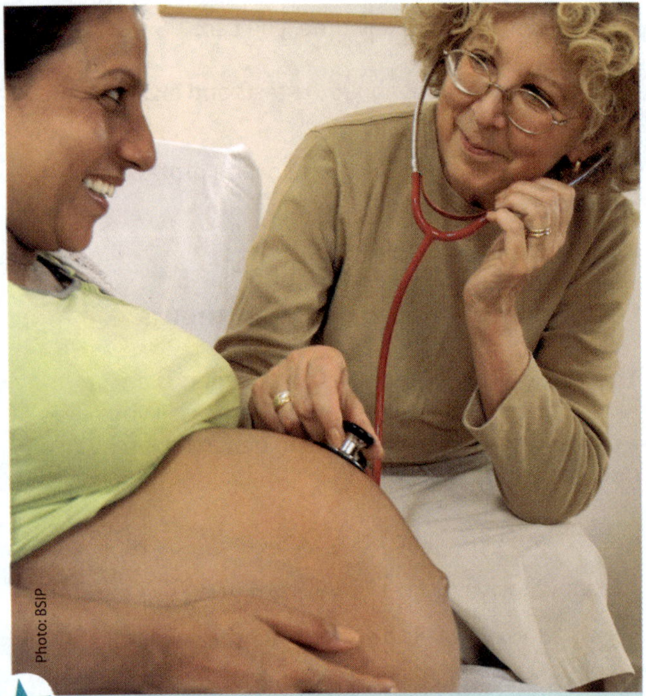

Your health professional will monitor the various aspects of your pregnancy with you.

Description of prenatal visits

During all visits, your health professional will check:

- Your weight;
- Your blood pressure;
- The size of your uterus (starting at about 20 weeks);
- The baby's heartbeat. Even though we begin hearing it at 10 to 12 weeks, your baby's heart has been beating since 20 to 22 days after he was conceived – about 5 weeks after your last menstrual period began.

Your first prenatal visit is usually between the 8th and 12th weeks. This allows sufficient time for parents who wish to undergo certain tests, such as genetic screening, which are best done between the 11th and 13th weeks of pregnancy. This visit will normally last longer than other appointments. In addition to the usual examinations, your health professional will ask you:

- The date of your last menstrual period, to determine how far along you are in your pregnancy and the due date for your child's birth;

- The state of your health before you became pregnant and how you have been since then. You will probably also be asked what medications you have taken, whether you have any allergies, whether you have ever had surgery or complications from anesthetics, physical ailments, or a physical or emotional breakdown of any kind;
- Whether you have been pregnant before, including miscarriages and abortions;
- What health characteristics you and the father have inherited, such as illnesses in your families, including heart disease, birth defects or hereditary diseases;
- Whether you have had gynecological problems in the past, such as surgery of the uterine cervix, or whether you or your partner have had herpes infection;
- About your living conditions and habits: tobacco, alcohol and drugs;
- About any sources of stress and tension in your life;
- What your job is, and whether it might be dangerous during pregnancy.

You will also have a complete physical examination.

Unless you have had one in the last few months, you will also undergo a gynecological examination and Pap test for cervical cancer. This may also be done later in the pregnancy. Your health professional may also recommend screening for sexually transmitted infections (STIs) such as chlamydia and gonorrhea, because they can go undetected and could harm your health and that of your baby. You may notice slight bleeding during the 24 hours after such an examination. Don't worry; the blood is not from the uterus but from the cervix, which is fragile during pregnancy.

Your health professional may prescribe lab tests and inform you about blood and urine tests, ultrasounds and screening for birth defects. If you aren't sure about taking these tests or think that others might be useful, now is the time to talk about it with your health professional so you can make an informed decision.

Blood and urine testing

Blood and urine tests can determine:

- If you are anemic;
- If you have an infectious disease you might give to the baby. If you have an infectious disease such as syphilis, HIV/AIDS or hepatitis B, you might be given certain medications during pregnancy, or your baby might be vaccinated at birth to reduce its risks of being infected;
- If your glycemia level (blood sugar) is normal;
- Your blood group and **Rh-factor**. If you are Rh negative for example, you may need certain precautions such as WinRho™ anti-Rh immunoglobulin at 28 weeks and perhaps after the birth. This treatment might prevent you from developing anti-Rh antibodies, which could harm this or a future pregnancy. WinRho™ can also be used in other situations, such as if you have a miscarriage, undergo **amniocentesis** or have bleeding after the first trimester (3 months);
- If you have rubella antibodies. If not, you will probably be advised to be vaccinated after the birth;
- If you have a urinary infection, whether or not you have symptoms.

▶ **Rhesus (Rh-) factor:** A characteristic of blood. A person can have a positive or negative Rh-factor.
▶ **Amniocentesis:** A procedure by which a sample of amniotic fluid is removed for tests.

Ultrasound

Your health professional will suggest an ultrasound exam between weeks 18 and 20. This is perfectly safe for the baby and allows to:

- See how the baby is developing;
- Determine the age of the fetus (if your menstrual periods were irregular or you weren't sure of the date of your last period);
- Determine the location of the placenta;
- See the baby's limbs and most of the organs – heart, liver, kidneys, stomach, bladder;
- Confirm the number of babies.

Although there is always the chance of a mistake, it is often possible during the ultrasound to see whether the baby is a boy or girl. If you want to keep the surprise, be sure to tell the technician and the doctor so they don't let it slip. Sometimes it is not possible to tell the baby's sex, but this is not a reason in itself to have another ultrasound.

Prenatal screening for Down syndrome

- Deciding to have a prenatal screening test can have serious consequences for you, your partner and your family.
- Before taking the tests, think about the decision you might have to make if you learn the baby has a chromosome abnormality.
- Health professionals can answer your questions and help you decide whether or not to take prenatal screening tests.

The most common chromosome abnormality is Down syndrome, also called trisomy 21. About one baby in 800 is born with Down syndrome, which limits intellectual development. This development can vary greatly from one child to another and can be affected in childhood or adulthood by the child's environment and how he or she is stimulated and supported. People with Down syndrome may also have health problems such as heart deformities.

There is no treatment for Down syndrome, but those who live with it have contributions to make as well as limitations to face. When given the chance, people with Down syndrome can grow attached to others and bring great happiness to themselves and those around them. Still, most will need some level of support for their whole life.

Down syndrome is not usually inherited. All women have a chance of bearing a fetus with this chromosome abnormality. The younger the mother, the lower the chance of having a baby with Downs.

Chances of having a full-term baby with Down syndrome

Mother's age	**Chance**
20 years	1 in 1,500
30 years	1 in 900
35 years	1 in 385
40 years	1 in 100

Prenatal screening

A screening test will show whether the baby has a small or large chance (low or high risk) of having Down syndrome. It will not harm the fetus.

If you want to be screened for Down syndrome, ask your health professional if it is available at your birthing hospital. If not, you can take the test at a private clinic at your own expense. Some private insurance may also cover the costs of these tests.

Results of prenatal screening

Prenatal screening will tell you whether the risk of having a Down syndrome baby is high or low.

- **If the risk is low**, your doctor will not advise you to have more tests. **But a low risk is not a guarantee that the baby will not have Down syndrome**. Because of natural differences between individuals, screening unfortunately does not detect all cases.
- **On the other hand, a high risk doesn't necessarily mean that your baby will be born with Down syndrome**. You will be asked to undergo another diagnostic test: amniocentesis with chromosome study. It's normal to be worried if you have to take this test. Still, most women who show a high risk in screening have a normal amniocentesis and give birth to a child that doesn't have Down syndrome.

Diagnostic test: amniocentesis

Amniocentesis with chromosome study is the most common prenatal diagnostic tool. It will determine with certainty whether a fetus has Down syndrome or not.

The test can be done after the 14th full week. A sample of amniotic fluid is taken from the uterus using a fine needle inserted in the belly.

Amniocentesis involves some risk of complications, which can include losing the baby. For this reason it is usually restricted to women showing a high risk in screening.

Results of amniocentesis

1) Most future parents learn that their baby does not have Down syndrome or any other chromosome abnormality.

2) When the results show that the baby has Down syndrome, the parents must choose between:

- Continuing the pregnancy and preparing to be parents of a child who, among other things, will be intellectually handicapped, although how seriously is impossible to predict;
- Ending the pregnancy.

3) In rare cases, amniocentesis will reveal other chromosome abnormalities. If this is your situation, your doctor will refer you to a specialist in genetics.

If you have to make the difficult choice of continuing or ending a pregnancy, you may need help. Don't hesitate to talk it over with loved ones and a health professional. You can also contact Down syndrome parent groups, which can provide sound advice based on members' own experience, to help you reach the decision that's best for you.

Association du Québec pour l'intégration sociale
This network will put you in touch with your local association for social integration.
514 725-7245
www.aqis-iqdi.qc.ca

Screening for Down syndrome

Blood tests

Blood tests will measure biological markers in the mother's blood. Using this information and the mother's age, it is possible to determine the risk that a baby will have Down syndrome. There are many ways to do these tests. Here are a few examples:

- A blood test during the **first trimester** of pregnancy, between the 11th and 13th weeks. This test measures two biomedical markers. It should be associated with nuchal translucency (neck fold).
- A test during the **second trimester**, between the 14th and 18th weeks. It is called the Triple Test because it measures three markers. There is also a four-marker test available.
- A two-sample test. The first blood sample is drawn during the **first trimester** (11-13 weeks), the second in the **second trimester** (14-18 weeks). This is called the integrated biochemical test and it analyzes results of the two tests combined with the mother's age. These tests can be associated with nuchal translucency.
- Other variations are also possible as knowledge of screening for Downs is increasing rapidly.

Nuchal translucency

An ultrasound test between the 11th and 13th weeks allows health professionals to measure nuchal translucency: the space between the skin on the neck of the fetus and the spine. If it measures more than normal, the risk of Downs or other chromosome abnormalities and heart deformities may be higher. Ultrasound screening must be combined with blood tests for more accurate results. Other ultrasound tests exist but they are not often used.

Source: ministère de la Santé et des Services sociaux du Québec

Problems during pregnancy

Warning signs

You should see your health professional quickly if you have specific problems during pregnancy. These problems include:

- Vaginal bleeding;
- The loss of amniotic fluid;
- Severe stomach pains or headaches;
- Fever;
- You don't feel your baby move for several hours.

Contact your health professional or Info-Santé if anything worries you. Go to the hospital if any of the above warning signs occur. You can also contact your hospital's obstetrics department if the problem occurs toward the end of your pregnancy.

Bleeding during the first months and miscarriage

Pregnant women often experience vaginal bleeding in early pregnancy. About half of women who bleed during the first three months will miscarry. In these cases, the bleeding usually happens several days after the pregnancy has ended. The bleeding may be brownish at first then become red, or it may be clear or dark red.

Contact your health professional if you experience bleeding. He or she will ask questions and examine you, then recommend what to do next.

The gynecological exam is important because it helps determine where the bleeding is coming from, the amount of blood lost, and whether the size of your uterus corresponds to the number of weeks you have been pregnant. If you are more than 10 weeks pregnant, your health professional may also try to listen to the baby's heartbeat. Hearing a heartbeat is a good sign and means the risk of miscarriage is much lower (2%). But if bleeding continues, the risk of miscarriage still remains. Your health professional will be able to decide whether or not an ultrasound is needed to check the condition of the fetus.

About 1 out of every 5 pregnancies ends in a miscarriage. Most miscarriages are caused by major **genetic abnormalities** or malformations. The likelihood of miscarriage also increases with the mother's age.

It's normal to feel sad and distressed after a miscarriage, and to experience a period of mourning. Some women also feel guilty, thinking about what they should have done or should not have done during their pregnancy. But miscarriages aren't related to stress, physical or sexual activity, food, or lifting heavy loads.

Ask for help from your health professional if you're not sure how to tell your children or loved ones. It's also a good idea to talk to a psychologist or social worker if your mourning continues for a long time, if you experience tension with your partner or if you need help with other problems.

▶ **Genetic abnormalities:** Errors in the genes, which are part of chromosomes in human cells. Genes transmit characteristics of parents to their children.

If you want to become pregnant again after a miscarriage, wait until you have at least one normal menstrual period before trying again. This will reduce the risk of miscarrying again. Your chances of having a normal pregnancy after a miscarriage are still excellent. But don't be in a hurry. Avoid rushing into another pregnancy. Take the time you need to mourn the loss of your previous pregnancy, and wait until you really feel ready for the next.

Bleeding after 12 weeks

Sometimes women experience vaginal bleeding after 12 weeks of pregnancy. You should be aware of the following if this happens:

- It isn't normal to bleed after 12 weeks and you should ask for an examination. Sometimes the bleeding does not mean the pregnancy is at risk, but this can only be determined through an appropriate evaluation.
- The bleeding may come from the cervix, which is more sensitive during pregnancy. You may bleed slightly after a gynecological exam, for example. In this case you don't need to be examined for the light bleeding.
- The cervix may also bleed more easily if you have a sexually transmitted infection.
- Bleeding may come from the placenta, and this can complicate the pregnancy. This situation requires immediate attention.

If your bleeding is clear red and you need to wear a sanitary pad, see your health professional quickly. He or she will determine whether the bleeding is from the placenta. In some cases, an ultrasound may be needed to find the source of the bleeding. Women with Rh negative blood may need to be given immunoglobulin (WinRho™).

Possible sources of fluid loss

Type of loss	Description	Quantity
Vaginal discharge	• More abundant and more liquid in the last months of pregnancy • May wet your underwear but not more • May soak a panty liner	The amount you lose can also help distinguish between vaginal fluid, urine loss and water breaking. To estimate the quantity: • Use a sanitary pad; • Check the pad 30 minutes later; • If your water has broken, the pad will be soaked and heavy.
Urine	• More often after physical exertion, movements, sneezing or coughing • Leaking stops after you empty your bladder	
Amniotic fluid (water)	• Continuous loss of a clear, odourless liquid	

Loss of amniotic fluid

You may also lose fluid during your pregnancy. This might be in the form of vaginal fluids, urine or amniotic fluid (water breaks). Your baby may be at risk if your water breaks before 37 weeks. See the table on page 103 to determine the type of loss you're experiencing.

If you think your water has broken or aren't sure, call the delivery room or go to the hospital or place where you are to give birth to determine whether you're losing amniotic fluid or not.

Severe headaches or stomach pains

High blood pressure does not usually cause symptoms during pregnancy. But if you have severe headaches, stomach pains, blurred vision or generally don't feel well, you might have preeclampsia: high blood pressure and protein in the urine. This condition can be dangerous for you and your baby. Have your blood pressure checked if you feel any of these symptoms.

See your health professional right away if:

- Your blood pressure is abnormal;
- The other symptoms get worse or are worrying you, even if your blood pressure is normal.

Fever

Being pregnant doesn't protect you against infection. If you have a cold and mild fever (about 38 to 38.4°C when you take your temperature orally), you can take acetaminophen to control the temperature and relieve the pain. You can also contact an Info-Santé nurse or your health professional for advice. But if your mild fever lasts more than 24 hours, or if you have a high fever (38.5°C or more), it can be harmful to the pregnancy or may suggest you have an infection that needs to be treated.

In the following situations, you should contact a doctor who can make a diagnosis and recommend appropriate treatment:

- You have a fever with a temperature of 38 to 38.4°C, when taken orally, that lasts more than 24 hours.
- You have a high fever with a temperature of 38.5°C or more, when taken orally at 2 different times.
- Your general health is poor, you feel unwell or you have severe chills.
- You're worried.

Your baby doesn't seem to be moving

Your baby will be more active at certain times of the day. You might also not notice him moving because you've been more active or distracted than usual. After 30 weeks of pregnancy, you should feel your baby move at least 10 times in a 24-hour period. You may not feel all of your baby's movements even though he's still active (remember the movements you saw on the ultrasound that you didn't feel). Toward the end of the pregnancy, you may feel your baby's movements differently, but you should feel him moving right up to birth.

If during the 3rd trimester, you don't feel your baby moving or he seems to be moving less than usual, rest and observe what's happening. If you feel less than 6 different movements over a period of 2 hours, quickly contact the birthing centre or go to the hospital to make sure your baby is okay.

Contractions before the 37th week

It's normal for you to feel contractions during your pregnancy that aren't related to labour. They're called Braxton-Hicks contractions and are irregular and felt in different ways, with or without pain. They may be due to sudden changes in your position, or because you've been standing for a long time. You may also feel little electric shocks in the cervix area or cramps that last a few seconds, similar to menstrual cramps. These are not contractions, but are reactions generally caused by your baby's movements.

But if you feel your uterus harden in a regular way, or if you feel pain, you may be having real contractions. The pain of the first contractions sometimes feels like that of menstrual cramps. If they are true contractions, they will last at least 20 seconds and happen at regular intervals.

If you feel regular contractions or pain before 37 weeks, you may be going into premature labour, especially if you have vaginal discharge. Contact your health professional or the hospital to evaluate the situation. Sometimes premature labour can be stopped if you get help fast enough.

From 37 weeks on, the same situation can mean the onset of labour, which is perfectly normal (see the section on delivery, page 127).

High-risk pregnancy

Some conditions create riskier pregnancies that need to be monitored more closely, often in a specialized clinic for high-risk pregnancies. This section describes high blood pressure, diabetes and twins.

High blood pressure during pregnancy

Some women have high blood pressure during their pregnancy. They are considered more at risk if they've already been treated for high blood pressure, if they've already had high blood pressure during an earlier pregnancy, or if they're expecting twins.

High blood pressure during pregnancy should be treated by resting at home, doing fewer activities, and sometimes taking medication to lower blood pressure.

If your blood pressure starts to increase, the protein levels in your urine will also be tested. If protein levels are also high, this means you have preeclampsia (high blood pressure with protein in your urine). This often means you need to be hospitalized to monitor both your condition and your baby's more closely. Sometimes labour must be

Differences between contractions and abdominal aches	
Problems	**Symptoms**
Heartburn	• Pain in the upper belly • Burning sensation due to excess acid
Intestinal cramps	• Pain throughout the belly due to diarrhea or constipation
Urinary tract infection	• Pain in the lower belly, and sometimes back • Frequent need to urinate in small amounts; false urge to pee, and sense of urgency; loss of urine • Burning sensation when urinating • Continued urge to pee after urinating • Sometimes, blood in urine
Ligament pain	• Stretching sensation or irritation in the lower belly, especially when you move, exert yourself physically, walk a long time, or turn in the night (ligament pain is more common in a second pregnancy and is not dangerous to you or your baby)
Uterine contractions	• Feeling of hardening of the uterus and pain • The first contractions may feel like menstrual cramps • The pain is regular and happens at regular intervals • The pain lasts at least 20 seconds.

induced, depending on the status of your pregnancy and the severity of the condition. Birth is the only way to treat preeclampsia. You and your medical team will decide the best time to deliver your baby.

Pregnancy diabetes

Diabetes during pregnancy, which is also known as gestational diabetes, is due to an increase in the level of sugar in your blood. The higher blood sugar level is caused by the placenta, which produces different hormones. Pregnancy diabetes is different from other types of diabetes. There is no risk of your baby being malformed. The main result of pregnancy diabetes is a larger baby, which can mean a more difficult labour for mother and child. Your baby may also have hypoglycemia at birth and have breathing problems.

The first step if you have pregnancy diabetes is to make sure you eat a balanced diet. You can meet with a nutritionist who will explain how to eat well. The diet for a woman with pregnancy diabetes is different from what is usually recommended for other people with diabetes since a pregnant woman must eat more nutrients to help her baby grow. Daily exercise is also encouraged, for example walking for half an hour.

If your blood sugar level (glycemia) is still high after eating well and exercising, you may be prescribed insulin. The treatment may sound complicated but it's not, and your medical team will guide you along. You may also be given 1 or more ultrasounds and extra tests to make sure your baby is doing well during the last weeks of pregnancy.

If you have gestational diabetes, it's recommended that you have another blood test after giving birth. It will check to see if your sugar level has returned to normal, which is usually the case. But you should also know that you will have a higher risk of diabetes later in life. Keep a normal body weight and exercise regularly to lower your risk.

Twins

You've just learned that you're expecting twins, triplets or quadruplets? If the arrival of a child was already going to change your life, how about several at once! You'll have to make some adjustments in planning your pregnancy, delivery and life after birth.

A twin or multiple pregnancy means that the mother is carrying more than one baby: twins, triplets, etc. Twin pregnancies are more common today than before, especially due to fertility treatments. In Québec in 2000, about 2.5% of newborns were twins.

There are two types of twins: identical and non-identical. In the case of identical twins, both babies come from the same egg and the same sperm. They have the same genes, they are the same sex and most of the time they share the same placenta. Non-identical twins come from two eggs fertilized by two different sperm, which grow side by side in the uterus. They are two individuals with different genes, and they may be brother and sister – they are not necessarily the same sex.

Here are a few tips to help you prepare for the arrival of twins at home:

- Try to find time to take care of yourself.
- Has someone offered to help during your recovery? Accept it but be clear about your needs. Make a list of household chores and a schedule, which can be adjusted later as needed.
- Ask for help during the weeks after your return home. If you don't have friends or family living close enough, ask your CLSC about groups in your area that can help.
- When cooking, make larger batches and freeze some. Your parents and friends can also help by bringing meals as gifts.
- Don't buy everything in double or triple. You can borrow furniture, baby carriages and clothes, or buy second hand.

TWO TYPES OF TWINS

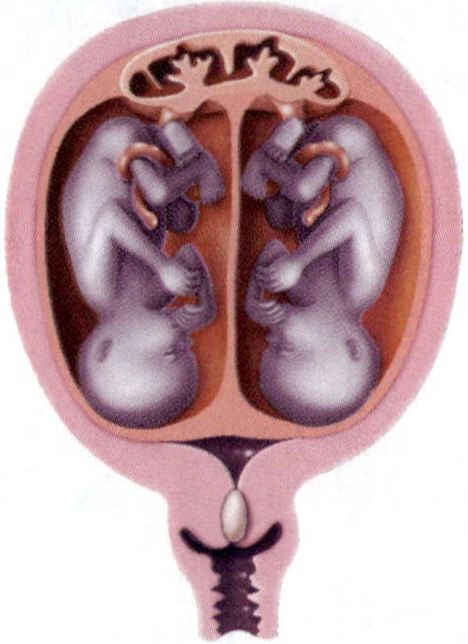

Identical twins

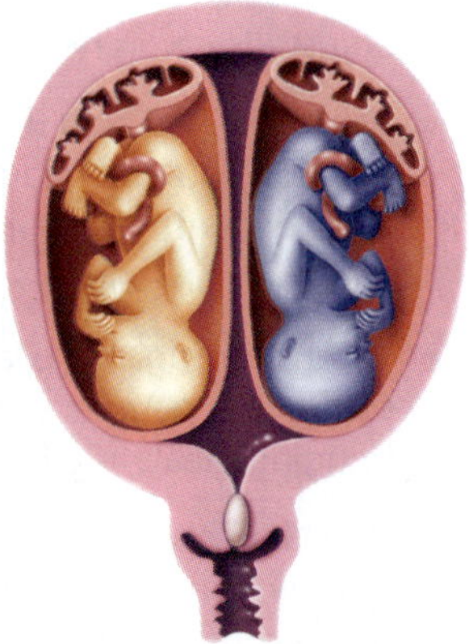

Non-identical twins

Twin pregnancies are considered high risk. If you are pregnant with twins you will benefit from closer monitoring, with more medical visits and exams. You will be advised to see an obstetrician who is familiar with this type of pregnancy and with delivering twins. Here are the most common problems that happen during twin pregnancies:

- Premature babies: The most common problem is premature labour, which can lead to premature babies. The risk of disease and death is higher in this case than for babies born at term.
- Twin-to-twin transfusion syndrome: Problems can happen with identical twins if the blood from the placenta is not shared equally between the two fetuses.
- Second baby: When twins are being delivered, the second baby is more at risk of complications and accidents due to the umbilical cord, the placenta or the baby's position.

You should plan your delivery with your doctor and the team that will take care of you. Your doctor will evaluate your situation and needs and discuss them with you. When the first baby is ready for delivery in a head-first position, which is the case in about two-thirds of twin pregnancies, vaginal delivery is generally recommended regardless of the position of the second baby. In 40% of twin pregnancies, both babies are in a head-first position. You should also plan for the location of your delivery. Women expecting twins are advised to give birth in a hospital, where all the specialized equipment and people, such as nurses, obstetric, pediatric and anesthetic care, are available.

During your pregnancy, you and other members of your family will also be planning for the arrival of your new babies. The best way is probably to talk to parents of twins. Their experience and tips will no doubt be helpful. There are associations of parents of twins in several regions of Québec. Ask your CLSC about the services and groups in your region that can help or provide information to you.

Multiple Births Canada
1 866 228-8824
www.multiplebirthscanada.org

Association de Parents de Jumeaux et Triplés de la région de Montréal
514 990-6165
www.apjtm.com (French only)

Association des parents de jumeaux et plus de la région de Québec
418 653-9607
www.apjq.net (French only)

Relationship violence

Some people have trouble talking about the problems they experience during pregnancy. Relations in your home might be very tense and some couples experience situations of domestic violence or partner abuse. All forms of violence can affect your health and that of your children, whether it's psychological, verbal, physical or sexual violence or financial domination.

These are examples of domestic violence:

Your spouse:

- Constantly criticizes you, your tastes, or your abilities;
- Puts down your relationships or stops you from seeing your family or friends;
- Controls your activities or how you dress;
- Makes fun of your physical appearance or sexual performance;
- Gets angry about anything and everything at home;
- Threatens to hurt you or uses the children to get at you.

Fear, shame and embarrassment can keep some victims of violence silent about their troubles. It's important to break the silence and talk to someone right away who can help and guide you. A health professional at your CLSC, where psycho-social services are offered, can help.

The staff at your CLSC will also know of organizations and resources available to help in your region.

SOS Violence conjugale
Bilingual telephone service open 24 hours a day, 7 days a week
1 800 363-9010
514 873-9010

CYCLE OF VIOLENCE

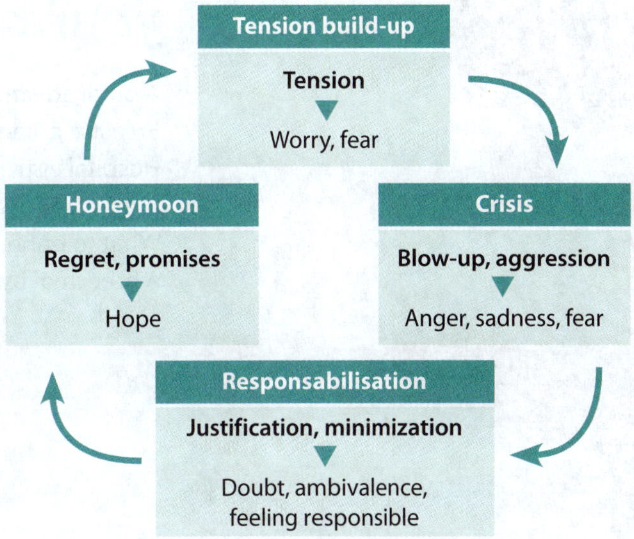

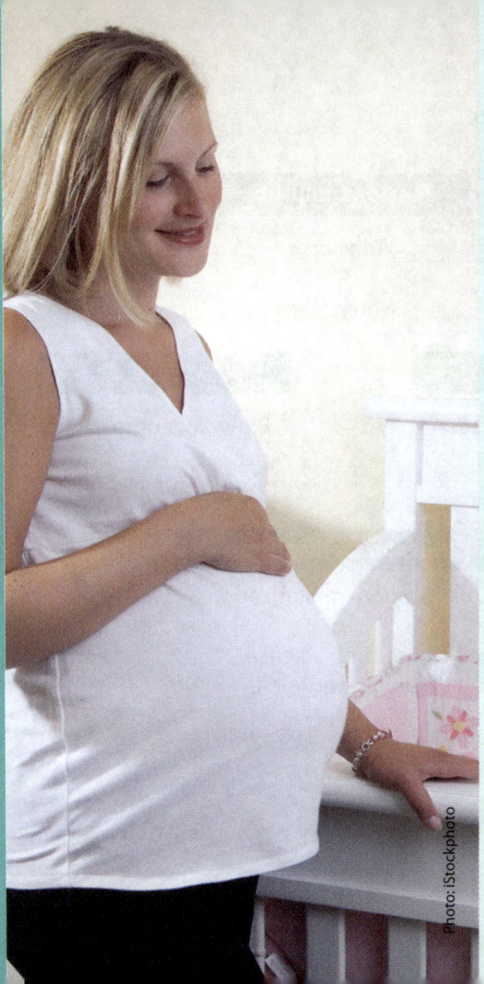
Photo: iStockphoto

Getting ready for your baby's arrival

A bit of advance planning

The arrival of every new child means that parents have to adapt to a new reality. At first, you won't be able to look after your home the way you usually do. Just taking a shower can become an adventure in itself! It's best to prepare ahead of time: arrange to have someone look after your children, cook meals and freeze them, accept that the house may be a bit disorganized. Ask yourself who can help: family, friends, neighbours, a community group. Also think about what won't be helpful; for example, company or advice that is not important. Your baby will be the star of the show; create a space to welcome and respect your bundle of joy.

Have you made arrangements to have someone look after your children when the time comes for the baby to arrive? Explain your children's routine to the person who will be looking after them.

Make sure to accept offers of help – if they suit you! There are community organizations that can help women who have recently given birth, for example by providing a few hours a week of housecleaning or babysitting. Find out what services are available in your region.

A suggestion for family and friends who want to offer a gift to celebrate the baby's arrival: why not offer "help certificates," which can be traded in for babysitting, cooking meals, housecleaning, etc.

Breast-feeding

It's a good idea to find out more about breast-feeding while you're still pregnant. You can go to breast-feeding information meetings, read about it, talk to women who have breast-fed or contact a breast-feeding volunteer or breast-feeding mentor.

Each breast-feeding experience is unique and each baby is different. If your first experience was difficult, it doesn't mean that you'll have difficulties with your next baby. It is very possible to breast-feed after a caesarean, if your baby is premature, or if you have twins. You may begin to breast-feed even if you aren't sure that you'll continue for several months.

A unique food

Breast milk is a living, fresh food that is passed directly from mother to baby. It adapts to the needs and age of your child. Babies like the taste of breast milk. Its taste varies slightly depending on the mother's diet, which gets the baby used to different flavours.

Breast milk is complete and is easy to digest. It is made of non-allergenic proteins, easily absorbed sugars, iron and enzymes that help the baby's digestion. It provides your baby with all the kinds of fat he needs. It contains high levels of omega-3 fatty acids and other essential fatty acids that help the brain and eyesight to develop. Breast milk provides the exact dose of vitamins and minerals needed for a baby's growth, while adapting to the maturity of his kidneys.

A gift for mom and baby

Breast-feeding protects the mother and baby against many illnesses. Breast milk contains living cells and antibodies that protect your baby against infection. No other food contains these things, not even commercial infant formula.

> The longer the mother breast-feeds, the greater the protection. Even a small amount of breast milk can make a difference.

Breast-fed babies are less likely to have anemia, gastroenteritis, diarrhea, respiratory illnesses (colds, laryngitis, bronchitis, etc.), ear infections and meningitis than non-breast-fed babies. When such illnesses do occur in breast-fed babies, they are less serious and require less hospitalization. Breast-fed babies are also better protected against many chronic illnesses.

Women who breast-feed are also rewarded. In the short term, breast-feeding reduces the risk of **hemorrhaging** after delivery. Mothers who breast-feed are less likely to experience anemia because breast-feeding delays the return of periods. In the long term, women who have breast-fed are less likely to get osteoporosis and to develop breast, ovarian or uterine cancer.

Practical and economical

Breast-feeding is practical for the baby because the milk is readily available, anytime. When your baby is hungry, he doesn't have to wait. Breast-feeding is also practical for the parents. You don't have anything to buy, wash, prepare, keep or warm up. If the mother wants to go out without the baby, she can express (pump) her milk so that someone else can feed the baby while she's out.

Breast-feeding makes family outings easier because the milk is always ready, day or night, at the movies, outside, while visiting friends or travelling.

▶ **Hemorrhaging:** Heavy bleeding.

Fathers and breast-feeding

As a father, you play an important role in the decision to initiate and to continue breast-feeding. Many women say that the support of their partner was key to breast-feeding success. This support can be in the form of encouragement or protection against negative pressure from those around you.

The mother will often need help with breast-feeding and you're in the best position to do so. You can help your partner get your baby latched on and help her find a comfortable position while she's nursing during the first few days. Little details, such as bringing her a pillow, a drink or a snack, are always appreciated.

As a father, you'll find many ways to be involved. Your baby needs to be held by you and to feel secure in your arms. He also needs you to change his diaper, give him a bath and dress him. To grow as an individual, he has a real need for experiences and emotional relationships outside his bond with his mother, who is the centre of his universe. This can only happen over time, with someone who is equally important to him, his father. Each father finds his own way of being involved in caring for his child.

Breasts and breast-feeding

You don't need to do anything special to prepare your breasts for breast-feeding. Whether your breasts are big or small, or your nipples long or short, your breasts were made to produce milk and feed your baby. Throughout pregnancy, they have been naturally preparing to breast-feed. Regardless of your delivery date, you will have breast milk to offer your baby.

Breast-feeding accessories

There are more and more products on the market: breast pumps, pillows, nursing pads and more. None of these accessories are essential. Generally speaking, you don't need to buy these accessories during your pregnancy. Support groups are a good source of information when it comes time to choose a breast pump or other breast-feeding accessories. Wearing a nursing bra is optional, but if you do decide to wear one, you should wait until the end of your pregnancy before buying one.

Hospital visit

During your pregnancy, you can find out about the different options available for giving birth (hospital, birthing centre) and their specific features (routine, rules, length of stay, rates and types of intervention). You may also visit them. These steps will often help you feel more secure.

> **Normally, you and your partner or the person who will be with you during delivery can visit the hospital where you will give birth. This will allow you to picture the birthing environment and to know what to do when you arrive.**

It's also a good opportunity to familiarize yourself with the route to the hospital, find the parking lot and find out about admission procedures. During this visit, the hospital staff will be able to answer your questions, tell you about the services available and explain how the team works.

Find out from your health professional or the person giving your prenatal classes how to go about arranging a visit.

Birth plan

Parents need to make decisions about treatments for both mother and baby at the time of birth. You will feel better prepared if you've taken the time to think about the following list. But keep in mind that no one knows ahead of time how the delivery will go. You can change your minds during delivery and you should stay open to any eventuality.

- Define your wishes and fears.
- Share your thoughts with your partner and with family and friends.
- Let the health professionals who are going to be at the delivery, and anyone else who will be with you, know of your preferences.

A birth plan is a tool that can guide you in thinking about how you want things to go. It also lets you communicate your wishes, verbally or in writing, to health professionals and others concerned.

There are many examples of birth plans available. You can ask for a sample from your health professional or from the instructor of your prenatal class or activity. Find out if the facility where you plan to give birth offers a model. You can also find examples of birth plans in books and on the Internet.

However you use it, remember that a good birth plan:

- is clear and short;
- is well prepared, given to your health professional and is gone over with him or her **before the delivery**.

Remember that a birth plan represents the ideal situation you want to experience, but things don't always go according to plan during delivery. Keep an open mind and have faith. And don't forget that if you feel powerless in the face of the decisions you need to make, you can ask your health professionals for the support you need. Trust them! They will help you throughout the delivery. They have experience, and their first concern is the well-being of you and your baby.

Here are a few tips to help you plan the birth of your baby as best as possible. Think about specific topics and find out about your rights during labour and delivery and after the birth of your baby.

Some hospitals offer a sample birth plan. You can also ask for one from your health professional or prenatal class instructor, or look for one in books or on the Internet.

Things to think about when making a birth plan

Topics	You have the right:
Who will be with you during labour and delivery?	• To be accompanied by the father of your child or the people that you choose; • To know that you may be examined by professionals who are in training (doctors, nurses, midwives).
What methods would you like to use during labour to lessen the pain, provide relief or make it easier to tolerate?	• To experience labour and the birth of your baby at your own pace; • To push and deliver in the position that suits you best.
What is your opinion on the possible interventions during labour and delivery?	• To be informed of the motives and reasons for all interventions (induction, stimulation, forceps, episiotomy, epidural, sedative, continuous monitoring, IV drip, etc.), to be informed of their effects on you and your baby and to refuse those that you don't want.
How do you want to deal with the unexpected during pregnancy, labour and delivery?	• To be made aware of the medical reasons for an intervention and the various possible options; • To be informed of the various types of anesthetic available and to choose the one that suits you; • To be accompanied at all times by the father or someone who is important to you.
How do you want to experience the first few moments with your baby?	• To have skin-to-skin contact with your baby beginning at birth and to keep him in your arms as long as you wish

Topics	You have the right:
Will you need to stay at the place where the baby was born?	• To share a room with your baby at all times, regardless of the number of occupants in the room; • To ask that arrangements be made so that the baby's father or the person who is with you can stay in the room with you at night; • To ask not to be disturbed by the institution's routines, according to your need for rest or privacy.
What do you think of the exams and interventions that may be suggested for you and your baby after birth?	• To refuse medications offered to you if you don't feel they are necessary; • To be made aware of the reasons for exams or interventions suggested for your baby and to refuse or delay them (eye drops, vitamin K injection, blood tests, etc.).
How do you want to feed your baby?	• To breast-feed your baby on demand and request that no supplement (water, artificial milk) be given to him; • To have available to you people who are familiar with breast-feeding to help if you need it.
How do you want to handle the unexpected after the birth of your baby (e.g., if you or your baby needs to be hospitalized)?	• To benefit from any measure that will help you stay constantly with your baby.

This information is adapted in part from the ***Grossesse et accouchement. Droits des femmes*** brochure published by the Association pour la Santé Publique du Québec (ASPQ).

What to bring to the hospital or birthing centre?

Suggestions for mothers

- Your health insurance card (medicare)
- Your complementary health insurance papers (if you have a private health plan)
- Your birth plan
- Comfortable clothes to wear during labour (if you don't want to wear a gown)
- Warm socks
- Massage oil
- Lip balm
- Tissues
- Your pillow
- Pyjamas
- A bathrobe
- Slippers
- A nursing bra
- Nursing pads
- Underwear
- Highly absorbent sanitary pads (hospitals and birthing centres don't always provide them)
- Your toiletry kit
- Snacks (muffins, granola bars, dried fruits, fruit juice)
- A book or magazines
- Clothing for when you leave
- A calling card (if you want to make long-distance calls)
- A list of your medications, if you take any

Suggestions for your baby

- Diapers (if they are not supplied)
- Pyjamas
- Undershirts
- A blanket
- A hat
- Clothing for when you leave (adapted to the season)
- A proper car seat (mandatory to leave the hospital)

Suggestions for fathers

- Comfortable clothing and shoes
- Food and drinks
- A camera with batteries and film (if needed)
- Something to read
- Your toiletry kit

For fathers who plan to sleep on site

- Your pillow
- Pyjamas
- A change of clothes

A breech baby

If your baby is in the breech position (when the baby's feet or bottom are in the lower part of your uterus, instead of his head), your doctor or midwife may suggest trying to turn the baby sometime around the 36th or 37th week so that his head faces down. This will increase your chances of having a vaginal delivery. This procedure, called external cephalic version, is done in the hospital.

External cephalic version is a technique, performed using only external manipulations to turn the baby so that his head is down. Generally, this technique is done after having checked the baby's position using an ultrasound. Turning the baby is sometimes impossible or may not be advised in some situations; for example, when there is a lack of fluid. After the baby is turned, a test for fetal reactivity is performed (monitoring) to ensure your baby reacted well to the change. There are fewer risks associated with turning the baby than with having a caesarean.

If turning the baby isn't possible, you can discuss with your doctor or midwife the option of attempting a vaginal delivery. Vaginal delivery of a breech baby requires a special evaluation and isn't done in every hospital. In most cases of breech presentation, a caesarean is required.

BREECH POSITION

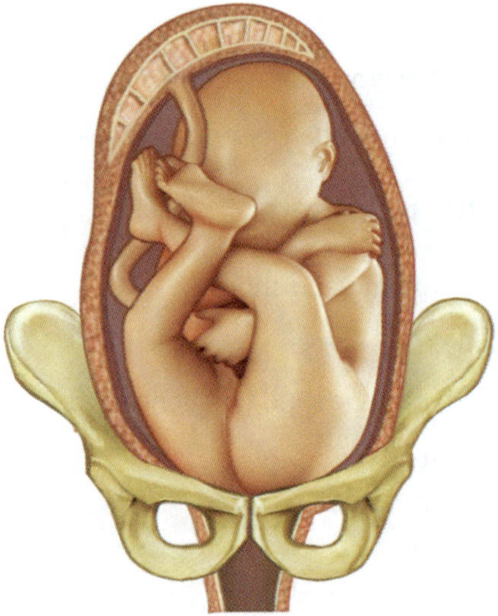

Illustration: Maurice Gervais

Delivery

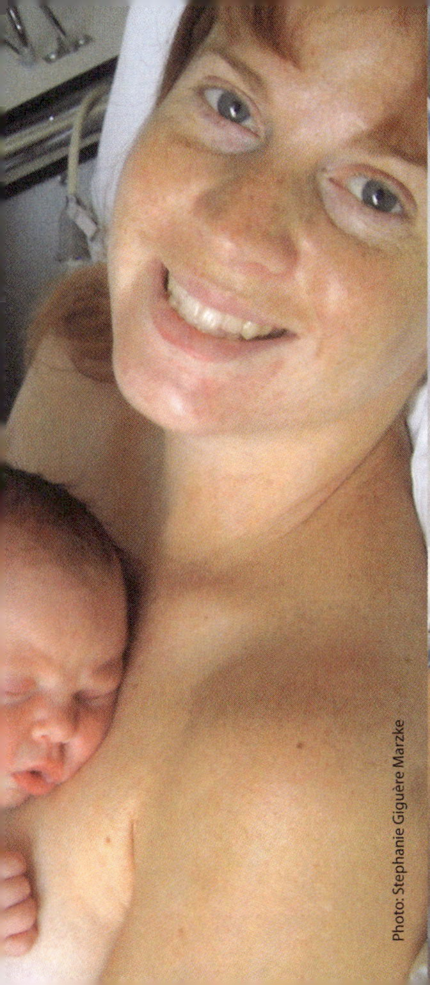
Photo: Stephanie Giguère Marzke

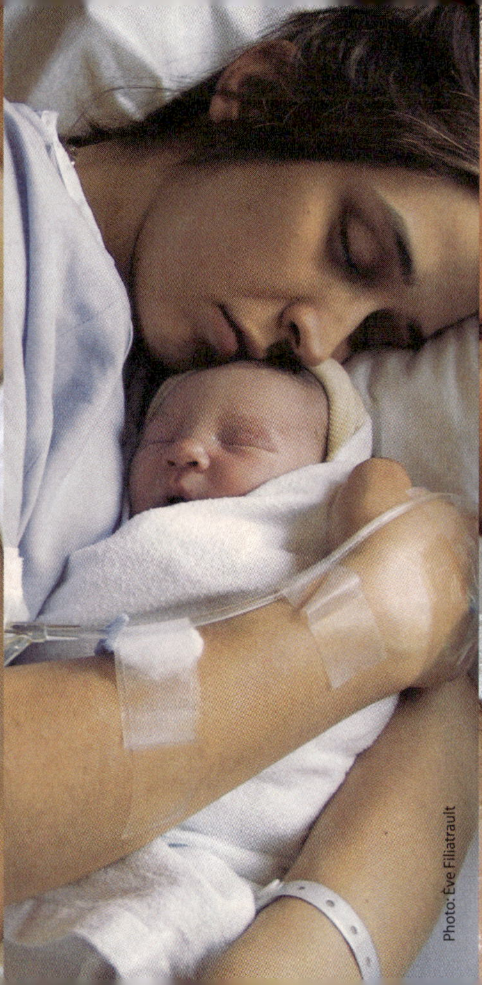
Photo: Ève Filiatrault

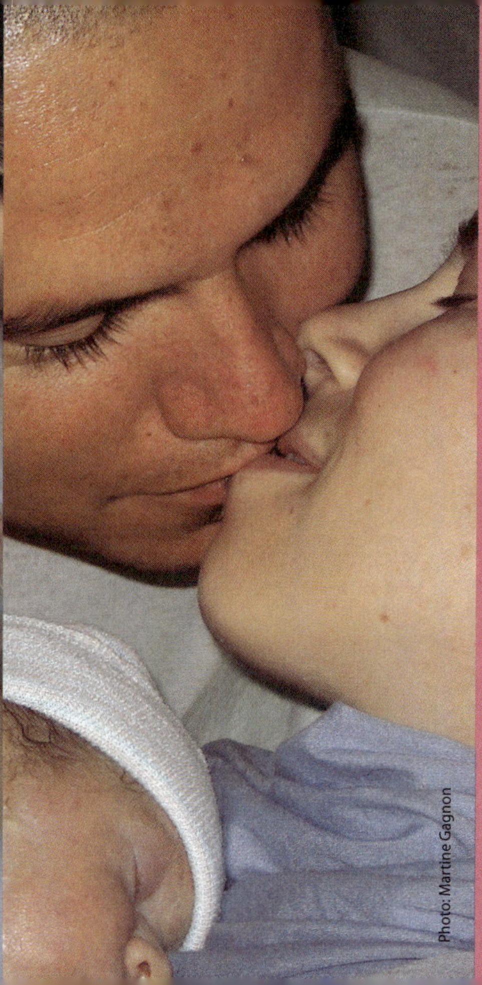
Photo: Martine Gagnon

Delivery

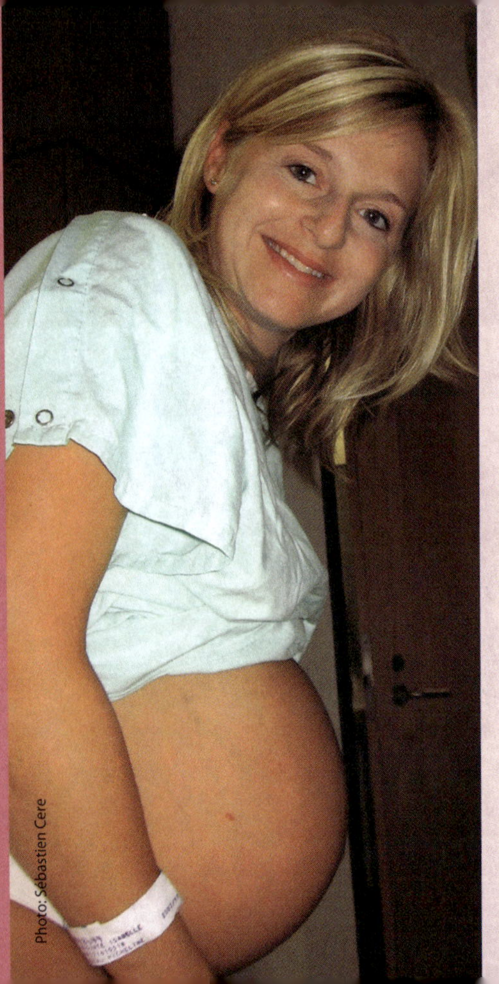

Photo: Sébastien Cere

The start of labour

Recognizing the start of labour

You will soon be bringing your baby into the world. Labour generally begins on its own sometime between 38 and 41 weeks after the start of your last menstrual period. However, delivery anywhere between 37 and 42 weeks is considered full-term. Your expected delivery date is not a deadline. Even if you haven't given birth by 40 weeks, there's still a good chance labour will begin on its own.

It might be better to give birth between 41 and 42 weeks than to wait until 42 weeks have passed. If you have completed 41 weeks and there is no sign that labour has started, you can discuss your options with your doctor or midwife. They may induce labour (see Possible interventions during labour, page 146) or have you undergo some tests (monitoring, ultrasound) to decide whether you can continue to wait for labour to begin on its own.

No one can predict when and how your labour will begin. Most women will recognize labour because of certain signs. It's normal at that point to feel excited or scared.

Passing the mucus plug

The mucus plug is made of thick secretions sometimes tinted with blood. It blocks the cervix during pregnancy. You may lose your mucus plug without even realizing it several days before you give birth or during labour. Even if you do notice it, this doesn't necessarily mean that labour has started. You need to wait for other signs.

Rupture of membranes

For some women (about 1 in 10), the rupture of the amniotic membrane signals the beginning of labour. The amniotic membrane is made of several layers; that's why it's also referred to as "membranes". This membrane surrounds your baby and contains the amniotic fluid around him. When it breaks, the amniotic fluid leaks out. It is often referred to as having your "water break" because the liquid that leaks out is clear like water, although sometimes tinted with a bit of blood. You may only leak a few drops or it may leak enough to wet your bed or your clothes. There may be enough liquid that it leaks onto the floor. At the end of your pregnancy, it can be difficult to tell the difference between normal vaginal discharge and amniotic fluid (see Possible Sources of Fluid Loss, page 103). Generally with amniotic fluid you will soak a sanitary pad.

What should I do?

When your water breaks, you should go to the hospital or birthing centre, even if you don't have any contractions. Staff will make sure that your baby is doing well and will check whether your membranes did actually rupture. (There is a larger amount of vaginal discharge at the end of pregnancy, which can be confused with having your water break.)

Labour should start in the hours after your water breaks. If the contractions take too long to start, if you are a streptococcus carrier or if you have a cervical infection, labour may need to be induced.

Contractions

For most women, labour begins with uterine contractions. You may have already felt your abdomen become hard during your pregnancy. These are contractions that, while sometimes uncomfortable, aren't really painful (Braxton-Hicks contractions).

Contractions experienced during delivery are different from Braxton-Hicks. Your abdomen gets tight and hard and the contractions become more and more uncomfortable. Generally, women feel pain in the lower abdomen, but for others the pain is located in the lower back and spreads to the front. Some women find the pain of contractions similar to menstrual cramps but stronger. Every woman will experience contractions in her own way. The feelings may even be very different for the same woman from one pregnancy to the next.

When should I go to the hospital or birthing centre?

At a certain point, it will be time to go to your birthing place to have your baby. Towards the end of your pregnancy, check with your doctor or midwife about when is the right time. It will depend on your previous deliveries, the distance you have to travel to get there and your health.

If you experience any of the following, you should go right away:

- Your contractions are regular and occur every 5 minutes or less; if you live more than 30 minutes away, you should leave when you are having contractions every 10 minutes;
- Your membranes rupture (your water breaks);
- You are bleeding;
- You don't feel your baby moving (see Problems during pregnancy, page 100).

Women often go to the hospital or birthing centre convinced that they're in active labour when they're actually still in early labour. If this happens, you'll be advised to go home and come back later. This allows you to get used to the contractions at home, in a familiar environment.

When labour begins or when in doubt, call your midwife or a nurse at the obstetrics department of your hospital. They will check with you to see if labour has started, and can answer your questions, give you advice and tell you when to come to the hospital.

Help from the father or someone familiar

A woman in labour needs to feel that she's not alone. During delivery, she needs to have someone with her that she knows and trusts. This may be the baby's father, a member of her family, a friend or a birth companion (also called doula). This company and closeness will help her feel better, and reassure and encourage her. This is an important life moment to share.

As a father you may feel helpless and powerless while your partner is giving birth, especially since this is an extremely important time for both of you. What do you do when the one you love is in pain and tells you she can't take it any more? How do you deal with all these emotions? There's no magic answer or flawless game plan, but you should know that your presence makes a big difference.

★ You don't need to be a massage expert to be useful during delivery! Don't be afraid to try different things. Your partner will tell you what feels good. Stay with her and continue what you're doing if your words and actions seem to be helping her.

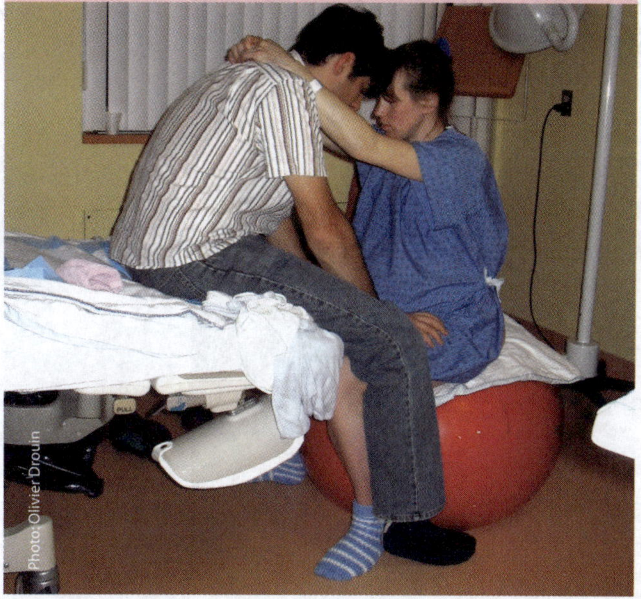
Photo: Olivier Drouin

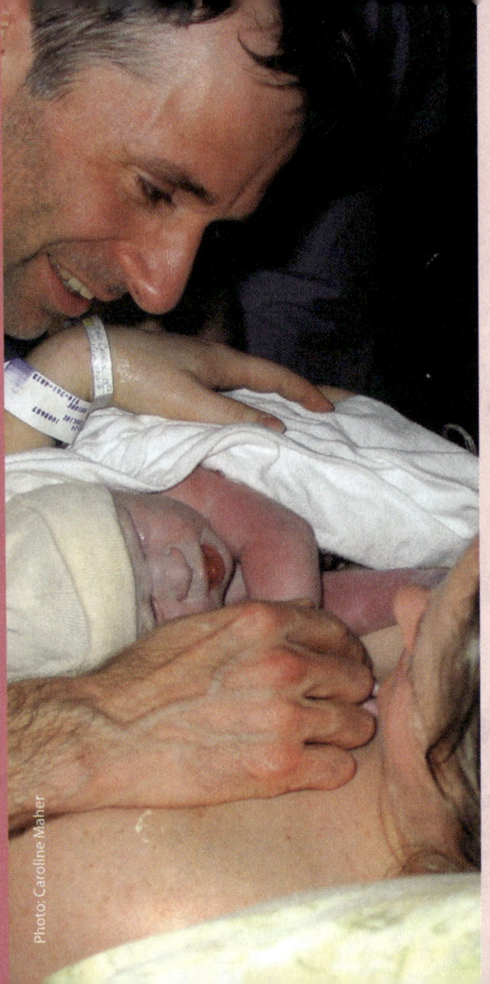

The stages of labour

Throughout labour, your body undergoes various changes that allow your baby to make his way to the outside world. Labour is divided into the following three major stages:

1st stage: opening of the cervix (also called dilation)
2nd stage: descent and birth of your baby
3rd stage: delivery of the placenta

It isn't possible to predict the length of each stage because they differ from one delivery to the next.

OPENING OF THE CERVIX

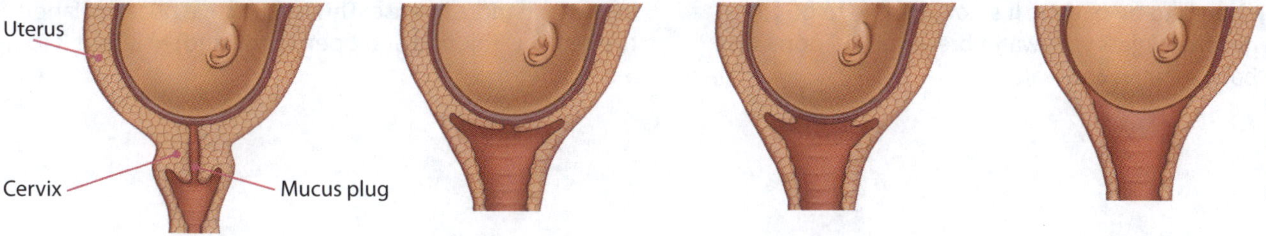

During pregnancy. The cervix is closed and thick.

Beginning of labour. The cervix has thinned (also called effaced).

During labour. The cervix is opening (dilating).

At the end of the 1st stage of labour. The cervix is completely dilated (10 cm).

Illustrations: Maurice Gervais

First stage of labour: opening of the cervix

The first stage of labour is the period when you have regular contractions. These contractions allow the cervix to open completely, until it is 10 centimetres (cm) wide.

Progression of labour

Early phase or "latent phase" of labour

Before getting to the actual stage of labour itself, you may have contractions without knowing how things will go next. Is this the start of labour or a false alarm? At the beginning, the contractions are not very strong. You'll be able to talk during a contraction. They are often irregular and don't last very long. Try to stay calm and don't forget to sleep and eat. Feel free to take a bath or shower if you like. Take this opportunity to come to grips with what's happening to you. This phase may be long or short; you'll need to be patient. It's not yet time to go to the hospital unless your water breaks or you don't feel the baby moving as usual.

If your contractions become weaker or stop, this is false labour. Something is happening inside you, but it's preparatory labour that is "ripening" the cervix.

If the contractions become regular (for example, every 10 minutes) and get closer together, more painful and longer (lasting 30 to 60 seconds), this may mean that you've gone through the latent phase.

Active labour

At some point, you'll feel that labour is progressing. The contractions are painful and getting closer together, longer and more intense. This is the active phase of labour: the cervix is thinned and open (or dilated) to about 3 to 5 centimetres.

The rhythm of the contractions gradually increases and the cervix opens over time to 10 cm (complete dilation). The contractions are often very painful at 8 or 9 cm. They reach their highest intensity just before the complete dilation of 10 cm. This phase can be compared to a storm. You may experience many strong emotions or you may want to scream. You may feel like you're losing control and that it will never end. This is normal. Try to open yourself up to the labour, breathe, visualize the baby starting to move down inside of you and stay in contact with him. Trust yourself, and don't be afraid to ask the person with you or your health professional to give you what you need.

Understanding and managing pain

The pain of labour is unique and has a reason. It signals the opening that will lead to the birth of your baby. These are changes taking place inside your body. They happen gradually. A rhythm develops and the intensity of the pain increases over time. The start of labour is hardest for some women; for others it may be when it is time to push. The pain is stronger during a contraction. The period between contractions gives you time to recover.

Here are some tips to help you manage the pain of childbirth.

Tips for managing the pain of childbirth

- Have someone with you: the baby's father, a family member, friend or birth companion (doula).
- Create a warm, calm and intimate atmosphere.
- Stay warm.
- Trust yourself and your instincts.
- Stay in the moment.
- Visualize what is happening inside you.
- Move and change positions as you need to (don't stay lying down); walk around during contractions.
- Relax.
- Breathe slowly.
- Take a shower or bath.
- Eat and drink as you need.
- Make noise, whisper, moan.
- Don't hesitate to ask for what might help you feel better.
- Have someone encourage and comfort you through their words and actions.
- Have someone touch you, massage you or hold your hand.
- Have someone sponge you with a wet compress (hot or cold).

In most hospitals and birthing centres, you can take a bath or shower. There are also large balls that you can sit and move on at the same time. Don't hesitate to ask for one if it isn't offered.

Massage can help decrease anxiety and make it easier to deal with the pain. You can easily be massaged during labour. Some women and couples learn methods to help make childbirth easier, like breathing and relaxation techniques, visualization, yoga, self-hypnosis and other approaches.

Some women like to have an acupuncture or acupressure specialist with them. These services are not covered by the public health system, so you would need to find out about the methods yourself, including their availability and cost.

Photo: Renée Desroches

For many women, being in the water helps manage the pain.

POSITIONS DURING LABOUR

STANDING

SITTING

SQUATTING

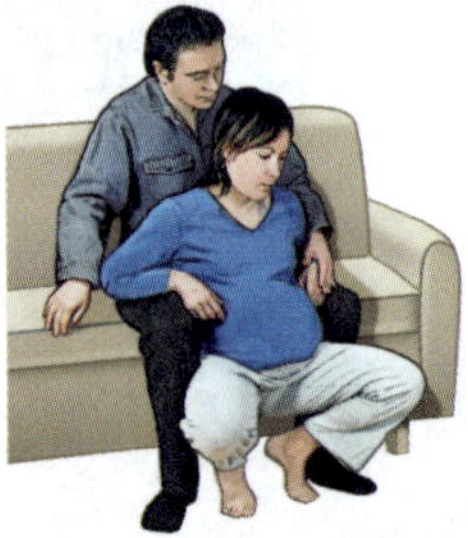

KNEELING

Illustrations: Maurice Gervais

Positions during labour

Throughout labour, you can explore different positions to help the cervix dilate and help you relax between contractions. Lying flat is often the least comfortable position.

Second stage of labour: descent and birth of your baby

The 2nd stage of labour begins when your baby is well descended into your pelvis and the cervix is completely dilated. The baby can now get through the cervix and descend into your vagina to be born.

Pushing

When your cervix is dilated to 10 cm, the sensations become different; you will feel the need to push. The contractions become a force within you, and all your energy is concentrated on pushing to help your baby be delivered. The time between contractions can allow you to recover between pushes. If you feel the need to push before your cervix is completely dilated, your health professional can tell you when the time is right to start pushing.

If you have an epidural, the pushing sensation is lessened and sometimes not even felt at the beginning of the 2nd stage. This feeling will come later, as your baby descends with the contractions. Normally, you can wait to push until you feel the urge to do so. Your efforts will then be more effective: you'll do a better job of pushing and won't have to push as long.

PUSHING POSITIONS

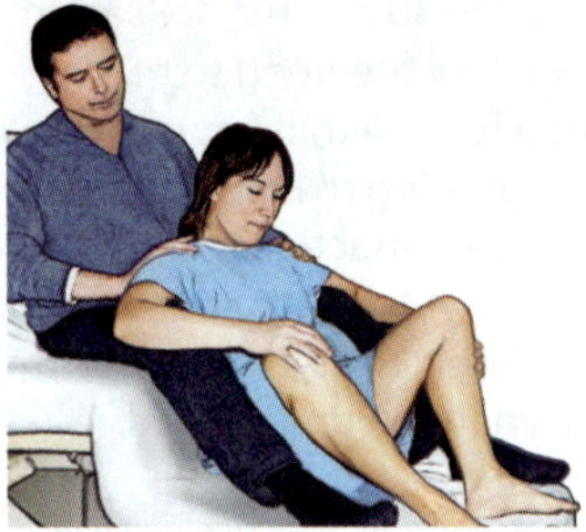

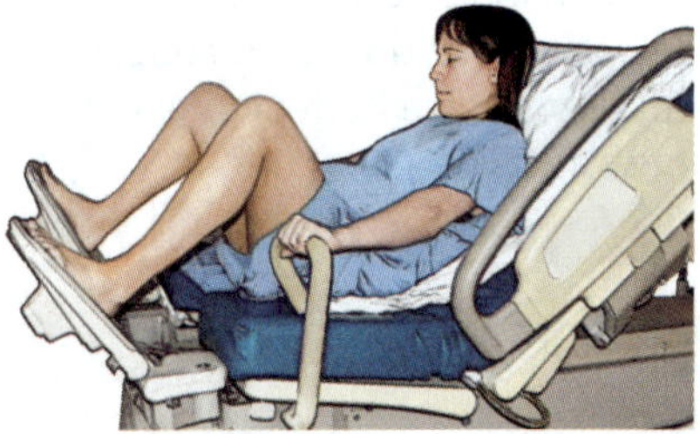

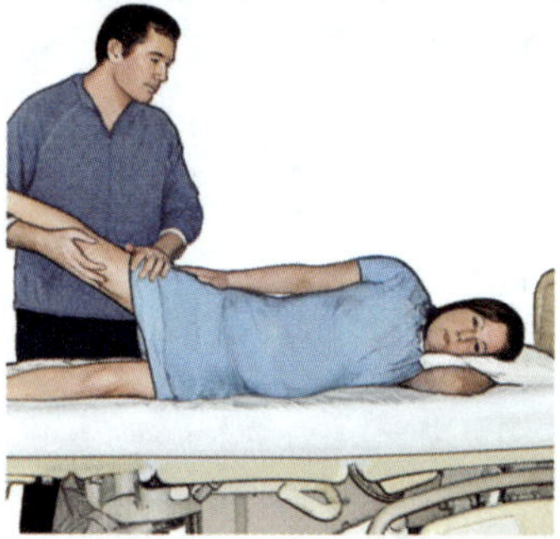

Illustrations: Maurice Gervais

Pushing positions

Get help from your partner or the person and professionals accompanying you to find a position that is comfortable and effective for you. Feel free to change positions when you want.

Birth of your baby

The time when you push is an intense experience for you and those accompanying you. As your baby prepares to enter the outside world, the top of his head will appear as a result of your pushing. If he likes, the father can get into a good position to see the baby's hair. If you like, you can also watch your baby's progress using a mirror set up in the birthing room. After the top of the head, the baby's face will be revealed. Another big push and the baby's shoulders and rest of his body will come out.

BIRTH OF YOUR BABY

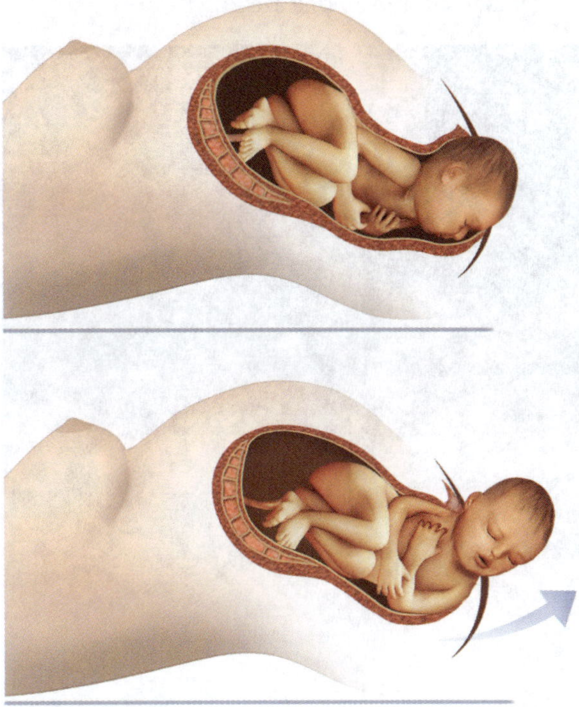

Illustrations: Maurice Gervais

The health professionals may ask the father if he wants to cut the umbilical cord.

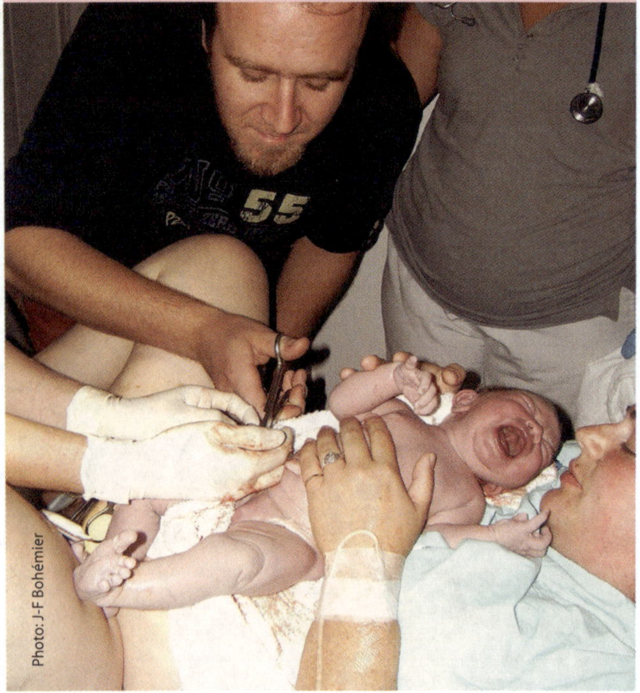

Photo: J-F Bohémier

Just after birth, your baby will announce his presence with his very first sounds. He will then be placed on your belly. The health professionals will dry your baby off and make sure he's doing well. If needed, they will clear the secretions out of his nose and mouth.

With both of you under a warm blanket, you can cuddle your baby with his skin against yours. Discover his face, his fists and feet, and meet his gaze. Your baby's instinct will be to nurse for both food and comfort. The professionals that helped with your delivery can help you start breast-feeding.

Third stage of labour: delivery of the placenta

Delivery of the placenta

Your baby is born, but the delivery isn't over. Contractions will continue for a little while to deliver the placenta.

After the placenta is delivered, your uterus will continue to contract to regain its original shape and to prevent hemorrhaging. The first few times your baby breast-feeds will stimulate the production of a hormone called oxytocin, which increases contractions of the uterus. If the contractions aren't strong enough, there is a risk of hemorrhaging. Your abdomen will then be massaged at the uterus to stimulate it to contract, or else oxytocin will be given as a medication for this purpose.

First moments with the baby

The next few hours are time to welcome your baby and get to know him. The health professionals, who up to this point have been helping very closely, will now be more discrete.

Your baby will again enjoy the warmth of your body, and discover comfort in his father's arms. He recognizes the voices of his parents. Your baby will stick out his tongue, blink his eyes, breathe more quickly, move his lips, turn his head… It's time to get to know one another!

Photo: Nathalie Peron

Your baby is born. It is time to welcome him and to get to know him.

Possible interventions during labour

Induction of labour

When should labour be induced?

Inducing labour is generally done in the following cases: if there is a rupture of membranes but contractions don't start, or if you have passed 41 weeks of pregnancy. In other rare situations, the health of the mother or baby are reasons for inducing labour.

Methods used to induce labour

There are different ways of inducing labour and the method chosen will depend on many things, including the maturity of the cervix and whether or not it is your first delivery. There may be several steps:

- The maturity of the cervix is assessed. If your cervix is still closed, a gel or small tampon soaked in hormones will be inserted to "ripen" the cervix through contractions. This will allow the cervix to become softer and effaced (thinner). The cervix will then dilate or open a few centimetres. Sometimes a catheter is inserted into the cervix with a small balloon on it that, when inflated, allows the cervix to open. These two methods may be a bit uncomfortable, but they help get your cervix ready so the rest of the induction can go well.
- Contractions may then be induced or intensified, if you are already having them, using a drug (oxytocin) given through intravenous drip.
- An artificial rupturing of your membranes can also be performed (breaking your water). This intervention is usually no more painful than a cervical exam and doesn't hurt the baby.

Stimulating labour

Once labour has begun, either naturally or by induction, your health professionals may suggest stimulating labour if your cervix is not dilating and your contractions are too far apart or not strong enough.

The frequency and strength of contractions are increased using a drug (normally oxytocin) given through intravenous drip. Once the oxytocin starts to take effect, you often need to continue taking it until your baby is born.

Monitoring the baby's health

During the active phase of labour, your baby's well-being is checked by listening to his heart with a fetal stethoscope or portable ultrasound machine. During this phase, the test is carried out every 15 to 30 minutes.

In many hospitals and birthing centres, electronic fetal monitors are used to check the baby: two devices are strapped to your abdomen with two belts connected to a machine that displays the readings. The monitor allows your health professionals to listen to your baby's heartbeat and make sure everything is going well. It also registers contractions and your baby's movements.

Electronic fetal monitoring can be done intermittently; for example, every 15 to 30 minutes. But if your baby needs to be monitored more closely, continuous fetal monitoring will be done. This means you will be connected to an electronic fetal monitor for a prolonged period of time. If the monitor bothers you or you'd like to move around more, you can ask if the frequency of monitoring can be modified to give you more freedom.

Hospital staff can explain what the display means. There's no need to worry if you stop hearing the baby's heartbeat: most of the time it's because the baby or mother moved and the device is no longer in the right place. Tell the staff so they can readjust it.

When and why is monitoring used?

When?	Why?
During the last trimester of pregnancy	To make sure your baby is doing well if: • You have health problems (diabetes, high blood pressure); • There are concerns about the baby (baby is moving less, small baby, lack of amniotic fluid).
During induction of labour with drugs; during stimulation of labour with drugs	To make sure your baby is doing well and to determine the frequency of contractions. Monitoring is done until the baby is born.
During labour	To make sure your baby is doing well, to determine the frequency of contractions and to see how your baby is handling them, if: • You had a pregnancy without complications and you're having a normal labour. Many hospitals suggest you be monitored for 20 minutes when you arrive and then every 15 to 30 minutes, based on the intensity of the contractions and how dilation is progressing (electronic intermittent monitoring); • There is any doubt about your baby's well-being, or if the situation requires more in-depth evaluation; • You ask for an epidural during labour. You will probably be connected to the monitor until the baby is born; • You are trying to have a vaginal delivery after a caesarean; • You had a high-risk pregnancy.

Drugs and epidural anesthesia

In hospitals, certain drugs can be used to ease the pain. The most common pain medications are narcotics or nitrous oxide, which decrease the feeling of pain and make the mother drowsy. These drugs cross the placenta and will get into your baby's body so they are not given at the end of labour. This prevents the baby from being drowsy at birth.

In most cases, an epidural anesthesia (epidural block) is suggested if other methods to deal with the pain are no longer working and you feel like you can't take it anymore. The epidural blocks the pain of labour but lets contractions continue. It can slow down labour because it may decrease uterine contractions and it prevents you from moving around as before. For this reason, it's better not to have an epidural too early, but rather to wait until labour is well underway.

An epidural is given by an anesthesiologist who inserts a needle between two vertebrae and injects a drug to freeze the lower part of your body. He or she then removes the needle but may leave a thin, flexible tube in place (catheter) so the quantity of medication can be adjusted during labour.

If you have an epidural, you will have to stay in bed, lying down or sitting up and you will be connected to an intravenous solution. You will probably be connected to a continuous fetal monitor, especially if you have been given drugs to stimulate the contractions. If the anesthesia is mild, you will be able to move your legs. The effects of the epidural may make it more difficult to know how to push when the time comes for your baby to be born. This is why vacuum extractors or forceps are needed more often to help deliver a baby when the mother is under the effect of an epidural. Epidurals do not increase the risk of having a caesarean.

Episiotomy

An episiotomy may occasionally be performed in situations where the baby needs help to be delivered more quickly. An episiotomy is a cut (incision) in the **perineum** made just as the baby is about to be delivered. The cut is then repaired using stitches and a local anesthetic.

Episiotomies are no longer performed automatically because they're found to increase the risk of deep tears to the perineum.

Caesarean

A caesarean is performed when the baby cannot be delivered through the vagina. A caesarean is a surgical operation that involves cutting the mother's abdomen and uterus to retrieve the baby.

A caesarean is performed only in an operating room at the hospital. If you are giving birth at home or in a birthing centre, you will have to go to a hospital and an obstetrician/gynecologist will then be responsible for your care.

Caesareans are safe interventions today and allow many women and babies to be saved. However, there are risks associated with this major surgery: infections, pain, bleeding, **thrombophlebitis** and a longer hospital stay.

If you had a caesarean the last time you gave birth, you may ask yourself how your new baby will be born: vaginally or by caesarean. There are many advantages to a *vaginal birth after caesarean section* (VBAC), but there is also a small risk of uterine rupture. In this case, an emergency caesarean is performed. There may also be consequences for the mother or baby. On the other hand, a planned caesarean includes risks of surgical complications for the mother. It can also increase the risk of minor respiratory problems in the baby after birth.

There are many factors involved in making a decision. Discuss your options with your doctor or midwife.

▶ **Perineum:** The part of the body located between the vagina and anus.

▶ **Thrombophlebitis:** Swelling of a vein due to the formation of a blood clot.

Vaginal birth after caesarean section (VBAC)

Positive factors	Negative factors	Contraindications (unsafe)
• Previous caesarean for a non-recurring reason: - Breech presentation - Fetal distress • Previous successful vaginal delivery • Labour begins on its own	• Previous caesarean because labour was not progressing beyond a certain point • More than one previous caesarean • Deliveries that are close together: less than 18 to 24 months apart • Unfavourable obstetrical conditions	• Previous classical or vertical caesarean (with a vertical incision to the uterus) • Uterus has previously ruptured • Previous uterine surgery (some types) • Certain abnormalities of the uterus • Placenta is not in the proper position or abnormal presentation of the baby • Other contraindications for a vaginal delivery

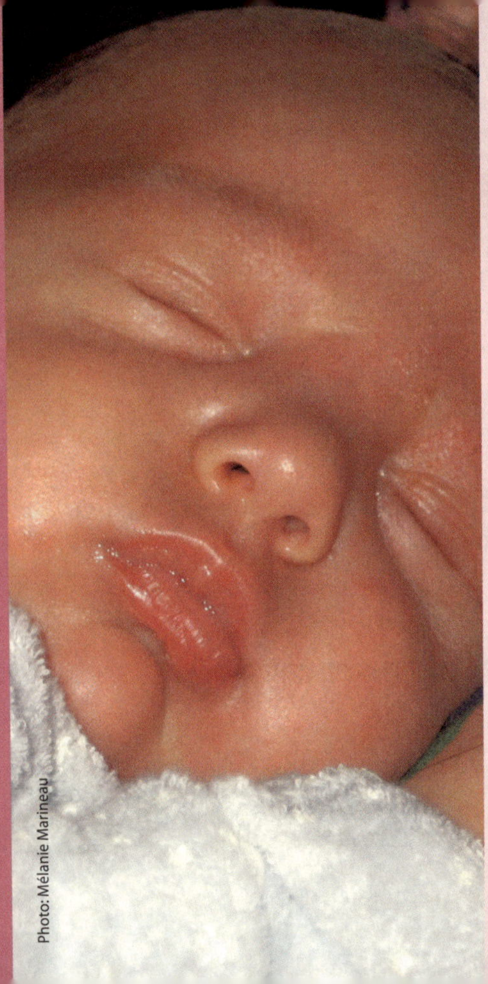

The first few days

Your child is born at last. Who does she look like? Her father? Her mother? Maybe a distant relative? If you've adopted a baby from overseas, she will probably remind you of her home country. Whatever the case, your baby is unique – and now you get to learn all about her.

Your stay at the hospital or birthing centre

> Your hospital stay is an ideal time to start getting to know your baby and learning how to look after her. Take full advantage.

Hospital stays are generally 2 days after a vaginal delivery and 4 days after a caesarean section. At a birthing centre, the stay is usually about 24 hours. More and more hospitals are encouraging parents to keep their baby with them in the hospital room. This gives you more time to get to know your baby and begin taking care of her, with a nurse nearby if you need help or advice. Keep your child close to you, sometimes skin to skin, to make her feel safe and connected. This is also true for dad, who is eager to share his newborn's first moments of life. Staying together will also let you nurse your baby on demand. This is a precious time. But keep a few minutes aside to complete the formalities always required by a birth.

When the unexpected happens

During pregnancy, you may have been asked whether you want a boy or girl. Most parents say they want a healthy baby. They know some babies are not born healthy, representing a major challenge. Sometimes the happy event doesn't happen as expected. Even in the best conditions, we can't always prevent the unknown. Deciding to have a family brings great happiness but also has its share of risk.

Birth	Care of premature babies
Before 34 weeks	Transfer to an intensive care ward for newborns in a hospital that has one. Your baby may: • Receive phototherapy if she has jaundice (exposure to light in an incubator); • Be placed in an incubator to keep warm; • Receive intravenous solutions; • Receive help breathing; • Receive help feeding.
34 to 37 weeks	Extra care, but less of it. Your baby may: • Receive help feeding; • Receive phototherapy if she has jaundice (exposure to light in an incubator); • Receive help breathing (only in rare cases).

Premature babies

The birth may come early, whether you were expecting one baby or twins. A baby is considered premature if born before the 37th week of pregnancy. The length of the baby's hospital stay will depend on how premature she is, and how well she gains weight.

Infection, malformation or other health problem

If your newborn has an infection, malformation or other health problem, she may be hospitalized at birth or in the next few days. This can come as a surprise to parents: "Didn't we say we wanted a healthy baby?"

If your baby has a chronic illness, find out about support groups for parents in the same situation. Help from people who have been through a similar experience can be very valuable.

A few suggestions for difficult moments

You may feel guilty, helpless and tired if your baby is hospitalized for a complication such as premature birth, infection, birth defect (whether discovered before or after birth) or other health problem. Whatever the situation, here are a few suggestions to help you get through these difficult hours.

You don't know what's happening

Be sure to ask questions about your baby's health and the treatment she's receiving. If you have worries about the care and treatment, ask if an alternative is available. She's your baby and you have the right to be involved in decisions affecting her.

Members of the care team will give you information if you ask. Check when is the best time for a discussion. If you never get to see the doctor, find out when he or she usually visits.

You need support

Be sure to ask for support if you think you need it. Specialized hospital teams include social workers and psychologists.

Your baby is in an incubator

Most parents want to be close to their baby. As parents, you have the right to be close to your baby at all times. Don't hesitate to ask for help touching your baby in the incubator or holding her in your arms or kangaroo style, skin to skin under a blanket. Feeling your presence will help your baby. If you're unable to take her out of the incubator, ask if you can put a scarf or piece of clothing that smells of you beside her.

You were expecting to breast-feed

Your baby may be able to breast-feed to some extent. Even if your baby is not yet able to suck, stimulate your breasts in the hours after birth. Express your milk until your baby can breast-feed on her own. Your milk can be kept in a refrigerator or even frozen until the baby is ready. At that time, supplements may be added if necessary.

Ask for help expressing your milk. Breast pumps are available in intensive care wards for newborns. Don't be discouraged if you get only a few drops the first few times. Your breasts need regular stimulation to produce what your baby needs. Being close to your baby or having a photo of her with you while expressing your milk will help increase your production.

If you weren't expecting to breast-feed, it's not too late to think about it. Premature babies have special needs, including the antibodies only your milk can provide.

You're spending a lot of time at the hospital

Every minute you spend with your baby is important. Find out if there are accommodations where you can stay close to your baby if you want to. If possible, ask other family members to look after your other children and to take turns staying close to your baby so you can get some rest. You won't always be able to be at the hospital, especially if you have other children. If the hospital stay continues, you need to rest and get ready to look after your baby once she gets home. Remember, your child needs you during and after her hospital stay.

Who may visit?

Some hospitals allow visits by children and members of the immediate family. Be sure that your visitors are not sick when they come to see your baby. Even an ordinary cold can be serious for a newborn.

It might be a good idea to involve your other children. Reassure them that what's happening to your baby is not their fault. Slightly older siblings may believe their jealousy of the new baby has caused the complication.

Death of a newborn child

It is rare today for children to be stillborn or die in infancy. The cause is usually extremely premature birth or birth defect. Whether it can be explained or not, losing a baby is always very emotional for the parents and family.

There are support groups for parents who lose a child. They can provide valuable help during the time of mourning. Such a loss will cause frequent episodes of sadness, anger and disbelief. The two parents may not experience their grief the same way. Either parent or the couple should feel free to see a psychologist, social worker or other health professional for counselling in the weeks and months after a death.

Screening for hereditary metabolic diseases

Your baby's blood will be tested in her first days for some inherited, or genetic, diseases.

She may also be tested for other inherited metabolic diseases, using a small urine sample taken on her 21st day. This is a voluntary program of the Québec health department, *Le Ministère de la Santé et des Services sociaux du Québec*. It's easy to participate. You will be given a urine sampling kit when you leave the hospital or birthing centre. One of the two envelopes in the kit contains the paperwork: an information pamphlet, a form to fill out, a sheet of blotting paper and a reply envelope. The other envelope contains 2 absorbent pads and instructions on how to use them. Read it carefully and be sure to follow all the steps so the tests are done correctly:

- Don't use disposable moistened wipes to wash your baby's bottom before taking the samples. Use a cotton washcloth.
- Don't use cream, oil or powder on your baby's bottom before sampling.

To take the sample:

- Put an absorbent pad in a diaper, with the plastic wrap toward the bottom of the diaper. Watch your baby and remove the pad as soon as she urinates. There must be no fecal matter on the pad. The blotting paper must be completely soaked.
- Put the urine-saturated pad on the blotting paper and press hard to completely soak both sides. If the pad was contaminated by fecal matter, don't put it on the blotting paper. Repeat the sampling with the second absorbent pad and then use it to soak the blotting paper. Let it dry on a clean, dry counter.
- Fill out the yellow information form, including your baby's estimated weight in kilograms or pounds, and how she's fed. This will help in understanding the results. Check your address and phone number.
- Once the blotting paper is dry, put it in the reply envelope along with the yellow paper, put on a stamp and mail it in.

If something abnormal turns up from the sample, you will be contacted so your child can receive the medical care needed. If all is well, you won't hear back about these tests.

If you forget on the 21st day, it's better late than never. Take your sample as soon as you remember.

Parents who send in the urine sample give their baby an early opportunity for screening. The diseases found are caused by proteins and their by-products, which the body absorbs poorly. This testing is important for your baby's health. To find out more, contact the provincial urine screening program, *Programme québécois de dépistage néonatal urinaire* at 819 564-5253.

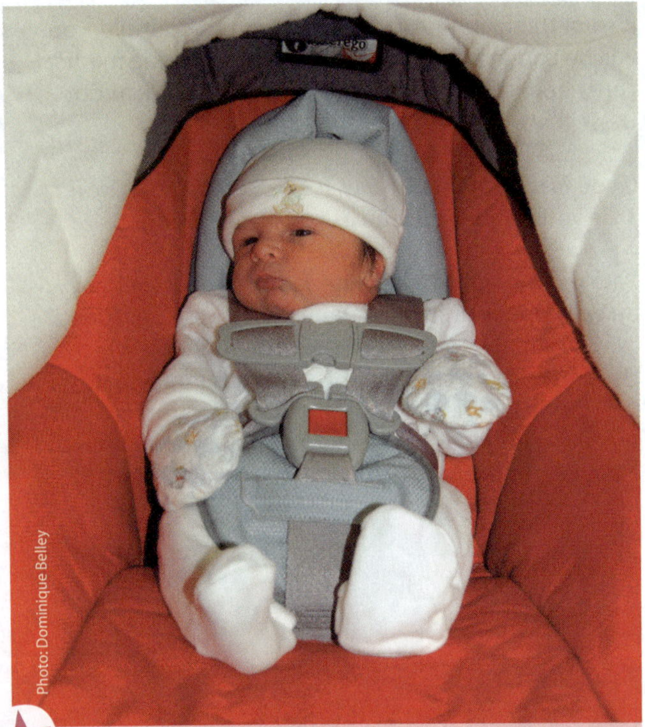

Photo: Dominique Belley

Babies are precious beings. Secure them for life!

The car seat: a requirement

If you travel by car, a car seat is essential to your baby's safety, from the moment you leave the hospital or birthing centre. Every year in Québec, more than 900 babies are killed or injured while riding in a motor vehicle.

The newborn seat

Baby car seats fit the shape of newborns weighing up to 9 kilograms (20 pounds) or shorter than 66 centimetres (26 inches). They hold babies comfortably in a half-sitting position and support the lower back. Follow the manufacturer's instructions closely.

Most car seats for newborns consist of two parts: a base that stays attached inside the car and a removable seat. Some are in one piece. To install the seat and the base properly, be sure to follow the instruction booklets for both the seat and the car. You can also have the installation checked by a police officer or at CAA-Québec. At the hospital, ask staff to help fit the straps to your baby's size.

Adjusting the harness before use

Adjust the car-seat harness to your baby's size. Make the adjustments before installing the seat in the car.

- Set the harness at the correct height. There are several slots in the chair back. Slide the harness through the slots just below the baby's shoulders so it wraps around them.
- Set the harness at the correct length. First, put your child in the seat and attach the harness by putting the metal tongue into the buckle. Make sure you hear it click. Then take the chest clip that connects the harness's two straps, and raise it to the middle of the baby's chest (the armpits). This will keep your baby from being thrown out of the seat in a crash.
- Finally, check the adjustments. If you can get more than one finger between your baby's body and the harness, you need to shorten it.
- Install the seat in the car. Place the seat facing opposite the direction of travel. Your child must be facing backward. That way, in a collision her head, neck and chest will be better protected from the shock. The safest place to put a newborn car seat is in the middle of the rear bench, near another passenger. Never put it on the front seat if the car has an airbag on the passenger side. Airbags are too dangerous for infants.
- Be sure the car seat is fully horizontal. Your baby should be at about 45 degrees, in a half-sitting position, so her head and back are well supported. If the seat of the car is too steep, slide a rolled-up towel under your baby's seat.

- Attach the car seat to the car. If it has a separate base, attach this to the seat bench with the seat belt or the strap for the ISOFIX or LATCH Lower Universal Anchorage System (see Car seat, page 513), and attach the seat to the base. If your child's seat is in one piece, slide the seatbelt through the slots made for it. If the seatbelt is not self-locking, install a metal safety clamp (usually sold with the car seat). This will prevent the seat from sliding during an impact.

See both your car owner's manual and the car seat instructions for recommendations on proper use of seat and shoulder belts.

Your baby is now ready to take her first car ride.

Physical recovery of the mother

Blood loss

For 1 or 2 days after giving birth, blood loss (lochia) will be more than during menstruation. Bleeding will then decrease and change texture. It may be mixed with mucus (a white substance). The colour will change gradually from pinkish to increasingly pale brown.

You may occasionally pass a blood clot. This may happen particularly in the morning, after urinating or breast-feeding. Unusual exertion or a caesarean section can also cause redder, more plentiful bleeding. The bleeding will start again about 10 days after delivery due to healing of the uterus.

Bleeding usually lasts for 3 to 6 weeks. Do not use tampons during this period. It's best to use sanitary pads without plastic linings since the lining can cause irritation.

! Consult your doctor or midwife if:

- You soak 1 regular sanitary pad every hour, for 2 hours in a row;
- You show signs of hemorrhaging: agitation, weakness, paleness, cold, damp skin, hot flashes and palpitations;
- You pass several blood clots bigger than an egg;
- The blood has a foul smell;
- You have a temperature of 38.0°C (100.4°F) or higher.

Contractions

You may feel contractions in the uterus, especially when breast-feeding. If you need to relieve the pain, speak to your health professional.

Healing of the perineum

Your perineum will be sensitive for some time, especially if you had stitches. You may experience a burning sensation when you urinate: don't hesitate to spray warm water on your vulva as you urinate. Relax when you're having a bowel movement. Don't worry, your stitches won't let go. To soothe the burning sensation, try a 10- to 15-minute bath, 1 or 2 times a day.

Let the stitches dry before getting dressed.

Constipation

It is normal not to have a bowel movement for 2 or 3 days after a vaginal birth and 3 to 5 days after a Caesarean section. However, beyond that time, you may be constipated. This often occurs after childbirth because of the pain stemming from the episiotomy, hormones, the medication administered, a lack of activity and dehydration.

If you are constipated:

- eat fibre-rich foods such as bran cereal, whole-grain bread, vegetables, fruits, legumes and nuts;
- drink plenty of fluids;
- go to the toilet as soon as you feel the need to;
- drink prune juice or eat prunes.

If these measures are not enough, use a laxative. Choose a fibre-based product such as Metamucil™. As a last resort, take mineral oil (available from a pharmacy) before bedtime, but only for short periods. Other laxatives can upset the mother or baby.

Hygiene

You can safely take baths as soon as you get home after giving birth. These quiet moments will give you a time-out for yourself. Hygiene is very important. These recommendations will help you avoid health problems:

- Take a shower or bath each day in a clean bathtub without oil or bubble bath.
- Change your sanitary pad at least every 4 hours.
- Always wipe from front to back.
- Wash your hands after using the toilet.

Don't give yourself a vaginal douche. Swimming is not recommended as long as you have lochia or heavy discharge.

Exercise

You can exercise the perineum to get your body back into shape after pregnancy and childbirth. Several times a day, contract the muscles of your pelvic floor, as if you were holding in urine, and then relax the muscles. You can do a series of exercises beginning the day after you give birth. You can gradually work up to 100 contractions per day toward the end of the first week.

> Two months after giving birth, you can gradually get back to your normal physical activity. There's nothing better to help you feel good about yourself!

It's best to wait a few weeks before starting any more of an exercise program. But you can spend time out of the house as soon as you feel ready. You'll find it's good for morale. Start by taking short walks – at first you'll tire more quickly and sometimes quite suddenly.

There are exercise programs designed for mothers and their babies. These activities are often organized by municipalities. Books and DVDs can also be helpful in setting up an exercise program.

Weight

Most women get back to their normal weight without any special effort. In a few months, your body will exhaust the fat reserves that accumulated during pregnancy. Eat a healthy diet. And be patient! The weight you gained over 9 months will not disappear in a few days.

Resist the temptation to lose weight quickly, especially if you're breast-feeding. Losing 1 to 2 kg (2 to 4 lb.) a month is reasonable. A woman who is breast-feeding should not follow a strict weight-reduction diet. A calorie-reduced diet can decrease your milk production and reduce your energy level.

All new mothers need lots of rest to recover from the physical and emotional demands of childbirth.

Get some rest

You're happy, but tired. This is normal. It will take a few weeks to get your usual energy level back. Be patient. You will experience many moments of happiness that occur between ordinary tasks. Take care of yourself and don't hesitate to ask for help when you need it. This will help prevent exhaustion.

It's a good idea to take the first few days after your baby's birth to rest in bed. If possible, rest between feedings. Breast-feeding can be a pleasant and relaxing time for you. It also helps you get to know your baby up close. If possible, rest all the time except when taking care of your personal hygiene, eating and taking care of your baby. Your partner can help you change diapers, get your baby latched on, bathe her, run errands and make meals. He can look after several things. If he isn't at home with you, ask a family member or friend for help during the first few days so you can rest. You shouldn't plan any activities in the week after your baby's birth. You'll need help up to the third week to take care of the housework, cooking and looking after other children.

Your baby will wake you up at night often, so it's a good idea to rest during the day when she's sleeping! Depending on your needs, you can nap twice a day or more during the first week. Taking a nap is a good idea for as long as your baby is waking at night.

Depression and the baby blues

After the birth of your baby it's normal to have mood changes and crying periods. You're tired and almost all mothers experience the baby blues for short periods of time. Hormonal changes are the reason for this temporary depression, which can last from several hours to 2 weeks. Try the following while you're adapting to your new role as a mother:

- Talk to your partner or someone close to you about how you're feeling.
- Try to get a bit more help in the short term from family and friends.
- Sleep when you get the chance.
- Have the father take care of your baby as much as possible.
- Talk to other parents.
- Get dressed and take care of yourself.
- Do activities with your baby.
- Take short breaks; have someone baby-sit once in a while.
- Enjoy skin-to-skin contact with your baby.
- Get out in the sun.

These tips will usually be enough to help you get over any depression.

But:

- if you've been feeling unhappy every day for a few weeks,
- if you're having trouble sleeping and have no appetite,
- if you're losing interest in your baby,

You may be experiencing postpartum depression.

In this case, it's best to talk to a doctor or psychologist right away. He or she can help bring a smile back to your face and allow you to enjoy motherhood.

The newborn

Fetal position

During his first few weeks of life, your baby will often take up the same position he did in your belly. We call this the fetal position.

Size and weight

Babies born from 37 to 42 weeks of pregnancy are said to be full-term. They usually measure 45 to 55 centimetres (18 to 21 inches) and weigh 2500 to 4300 grams (5.5 to 9.5 lb.).

It's normal for a baby to lose up to 10% of his weight in the first few days of life. He eliminates his meconium and first stools. He also loses water because he was immersed in liquid throughout the pregnancy. And he's only drinking a little milk at a time. If born at term and in good health, he will be back up to his birth weight at 2 or 3 weeks old.

Skin

A newborn's skin colour can vary from pink to dark red. His hands and feet are sometimes paler and may stay reddish for up to 48 hours. The skin may also be mottled. This is due to cold – your baby is still learning to control his own temperature. In most cases, the mottling disappears once your baby is in a warm place.

The skin is usually smooth, soft and transparent in places. It may wrinkle and peel, especially on the hands and feet. It is sensitive to heat and cold. At birth it may be covered with a whitish coating which will be absorbed in a few hours or days. Some babies, even premature ones, can also have skin covered with a fine down which goes away after a few weeks.

Eyes

The eyes of white-skinned newborns are blue-grey or slate blue. Darker-skinned babies often have dark eyes at birth. The eyes usually adopt their permanent colour at about 3 months old but may change up to 1 year. Newborns usually cry without tears, which appear at 1 or 2 months.

Head

Your baby has a delicate neck, but should be able to turn it sideways easily. If he has trouble moving it and it seems to hurt, he may have a stiff neck. If the stiffness persists, get advice from a health professional.

The baby's head is large and heavy. It needs to be supported when you pick him up.

Photo: Isabelle Leduc

Pressure during labour and delivery sometimes deforms the baby's head. It will regain its round shape in a few weeks. The bones of the skull are not yet knitted. They are attached by a diamond-shaped membrane, the anterior fontanel. Located on top of the head, the anterior fontanel is supple to the touch and forms a small depression when your child is sitting. You can sometimes see it beating with the heart. A smaller triangular fontanel is located on the back of the head. Fontanels are the most fragile areas of the head but you can safely wash them and touch them gently. The bones of the skull will knit between 9 and 18 months, and the fontanels disappear.

A bump or swelling containing blood and/or other liquid may be visible beneath the scalp. It will cause the brain no harm and disappear without a trace, usually in a few days.

Genitals

In **girls** the labia minora are swollen for 2 or 3 days after birth. There may be a whitish deposit between the lips of the vulva. Don't clean it off – it is excellent protection against bacteria.

During the first week, a few drops of blood may drip from the vagina. Don't worry; this mini-menstruation is caused by extra hormones coming from the mother before birth.

In **full-term** boys, the testicles have usually descended into the scrotum, which is purplish red. If they haven't, tell the doctor. The foreskin is the skin covering the head of the penis. Don't try to force this skin to move. It would be painful and might injure your child. Leave it to nature – in 90% of boys it will dilate and descend naturally at about 3 years old. In only a few cases this won't happen until adolescence. Circumcision is an operation in which all or part of the foreskin is removed. It is not recommended because it serves no purpose. Some parents call for circumcision for religious or cultural reasons.

Swollen breasts

Both boy and girl babies may have swollen breasts, which may even produce a little milk. Do not try to release any milk. Everything will take care of itself in a few days.

Spots

The newborn may have small red spots between the eyes, on the eyelids or along the back edge of the scalp. They turn white when touched under slight pressure, and become more visible when your baby cries. They will disappear during the first year. Babies sometimes have bluish spots on the buttocks or back, which should be gone by the age of 3. Other marks are permanent.

Sneezing

It's normal for your baby to sneeze often. Because the hair inside his nose hasn't grown enough, he may sneeze up to 12 times a day to eliminate secretions that interfere with his breathing. It's not because he has a cold.

Hiccups

Your baby may also get the hiccups, especially after feeding. This isn't serious. It won't hurt him and the hiccups stop by themselves in a few minutes. Putting him back on the breast may also end his hiccups.

The need for warmth

Newborns need warmth but not too much.
They shouldn't perspire. If the room temperature is comfortable for you, it is for him too. A temperature between 20°C (68°F) and 22°C (72°F) is perfect.
Use light blankets; add and remove them according to the temperature. Don't wrap him up too much.

Urine

A baby who is drinking enough will urinate regularly. His urine is pale yellow and has no detectable smell. During the first week of life, he will urinate more and more often. By day 5, he will be wetting at least 6 diapers a day. (See chart on page 328).

It's normal to sometimes see orange spots on diapers. Make sure your baby is feeding properly and often enough, wetting his diapers with plenty of urine, and gaining weight normally (see Baby's growth, page 454 and 455).

If your baby is urinating less often than usual, his urine is dark and has a distinct smell, it may be because he has a fever, because he's overdressed or simply because it's very hot. Increase the number of feedings or, if you're using a commercial baby formula, give him more water. In this case, it is recommended to take his temperature. If a baby under 3 months has a fever, see a doctor immediately.

Stools

During the first 2 or 3 days, the stools will be very dark, green or even black, and sticky. This is meconium; your baby is eliminating the residue remaining in his intestines from before he was born. Colostrum, the mother's milk during the first few days, has this cleaning function. Then during the first year the frequency and consistency of defecation will vary depending on what the baby is fed. You will gradually learn to recognize your child's normal feces. See your doctor if his stools are red or black because this may indicate blood.

During breast-feeding, stools may range from mustard yellow to yellow-green. They are liquid or semi-liquid and smell of sour milk.

During the first 6 weeks, newborns may have up to 10 bowel movements a day. After that, most babies have 2 to 5 plentiful movements a day as long as they're breast-fed; others have only one movement a week. If your baby is defecating infrequently but the stools remain soft, there should be no problem.

If your baby's stools suddenly change from soft to liquid, there may be a transient trouble. Some medications can cause a change. For example, an iron supplement may cause black or dark brown stools.

If your baby is healthy and developing normally, don't worry about his stools.

Jaundice

If your baby's skin is yellower than normal he probably has newborn physiological jaundice. It can affect 60% of full-term babies and 80% of premature babies. In full-term babies, it usually begins after 2 or 3 days of life, grows worse at 3 or 4 days and is gone after the first week. It can persist for several weeks in premature babies.

Physiological jaundice is caused by an accumulation of orange pigment called 'bilirubin' in the blood. This brings a yellow colour to the skin and whites of the eyes.

Bilirubin is partly eliminated in the newborn's feces. Jaundice is stronger when your baby isn't feeding enough and his intestines aren't working very much.

Jaundice can last up to 2 months in some breast-fed babies. If your baby is developing well, gaining weight, experiencing normal bowel movements and urination, this form of jaundice will cause no problems and need no treatment. Breast-feeding can continue normally.

What should I do?

It isn't easy to measure the intensity of yellow colouring in a newborn baby. Look at the skin and whites of the eyes. If you find your child to appear very yellow, if he seems drowsy and is not feeding well, you should see your doctor, the CLSC nurse or the hospital nursery. If needed, the level of jaundice will be measured by a blood test or a machine that reads the skin colour. If necessary, your baby will be admitted to hospital and treated under phototherapy lamps. But in most cases of newborn jaundice, no treatment is needed. Your baby needs feeding more often. Offer him 8 to 12 feedings per 24 hours.

Umbilical cord

At birth the umbilical cord is white. It darkens while drying out and usually falls off by itself between the 7th and 20th days, although it may hold on for a month.

Caring for the umbilical cord

A clean umbilical cord neither smells nor leaks. If in doubt, ask a health professional.

- Clean around the umbilical cord every day until the navel heals.
- Gently wash the area with a Q-Tip-type cotton swab soaked in lukewarm water. Don't use alcohol, which will delay the cord's departure.
- Next, dry the area thoroughly with a dry swab. The navel must stay dry, so don't let diapers or compresses cover it. To prevent irritation, fold diapers below the navel.

- Also, dry the navel after your baby's bath. Wiping the edges and folds of the umbilical cord with a cotton swab won't hurt and will keep the navel dry.

The cord can stay partly attached for 2 or 3 days and may leave spots of blood on diapers and clothing. After it falls off, a few drops of blood may spill from the scar when your baby cries. This isn't dangerous and the navel will heal by itself.

Clean around the umbilical cord every day until the navel heals.

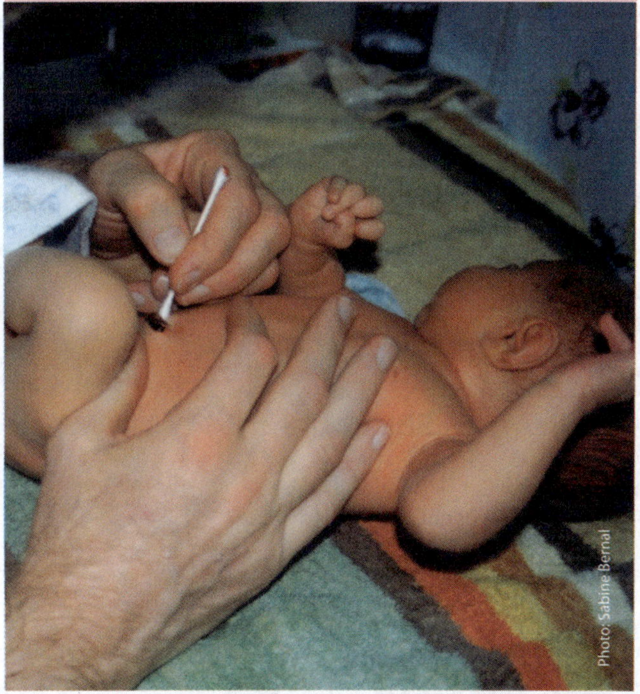

Photo: Sabine Bernal

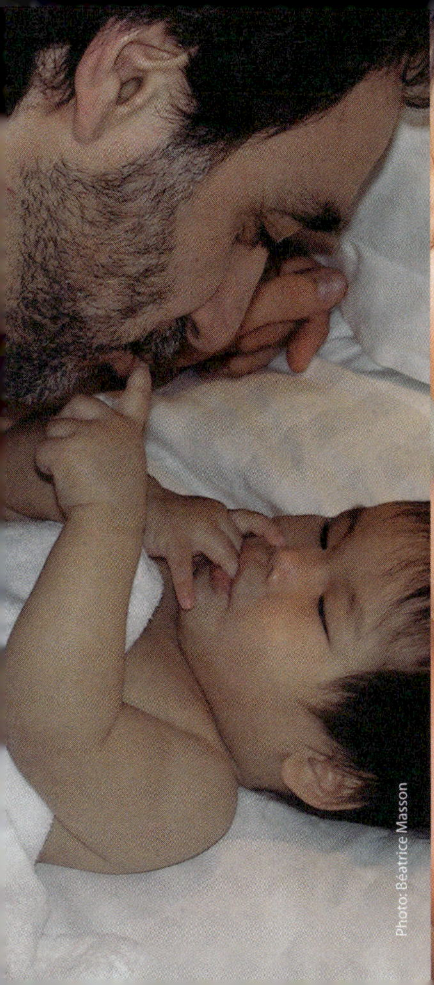

Photo: Béatrice Masson

Photo: iStockphoto

Photo: Marie-Josée Soucy

Family

Photo: Martin Perreault

Being a father

You aren't born a father, you become one.

Fatherhood is an exciting adventure that you can start enjoying from the time of conception. In Québec, more and more fathers are sharing the secret of how happy and proud they are to become parents.

We haven't always talked enough about fatherhood. It wasn't that long ago that our society saw fathers simply as providers. Today, they fill a growing variety of roles.

It's up to you to decide what kind of father you want to be. What did you like about your own father? What would you have liked him to do more? What kind of relationship do you want to have with your baby? Maybe you would like to be the type of father who:

- Plays with his baby and enjoys other activities together;
- Takes care of his child, feeds her, changes diapers, prepares meals and gets her ready for bedtime;
- Shows the child his affection;
- Educates his child and takes responsibility for her, follows the vaccination record booklet, books the babysitter and makes plans for his child;
- Provides for his child – yes, it takes money;
- Enjoys talking about his baby, carries a picture of her and shows his pride.

You can begin your relationship during pregnancy; as soon as her mother begins changing shape the baby will start hearing your voice, then listening to it and recognizing you. You can talk to her, sing a little song and touch her mother's belly. These will be among the first of many magic moments.

It's up to you to take advantage of your strong points, accept your weaknesses and maybe even work on improving them.

Get involved. You are unique and very important to your child. Getting close to your baby as early as possible will help the two of you form a solid bond (see Bonding, page 259). But first decide what role you want to play in your child's life. You may even have to assert yourself.

A new role

It takes 9 months to prepare for the arrival of a baby. Today, it's easy for a father to follow the pregnancy closely. Many fathers are present for the ultrasound, take part in prenatal meetings, and touch mother's belly to feel the baby move. Together, parents dream that their baby's birth will be a celebration.

Life changes when your baby is born. Your schedule is upside-down, your home is upside-down, your partner is exhausted. Your time as a couple doesn't seem to exist anymore. What's happening?

Don't panic – most parents go through this.

> Like so many fathers, you will adapt to your new life.

First, identify your emotions – The birth of a child will put you through a wide range of emotions. Some are positive, like the happiness, wonder and pride of fatherhood. But feelings of insecurity, disruption and clumsiness are harder to live with. The first step is to recognize your feelings. It's important to give names to your emotions, even if they're hard to think and talk about. You surely have someone experienced you can talk to, who can help you be more comfortable in your new role as father.

Take part in caring for your baby – There's no recipe for the perfect parent. Getting involved in day-to-day parenting chores will build your confidence. You may not do everything the same way your spouse does. The important thing is to agree on what to do, while respecting each other's different opinions.

Nurture your relationship as a couple – At first, new parents sometimes have the impression they never stop and can't take time to enjoy a quiet meal together. This can put your relationship to the test. But things will be easier as soon as you both establish your new routines. Make room for private time together. Try to understand your spouse's feelings during the post-partum period (see Depression and the baby blues, page 167). Once you've settled into your new roles, you will rediscover the desire for intimacy, although perhaps not both at once.

With a little help from your friends – The support of family and friends can be extremely helpful while you're adapting to the new situation. If people offer to help, accept. But don't let anyone take over your space. Delegate household work and meal preparation, and stay with the routine you need to learn about your new responsibilities. Be sure to protect the privacy of your life as a couple and family.

Advice from dads

The arrival of a baby is a wonderful thing but it takes a lot of work!

There is no magic recipe except to be prepared. Take the first steps toward finding your place as a father. Here is some advice from experienced fathers:

During the pregnancy:

- Join in the preparations (names, clothing, the bedroom, toys, etc.).
- Follow your baby's growth in the mother's womb.
- Share your feelings about the unborn baby.
- Discuss how you see each other's role.
- Let imagination and tenderness guide your sexuality.

During the baby's birth:

- Be there to provide your partner with anything she needs.
- Be aware of her emotions and share your feelings with her.
- Speak with staff in the delivery room.

During the baby's first weeks:

- Be as available as possible around the time of your baby's arrival.
- Take full advantage of the parental leave available to you during the coming months.
- Encourage the breast-feeding mother.
- Get involved in household chores without being asked.
- Encourage Mom to go for a walk so you can be alone with your baby.
- Take the baby for a walk in the stroller.
- Relax with Mom while your baby is sleeping.
- Prepare your partner for your first outing – it will be easier for you than her.

At any time:

- Be present and dare to act.
- Believe in your own importance. Have confidence in yourself.
- Take the time to share your ideas with your partner.
- Give yourself the chance to learn and the right to make mistakes.
- Share your joys and worries with those close to you.
- Compliment Mom; don't criticize or complain.
- Don't let anyone push you aside. Remind them gently that you are the father.

Find occasions to share what you're going through with other fathers and couples in similar situations. If you don't know any, you can contact your local family centre, the *Maison de la famille*, or the CLSC. For information on community groups in your region that support families, contact the Québec federation of family community groups, the *Fédération québécoise des organismes communautaires Famille* at 450 466-2538 or www.fqocf.org.

You're guaranteed to have some tough moments. Not everything about having a baby is what you expect. Once again, don't worry about it. You'll learn more about parenting every day.

When the reality of your daily life and work get back on schedule, be sure to set aside time for yourself, for your partner, and with your child.

Feeding your baby together, as a couple

During the first 6 months, breast-feeding is best for your baby. You can be a big help to both your wife and your baby. The breast-feeding mother needs encouragement, especially when she's having a hard time.

You can also help the breast-feeding mother by pitching in around the house: cooking, laundry, groceries, etc. You can get to know your baby too: changing diapers, holding her in your arms, rocking her, singing songs, giving her a bath or just bringing her to Mom at feeding time.

Then you can put her to sleep lying on your chest. Baby boys and girls alike all need the comfort and reassurance of physical contact with Dad.

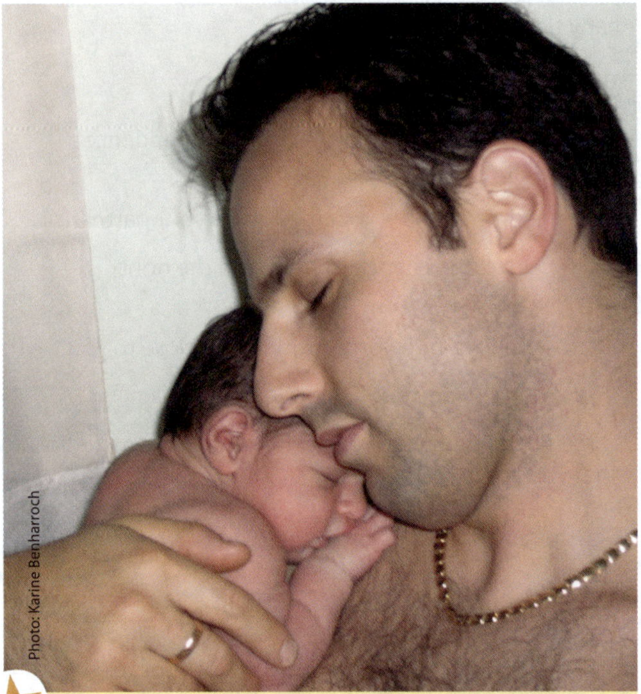

Photo: Karine Benharroch

Physical contact with Dad brings baby comfort and reassurance.

Importance of the father-child relationship

A father's relationship with his child is not the same as the mother's, but it is very important for your girl or boy. Fathers often develop relationships with their children by playing with them. These ties will grow stronger with time. Fathers tend to be firmer than mothers, and more physically active with their child, encouraging her to explore her surroundings and become independent.

The child's relationship with her father will have a definite effect on how she relates to other children and adults.

Both parents should agree on family rules. A shared approach to discipline will be valuable for years to come. Everything is easier when the parents can count on each other's support. The whole family benefits.

Fathers everywhere

Resources intended for family support, such as community groups, medical clinics, CLSCs and daycare centres, increasingly recognize the role of fathers and reach out to them. You can ask to be included in appointments and activities. This isn't happening everywhere yet but by asking to be involved more you will be helping fathers take a bigger role in the lives of their babies.

Let your children teach you about fathering. They won't insist on perfection; they just want you to be there. They are saying "my dad is important. He's the man in my life."

We encourage you to read the chapter "Being a mother" as well, to learn a few things about motherhood. Asking questions and listening to your partner will help you both discover your new lives as parents.

Family

Photo: Nicolas Delaitre

Being a mother

The birth of a child is a very emotional event. Becoming a mother will bring you great joy and deep attachment to your child. Once your baby is born, you will start learning about being a mother. As you did during the pregnancy and birth, you may need some professional advice and assistance.

A new experience as a woman

Most women want to express themselves through work, friendship and love, as well as being mothers. Following this route may take some years. You may have had to be very patient before having your first child. On the other hand, you may go through pregnancy without planning it.

Holding your infant in your arms for the first time is very moving. Your baby's arrival will show you things about yourself that you never noticed before. You may have some doubts about yourself as a mother, but you'll grow and change as your child does too. This tiny person now depends completely on you and his father.

Becoming a mother is a big new step in life.

All too soon your baby will be a child, then a teenager and adult. Whether cuddling your baby, feeding, bathing or changing him, try to enjoy the moment. These memories will lift you when you're down, and will stay in your heart forever.

Many women who become mothers develop a new passion, finding out everything they can about family life. Some develop special skills and want to share them with other moms or get involved in various family community groups. Some decide to stay at home and raise their children full-time, while others go back to work either full- or part-time.

Have confidence in yourself

Do you worry about your ability as a mother? It's normal. There's no school where you can learn this job. Are you afraid of being clumsy when giving the baby his bath, or not understanding why he cries, or panicking when he catches his first fever? Don't worry about it.

Your first experiences with your baby will be moving and intense. Even though you may have doubts, you're getting to know your child better every day.

Have confidence in yourself and your partner. Listen to your intuition for answers to your questions. You may be surprised at how comfortable you become while doing things that used to make you nervous. You'll also see your baby becoming less and less fragile. Understanding his needs gets easier each week. You'll learn from your experience and become more sure of yourself.

For most women, it takes about 2 years to fully balance life as a couple, friends, work and the new job of mother.

With a baby, your days are very busy. At first it's quite tiring. There is no miracle cure for this, but there are many magic moments, like your baby's first smiles and affection. You will quietly master your new role, discovering your strengths and your own way of doing things. Routines are built through time and teamwork, and daily chores become easier.

Rest and more rest

As long as your baby is waking up at night, try to take naps during the day. If possible, ask those close to you for help taking care of your baby – and of you too!

Above all, don't demand too much of yourself. A little dust around the home isn't the end of the world. The good times you spend with your baby are worth a lot more.

Photo: Alexandra Houde Brosseau

Rest is not just for getting over childbirth. The baby's first months take lots of energy.

Sexual desire

Many women say they feel less sexual desire after giving birth. The reasons behind this include fatigue, adapting to the role of parent, the time and effort required in taking care of a baby, physical or emotional complications, and changing hormones. Once you've adapted to the new situation, you will likely regain your desire for intimacy and sexual relations. It's important to follow your own pace and try not to feel guilty if your feelings are slow coming back.

Most couples start having sex again a few weeks after their child is born. It may take longer, for example, if your vagina and perineum, or pelvic floor, are still sensitive, if you're still bleeding or if you're very tired.

Don't wait until you have lots of free time before allowing yourselves some loving moments together. Take advantage of your baby's sleep time. Ask someone close to you to take care of your baby for a few hours while you go out together as a couple to enjoy a change of pace. Romantic outings are important for you as a couple.

Motherhood and fatherhood are a good occasion to discover a different type of intimacy, full of kisses, caresses and affectionate gestures.

Hormones released during breast-feeding may prevent the vagina from lubricating itself adequately. You can use a water-based genital lubricant to make sexual activity more comfortable.

Motherhood and fatherhood are a good occasion to discover a different type of intimacy, full of kisses, caresses and affectionate gestures.

Birth control

Bringing a child into the world and taking care of that child takes a lot of energy. It's best for your health and that of the child not to have another pregnancy right away. Feel free to ask your doctor, a midwife or the CLSC nurse about family planning. Whether or not you are breast-feeding, think about birth control early on. If you're not breast-feeding, ovulation can begin as early as the 3rd week after vaginal or caesarean delivery. If you are breast-feeding exclusively, ovulation may be delayed. But don't depend only on breast-feeding to prevent pregnancy; use a method of contraception to prevent an unplanned pregnancy.

Birth control methods while breast-feeding

The following contraceptive methods may be used if you are breast-feeding:

The condom – You can use lubricated condoms as soon as you resume sexual activity. Don't use spermicidal foam or condoms coated with spermicide (benzalkonium or nonoxynol-9), because these products can cause vaginal irritation or vaginal infections and increase the risk of transmitting HIV if you or your sexual partner is infected. Use of a condom every time you have sexual relations is a simple and effective contraceptive method and is often the most appropriate method at this stage.

Intrauterine device (IUD) – The doctor can insert a copper IUD immediately or in the 48 hours following vaginal or caesarean delivery. Otherwise, you will have to wait 4 weeks before having one inserted. The levonorgestrel IUD (Mirena™) normally has no undesirable effect on breast-feeding or on your baby's growth and development. It is recommended that you have it inserted 4 or more weeks following vaginal or caesarean delivery. It is important that you abstain from having unprotected sex during the 2 weeks before your appointment to ensure that you are not pregnant when the IUD is inserted.

Progestin-only birth control pill (Micronor™) – Depending on your situation, the doctor or nurse can recommend that you start taking progestin-only contraceptive pills beginning the 21st day after vaginal or caesarean delivery (the day of your baby's urine screening test for hereditary metabolic diseases, see p. 158). The progestin-only pill normally has no undesirable effect on breast-feeding or on your baby's growth and development.

Contraceptive injection (Depo-Provera™) – Depending on your situation, the doctor or nurse can recommend that you start taking contraceptive injections beginning the 21st day after vaginal or caesarean delivery (the day of your baby's urine screening test for hereditary metabolic diseases, see p. 158). Contraceptive injections normally have no undesirable effect on breast-feeding or on your baby's growth and development.

Diaphragm or cervical cap – You can use a diaphragm or cervical cap beginning 6 to 8 weeks after delivery, when the uterus and vagina have recovered their shape. However, to be sure it is effective, ask your doctor to check that the device is properly fitted. Using a spermicide with either of these methods may cause the same problems as mentioned above (section on condoms).

Combined hormonal contraceptives (all the common birth control pills containing estrogen and progesterone, the contraceptive skin patch and the vaginal contraceptive ring) – Do not start using a combined hormonal oral contraceptive immediately after vaginal or caesarean delivery. Combined hormonal contraceptives are not the ideal choice of birth control methods if you are breast-feeding because they may reduce the quantity of breast milk. Based on your situation, it is suggested that you wait at least 6 weeks after vaginal or caesarean delivery before beginning this type of birth control.

If you use hormonal contraceptives (combined hormonal contraceptives, progestin-only pill, contraceptive injection, levonorgestrel IUD (Mirena™)), pay attention to your milk production as well as the baby's growth and satisfaction while nursing. If you notice a problem, contact a breast-feeding consultant (IBCLC), your midwife, doctor or a CLSC nurse.

If you want to use the Lactational Amenorrhea Method (birth control method that requires exclusive breast-feeding and conditions for which it is best to get specific help), contact your midwife or a breast-feeding consultant (IBCLC), or a CLSC nurse. You may also consult the Web sites of the Association québécoise des consultantes en lactation diplômées de l'IBLCE (AQC) at www.ibclc.qc.ca, Serena (organization promoting natural family planning methods) at www.serena.ca (514 273-7531 or 1 866 273-7362) or the World Alliance for Breastfeeding Action (WABA) at www.waba.org.my/resources/lam/index.htm#LAM.

If you prefer natural birth control methods (Billings, sympto-thermal methods), first consult Serena. Otherwise, contact your midwife, doctor or a CLSC nurse. These methods require attention, but they are effective and can be very satisfying when your regular menstrual cycle is re-established.

Do not stop using a method of birth control unless you are immediately beginning another method. In order to avoid having unprotected sex, always have condoms on hand. Find out more about birth control methods by visiting the contraception Web site presented by the Society of Obstetricians and Gynaecologists of Canada: www.sexualityandU.ca.

Birth control methods when not breast-feeding

If you aren't breast-feeding, refer to the previous section for use of the following birth control methods:

- Condom
- Diaphragm or cervical cap
- Natural birth control methods

Intrauterine device (IUD) – The doctor can insert a copper or levonorgestrel IUD (Mirena™), immediately or in the 48 hours following vaginal or caesarean delivery. Otherwise, you will have to wait 4 weeks after vaginal or caesarean delivery before having one inserted. It is important that you abstain from having unprotected sex during the 2 weeks before your appointment to ensure that you are not pregnant when the IUD is inserted.

The progestin-only pill (Micronor™) and contraceptive injection (Depo-Provera™) – You can begin either of these methods immediately following vaginal or caesarean delivery.

Combined hormonal contraceptives (all the typical birth control pills that contain estrogen and a progestin, the contraceptive patch and the vaginal contraceptive ring) – You cannot use combined hormonal contraceptives during the first 3 weeks after vaginal or caesarean delivery because they can increase the risk of a blood clot in the leg (deep vein thrombosis) or in the lungs (pulmonary embolism). After 21 days, the risk of these conditions is very low, and your doctor or nurse may allow you to begin taking combined birth control pills.

In an emergency

If you have unprotected or poorly protected sex, you can use emergency birth control methods.

Copper IUD – If it is not contraindicated for you, your doctor may insert a copper IUD up to 7 days after the unprotected or poorly protected sex took place, but not before 4 weeks following vaginal or caesarean delivery.

Emergency contraception (EC) pills, (the "morning after" pill) – It can be used up to 5 days after the unprotected or poorly protected sex, at any time after delivery. The sooner it is taken, the more effective it is. Your pharmacist can prescribe it. He or she has been trained to provide it since January 2002.

! The progestin-only emergency contraception pill (Plan B™) normally has no effect on breast-feeding. But an emergency contraceptive pill also containing estrogen (a product other than Plan B™) may reduce milk production for a brief period. Consult a support group, breast-feeding consultant or the CLSC nurse to help you re-establish your milk production.

Feeding Mom

Canada's Food Guide is the best way to make sure you get all the foods you need. Eat a variety of foods every day chosen from the 4 food groups: fruits and vegetables, grain products, dairy products and substitutes, and meat and substitutes. Refer to Canada's Food Guide on page 35.

Eating well after you give birth helps:

- Rebuild your food reserves;
- Maintain a good level of energy;
- Reach and maintain a healthy weight;
- Maintain and improve your health.

It's a good idea to continue your healthy eating habits after giving birth.

If you are breast-feeding:

You do not need to eat perfectly to produce good milk. If your diet is very different from the recommendations in Canada's Food Guide, your health is likely to suffer more than that of your baby.

Eat regularly and adequately. Have snacks as well as meals if you're hungry. Fruits, vegetables, muffins, bread, nuts, cheese and yogurt are good choices.

Pay attention to your thirst. Drink water, milk, fruit and vegetable juice and broth. If your urine is dark or cloudy, it's a sign you aren't drinking enough. But drinking large amounts of liquid will not increase your milk output.

Coffee, tea, herbal tea, chocolate and drinks

Caffeine enters breast milk. Too much of it can make your baby nervous and irritable. Coffee, tea, chocolate and cola-type soft drinks contain caffeine. You can consume them in moderation – about 2 cups a day. Energy drinks are not recommended while breast-feeding.

Coffee can be replaced with cereal-based drinks and herbal teas. Chicory, linden, mint, rose-hip, and fruit teas are good. Let the herbal tea steep no more than 3 to 5 minutes.

Fish

Your diet should include some fish. But some species contain pollutants that enter the breast milk and can harm your baby. You can gain the benefits associated with eating fish while reducing your risk of exposure to contaminants including mercury if you:

- Choose light canned tuna over white canned tuna;
- Limit your consumption of the following fresh or frozen fish to once a month: shark, swordfish, marlin and tuna (this doesn't apply to canned tuna);
- Eat bass, pike, wall-eyed pike, muskellunge or lake trout (grey trout) only occasionally. If you eat game fish regularly, you should find out about the contamination level of the fish based on where they were fished as well as the recommended frequency for eating them. Consult the Guide de consommation du poisson de pêche sportive en eau douce (www.mddep.gouv.qc.ca/eau/guide) or call the ministère du Développement durable, de l'Environnement et des Parcs at 418 521-3830 or 1 800 561-1616.

Take note

Some foods change the taste of breast milk, but infants usually get used to it. If your baby seems to be reacting badly to the food you're eating, try not eating it for a few days, then reintroduce it while watching your child's reaction (see Lactose intolerance, page 438).

We don't know of any food that increases the production of breast milk. But if you're feeling tired, a milk-based drink can provide calories and nutrients that will give you a boost of energy.

Even if members of your family have food allergies, it is not recommended that you stop eating the most highly allergenic foods while breast-feeding. There is no proven link between the food you eat while breast-feeding and the risk of developing food allergies. If your baby is diagnosed with an allergy, you must change what you eat. Rebalance your diet with a dietician.

If you are a vegan, eating no animal products, meat, fish, eggs or dairy products, and you are breast-feeding, you need to take vitamin B_{12}. Eat foods containing plenty of protein, iron, calcium and vitamin D. It would be wise to consult a dietician, who can recommend supplements if needed.

Family

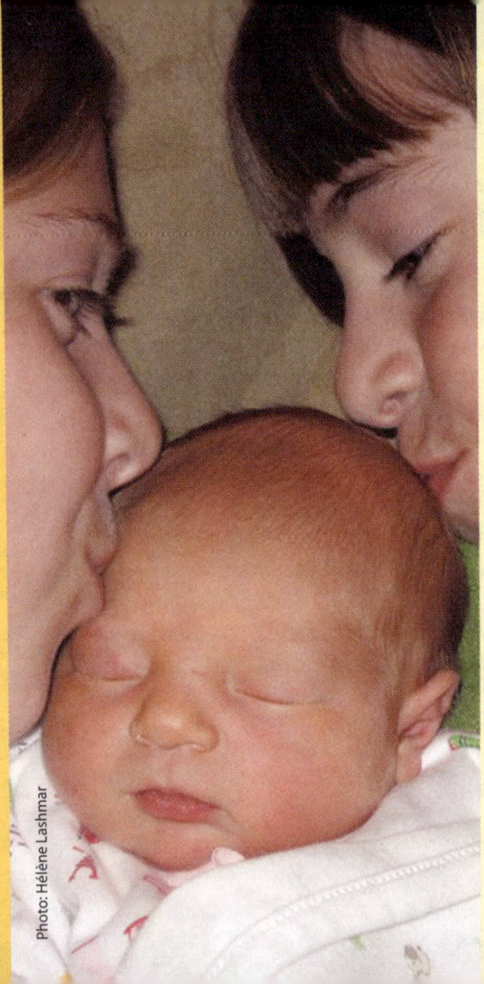

Photo: Hélène Lashmar

Growing as a family

Togetherness

The birth of a child gives new meaning to a couple's life together. Parents are now partners in a new project. Your way of life will change. You have to care for a child and lead her through the various stages of growing up. But there's more than one way to be a team.

Children have physical and emotional needs. Fathers and mothers each react in their own way. Remember that your child needs:

- To feel wanted;
- To be herself and have the right to express herself;
- To have a place in the family;
- To be able to count on her parents;
- To live in a pleasant, safe, honest and open atmosphere;
- To have rules for life in the home;
- To identify with role models;
- To love her father and mother freely, without feeling like a hostage between them.

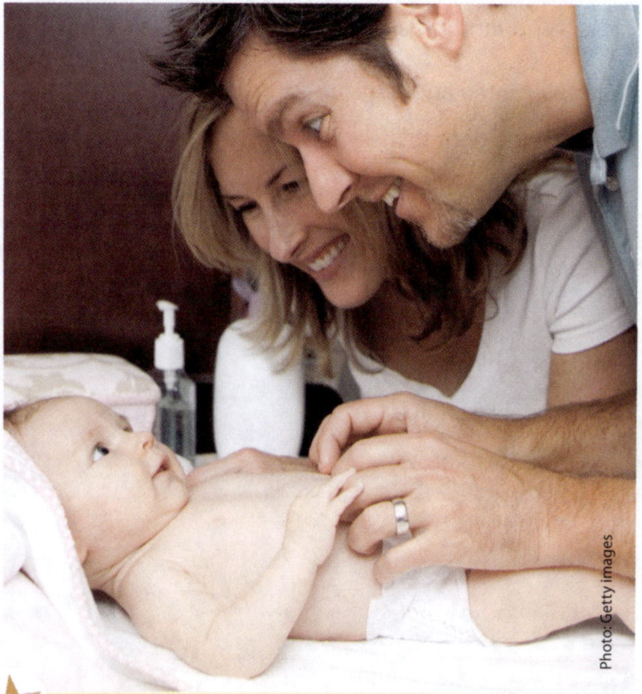

Photo: Getty images

The members of a solid team know what each other needs.

Fathers and mothers also need:

- To feel wanted and respected;
- To have the right to make mistakes and learn;
- To accept their differences and be able to take their places;
- To share their roles and responsibilities;
- To find time and space for themselves;
- To communicate and be heard;
- To live a pleasant life;
- To continue to grow.

Being partners is better

Working together with your spouse will allow you to support each other, grow together, feel happiness, spend more time with the children and do things in different ways. It will also help you improve at communicating, sharing, respecting and listening to each other. Don't deprive yourself of this very rewarding experience.

But it's not always easy

Parents marvel as they watch their children grow day by day. But they also face the challenge of combining a lot of different roles at once.

In many cases, time can be short; it may be hard to negotiate with your spouse; you may become tired and impatient; and you may have financial worries. These challenges may be caused by differences in education, the sharing of work and responsibilities, changes in the broader family life, conflict between the two of you, ineffective communication, the stress of everyday life, and prejudices between men and women. With a little time and patience and lots of love and respect, you'll learn to strengthen your team.

Building togetherness

Here are a few ways to help you learn to work together:

- Set a time in the household schedule to settle your differences once things quiet down. It's not always easy to find a solution, don't worry about it;
- Don't make accusations, and admit your share of responsibility for a conflict;
- Appreciate the things your partner does well;
- Know your own limitations;
- Take each other's abilities and interests into account when dividing work and responsibilities;
- Have the confidence to let each other do things your own individual ways;
- Seek outside help if you need it. Just talking to a third person can often lead to a solution;
- Talk to each other. It's important to speak, but also to listen. Take all the time you need;
- Identify the strengths of your team so they can help when you need it.

Sharing the chores

During your baby's first months you will often find yourself short of time. Share the responsibilities according to your interests and schedules. Share the fun too. If one of you feels overwhelmed and has to ask for help every day, your relationship as a couple will suffer. A clear, fair sharing of the chores will help keep things pleasant. All parents need rest. Give yourselves each time alone with your baby and time off for yourself.

You don't need to be perfect

Parents must accept their mistakes and correct them. Don't be discouraged; everybody makes mistakes, questions themselves and feels insecure. Be willing to learn more about family matters. Even more, recognize that your spouse has the same right. You can help each other. Don't let the adventure of parenting turn into hard labour.

Am I being too strict? Am I spoiling the baby? Parents are always asking questions like this. There's no right answer for all situations. Today there are many types of families. Decide on your roles as parents according to your values, needs and abilities.

Children need love and support but they also need rules and limits. As a parent, you will sometimes be loving and affectionate. But you will also sometimes be an educator enforcing the rules. You'll find your own way to combine the two roles.

Invest in yourself and in your relationship as a couple

Make sure to take care of yourself and take time with your partner, for your sake and that of your child. You'll sometimes feel you're forgetting yourself to care for your baby. At other times she will bring you great joy, give you energy and make you proud. When you feel the need, give yourself an outing or a day off as a loving couple. Continue to share entertaining activities and projects together. Enjoy yourselves.

Communicating is a good way to sustain your relationship as couple. Pregnancy and a child bring big changes and require both parents to adapt. Talking about your feelings, your worries and your happiness can help keep you close.

If you're a single parent, it's also very important to take care of yourself. It will do a lot of good to take a nice hot bath, enjoy a meal with friends or go out.

Grandparents

Becoming a grandparent gives you a unique new opportunity to enjoy a child's first moments. You will also witness the beginning of a new family. Many factors shape a grandparent's role in the new family: distance, work, relations with the new parents, and the desire to be involved.

The pregnancy is a good time to talk about the grandparents' new role. Do we want them to be present during the baby's first days? How should they be involved in her education? How can they best help the new family? The first few weeks will be easier for the new parents if someone else is helping them look after things. Home-cooked meals are a statement of love and solidarity that anyone can make.

It takes time to develop a good relationship with a grandchild. A close attachment, pride and protective instinct combine to create a lifelong bond. Time and distance may separate grandparents from the baby, but you will gradually find ways to keep the relationship close.

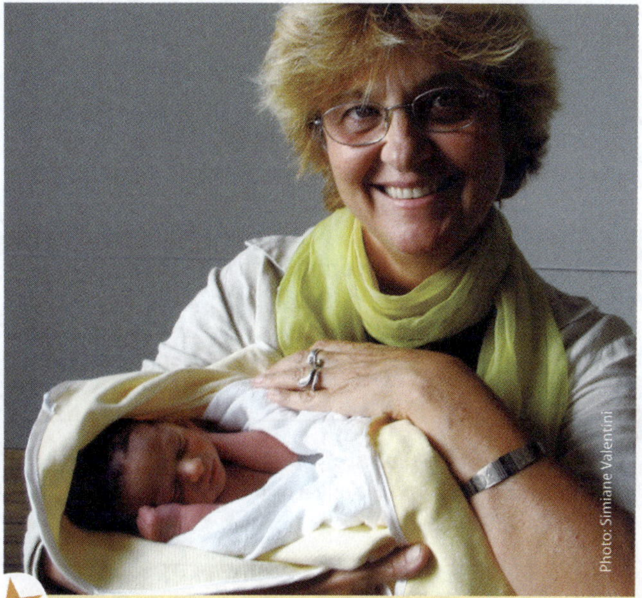

Photo: Simiane Valentini

Grandparents may do things differently, and practices have changed a lot since their day. This guidebook, *From Tiny Tot to Toddler*, may be a handy way for grandparents to update their knowledge with the latest advice.

The new family reality

No matter how big or small, every member of the family needs love and attention. Sometimes you have to find new ways to keep everyone happy. This is important.

If you've made a new family with a new mate, you already know about change. The coming of a new child will be an opportunity to reconsider everyone's place. There is no instruction booklet for this, or any single way to do things. You'll find out what's best for every member of the family.

> Time and patience are your best friends while everyone is fitting in. You're not the only one in this situation.

There are more and more blended families. Don't be shy to talk about your situation with relatives and friends.

If you need support, contact the CLSC or community groups in your area. There are also a number of good books on the subject.

Reaction of older children

A child of any age can be jealous of a new baby in the family. This is a normal reaction. It's important to prepare for this before the birth. Even so, the older child may behave differently for a few weeks. He needs time to get used to his new situation and to understand that he still has a big place in your heart.

The older child may return to earlier behaviour (e.g. bedwetting, thumb-sucking, stuttering, asking for the breast). Don't blame him; these are normal reactions. Keep showing him tenderness; he'll quickly become

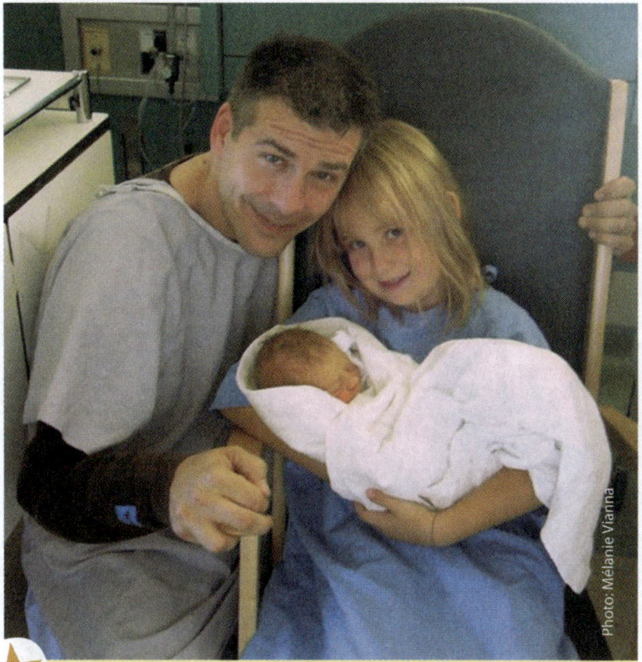

Make sure that friends and relatives show as much interest in the elder child as in the new baby. A little special attention will make her feel better.

attached to the baby. If you give him little chores to do, he'll feel useful like a "big" child. Tell him what you're doing with the baby and remind him that he's been through it all himself when he was small. If he wants, sing to him, rock him and tell him you love him as much as ever.

Taking baby for a walk

Babies need fresh air, light and outdoor walks. A healthy baby can go outside every day, even in winter, as long as the temperature seems reasonable, down to about –12°C, and it's not too windy. She'll have fun, be distracted and get plenty of oxygen. Babies can't tell you if they're cold, so her extremities – head, hands and feet, which get cold first – must be well covered.

The first outings should be relatively short: about 20 to 30 minutes. They can gradually get longer, provided your baby stays comfortable. The wind can be harmful to infants so use the carriage or stroller hood for protection. Chilblains are more common when the child isn't moving much. When the temperature is below freezing, it's better not to use a front baby carrier. If you're using a backpack carrier with an older child, don't stay out in the cold too long.

Babies don't like hot summer weather and must be kept out of the sun (see Sun, page 532). If it's very hot – 25°C or more – a short, lightweight garment and diaper will be enough. Your baby can sleep in her room with the window open. If the temperature is milder, say 21°C for example, she may want to sleep outside, in the carriage with a mosquito net, out of the wind and sun. The carriage needs to be long enough for the baby to stretch out. Babies must always be buckled in and kept under a watchful eye.

Photo: Isabelle Bouter

Baby carriers are fun and practical.

Baby carrier

Your baby likes to be snuggled up with her father or mother, even when taking a walk. You can begin to use a front carrier when your baby is able to hold her head up without help and a backpack carrier when your baby is 9 months or older. Certain precautions must be taken to avoid injury:

- Use a baby carrier adapted to your size and the baby's weight. Adjust the straps to keep her head upright and her shoulders and back straight;
- Make sure that her breathing is not blocked by clothing, a blanket or the carrier's fasteners;
- Make sure that your baby is well dressed and not cold in winter. She must be able to move her legs to avoid chilblain;
- Hold your baby when you bend over;
- Go up and down stairs carefully. Avoid using a baby carrier during activities where you could fall, for example, biking or walking on an icy sidewalk;
- Don't use a baby carrier when cooking, thus avoiding potential burns;
- Don't take a nap with the baby in the carrier.

In the stroller or carriage

You can choose from many styles of strollers and baby carriages. Models that switch from carriage to bed to stroller are practical year-round. Those with seats for your baby to sit or lie down are an excellent way to get around. Umbrella strollers are handy but light, and can tip over.

Always buckle up the safety belt and keep a close eye on your baby. It's convenient to hang a few shopping bags from the stroller or carriage, but be careful not to overload it, which can make it tip.

At 1 year old, baby is ready for her first bike ride.

On your bicycle

The safest bicycle seats have a headrest and leg protectors. Your baby must sit up straight with her shoulders strapped in and head supported. Of course she must be wearing a helmet – like yours! Be sure to find out the seat's maximum weight capacity, and whether it's made to go with the bicycle. It must be properly installed, and the straps adjusted to fit your baby. Never leave your baby in the seat when you're not on the bicycle – it could easily tip over.

A trailer has more space and can carry two children. They must be belted in for safety and the bicycle will need a flag.

Don't go fast on your first family bike ride. The extra weight will make it harder to stop your bike.

Bicycle paths located away from roads are safer and usually more pleasant. Whatever route you choose, be careful at intersections.

In the car

You must always use a car seat adapted to your child's weight and height.

It isn't wise to buy a second-hand car seat from someone you don't know. You should know the full history of your baby's car seat.

A second-hand car seat must meet the following standards:

- Be complete with all parts and in good condition;
- Carry the seal of approval of Transport Canada and the manufacturer;
- Include the instruction booklet;
- Have never been in an accident;
- Have never been subject to a manufacturer's recall (you can check this with CAA-Québec).

All child car seats and booster cushions sold in Canada must display an expiry date or useful lifespan. This date is intended to warn buyers not to use it for too long. Anyone using a chid car seat and cushions after the date indicated does so at their own risk. The lifespan varies from 6 to 8 years depending on the maker.

By air

If you're traveling by air with your baby, you can carry him in your car seat if it meets the standard NSVAC 213, 213.1 or 213.2.

By taxi

If there is no child car seat, your child must wear a seat belt unless she is too young to sit upright by herself. In this case, buckle up your seat belt and then hold the baby in your arms.

Children less than 12 years old must be seated and buckled in on the back seat, the safest place in the car.

Family activities

Most children like the outdoors. Municipalities often provide enjoyable activities at low cost. In summer, many organize free outdoor concerts. Contact your municipal recreation department to find out more.

Your energy will return once you've finished adapting to life with your new baby. Many parents then get the urge to do things as a family. This is a good idea. Family activities can continue with the baby, depending on your energy level. Even very brief outings strengthen family ties. The adults feel more fulfilled and satisfied, parents less isolated. Try a few little escapades as soon as you feel like it.

Take your child outside in a carrying sling or in a stroller in summer or on a sled in winter. In summertime, picnics in the park can be a lot of fun. If the weather's bad, take your baby on visits with friends.

Ask friends who have children about their favourite family activities. And have a good time!

There are lots of things to do on outings with your baby, such as swimming at the pool, storytelling afternoon at the library and children's shows. Some libraries have a kit named "Une naissance, un livre."

Getting a babysitter

Does Mom want to get out by herself, go for a walk or see friends? Dad is there to take care of baby too. It can be a good opportunity to be alone with your child and gain confidence in your abilities as a father. If you want to go out as a couple, you'll need to entrust your baby to someone else. Choose someone you know or who has been recommended by other parents.

The person who looks after your baby must be over the age of 14. If you choose a teenager, pick one who has experience and has taken a babysitting course. Have him or her come for a visit before you go out.

Watch how your baby reacts to him or her. Before leaving, make sure you leave the phone number where you can be reached and the approximate time you'll be home.

Information to give the babysitter:

- Baby's name and age
- Bedtime and feeding schedule
- Phone numbers where you can be reached in case of emergency

See page 618 for information about daycare services.

Twins

If you give birth to twins, your life during the first few months will revolve around feedings, diapers, baths and naps. You'll have the same routine as all parents – but doubled! You'll also be doubly amazed by the things that get done each day.

Even identical twins will probably have different schedules. To make things easier, keep a notebook of each one's schedule. This will also be helpful to anyone who comes to give you a hand. If friends are looking for gift ideas, you can ask for diapers, home-cooked meals… or a few hours off. You'll need help looking after the babies and doing household chores. Get help from your family, friends or a CLSC. Why not post a list of things to do on the fridge as a guide to those lending a hand?

Even if you're the very busy parents of twins or triplets, make sure to set aside time for yourself and yourselves as a couple. You're more than just parents! If the weather is good, get out of the house with your babies. This will break the routine and give you the chance to chat with other people. People will admire your twins and you – making you feel proud and rewarded.

To find out more, contact:

Association de Parents de Jumeaux et de Triplés de la région de Montréal inc. (APJTM) 514 990-6165 or www.apjtm.com (Web site in French only)

Association des parents de jumeaux et plus de la région de Québec inc. 418 653-9607 or www.apjq.net (Web site in French only)

Photo: Anita Chan

Your twins may look alike but they're 2 separate people. As parents, you can encourage differences and characteristics that are unique to each of them. Over time you'll discover what sets them apart.

Being a parent of a baby who is "different"

The need to know

Some parents learn during pregnancy that they will have a baby who is different, while others only find out at birth or in the hours, days, weeks or months that follow. In some situations, it's parents who notice their baby is different. Sometimes it's hard to make a definite diagnosis. These are difficult times of worrying and waiting. Having a diagnosis often makes it easier to know the best way to act, but this is not always the case. Your intuition and knowledge of your baby are valuable assets. There are many advantages to developing a good relationship with all the health professionals dedicated to your baby's well-being.

Medicine has come a long way in the past several years. It is now sometimes possible to identify the cause of a baby's health problem or deformity. It may be a genetic or metabolic illness, a birth defect, a neurological disorder or a syndrome.

A baby with health or growth problems often requires more care and has greater needs. It will take courage and a lot of love. Don't forget that parents also have needs as they continue in their adventure to adapt.

Help

There are support groups to help you come to grips with the situation and your baby's health. Some services may also help you care for your baby. Don't hesitate to ask for help. You shouldn't forget that you just gave birth and still need to rest, despite the emotional strain, errands, appointments, medical investigation and hospitalizations.

Having a diagnosis for your baby is an important step. As soon as a diagnosis has been made, don't hesitate to register your child on the waiting list of a rehabilitation centre that may be able to help her. Unfortunately, the waiting lists are sometimes long. Different associations can provide information and sometimes support for many health problems. Don't hesitate to ask questions of the health professionals and parents you meet.

Services differ from one region to the next. You'll find the resources that suit you best by exploring what's available. The Web site www.laccompagnateur.org provides a wide variety of practical information that can guide you in your search for information about your "different" child.

Financial support is available. For information on the Supplement for Handicapped Children provided by the Régie des rentes du Québec, go to page 580. To know more about Child Disability Benefit (CDB), see page 576.

Take time

When you bring a so-called different child into the world, ill or handicapped, you're transported into a world of doing. This means you take care of her, stimulate her, give her medication, feed her and so on. All these tasks mean you lack the time and energy to simply be with your new baby. "Being" with your baby who is different means spending time massaging her; stroking her; watching her sleep; just looking at her without worrying about her physical care or medication; telling her your sorrows; and expressing your love, etc. Forming a bond with your baby is as important for you as parents as it is for her. This contact without any obligation to "do" will help you come to grips with and adapt to the situation.

Support groups

A number of community groups are dedicated to helping young families. Some focus on general parent-child relations, others focus on specific needs. Contact the CLSC in your region for more information.

There are also breast-feeding support groups for mothers. Don't hesitate to contact them! They offer valuable advice. They've helped many women overcome problems in order to have a pleasant breast-feeding experience.

For a list of lactation consultants:

Association québécoise des consultantes en lactation diplômées de l'IBLCE 514 990-0262 or www.ibclc.qc.ca
Telephone support from recognized leaders. Books and breast-feeding accessories for sale.

La Leche League

1 866 255-2483 or www.allaitement.ca or www.lllc.ca

Telephone support, breast-feeding support meetings, prenatal information sessions, training and information, rental and sale of breast-feeding accessories.

Nourri-Source

514 948-9877 / 1 866 948-5160 or www.nourri-source.org (in French only)

Regroupement Naissance-Renaissance

514 392-0308 or www.naissance-renaissance.qc.ca (in French only)

There are also support groups for fathers that promote discussion and sharing, and play an important role in promoting the father's involvement.

Community organizations

Many community groups offer services to families. Are you aware of them?

These community organizations, volunteer groups and social economy services have grown over the years to support parents in their new job. Don't be afraid to contact them: their staff have the skills required to help you. They can make life easier for you and your baby in many different ways.

Specifically, they offer the following kinds of support:

- Prenatal classes to help you prepare for the birth of your baby;
- Qualified birthing coaches to help you during delivery;
- Breast-feeding support;
- Household help for everyday tasks or to help entertain other children;

- Get-togethers for parents to share experiences;
- Fathers' groups;
- Support in educating your child;
- Parent-child activities;
- Workshops and meetings;
- Support groups for immigrants.

Take advantage of these services as soon as you're expecting a child. This will help you prepare for your baby's arrival. But it's never too late to get information: parenthood is for life!

At every stage of life, sharing your experience with those in your community can be enriching for you and for other parents. Find out about the organizations in your neighbourhood by contacting your CLSC. You'll find information, help, a break, solutions, friends, a babysitter… or even the desire to become a volunteer!

Budgeting for baby

More expenses and less income can be an added source of stress, so try to keep life simple. There are different types of economic support that may be available to you. All this information can be found in the Becoming a parent section.

Take advantage of your pregnancy to make your needs known to people around you. You may be surprised by the willingness of family and friends to help out and share supplies, clothing and baby necessities. You can also explore the treasures to be found in thrift shops, garage sales, second-hand clothing stores, used furniture stores and bazaars held by church and community groups.

Photo: iStockphoto

Preparing for a baby's arrival requires a few necessities. But there's no need to spend a fortune!

Are you worried about the costs that come with a first baby? Check out the *Un bébé à bas prix* guide published in 2000 by the consumer association ACEF. The guide is available (in French only) for $7 (plus $2 for shipping) by calling 514 257-6622.

If your family is having trouble adjusting financially to your baby's arrival (debt, trouble paying regular and other bills, etc.), there are about 30 consumer associations in Québec that offer free budget consultation services.

For the name of the association nearest you, contact the Union des consommateurs du Québec at 514 521-6820 or 1 888 521-6820, or the Coalition des associations de consommateurs du Québec at 514 362-8623 or 1 877 962-2227. You can also visit the following Web site that lists these associations: www.consommateur.qc.ca (in French only).

Choosing clothes

As diapers will be part of your baby's wardrobe for about two and a half years, you'll find more about them in the section Caring for your baby, page 242.

Regarding clothing, there's no need to buy lots of clothes of the same size because your baby will grow quickly. The size indicated on the tag can be deceiving: even if your baby is only 1 month old, a size 3-month garment may be too tight.

The choice of clothing is often based on the weather. In summer, a diaper and a light garment or undershirt may be fine. Dress your baby more warmly if you have air conditioning. In winter, your baby will be very comfortable in pyjamas with feet. Your baby's toes shouldn't be curled up in pyjamas that are too short. Check whether your baby is too hot by touching the back of her neck: it shouldn't be damp.

When Dad is dressing the baby, his choice of clothing may be different from what Mom would choose. Priorities are not necessarily the same. For some, it's the choice of colours, for others, the comfort or convenience. Teamwork between mom and dad is more pleasant when each other's differences are recognized and welcomed. It's also important to feel appreciated for wanting to be involved.

Caring for clothes

If your baby has sensitive skin, wash her clothing with mild, unscented soap. Rinse the clothes twice to get rid of any trace of soap. Poorly rinsed clothes are often the cause of skin irritations.

It's best to wash new clothes before your baby wears them. Watch out for fabric softeners: they irritate the skin of some newborns.

First shoes

Babies normally have flat feet until they are 3 years old. The arch takes shape as the muscles develop. Letting your baby go barefoot in the house and outside in the summer about half the time is excellent for her feet. There's no need for shoes before your baby takes her first steps.

It's best to take your baby to the store with you when buying shoes. The shoes should fit properly at the heel and be about 1.25 cm (½ inch) longer than your baby's feet. Have your baby stand up so that you can measure the space between her longest toe and the tip of the shoe. You can also measure the inside of the shoe with a measuring tape and compare this measurement with the length of your baby's foot when she's standing.

Shoes should have a semi-rigid sole. You should be able to bend the front of the sole using slight pressure. Shoes protect the feet and keep them warm. Booties that offer more support aren't necessary, although they are easier to keep on. Socks should not squish the toes.

When your child is between the ages of 12 and 36 months, check her shoes every 3 months to make sure they fit properly. You can buy your baby's first shoes when he starts walking.

EcoLogo-certified!
You'll love their very nature.
If you want to make the best choice, Hertel and La Parisienne products are ideal for all your washing and cleaning needs. Plus, using EcoLogo-certified products helps you care for the environment while you care for your children.
La Parisienne 2
Hertel
Biodégradable
MULTI
MULTI-PURPOSE
MULTI-USAGE
La Parisienne
Biodégradable
PRODUCT OF
QUEBEC
ENVIRONMENTAL CHOICE
CHOIX ENVIRONNEMENTAL
The EcoLogo is an internationally recognized certification symbol that belongs to the Government of Canada-Environment Canada. It tells consumers that the product is in the "environmentally preferable" category of Canadian products, based on a set of requirements and standards that aim at sustainability. Multi-purpose ultra-concentrated perfume-free and dye-free Hertel cleaner, La Parisienne perfume-free and dye-free double-concentrated laundry detergent and La Parisienne 2 chlorine-free whitening agent have received this certification. To find out more visit: www.hertel.ca and www.laparisienne.ca

Assistance

La ligne parents

If you are suddenly worried about your child, you can call La ligne parents (1 800 361-5085 or 514 288-5555). This is a free telephone support service available throughout Québec. Don't hesitate to call; staff will be happy to provide information even if the situation doesn't seem serious. In the Montréal area, you can also contact Éducation coup-de-fil at 514 525-2573 or 1 866 329-4223 or visit its Web site: www.ligneparents.com.

Info-Parents guide

If you're looking for written material, try the *Guide Info-Parents*, published by Éditions de l'Hôpital Sainte-Justine (in French only) or visit the following Web site: www.chu-sainte-justine.org/editions. The guide and the Web site provide a list of books, associations and Web sites that can answer parents' specific questions.

Adaptation problems

Does your child have sleep or behavioural problems? Does she seem overly nervous or sad? Talk to a doctor or a trusted health professional. Don't feel guilty; if earaches are a reason to consult, there can be many other reasons. A CLSC social worker can help or direct you to the appropriate person. The Ordre des psychologues du Québec can also refer psychologists in your region who work with children. If you have a limited budget, some insurance policies and most employee assistance programs will reimburse part of the expenses.

Specialized services

Do you think your child needs a special service? Various professionals can help (see Who can help your baby? page 447).

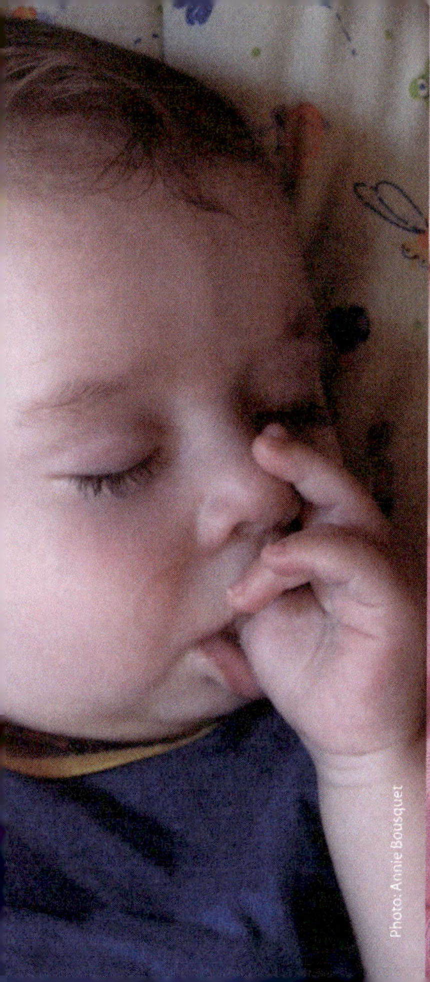

Photo: Annie Bousquet

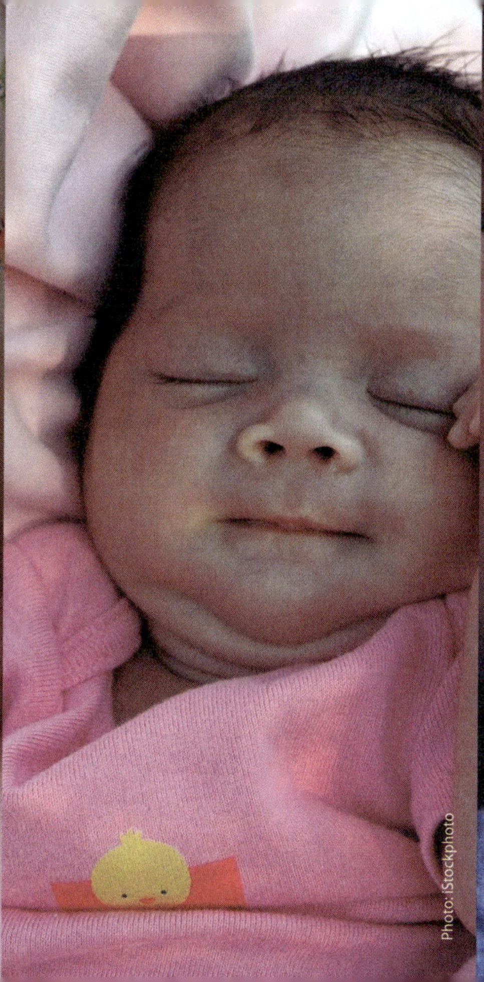

Photo: iStockphoto

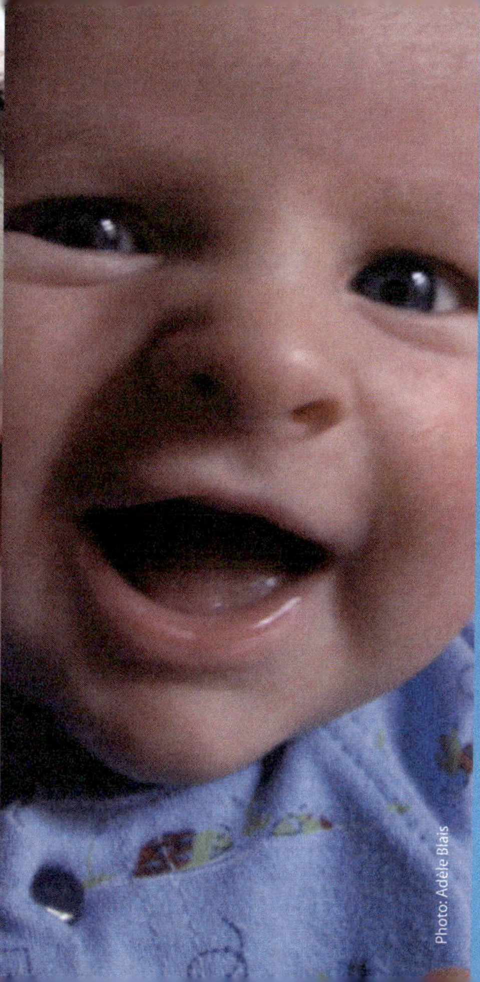

Photo: Adèle Blais

Your baby

Photo: iStockphoto

Talking with your baby

Un, c'est bien, mais dix, c'est mieux !

Soyez bien outillés pendant plus d'une année avec Le Magazine **Enfants Québec** !

Pour en savoir plus, visitez notre site au www.enfantsquebec.com

Postez cette carte réponse préaffranchie dès aujourd'hui
et obtenez votre premier numéro d'essai **gratuit** !

POSTES CANADA
CANADA POST

Port payé si posté au Canada | Postage paid if mailed in Canada

Correspondance-réponse d'affaires | **Business Reply Mail**

1813994 **01**

1000010244-J4R1K5-CR01

LE MAGAZINE ENFANTS QUÉBEC
300 RUE ARRAN
SAINT-LAMBERT QC J4R 9Z9

En famille

Vivre le quotidien et la vie à la maison;
À chaque âge son approche;
Petits et grands.

En société

La garderie, l'école, l'environnement;
Questions en matière d'éducation.

Par plaisir

Fantaisies et rencontres de stars;
Alimentation et nutrition;
Mode in Québec et des conseils d'achat.

Et plus encore dans le magazine…

Your baby starts "talking" to you from birth onward. She cries, moans, babbles, wriggles and sometimes nurses intensely. By paying attention to all this, you are communicating with your baby. You can also talk to her with loving words; tell her what you are doing as you take care of her. She will feel safe and secure just at the sound of your calming words.

Your baby will listen more than talk during her first two years of life. This is normal because her brain is still growing. She is absorbing what she hears. She will learn to talk by repeating the sounds and words that she hears.

Crying

A baby never cries without a reason. Some babies cry more than others because no two are alike. It can be hard understanding a newborn sometimes, but with time you will get to know her just by being together. Her reactions will help you understand what she likes and doesn't like.

Photo: Anne-Marie Fortin

She feels safe and happy when she hears your voice.

For example, you'll discover different cries that mean different things:

- "I'm hungry, I'm tired!"
- "My diaper is dirty, I have gas!"
- "I'm too hot, I'm too cold!"
- "I need to burp, I need to suck!"
- "I'm bored, I need affection!"
- "I want to play with you, I need your attention!"
- "I'm having a bad day and I don't feel good!"

Sometimes, despite all your efforts, you won't understand why your baby is crying. When that happens, just try to stay with her and be calm. It will teach her that she can trust you.

During her first nine months, your baby doesn't have any real sense of time and can't handle being uncomfortable very well. She needs you to take care of her quickly. This way she learns that you are attentive to her and ready to respond to her needs. Comforting a baby every time she cries will not spoil her.

It is important to respond to a crying baby. She needs parents who are able to understand her unhappiness, anger and fear. This will help her feel loved.

Starting at 6 months of age, some babies might cry so hard they convulse and turn blue – in what is called a breath-holding spell. It will last less than one minute. The baby shrieks until she stops breathing for several seconds. She turns pale or blue, can no longer sit up and may fall. This will likely upset you too, but stay calm. Stay with her and reassure her. She will quickly start breathing again on her own. Your child's health is not in danger. However, if the breath-holding spell occurs before the age of 4 months or lasts for more than one minute, it's a good idea to talk to her doctor.

Colic or excessive crying

Your baby is in good health, but cries heavily for more than three hours a day, especially at the end of the day or in the evening, often at the same time. Her face is red, her fists are clenched and her legs are curled up on her tight belly. She may have gas. It is very hard to comfort her. Between bouts of crying, she is cheerful and seems satisfied. She is gaining weight normally.

Little is known about this intense crying, which is often called colic. Colic seems to happen with some babies as they adapt to their new environment outside the womb and it may be because they are more sensitive. Breast-fed babies can also suffer from it. Colic occurs around the age of 2 to 3 weeks and decreases greatly around the third or fourth month. The most difficult period is around the sixth week. A doctor can diagnose colic at one of your baby's checkups. Medication is not usually recommended to treat colic.

This is a soothing position for your baby.

What to do?

Make sure your baby is not hungry, cold or hot and that she doesn't need a clean diaper or to burp. Check that she doesn't have a fever and that she's drinking enough milk to satisfy her needs.

Here are some ideas to help soothe your baby:

- Find a calm area; play soft music.
- Speak softly to your baby and touch her. Place her on your stomach with her skin against yours, in a warm place. Massage or caress her.
- Many babies calm down while nursing: it satisfies their hunger while comforting them.
- Move her around, walk or rock her. A walk in a stroller, a car ride or an infant carrier often helps.
- Give her a bath. Some babies love water.
- Put her on her stomach on your forearm with her back against your stomach and her head in the crook of your elbow. Support your forearm on your abdomen with your hand between her legs. This is the "anti-colic" position.

If your baby is inconsolable

When you are tired or impatient, it's good to rely on your partner or someone you can trust who can give you a hand. Have someone replace you so that you can get out of the house or take a break from your baby's crying. When you come back, you will be able to pass along your sense of calm.

What if you are feeling overwhelmed and have no one to replace you? Put your baby in a safe place, like her crib, close the door and leave the room for a few minutes. You need a break. Seek help: a babysitter, relative, doctor, CLSC, volunteer centre or contact La ligne parents help line at: 1 800 361-5085.

Never shake an infant: you can cause permanent brain damage or even kill her.

Intense crying can also be a sign of allergies or other problems. Read the "Health" and "Food-Related Problems" sections of this guide.

The need to suck

All newborns have the reflex to suck. Sucking the breast is natural and ideal for your baby. It is more satisfying than any replacement.

Not all newborns need a pacifier (soother). Many are content with the breast.

If your baby sucks her thumb or fingers, encourage her to change this habit as soon as possible: try a pacifier because it's easier to control. Your baby may occasionally need her pacifier for comfort but she should not have it in her mouth all the time. Gently remove the pacifier when it's no longer needed, to avoid creating a habit.

A pacifier can act as a gag. Don't be too quick to use it to calm your baby. She is trying to tell you something through her cries. Be attentive to find out what she really needs.

Sucking her thumb, fingers or pacifier can sometimes change the position of her teeth. Around the age of 2 or 3, help her gradually give up this habit. It's important she stop before her first adult teeth come in. The dentist or dental hygienist can give you advice. Sucking a pacifier can sometimes affect your child's pronunciation. A child who talks with a pacifier in her mouth is hard to understand and she will not learn to express herself properly.

To attach a pacifier to clothing, use the clips designed for this purpose.

! Never hang a pacifier around your baby's neck or wrist or attach it to her crib. The string could injure or strangle her. Don't use a safety pin.

Choosing a pacifier

If your baby needs a pacifier, choose one for her age. There are several silicone and latex models.

If your baby uses her pacifier for chewing, give her a teething ring instead. The pacifier disk must remain outside her mouth. If the baby chews it, it could break and she could swallow the pieces and choke.

Cleaning the pacifier

Before using a new pacifier, disinfect it according to the manufacturer's recommendations. Each time your baby asks for it, wash it in hot, soapy water and rinse it. Do not put it in your mouth; you may give her cavity-causing bacteria. Pull on the disk to make sure it is properly attached to the nipple. This safety precaution is important, especially when your baby has teeth.

Check the condition of the nipple regularly. It must be very flexible. If it has changed colour or shape, is sticky or cracked, throw it out immediately.

Recommended by Health Canada

Health Canada suggests you replace pacifiers after two months of use, no matter their condition.

Touch

Touch is the first sense a baby develops, while in the uterus. It is important throughout pregnancy: when your baby rubs against the uterine wall, when you rub your belly to feel her, and so on. After birth, breast-feeding is a form of complete, warm, reassuring and satisfying contact.

Touch fulfills to a need that is as important as drinking and eating.

Touch is a form of communication newborns seek. Holding her against your chest or your shoulder, and the way you rock her is comforting. Your caresses help her feel well, and calm her fears. Your kisses encourage her awareness of life. Through touch, you are showing your love.

Your baby will be thrilled if you like giving her massages! Massaging an infant is easy and relaxes her. It helps her body work properly and promotes her growth. It also helps you learn her expressions – you'll feel like a better parent!

You can begin the massage on your baby's temples or the soles of her feet. Repeat the movements that she seems to like and follow your intuition. There are good books available about baby massage, or you can contact your CLSC. Baby massage workshops are also available.

The following basic guidelines will help you give a successful massage:

- Choose a time when your baby is awake and receptive, preferably not too close to a feeding;
- Make sure the room is warm, comfortable and cozy;
- It's best to sit on the floor;
- Use a firm but gentle touch with your entire hand to avoid tickling her;
- Use a small quantity of vegetable oil (such as sunflower) warmed in your hands for pleasant contact. Try the oil on a small part of the body first to make sure there's no allergic reaction;
- Stay relaxed and be attentive to your baby's preferences.

Use bath time if there isn't a better routine time for the massage. Wash your baby with your hands rather than a cloth. Take the time to rub her body with cream. She'll appreciate this contact and the time you spend with her.

Taste and smell

Newborns already have a sense of taste and smell. Very early on, they are able to recognize their mother by her smell. The scent of milk draws your baby to the nipple to satisfy her hunger. Sucking gives her an intense feeling of well-being. The taste of breast milk can vary depending on the mother's diet. When the father takes her in his arms for the first time, the newborn will also recognize her father's scent. It is good for father and child to share skin contact in the first few hours after birth.

Hearing

Your baby can hear at birth, and even before she is born. She is especially sensitive to the voices of her mother and father, possibly because she has often heard them while she was in the womb. She may turn her head toward your voices. Familiar sounds reassure your baby. Calling her in a soft voice can often calm her. Loud noises will startle and disturb her.

Most babies born in Québec have normal hearing. At birth, about six babies in 1,000 may have hearing problems. However, it's difficult for even the most attentive parents to evaluate a baby's hearing during the first few months of life. Some hospitals are beginning to offer screening for deafness at birth through a simple, quick and safe test. The test is normally given while the mother and baby are still in hospital.

If your baby doesn't have this test, you should make sure she reacts to the sound of voices and noises without seeing what is making the noise, for example, the sound of a dog barking behind her head or the doorbell ringing. Normally around the age of 6 to 9 months, she will turn towards the sound of the noise. If this doesn't happen, it's a good idea to talk to your doctor who can direct you to resource people that can help (audiologist, ORL or ear, nose and throat doctor).

The ears of newborns can stick out somewhat. Nothing can be done to correct it at this age. You can talk to your doctor about it before your child starts school.

Eyesight

From birth onward, an infant can see faces, shapes and colours, and prefers faces and geometric shapes. Sight is an important way for your baby to communicate.

At the age of 1 month, she will look for and at light that is not too bright. At 2 months, she can start seeing the difference between colours and can use her eyes to follow a person or object that moves slowly. Her field of vision increases to that of an adult's at about 1 year. As control of the eye muscles isn't fully complete before 6 months of age, infants sometimes become cross-eyed. If Strabismus (being cross-eyed) continues beyond the age of 6 months, you should see a doctor or an optometrist.

A child will rarely complain of a vision problem. Your baby won't know the difference; she will think her vision is normal. Almost 25% of children under the age of 6 have eye problems, but only 15% of parents consult an eye specialist (optometrist or ophthalmologist) each year. Any vision problem should be corrected before age 8 or it will become permanent and may affect your child's ability to learn and work in the future.

Early signs of vision problems

Your baby may have vision problems if she:

- Doesn't follow moving objects with her eyes;
- Blinks often;
- Is very sensitive to light and has very watery eyes;
- Hides one eye to look or focuses by turning her head;
- Cries when you cover one eye;
- Bumps into things and has difficulty getting her bearings;
- Seems cross-eyed (after 6 months of age).

Life begins here

Mamanpourlavie.com, a portal for today's mommies and daddies!

It takes only a few *clicks* to find answers to your questions

- Many new articles and special reports **to keep you informed.**
- A forum **to keep you in touch.**
- A weekly newsletter **to guide you.**
- A team of specialists **to reassure you.**
- A customized pregnancy calendar **to accompany you.**
- Events and activities **to stay in contact.**

Mamanpourlavie.com, a growing community
that you can count on every day
of your new parenting life …

mamanpourlavie.com
a living portal at parent's service

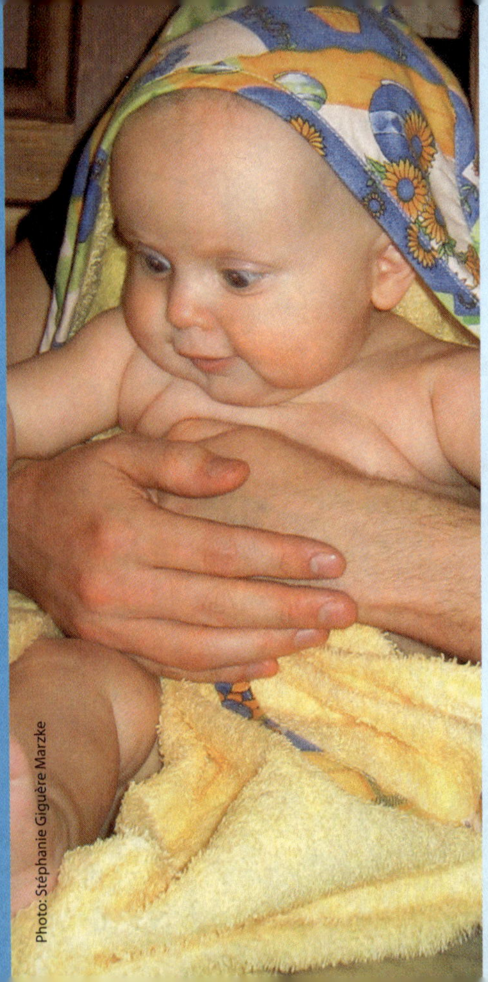

Photo: Stéphanie Giguère Marzke

Caring for your baby

Picking up your baby

Until he is 3 months old, always support your baby's head and back. You can wrap him in a small blanket when you pick him up. Babies like to be rocked since it reminds them of the movements they felt in the womb.

Hold your baby often. You won't spoil him by satisfying his needs for comfort and love.

Mom and Dad – don't be afraid! Your baby isn't as fragile as he seems but he does need to be handled gently and lovingly.

Baby's bath

Everyday care is a source of fun and joy. Bath time is a special chance for fathers and mothers to get to know their baby.

You can give your baby a sponge bath or wash him in the tub. Your baby should feel comfortable if the water is the right temperature (body temperature). Some parents prefer giving their baby a sponge bath until their navel has healed, although bathing in the bathtub won't increase the risk of infection. Being in the water of a bathtub helps keep your baby warmer.

When to bathe your baby

You can give your baby a bath anytime of day as long as he is awake. During the first few weeks of your baby's life, you don't need to bathe him more than two or three times a week. But you should wash his face, neck, bottom and genitals every day.

Preparing the bath

Get the following items ready before undressing your baby:

- A wash cloth and towel;
- Mild, unscented white soap, with neutral pH if needed;
- Unscented moisturizing lotion or cream (for dry skin areas);
- Zinc oxide cream or Vaseline;
- A pair of small nail scissors;
- Clean clothes;
- A diaper.

Here are a few suggestions. The room temperature should be between 22°C and 24°C (72°F and 75°F). The bath water should be body temperature. It is best not to add bubble bath or similar products since your baby has sensitive skin.

Soap removes the natural protection of a baby's skin and can cause irritation. During the first two to four weeks, you can use mild soap, but not more than three times a week. It is recommended that you use soap especially on the baby's hands, bottom and genitals.

Sponge bath

To avoid having your baby get cold, don't undress him right away. Here's how to give a sponge bath:

Wash his head and face with clear water.

Wash around the eyes. Start with the inner corner close to the nose and clean towards the outer part of the eye. Use a different corner of the washcloth for each eye. Then with another corner of a wet washcloth, gently clean outside and behind each ear. Don't push the cloth too far into the ear. Don't use cotton swabs since they can damage the eardrum and push the earwax farther into the ear. Use another corner of the washcloth to clean your baby's nostrils. Clear your baby's nose if it is blocked by mucus (see Stuffy Nose, page 500).

You can give your baby a sponge bath or wash him in the bathtub.

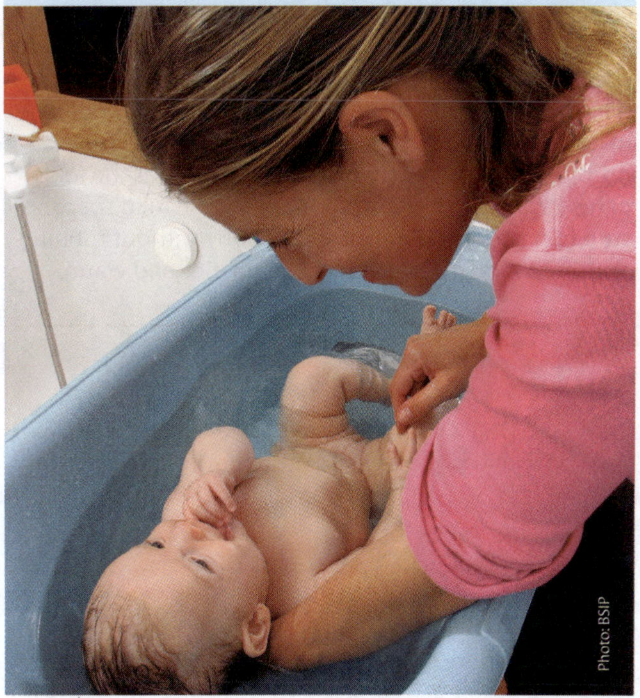
Photo: BSIP

If needed, wash his head once or twice a week with a mild, unscented soap or baby shampoo. Gently rub the baby's soft spot (fontanel). Rinse well with clear water and gently dry.

Carefully wash the folds in your baby's neck. Undress him and remove his diaper. Using a washcloth dipped in lukewarm water, quickly wash the whole body without rubbing. Don't forget the underarms as well as the folds of his thighs and his bottom. You may use mild soap; be sure to rinse well. Gently dry your baby without rubbing and wrap him in a towel to keep him nice and warm.

> **!** Never leave your baby alone for any reason… not even for a second. A baby can drown in 2.5 to 5 cm (1 or 2 inches) of water. If the telephone or doorbell rings, take the time to put your baby in his crib or bring him with you. You may also decide not to answer.

In the bathtub

Bathe your baby in a plastic tub, a clean sink in the bathroom or kitchen, or even in the bathtub with you.

Between 8 and 12 cm (3 to 5 inches) of water at body temperature is enough to keep your baby warm. You can put a washcloth in the bottom of the tub to keep your baby from slipping. Support his head and neck with one hand and his bottom with the other. Place your baby in the water gently so you don't frighten him, then wash and rinse him well.

Baby seats with suction cups that stick to the bottom of the bathtub are not recommended. In recent years, too many babies have drowned using these seats while their parents thought they were safe. Nothing replaces your supervision.

Genitals and bottom

Wash the genitals and bottom with warm water at every diaper change. This should be done for both newborns and older babies. Do not put scented products in the water (bubble bath, bath oil) as they may cause irritation.

In the case of baby girls, gently clean the vulva by separating the outer lips of the vagina. Work from the front to the back to prevent stools from entering the vagina and urethra. Rinse well.

In the case of baby boys, wash the penis and scrotum. Rinse well. The foreskin is not loose at birth. It's not a good idea to dilate it (stretch it) to clean it.

After the bath

Once the bath is done, wrap him in a towel to keep him nice and warm. Dry your baby quickly and remember to dry the folds of his skin, without rubbing. Using powder is not recommended because it can cause breathing problems if it gets in the lungs.

Cutting your baby's nails

During your baby's first week of life, his nails will be stuck to his skin. You don't need to cut them because you may hurt him. After several days, the ends of the nails will come away from the skin. You should cut his nails when they grow to the point where your baby scratches himself.

You can cut your baby's nails after his bath when they're softened by the water or when he's sleeping. You should cut the toenails straight across using a small pair of scissors or nail clipper. This will keep them from becoming ingrown. Fingernails should be rounded so he doesn't scratch himself. Nails grow quickly so trim or file them regularly.

Choosing diapers

Diapers will be part of your baby's wardrobe for about two and half years. Should you buy disposable or cloth diapers? The choice is up to you. Cloth diapers are less expensive and more environmentally friendly. Disposable diapers cost more and can irritate the skin of some babies. But they're practical.

Disposable diapers

Disposable diapers contain crystals that convert urine into a safe gel and separate it from the stools. This stops the urine-stool mix that bothers a baby's skin so much. If you choose disposable diapers, be sure to keep an eye on your baby's skin because some scented disposable diapers can irritate it. Regular diaper changes are important; disposable diapers give the impression that they're dry even if they're not.

Cloth diapers

The new cloth diapers are easy to use. They fit well thanks to fasteners (Velcro or snaps) and leak-proof gathers. Many models have removable or semi-removable liners that make washing easier. But if you're looking for another cheaper option, traditional diapers fastened with safety pins are still available.

Cloth diapers are less absorbent than disposable diapers. Some brands of cloth diapers offer a more absorbent night-time diaper or a second absorbent liner to put in the diaper. Diaper covers that let your baby's skin breathe are the best type to use.

Washing diapers

Follow the manufacturer's instructions when washing cloth diapers. Some manufacturers recommend soaking the diapers before washing; others do not.

Cleaning

Empty the stools in the toilet. Disposable, biodegradable liners make it easier to remove the stools. The liners can be flushed down the toilet. If you use disposable diapers, empty the stools into the toilet and then throw the diaper in the garbage.

Washing

Washing is a very important step. The diapers can irritate your baby's skin if they're not washed properly. Follow the steps below to avoid irritation.

- If the manufacturer recommends soaking the diapers, wring them out thoroughly when you take them out of the soaking bucket or spin them in the washing machine.
- You should use unscented detergent and wash in hot water. The water should be lukewarm if the diapers have a waterproof coating.
- They should be rinsed in water only, with no fabric softener; some manufacturers recommend rinsing the diapers twice.
- Dry the diapers in the dryer at medium heat or hang them to dry. Drying them in the sun helps whiten them. Some diapers that have a waterproof cover should not go in the drier.
- Wash and rinse diaper covers often. Always wash diapers separately from clothing. Do not use detergents for delicate clothing; they leave a sticky deposit on diapers and reduce the amount they absorb. Do not use fabric softeners; they can irritate the skin and make the diapers less absorbent.

Specialized diaper services are available in some regions. This will make your life easier. Simply follow the diaper company's recommendations for storing dirty diapers.

Diaper changes

Change your baby's diaper every time he has a bowel movement. Diapers should be changed often to prevent irritation.

A few tips:

- Wash your baby's bottom and genitals every time you change his diaper, whether he is a newborn or older.

- To prevent irritation, occasionally apply a thin layer of Vaseline or unscented zinc oxide such as Ihle's paste™, Pâte foufounes™ or Zincofax™. Don't overdo it. Too much of these products can get onto the Velcro fasteners of cloth diapers and make them sticky and the diapers less absorbent.
- Disposable diaper wipes can cause irritation. They should be used only on healthy skin or when soap and water are not available.
- To avoid contamination, always wash your hands after changing your baby.

Your baby loves to hear you speak or sing songs to him.

A little bit of music, a rattle, pictures on the wall, a mirror, mobile, or, when he is a little older, a storybook, can distract him and make this a pleasant time.

Take this opportunity to caress, tickle and kiss your baby.

Make diaper changes an enjoyable time!

Your baby

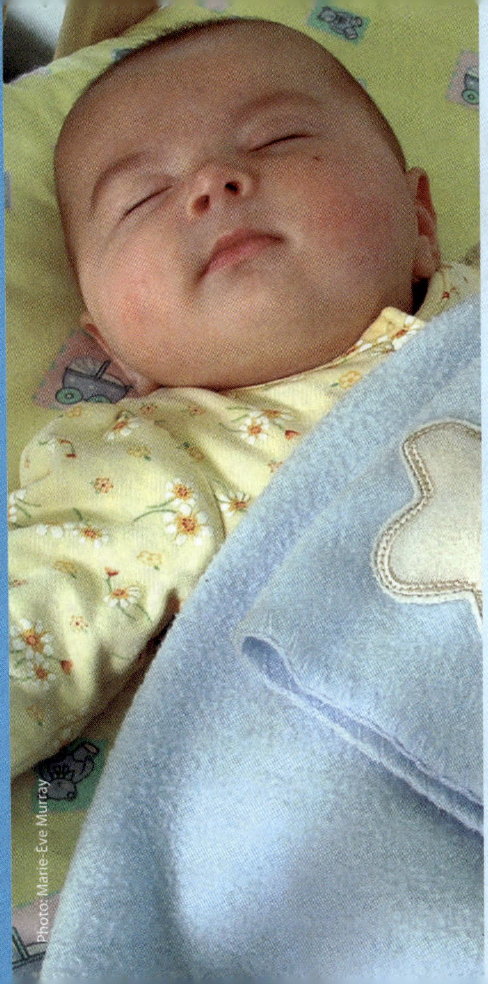
Photo: Marie-Eve Murray

Sleep

Sleeping safely

Your baby should sleep on her back on a firm mattress in a crib that meets Canadian safety standards, from birth onwards. The blanket should be the only extra thing in the crib.

Recommended by the Canadian Paediatric Society

Tragically, every year there are reports of deaths of babies who were sharing their parent's bed. For this reason, the Canadian Paediatric Society states that during the first six months of life, the safest place for a newborn to sleep is in her parents' room in her own crib.

★ For her own safety, your baby should sleep on her back, in her own crib.

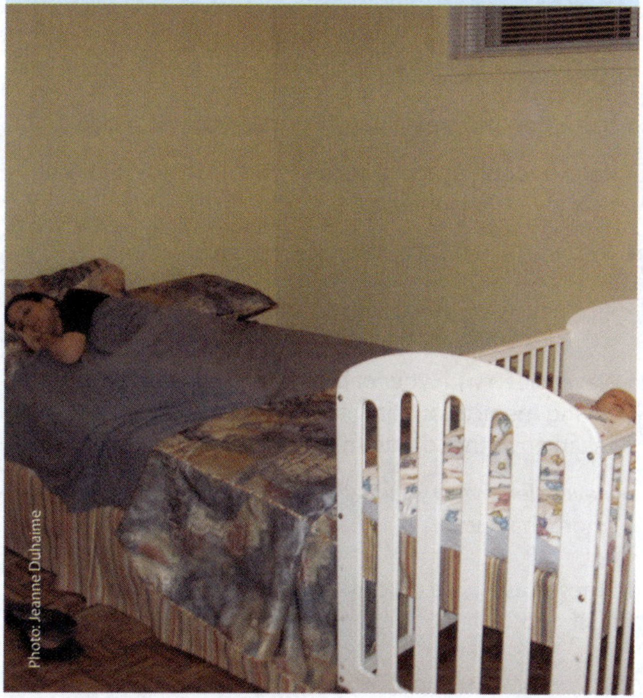
Photo: Jeanne Duhaime

Do you sleep with your baby?

To avoid an accident, make sure you:

- Do not sleep on a couch or similar piece of furniture (armchair) with your baby;
- Use a firm mattress (no soft surfaces or water beds);
- Keep enough distance between the mattress and wall that your baby doesn't get stuck;
- Never let a newborn sleep alone in an adult bed.

And:

- Never sleep with your baby if you have been drinking, taking medication that makes you drowsy, or have taken any other drugs (marijuana, crack, etc.);
- Never sleep with your baby if you are extremely tired (more than usual).

In these cases, it is much safer for your baby to be in her crib.

If you are unable to sleep well when you're in the same room as your baby, you could have her sleep in a secure crib in another room. The quality of your sleep is very important.

Your baby must sleep in a safe place even when you are travelling. Never, under any circumstances, put your baby to bed in an adult bed and don't use pillows. If you don't have a crib, a blanket placed directly on the floor can act as a temporary safe bed for a baby who is less than 6 months old. Using a playpen or a mattress on the ground can be a solution for putting your baby to bed when you are travelling.

A car seat should be used only for transporting your baby in the car. Car seats and baby seats should not be used in place of a crib as they are not a safe place for sleeping. If she wakes up, it is important to change your baby's position. She needs to spend time in your arms. She can play near you while she is on her back or her stomach. When she is awake, this position is very important for her development.

The car seat should be used every time you transport your baby in a vehicle. It's best not to leave your baby in her car seat for more than one hour during her first few months of life. She may fall asleep in her car seat. During trips, frequent stops are recommended so that you can change your baby's position and hold her. Car seats should not be used to replace a crib as they are not as safe for sleeping.

When you go for walks, your baby will be safest and most comfortable sleeping on her back in a stroller. The back of the stroller should fold down flat or almost flat, and your baby should be properly strapped in.

Most babies enjoy being carried in front baby carriers. Many babies will fall asleep due to the warmth and the walking motion.

> ! Be careful; your infant is not safe in her baby carrier if you are sleeping or lying down while wearing the carrier.

Sudden infant death syndrome

The sudden death of an infant under the age of one usually occurs while the baby is sleeping. We still do not know the cause of Sudden Infant Death Syndrome (crib death).

The main risk factors for Sudden Infant Death Syndrome are:

- being exposed to her mother's smoking during pregnancy;
- sleeping on her tummy;
- ending up with her head completely covered by blankets.

Here are some recommendations to reduce the risk of Sudden Infant Death Syndrome:

- Avoid smoking during pregnancy. Tobacco by-products absorbed by mothers who smoke are passed from the mother's blood to the baby's blood via the placenta.
- Place your baby on her back to go to sleep. Tell anyone who looks after your baby to do the same. Healthy babies won't suffocate when they sleep on their backs. When your baby begins turning over on her own, you can allow her to sleep in the position that she prefers without any danger.
- Avoid using comforters because they can easily cover your baby's head as she moves around.
- Avoid using pillows, bumper pads or other similar items in your baby's crib. Your baby could suffocate against these objects if she is on her stomach or accidentally turns onto her side or stomach.

You can swaddle your baby in a blanket. There is no risk in swaddling a baby that is sleeping on her back.

Infant sound and movement monitors do not replace these precautions. All these safety measures must be followed even if you use a baby monitor.

Preventing a flat head

Sudden Infant Death Syndrome happens 50% to 70% less often since paediatricians have recommended that infants sleep only on their backs. But if a baby always sleeps in the same position, in her crib or car seat, she may end up having a flat head. The medical term for this is positional plagiocephaly.

Since the bones of the baby's skull are still soft, the part of the head lying on the mattress flattens with pressure. A slight flattening of the head will disappear on its own. A more pronounced flatness may be permanent but will not harm your baby's brain or development.

Photo: Sarah Witty

Your baby needs to spend some time on his tummy every day.

Recommended by the Canadian Paediatric Society

To prevent a flat head, the Canadian Paediatric Society recommends changing your baby's position in the crib every day.

- One day, place your baby with her head at the head of her crib.
- The next day, place her head at the foot of the crib.
- Make sure she is always looking towards the room, not towards the wall.
- You can also put a mobile on the side of the crib facing the door to encourage your baby to look in that direction.

Your baby needs to be placed on her tummy for short periods of time every day when she's awake and is with a parent. This will help her grow and prevent flat spots from forming on the back of her skull.

Sleep in the first weeks

Your baby will sleep and wake according to her needs and feelings. Some babies wake almost only to nurse. Others are awake longer from their first days out of the womb. The amount of time they stay awake will be longer as the weeks pass.

As with adults, newborn babies go through different sleep cycles: drowsiness (light wakefulness), calm sleep and agitated sleep. When your baby is in her agitated sleep cycle, she may make sucking movements, frown, cry, smile, jump, tremble, groan, breathe hard or move. This is normal. No need to wake and comfort her.

Babies feel safe when they smell the familiar scent of their parents. They might even sleep better with an item of your clothing nearby.

Sleep at around 4 months

At 4 months, the average amount of time a baby sleeps is 14 to 15 hours per day. Babies will start to sleep longer through the night.

At about 4 months, babies usually have a more regular and predictable daily routine. Because you've paid close attention to your baby from the time of birth, she will feel safer and more secure. She will be able to wait a bit longer for things. She learns to comfort herself by putting her hand in her mouth. Little by little she learns to fall asleep on her own. Beginning at between 4 and 6 months, some babies won't need to feed during the night anymore. Others will still need to – possibly even more so than during the weeks before (see First few months, page 316).

The bedtime routine helps your baby get ready to sleep.

> Gradually you will recognize more and more of your baby's signs of fatigue.

Bedtime routine

It's a good idea to make bedtime a relaxed, happy time. Repeating the same actions every night will create a bedtime routine that makes going to sleep easier. Turn on a night light in the hall and leave the bedroom door partly open. If you stick fairly close to your routine each day, your baby will start to understand when it's bedtime. For example, develop a routine of a warm bath, quiet game, a story, soft music or a song. A lot of parents enjoy this time of the day with their baby, and take the time to rock her to sleep. Others prefer that the baby learns to fall asleep on her own.

If you want, once the routine and quiet time are finished, put your baby in her crib even if she isn't fully asleep. When your baby learns to go to sleep on her own it means she can go back to sleep on her own in the middle of the night if she wakes up during a period of light sleep.

> There's no right or wrong way in your bedtime routine. The important thing is for you to feel comfortable with the routine you choose.

Sleeping through the night

Sleeping through the night is what adults do; babies have different sleep patterns. A baby's sleep schedule can in fact vary quite a bit from one baby to the next. "Sleeping through the night" generally means five or six hours of sleep between 11 p.m. and 8 a.m. About 70% of 3-month-old babies sleep five hours at night; 85% do at 6 months, and 90% at 10 months.

Follow your baby's rhythm and needs. When feeding at night, you can keep things calm and quiet so she learns the difference between night and day. For example, keep the lights very dim and resist the very natural urge to speak to her.

Sleep after 6 months

Most babies between the ages of 6 and 12 months sleep 8 to 10 hours a night for a total of about 15 hours a day.

Sometimes, 6- to 12-month-old babies start waking up again in the night. This is the normal period for separation anxiety. You might also notice during the day that your baby reacts more strongly when you leave her, when you go to another room or when you put her to bed. When she wakes up crying at night, you can reassure her simply by being there and talking softly to her. Often, just your voice and touch will make her feel better. Remember that it's normal for babies to have wakeful periods. Your baby can learn gradually to go to sleep by herself.

Remember that whatever your baby needs to go to sleep is the same as what she will need to go back to sleep when she wakes in the middle of the night. If she needs to be breast- or bottle-fed or to be rocked to go to sleep, she will probably need you to help her go back to sleep when she wakes in the middle of the night. If you want her to learn to go back to sleep on her own, you need to teach her first to go to sleep on her own in the evening. If she does need you there, you can try teaching her to go to sleep on her own by gradually decreasing the amount of time you stay with her each evening.

If your baby cries a lot at night, you should check to make sure she's not sick. Take her temperature. If it happens often, talk to your doctor. He or she can reassure you about your baby's physical well-being and support you during the difficult period.

If your baby doesn't have any health problems, think about your bedtime routine and see if it can be improved to encourage sleep.

Sleep between 1 and 2 years old

A 1- or 2-year-old child sleeps 8 to 12 hours per night. Generally, up to 18 months, your child needs two naps per day, one in the morning and the other in the afternoon. Beginning at about 18 months to 2 years, she may need only one nap. Sometimes she will be in a bad mood when she wakes up. Be patient and wait a bit before getting back to regular activities. Remember that each baby's sleep needs are different, and they decrease as she grows.

Sleep problems

A lot of children aged 1 or 2 cry at bedtime. They are going through a normal period of separation anxiety, which can last to 18 months or more. Their fears make it harder for them to be without you at bedtime. Keep your bedtime routine with a gentle firmness. This will help reassure your child.

Nightmares and night terrors

Beginning at age 1, many children have night terrors. The child may scream and cry, yet seems to be sleeping deeply. You don't need to wake her or do anything in particular, unless you think she might hurt herself. If you can't console her, don't worry, she will calm down soon.

If she wakes up in a panic and seems very awake, she probably had a nightmare. Being there to reassure her will help her fall back to sleep calmly.

And don't worry, night terrors and nightmare problems generally go away as your child grows. Several books offer tips on how to teach older children to deal with the problem.

Disturbed sleep

If your child wakes up at night, try the bedtime routine we suggested previously for children over the age of 6 months. If you have trouble creating a bedtime routine, or if your child keeps waking up at night despite your routine and you're concerned, talk to a health professional.

Your child's sleep is disturbed if:

- She wakes often during the night (more than two times);
- She wakes for a long period during the night (more than 20 minutes);
- She needs you when she wakes at night;
- She wakes more then four or five nights out of seven;
- She's woken up during the night for at least three months.

In these cases, getting help is a good idea. Reading about the problem or talking to a professional can be useful.

Photo: Langis Michaud

Your baby

Your child's development

Children grow and develop gradually. But some days the progress is surprising and delightful! Your child needs simple but essential elements to grow in mind and body. He needs food, physical care, sleep and security. He needs to develop significant relationships with the people who take care of him, and in whom he trusts. For this bond to be created, your baby needs to be:

- Loved as he is, with all his strengths and weaknesses;
- Surrounded by love and be touched;
- Encouraged and supported with gentle words;
- Stimulated by people who talk and play with him;
- Guided in his experiences by a few clear rules.

Bonding

In order to grow, a child needs to develop a bond of trust with one or more people who are sensitive to his needs and who reassure him when he is afraid. This bond known as "attachment" is created through the daily care, affection and attention you give to your baby and the time you spend with him.

Photo: Nicolas Delaitre

Bit by bit the bond between you and your child grows through the care, affection, attention and time you give him.

Sense of confidence

Your baby sends you signals (sounds, crying, arm and leg movements, frowns, etc.) to express his needs. You learn to understand them as you try to respond. It is important to pay close attention to these signals to determine the appropriate response to his needs. Your response should also be prompt and reassuring for the baby, especially when he is crying. That's how he'll gain confidence in you. Your baby will know you're there for him.

Here's an example of a prompt and reassuring response: as soon as your baby begins to cry, Dad picks him up. When Dad realizes that the baby is colicky, he takes him out for a walk in the baby carrier. If this works to relieve your baby's end-of-day colic, then he's reassured that his parent is there for him.

If your baby has confidence in you, he will have confidence in himself. This sense of confidence is necessary for your child to explore his world. He will feel safe if he knows his parent is there to help and comfort him in a moment of trouble. Some more sensitive children need more time to feel confident.

Since children gain confidence from the people that take care of them regularly, it's normal for them to react against separation from their parents. It is usually around the age of nine months that toddlers have a difficult time coping with separation. When you're back together with your child, he may show he was unhappy about the separation or instead show his joy at you being there again. After a bit of time close to his parents, he will feel safe and confident again.

Here are a few tips to help your child gain confidence:

- Hold him often in your arms, with his skin against yours, especially when he cries.
- Take time to play and talk with him.
- Learn to get to know him and to take his personality into account.

Temperament

From birth, a newborn has a character and manner of his own. Each baby has his own ways. Here are the kinds of differences you can see in babies:

- How energetic they are;
- How regular they are in terms of appetite, sleep and bowel movements;
- Their reactions to new experiences;
- Their ability to adapt to new things;
- Their sensitivity to noise, light and texture;
- How much they react to good and bad events;
- Their mood;
- Their ability to concentrate;
- Their ability to persevere.

Take time to observe your baby to get to know him. Your observations are important. They will help you adjust how you treat and care for your child. You'll also learn to guide your child in his learning and discoveries.

Some babies are considered "easy." They wake and eat according to a regular schedule. They're generally in a good mood and are somewhat active. These babies, like others, also need a routine but they adapt well to changes and new situations. In response, their parents simply learn their own way of taking care of them. Some activities are suggested in the section of this guide on stages of development.

Other babies are "more sensitive." The care and attention they need change from one day to the next. They don't adapt as easily to new things and sometimes cry a lot. They may be irritable for a number of reasons. Some are more sensitive to light, others to noise and others to movement.

These children require flexibility and patience. Daily care becomes a routine that is good for them and reassures them. It's important that you keep up your efforts to give warm and constant care even when your child is irritable and unhappy. Your presence and your calm make them feel better.

If your six-month old baby is very active, you can help him focus his attention and concentration. Looking at children's books with him for several minutes is helpful. Over time, his interest and attention increase.

Some babies are more "cautious." They're calm and take time to observe before acting. They're a little more timid about new activities. They take their time, and may resist change. Because they often make less noise and require less attention, they may seem to be more independent. But even though they take their time, they understand and learn to explore, to socialize and to play with others.

It is good to encourage them to discover new things at their own speed. Your child will feel understood, respected and encouraged in his learning. Be sure to take plenty of time to play often and regularly with your child even if he's calm and undemanding. Quiet children need physical games too.

To interact is to stimulate

Children need a lot of contact with the people around them, especially their parents. From the time they're born they have everything they need to interact: sight, hearing and touch. As they grow, their ability to interact improves.

You can enjoy great times with your baby while caring for and playing with him. Use those times to stimulate your child's abilities. Interaction with your child creates a happy relationship that allows your baby to get to know you and learn to predict what comes next. After 6 months, he needs you to be able to relate to objects and the world around him. You are introducing him to life outside the womb.

Your baby understands language several months before knowing how to express himself. Speak to him, use words to describe what you are doing and your actions. "Look, Mummy's going to feed you now." "Daddy is giving you a bath." Don't be afraid of repeating yourself; he is taking in what he hears and learning to remember.

Playing to learn

Playing is essential to your child's growth. Through play, he shows his joy for life and discovers his body, family and home.

All children love playing for two very good reasons: it's both fun and instructive.

Mum and Dad's games are different but they also complete each other. Play is like your child's first schooling. Your child learns skills and gains confidence in himself. He will make his greatest discoveries during the first two years of his life.

He will learn to:

- Crawl, walk, climb, run and dance (general motor skills);
- Use his hands and fingers to hold and handle objects and develop hand-eye coordination (fine motor skills);
- Understand language, talk, interact;
- Develop his intelligence;
- Get to know the world around him and his place in it;
- Be proud of his successes and develop a sense of confidence.

Toys

The toys you choose should be appropriate for his age and be safe (see Toys, page 521).

Be sure to give him stimulating toys. For example, a dog on wheels that he has to pull is better than a battery-operated puppy that he just has to watch. And be sure to take time to play with him. He needs help learning to discover his new playthings. Time with Mum and Dad is always better than a more complicated toy, especially if it's forgotten in the bottom of the closet.

The best toys aren't the most expensive. Many household objects can amuse young ones: pots, plastic utensils, bowls and of course the quintessential cardboard box (beware of staples!), which becomes a house, tunnel, car, hat and so on.

Instead of filling your child's toy box, rediscover your own childhood joy. Have fun with your little one! Help stimulate his growth – and yours! Play with him, pamper him; you'll discover the joy of being together.

A few suggestions

- Store some toys for awhile. When you take them out again, your child gets to discover them all over. That way you can rotate the toys in your house or even trade with friends.
- Toys play different roles at different ages. At first, your baby will handle them and put them in his mouth. Then he will figure out how they work or start piling them on top of one another.
- After very active games or before bedtime, it's a good idea to choose a calm activity. Read a story, rock the teddy bear to put him to bed, hum a lullaby.

Questions about language

Babies begin communicating from the time they leave the womb. Slowly they learn the language that will let them express themselves and interact with the people around them. The step-by-step development of language is described beginning on page 276.

Parents may worry about how well their child is learning language. Before worrying, remember that children learn at different speeds. Some are slow to speak, others are quick. Temperaments are different too: some children are quieter, others like to talk.

In this section, we will try to answer the most common questions from parents about language.

It's best to put yourself at your child's level so he can see your face when you speak.

How should I speak to my child?

Use simple words and sentences that are not much longer than your child's. Speak more slowly and repeat what you say often. Your child will no doubt come up with words like "wawa" for water, "woof-woof" for dog, and "banket" for blanket. Help him learn the right words. When he says "wawa," offer "Yes, water." You can also use words and sentences to describe what you and your child are doing. As he grows, you will naturally adapt to his level.

He doesn't talk; what do I do?

It's important not to pressure your child. Keep your interaction enjoyable. Try these strategies to get him to express himself:

- Create funny situations that will interest him. For example, pretend to try to put his boots on your feet, or pretend to fall asleep when you're playing with him;
- Try to avoid responding to his needs before he asks. He will no doubt find sounds, words or gestures to express what he wants;

- Ask questions that require more than a yes or no answer. For example, "What would you like to eat?";
- Offer a choice when he points to what he wants: "Would you like an apple or a banana?";
- Say the beginning of the word or sentence: "You want the ba…" (balloon); or "You want the…" (balloon);
- Place things out of reach so he has to ask for them;
- Encourage all his attempts at using a new word and congratulate him.

I don't understand what he's saying. What do I do?

Without blaming him, tell him that you don't understand.

It's important to encourage all his attempts to communicate, even if you don't understand. If you understand a few words, try to ask about the rest of the sentence: "Something happened to your teddy bear?" If you have no idea, ask him to show you.

His pronunciation is wrong; what do I do?

When a child learns to speak, some sounds come early, like *p*, *b*, *m*, *t*, *d*, *n*, while others develop later. The *r* and *l* sounds appear between 2 to 2 ½ years and 5 years. The *s* and *z* sounds appear at around 2 to 2 ½ years, but they're often deformed or spoken from the tip of the tongue in 5- to 6-year-olds. The *sh* and *j* sounds appear at around 3 ½ years and may be learned at only 7 years in some children – no reason to worry before then. Many children replace *sh* with *s* and *z* (e.g., shoe → soe, jam → zam).

To help your child learn to say sounds correctly, repeat the words in the right way, emphasizing the sound he mispronounced. For example, if he says "woud" for "loud," help him by stretching the correct sound and saying it louder: "LLLLLLoud." Don't force him to repeat it. And keep your conversation enjoyable by not repeating too often. What he says is so much more important than how he says it.

When should I see a professional?

Remember that to speak your child needs first to be able to hear. If you're worried about your child's hearing, talk to your doctor, who can refer you to an audiologist, a doctor who specializes in hearing.

Some aspects of learning to speak and communicate are very important. We encourage you to ask for advice from a health professional if:

At about 6 months, your child does not react to your voice or noise. He doesn't babble and doesn't smile.

At about 12 months, he stops making sounds. He doesn't react to familiar words, like his name and the names of people close to him, his teddy bear and favourite games. Your child doesn't look you in the eye, and doesn't seem interested in communicating through gestures or sounds.

At about 18 months, he isn't using any words. He doesn't point. He doesn't understand simple and familiar instructions, such as "give" or "come here."

At about 24 months, he doesn't combine two words, and expresses himself mainly with gestures. He doesn't imitate sounds or words.

At about 3 years, strangers are unable to understand him. He doesn't speak in sentences. He doesn't try to communicate. He doesn't understand simple sentences. He's not interested in other children.

Recommended by a health professional

Some situations can increase the risk of language problems. You should talk to a health professional about such situations, which are listed below. Together, you will be able to decide if a special consultation is required.

- Low birth weight;
- Prematurity (less than 37 weeks);
- Lack of oxygen at birth;
- Speech, language or learning difficulties in the family;
- Hearing problems in the family;
- Drug or alcohol consumption during pregnancy;
- History of repeated ear infections;
- Your child speaks loudly or needs things repeated often.

Should he see a speech-language pathologist?

Language is essential to your child's growth and ability to communicate. When he gets to school, he will need to be able to express himself and be understood. If you notice that his speech is delayed or he has specific troubles, it would be worthwhile to see a speech-language pathologist. Your doctor can help you find one. The local CLSC, hospital or rehabilitation centre might offer such services. Schools also offer support, but it's better to help your child before he gets to school. Waiting times for seeing a speech-language pathologist lead some parents to pay for one through the private sector.

A complete list of speech-language pathologists and audiologists in your region is available through the Ordre des orthophonistes et des audiologistes du Québec. www.ooaq.qc.ca or 514 282-9123 / 1 888 232-9123.

Setting limits

All children need limits. As parents, you respond to this need according to your values but also taking into consideration your child's character, age, and physical and emotional needs. It is important for him that the rules in your family be simple and clear.

Providing clear, simple rules

Love also means setting rules. Rules exist to help keep your child from getting hurt, from hurting others and to teach him to respect others and the world around him. He needs rules and limits, but since he doesn't know what they are, he needs you to teach him.

We usually begin to teach a child rules when he starts to move around on his own with ease; in most cases, that's at about 9 months. From that age on he's able to learn simple rules.

Your little one will follow a rule if you explain it to him taking into account his age and his ability to understand and remember what you are asking him. Teach him one rule at a time and go on to the next only when the last one has been well integrated into his day-to-day routine.

At the age of 18 months, take time to explain the "why" of a rule. Use clear, simple, descriptive language that shows him exactly what you expect from him. This will make it easier for him to understand, accept and respect this rule.

Learn to say NO

Be consistent: when you say no, stick to your word. For example, if you've just told your child he's not allowed to touch the oven door, but he tries to do it anyway, you should say NO firmly.

You can then move him away from the door and offer him a toy as a distraction. If he starts playing with it, praise him. If he cries, repeat no softly, taking care to reassure him. If he is old enough to understand, explain why this is not allowed. If he gets up and returns toward the oven door, simply say no once again and repeat the process. Usually it takes several times, so don't be too discouraged.

Individual parents have their own style of educating their children, probably learned from their own parents; they can be adapted to today's realities. Some are more permissive, others more strict. The most important thing is to be aware of your own approach and to respect your children.

Keep the emotional bond

From the time your baby was born, you've created a strong emotional bond with him. This will help you a lot when it comes to setting rules. A child who feels loved, understood and respected will be much easier to guide than one who doesn't feel appreciated.

Simple, clear instructions are followed more promptly.

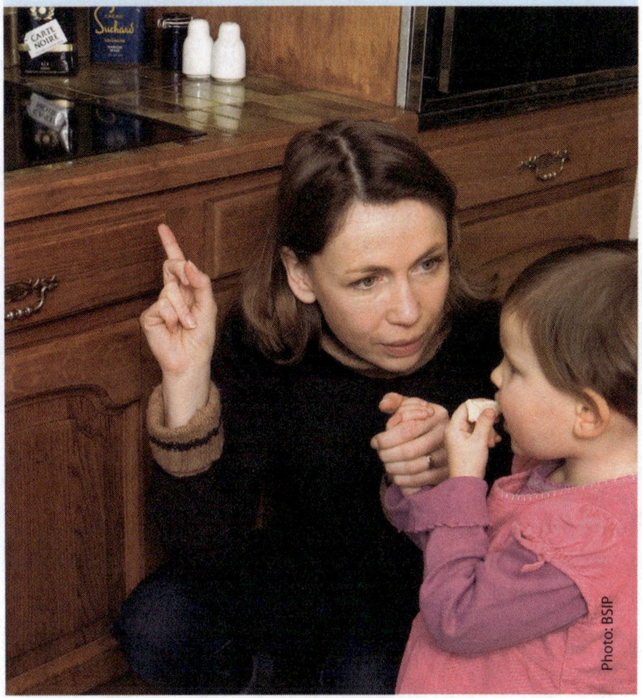

Photo: BSIP

Discipline is necessary

Discipline exists first to keep little ones physically and emotionally safe. It also makes living with others possible – for your child today and in the future. For discipline to work, both parents must decide together what is and isn't allowed. That way, you can set clear rules without contradicting each other.

Clear rules for staying physically safe – This means preventing behaviour that could be dangerous for your child and that could result in him being hurt. For example, you don't allow him to climb something that's not stable. You can make discipline easier by not having too many unsafe things around – make your house safe.

A routine for emotional well-being – Your child needs a routine. He likes things to happen in about the same order each time. That way he can learn to predict what's happening and how it will affect him. He will feel reassured if meals, bedtime and leaving for daycare follow a predictable routine.

Rules that teach cleanliness and politeness – On the one hand, you teach your child to eat with a spoon, put objects away, use the potty and brush his teeth morning and night. On the other hand, you can also teach him some basic rules that will make his life in the outside world easier later on:

- Washing his hands before meals;
- Saying please and thank you;
- Not talking at the same time as someone else;
- Waiting his turn.

A few tips for making discipline easier

- Place yourself at eye level with your child so that he looks at you and is listening when you teach or repeat a rule.
- Be sure to get his attention before explaining a rule; avoid having him be distracted by noise or a game.

- Use games to pass on some aspects of discipline. For example, little ones love to be with their parents and to imitate them. Playing a game of pretending to be a grown-up can help teach your child to pick up his toys and clothes.
- Congratulate your child with a kind word or a smile each time he listens and follows a rule.

Reward good behaviour

Help your child learn good behaviour through the rules you set by congratulating more than scolding. Put more time and energy into encouraging than arguing. Work to guide him toward acceptable and good behaviour. The results will be much better than constantly having to reprimand.

A child that is given too many instructions and scolded too often is likely to become upset or discouraged.

Recognize and congratulate your child's good actions. This will teach him about your expectations and reassure him about his skills and abilities. A child's self-esteem grows through his daily experiences; this is how he develops a positive image of himself. Success and happiness, like frustrations and problems, will teach him about life.

The challenge for parents is to balance encouragement and correction.

Teach patience

Between 9 and 12 months, you can start teaching your child that he can wait a few minutes before getting what he needs. But be sure to be reassuring during these first waiting periods. Keep talking with him, saying for example, "Mommy's on the phone; I'll be with you in two minutes," or offer him a toy.

This will help him learn to be patient little by little in daily situations, for example, while you're making supper, taking care of another child or answering an important phone call.

Don't hesitate to acknowledge your child's good behaviour and to congratulate him on it.

The terrible twos

During this infamous time of no-no-no, which is usually between about 18 months and 3 years, children experience the need to go against anything asked of them. They are in fact going through their first assertiveness crisis. They are testing what they've learned and learning more. Little by little, they understand that not everything is allowed, that there are consequences to our actions, and that rules and limits are part of living with others. Avoid confrontations. It's a good idea to offer choices within limits that are acceptable to you. This will satisfy his need for independence. For example, if the child has to put away his toys, ask if he would like to pick up the blue blocks or the red blocks first.

He won't follow the rules?

Your job of parent-teacher isn't easy. But it's crucial. The sooner your child learns the rules of the house, the easier and more enjoyable it will be to live with him. You'll have more time to do interesting things together. It will also be easier for him to accept rules in other situations, like at daycare. Your household rules get him ready for life outside home, where the rules will be similar to yours.

When the rule is essential to your child's well-being, such as bedtime, don't hesitate to keep your word. Be persistent without being aggressive. Avoid repeating an instruction over and over without making sure it's respected; otherwise your child will learn that he doesn't need to obey.

If your child refuses to follow a rule you've taken care to explain, you must be firm. It will show in your face and the tone of your voice. Don't hit your child. It will only teach him to be afraid, to be disrespectful and to be aggressive. It will teach him to hit to get what he wants, because that's the model you'll be showing. There are more effective ways.

Be firm – Firm means clear and consistent. Some children need more rules and supervision than others. As parents, you are in the best position to adapt to the needs and character of your little one.

Look at a common example: the grocery store crisis. Your little angel throws a devil's fit because you won't give him the candy he sees. He cries, kicks and screams. He even tries to hurt you and rolls on the floor. Obviously, everyone is now watching, some who understand, others who don't.

What do you do?

Withdrawal – In this kind of situation, a good trick is to say "enough!" with a firm tone and get your child out of the situation. Once away and at a distance from spectators, explain calmly but firmly to your child that you will not continue getting the groceries until he understands that he will not be getting any candy. This kind of radical change in the situation should surprise him and get him to change his mind.

Wait for the calm to return before going back to get your groceries. It may seem that you're wasting time, but the limits you're setting with your child are essential and will save you time in the months ahead.

This approach – called withdrawal – means you remove your child from a difficult situation for several minutes to explain what you expect of him. It's better than punishment, which often leaves the child not understanding why he's being scolded or what's expected of him.

> Love, respect, flexibility, patience and persistence are the qualities you have that will allow you to teach your children well.

Worthwhile efforts

Couples need to work together to create healthy discipline. The daily and necessary efforts you make are an investment in the future. By gradually teaching your child the rules of life as a family and as a society, you are making him able to follow the rules on his own later in life.

Many books are available in stores or libraries if you would like to read more about discipline.

Stages of growth

Here are a few tips to help guide you on the great adventure of being a parent. They offer guidelines on your child's growth and give you some ideas for ways to have fun with him.

Remember that the ages we use are only approximate. Children grow at their own individual pace and may learn new skills sooner or later than expected.

The age of a premature baby (born before the 37th week of pregnancy)

Babies born early must make up the weeks they lost in their mother's womb. This doesn't happen magically when they're born but takes place slowly over the first 2 years. Use your baby's corrected age when looking at progress on growth charts and comparing with other children. If not, you may expect too much.

To correct the age of a baby born before term, count from the birth date that was expected. For example, if the expected birth date was March 1st but your baby was born on January 1st, he is two months early. In this case, when you calculate your baby's corrected age, subtract the two months from his actual age. On April 1st, his real age will be 3 months, but his corrected age is 1 month.

We encourage you to consult the Association des parents d'enfants prématurés - Préma-Québec (see Associations, agencies and support groups, page 631).

The following pages offer information about different levels of growth at each age:

- Motor skills;
- Communication and language;
- Understanding (cognitive growth);
- Relationships (socio-affective growth).

Birth to 2 months

Fine motor skills

During his first few weeks, your baby moves but has little control over his movements. His senses are awakening. If you touch the inside of his hand, he'll try to grasp your finger. He will look at a mobile over his crib. Around 1 month of age, his eyes will follow a moving object. Shake a rattle near him and he will react to the sound.

The baby's fine motor skills are poorly organized and his movements are not voluntary. This is normal. This is the reflexive stage, which will disappear as the brain matures.

Moro's reflex means that your baby will jump when he hears a loud noise or is moved quickly. This is not a sign that your baby is nervous.

The sucking reflex is well developed. This allows your baby to feed himself or to calm down by putting his hand in his mouth.

An offshoot of the orientation reflex will make your baby turn his head if you tickle his cheek or arm. It helps your baby look for the breast.

The automatic stepping reflex appears when babies are held standing. He will try to walk on the examination table (the doctor can show you this). Your baby can't support his own weight yet, nor will stimulating this reflex help him walk sooner.

Understanding

Watch your baby and you will see he is born with some extraordinary abilities. He does exciting new things every day. He is not too small to play, and can imitate some gestures like sticking out his tongue and opening his mouth. He can tell the difference between black and white and bright colours.

Relationships

Newborns immediately begin recognizing faces, and their memory is growing. They look for your face, and can find it. Their emotions are intense and hard to control; they need your help in doing so. Their emotions are expressed through everything from crying to cooing and babbling.

Language

Crying is your baby's first way of communicating. At first, babies cry as a reflex, not by choice, usually when something is bothering them. They have different ways of crying to tell you about different needs, such as food or sleep. They coo from the earliest months. They don't understand the meaning of words but can sense emotions such as joy, anger and tenderness in your tone of voice. They react to loud noises. Your baby recognizes your voice and likes to hear it. In his own way, he is already communicating!

Activities

Talk with him. Talk softly. Tell him a story or sing him a song. Imitate the sounds he makes and watch for his reaction. By doing this, you will be helping him to pronounce sounds and learn tones and rhythms. He will want to join in the conversation. Say his name often; soon he will recognize it. Move around while calling him; he will move his head in the direction of your voice. Do this often. It is important for learning speech.

Look at your child when he is in your arms; both of you will get to know each other better.

Photo: iStockphoto

From 2 to 4 months

Fine motor skills

Your child is beginning to control his head movements and hold his head up better and better.

He is becoming more active. When lying face down, he raises his head and pushes up bit by bit using his arms. He moves his legs and explores his hands and feet. He loves to be touched and kissed and nuzzled, and for you to move his feet like pedals and to play with his hands. He will grab a rattle and try to suck on it. Don't be surprised; for quite a while he will try to put everything in his mouth. This is how he learns. You'll see him playing with his tongue and saliva and making bubbles.

Language

Your child will make different sounds depending on what he needs. He's moving toward babble ("dada, mama, baba"). He reacts to familiar voices and the sound of his toys. He will also smile in reaction to your stimulations. He doesn't understand words yet, but likes it when you hum or sing to him because he recognizes your voice and feels safe. He pays attention to the tune and your gestures. If he cries, talk softly, he may calm down. He may pay attention to music.

Relationships

The first social smile usually appears in the second month. The human face interests the baby, who answers a smile with a smile. At 2 months, he starts becoming interested in other babies and may become excited when he sees one. At 3 months, he is becoming more and more aware of other members of the family.

Understanding

Your baby repeats pleasant actions he has learned by accident, such as sucking his thumb and putting toys in his mouth.

Activities

Touring the home. Give the baby a detailed tour of your home. Show him and tell him what's in it. He will try to grab things, practicing his hand-eye coordination.

Photo: Étienne Carrier

Tickling. At bath time or while playing, help your child discover textures. Tickle him with a toothbrush, paper tissue, teddy bear, dry washcloth, plastic toy, etc.

From 4 to 6 months

Fine motor skills

Your baby is stronger now and holds himself better. He has probably doubled his birth weight (see Growth, page 452). Lying on his back, he raises his head, pedals and puts his feet in his mouth. If you pull on his hands, he rises and his head follows the movement. His back is straight but he still needs to be supported. Lying on his front, he rolls over onto his back with pleasure. He looks at his hands, puts them in his mouth, grabs things easily, holds them well but sometimes drops them. He will follow objects with his eyes but may sometimes squint. His vision is very good and he can distinguish small details.

Understanding

He likes fairly big, coloured objects hanging within reach. He enjoys looking at them, touching them and turning them around. He knows that if he moves the rattle, it will make a noise. He also knows that if he babbles, you'll pay attention for a longer time. When he drops something, he doesn't look for it.

Language

He expresses his needs by yelling, crying and babbling. He is improving the babble with sounds that respond to yours. He roars with laughter and sometimes shouts for fun. Exploring his voice, he tries sounds, repeats them and tries to imitate others. He watches people talking to him and looks for the source of a noise. When he is babbling, answer him. He will find out he can affect the world around him and learn to take turns speaking. Talk to him often.

Relationships

Now that your baby is more aware, he will be more active in seeking your attention. He may cry because he's bored and hopes you will come and move him around and babble with him. He may even interrupt feeding to look at mom and dad. It's a good idea to keep him in the same room you are in and talk to him. You can pick him up as often as you want, even if he's not crying.

At this age, the child is interested in the people around him. He looks for the sources of noise. He also recognizes family and friends. Take advantage of this to check:

- If he reacts when you smile at him;
- If he stops crying when you talk to him;
- If he turns toward you when you say his name;
- If he follows your movements without constantly squinting.

If he shows little reaction and you are worried, don't hesitate to talk to the doctor about it.

Activities

Lying face down. Place your child on his belly and put some safe and interesting objects in front of him. He will want to reach out, grab them and handle them.

Rattle. Your child will want to shake a rattle to make noise.

Lying face down, your child will learn to coordinate his movements and learn shapes and textures.

From 6 to 9 months

Fine motor skills

He is starting to move around on his belly. He rolls over. He's learning to crawl, backwards first, becoming more skilled and moving faster. Lying face down, he holds himself up with his arms. You can get him to move forward by offering him a teddy bear or a small ball. He can grab smaller and smaller objects and move them from hand to hand.

He holds the breast with two hands while feeding. He may even turn around while suckling to watch what's going on around him. His teeth sharpen and he will probably learn the joy of biting. He is beginning to eat solid food. To be safe while eating, he must be close to you and fully secure in the highchair. He likes to play with his bowls and food. At about 9 months, his hand-eye coordination will improve. He can drink by himself from a bottle with a spout.

Language

Deliberate communications begin at about 7 months, mainly by gesture until 18 months. Meanwhile, the baby's babble is becoming more diverse and sophisticated, copying the sounds he hears. He is interested in people who talk to him, looking at them and answering to his name. He now starts using a few familiar words ("daddy, baby"). By about 9 months, your child understands familiar gestures. If you hold out your hand and ask for his toy, he might give it to you. A baby understands language before he tries to use it voluntarily. At this age, your child understands many words even if he can't yet say them.

Understanding

He likes mirrors and articles he can handle, turn and move. He enjoys large plastic cubes. He is fascinated by noisy games and will bang things against each other or the table, walls and floor. He likes squeeze toys that make noise. He will play the same game over and over. He doesn't throw things on the floor to make you angry – he's learning how to throw and how things fall. Your child learns from the things you do with him. He is gathering knowledge and putting it to use.

At about 8 or 9 months you will notice that your child likes to look at his cubes, his teddy bear and his bowl from every angle – top, bottom, left, right, back and front. He's learning perspective. In front of a mirror, he tries to capture his image and yours; he examines himself. Tell him that it's him, and say his name, which he has known for a long time now.

Relationships

The baby is discovering his body and his parents' faces. He feels the need to touch them, to put his fingers in their mouth, nose and eyes. He pulls at their clothing. He laughs at the faces they make and becomes something of a tease. He tries to attract the attention of other babies by smiling and babbling when they meet. The fear of strangers may make him cry when he sees unfamiliar faces.

The tunnel. A big cardboard box with holes in both ends makes a fine tunnel to crawl through. Be sure to remove any staples first. Get down on all fours with your baby and you'll see the world from his point of view.

Photo: BSIP

At 8 or 9 months, it will be hard to separate your child from the person who takes care of him the most. He will cry when you leave. Try playing peekaboo so he will understand that you're not disappearing forever when you leave. He'll learn to keep an image of you in his mind.

After you have left or when he wakes up, he may be worried to discover you aren't there. Always tell him, particularly if he's taking a nap, that you are going away and will be back soon. A child may become attached to substitute objects such as a doll or blanket to make up for absent parents. Be careful of this precious article and wash it secretly. Keep an identical spare if possible and switch on laundry day.

> **!** Help make your baby's separation from Mom easier by having Dad also spend lots of time with him. This will make it easier for your child to turn to another person in the family circle (see Importance of the father-child bond, page 185).

Activities

Parts of the body. You can now play at identifying parts of the face. Then name parts of the body.

Peekaboo. Several times in a row, hide your face behind your hands then reveal yourself while calling "peekaboo." Start the game over using his favourite toy; he will be surprised and happy to see it reappear so quickly. At this age, children think that people or things they can no longer see have really disappeared.

Mirror, mirror on the wall… Put yourself and your baby in front of a mirror. Make lots of smiles and faces; he is learning to recognize both you and himself. Make noises with your mouth and he will try to answer them.

The wide world. Whatever the season, take him outdoors. It's good for his health and yours. Help him discover the world around him – trees, birds and flowers – and other children.

Blocks, balls, bottles. Give him blocks to pile, balls to push and floating toys. In the bathtub he will play with plastic bottles and small containers; he will love to fill and empty them. Don't use toys that don't drain because they make a fine home for bacteria and other nasty microbes.

Words and books. Reading stories is a good way to learn new words. Choose a book with simple colour pictures.

From 9 to 12 months

Fine motor skills

Your little one will want to explore every corner of the home. He races around on hands and knees and disappears before you know it. He's becoming more and more independent. He may not walk yet but he can stand up, squat and bend over. Using furniture for support, he stands up, takes a step or two and falls down. And starts over! His hand coordination is improving and he is becoming more and more capable of doing things. He picks up crumbs and tiny objects and holds them between thumb and forefinger. He still puts things in his mouth because that's how he discovers. So pay attention!

Your baby can move very quickly on all fours!

Photo: Mireille Simard

Language

Your child can understand what you tell him, especially if you speak plainly and use gestures as well as words. This is the stage when your baby starts to follow simple instructions (e.g., show me your nose). He knows "bye-bye" and "clap" and how to hide. He is beginning to communicate for specific reasons, to get something or attract attention. You have to know what he wants because he illustrates his babble with gestures while saying "ba ba ba, ma ma ma" and so on, holding out his hand and eventually pointing to the thing he wants. He turns when his name is called and imitates the sounds you make. He also still enjoys noise-making toys, and can locate the source of a familiar but hidden noise or voice (from several metres away).

Relationships

He is becoming very sociable. He and the children he plays with are beginning to imitate each other. He cries when he can't see you any more. You are still the centre of his life but he is exploring the world around him with great curiosity. It can put your patience to the test but this curiosity is a sign of good development. He can begin playing alone, but would much prefer that dad be there to give him a friendly hard time. He still doesn't play with the same toy for very long, and he can choose between a stuffed animal and a doll.

Understanding

Your child enjoys imitating you. He is beginning to show interest in books and music. He really enjoys games of emptying and filling. He is able to use his knowledge in new situations. If you prevent him from taking something, he will look for other ways to get it. He can coordinate several actions to achieve a goal, such as crawling across the room to get a toy.

He links events and reactions, such as how his parents react to his crying. He is fascinated by the results of his actions, and may pull on the tablecloth to get the glass of milk on the table.

Activities

A ball. Sit on the floor face to face with your legs open. Roll the ball between his legs. Ask him to send it back the same way. He will be proud of himself when he sees you're happy he succeeded.

A toy chest. Give him a box full of colourful, washable toys such as balls, blocks, stacking rings and fabric animals. Keep him fairly near to you. He'll start playing by himself.

Smells. Use mealtime to introduce your baby to different odours, such as bread, meat, fruit, vegetables and spices. This will help develop his sense of smell.

Books. Let him handle his first books, made of cardboard or cloth. Point at things on the pictures and tell him their names. He will learn to identify them and later to name them.

Photo: iStockphoto

A cupboard for baby. Give him permission to go through a cupboard located away from the stove and full of plastic containers in various shapes and colours. While he plays with them you can work quietly in the kitchen. Don't forget to use security locks on all the other drawers and cupboards.

From 12 to 15 months

Fine motor skills

Your baby now weighs three times as much as when he was born (see Growth, page 452). He can walk, or almost. But there's no rush. Children grow at their own pace. Maybe he prefers to wait until 15 to 18 months. Don't push it. He'll soon be climbing on the furniture and moving chairs around you.

He is very capable on all fours and can climb the stairs this way. He is learning about shapes, putting small cubes inside big ones, balls in holes, rings on a cone.

Understanding

He sorts objects by shape and colour. And he likes testing different actions. For example, if he drops an article down the stairs he'll throw another one down to see what happens.

Language

Children generally say their first words at about 12 months. A baby's first words will refer to people close to him (e.g., mommy, daddy) and to familiar articles (ball, doll). It's important to know that some words will not match adult speech (e.g., banky for blanket). He recognizes the names of familiar people and things. He enjoys repeating what he hears and continues to babble.

Relationships

Your child is very sensitive to his parents' emotions, especially in unfamiliar or threatening situations. A parent's worried or confident expression will affect his behaviour and feelings. Your young child is more sensitive to family mood than anything else.

During your baby's one-year medical exam, the doctor will ask you some questions about your child's growth; for example:

- Does he turn toward you when you call his name?
- Does he look directly in your eyes?
- Does he point at things to show his need or interest?
- Is he beginning to pretend (feeding baby, talking on the phone)?

Activities

Decorating the refrigerator. Your child will have fun with fridge magnets. Moving them around helps teach the finger and thumb to pinch, and improves hand-eye coordination. Careful! Be sure the magnets are firmly assembled and too big to swallow (see Toys, page 521).

Photo: Stéphanie Giguère Marzke

The falling tower. Show him how to make a stack of three or four blocks. Put one down and ask him to add a second, and so on. Then tell him to knock the stack down – and start over.

Mastering the stairs. Once he starts walking, there's a new game he'll love: going downstairs backward.

Nursery rhymes and chitchat. Chatting with him frequently is a good way for your baby to learn language skills. He will enjoy having body parts named, for example. To add to your choices, your local library may have tape cassettes of the nursery rhymes and songs that children love so much.

From 15 to 18 months

Fine motor skills

By now your child is walking. He happily struts around with legs apart and arms out for balance. It's a good time to buy him some soft shoes for walking outdoors (see First shoes, page 220). He climbs stairs on all fours, goes downstairs backward, gets into cupboards, climbs on chairs and touches everything. He's learning to handle screw tops, door handles and the pages of a book. He helps you dress him, and undresses quickly and throws away his boots. He can take a few steps sideways or backward. He can roll a ball toward an adult.

He can also draw pictures with a large crayon. He can stack two or three cubes and put things in a bowl. He likes to fill and empty containers.

Careful! He still puts things in his mouth, including stones. He is so excited he wants to eat and sleep less.

Understanding

He is still experimenting with gravity, dropping things on purpose from his highchair. Throwing things is still part of his learning program. He looks for various ways to do what he wants and tries out new behaviour. For example, if he steps on a plastic duck it makes a noise. He may then try to squeeze it in his hands or sit on it to make the same noise. He's starting to solve problems by trial and error.

Relationships

This is the beginning of independence, and a very important time in a child's social development. It can be very hard on parents. He will follow you and imitate the things you do around home – toilet, housekeeping, toothbrushing, preparing meals. Lend him a cleaning cloth, a spoon and a bowl. Name the things he does. Invite him to imitate the sounds of things he hears: cars, airplanes, the vacuum cleaner, dogs and cats. He likes to pretend he's on the phone. Play music for him and he will dance to the rhythm. Play chase and hiding games with him and he'll be delighted. He loves playing in sand and splashing water.

Baby follows you and imitates you.

Photo: François Gervais

Rather than responding to what he wants before he asks, let him express his needs.

Language

He is starting to grasp simple instructions (e.g., "go get your teddy bear") and depending less and less on your gestures. When he hears a noise, he looks toward the source of it. By 18 months, he knows at least 18 words that his parents understand, and he speaks one word at a time. He says "daddy" and "mommy" and a few useful terms such as "down", "wait" and "more". He may name some body parts (nose, eyes), pets (dog, cat), and articles of daily life (ball, car). He tries to repeat words and imitate the sounds of animals. Give him time to talk and encourage conversation, because he will learn through practice. When he says a word, add more words to it. For example if he says "turn", you say "yes, the top is turning fast."

Activities

Puzzles and a tool box. He is becoming more capable with his hands. He loves toys he can put together and take apart, nesting and stacking games. It's time for his first jigsaw puzzle (with large parts), a plastic tool box and some big building blocks.

A pull toy. He likes to push and pull a vehicle. Give him toys with long handles, carts, wagons, balls and boxes full of various things. Tie a piece of string to an empty shoe box and suggest that he put his teddy bear in it. This makes a great sled.

Drawings. Give him paper and non-toxic wax crayons. Show him how to doodle and he will immediately see the link between action and result. After praising the artist, hang the masterpiece on the fridge.

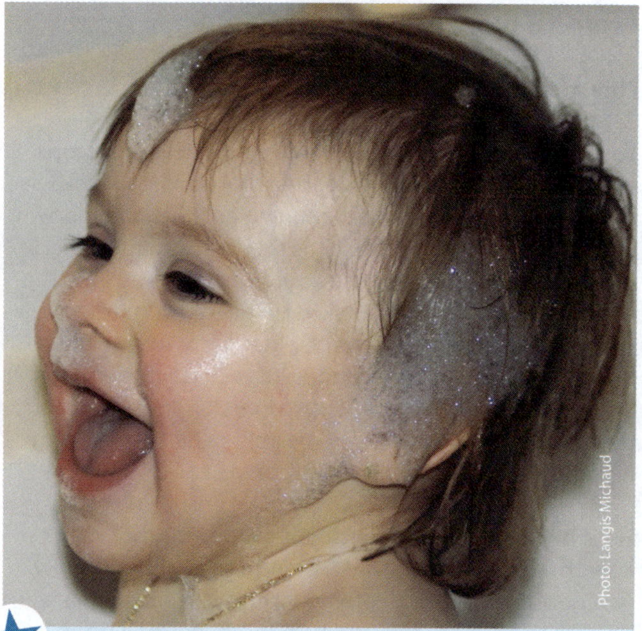
Photo: Langis Michaud

Bubbles. You can blow bubbles for him to catch in the bathtub. He will get very excited so be sure to keep him sitting down. This will be just as much fun outside on the grass.

From 18 to 24 months

Fine motor skills

Your child has a wild need to move now. He runs, stops, starts, stops again, legs wide, chest forward, crouches as if urinating, stands up, starts running again and falls down. He bumps into everything. He kicks his ball to move it. He dances by spinning around and around when he likes the music. He loves playing outside. He needs room to walk, jump and run the way he wants. Teach him to rest when he's tired by sitting cross-legged. It's a good position for the legs. By about 2 years he can do a standing jump and between 2 and 3 years he will be able to hit the ball with his foot. He will also learn to walk on his toes.

He is becoming more coordinated every day. He may be able to run a piece of string through something hollow or a bobbin of thread. Between 2 and 3 years old, he will be able to hold scissors and turn the pages of a book one at a time.

He doesn't want help at the table. He holds his spoon well but still has trouble getting it to his mouth. He willingly splashes his soup on himself. He can easily take off his hat and socks, and you can encourage him to dress himself by choosing clothes that are easy to put on.

Language

By about 18 months, your child will clearly understand simple sentences like "go get your ball" with no gesturing. He will also turn his head toward a noise. By 24 months, he can do what you ask (e.g., point at a picture in a book). He likes listening to little songs and stories. By 30 months, he can correctly answer questions about who, what and where with words and actions. His vocabulary is now growing quickly. From the 18 words he knew at 18 months, he has learned 100 by 24 months. The first 2-word sentences appear at about 2 years (e.g., daddy gone, more milk), and grow to 3 words by about 2 ½ years. At this age, your child is also starting to use small words like "me" and "one."

Little conversations will soon become possible. You'll be able to talk with your little one about an event or a thing. Don't worry if he still can't pronounce all the sounds and syllables. Children make lots of language mistakes at this age.

Relationships

Your child is becoming more self-assured and independent. Do you feel the distance is growing between you? In fact, he's discovering the world around him. He sometimes talks a lot and continues to imitate you. He feeds his teddy bear, washes it, walks it and puts it to bed. He's playing the role of mother and father.

At 2 years old, he wants to do everything by himself: eat, drink and undress, mainly. He loves learning. Sometimes he makes a mess but never mind. Let him experiment while you watch. His success will make him confident.

Your child will have fun with you or with an older child but not yet with a toddler his own age. He may find it hard to lend his toys but you will gradually convince him to share. It will be easier at 3 or 4 years. Many children go through a phase when they push, bite and hit. Say NO clearly but don't hit or bite your child.

Understanding

Between 18 and 24 months, he learns that objects exist even when he can't see them. When your child sees an object moved from one place to another, he looks for it in the last hiding place. He also looks for articles he hasn't seen moved.

Your child can understand symbols now, and can think of people, things and events he doesn't see. He can imitate someone who isn't there, or pretend to. He can draw objects. At about 2 years old, he will be able to sort articles based on common characteristics such as colour.

She loves to hear the same stories over and over because she identifies with them.

Photo: Langis Michaud

He is also beginning to understand cause and effect. When your child bangs on things with a spoon, he realizes that each one has its own sound.

Activities

A story every night. As often as possible, take the time to read your child stories. Point out pictures by naming objects and actions. Ask him to turn the pages and let him handle the book.

Your child will learn that reading goes from left to right and from the top of the page to the bottom, and that stories have a beginning and an end. He will express his emotions. This is a great time to share precious moments of pleasure and togetherness. Choose books he likes. You can go to the library, and ask family members to give him books as presents.

Other word games. Writing is everywhere. While taking a walk, satisfy his curiosity by reading things that attract his attention: posters, the names of stores, advertising, road signs, etc. He will learn to recognize logos, which is the first step toward understanding words.

The sound of music. He is also discovering music. Listen to CDs and cassettes and sing his favourite songs with him. He often prefers songs accompanied by simple gestures. Since he is using toys with more ability, you can provide him with simple instruments like drums, a xylophone and cymbals.

Free creativity. It's time to use toys that let him create things. He likes finger painting, modelling clay and mud pies. Say something about what he makes. He will want to talk about it. Don't forget to show off his handiwork – he will be very proud of it.

Long live the outdoors. Your child needs to move. He needs space to run and jump. Play with him outside in your yard or the park as often as possible. He likes playing outside and it's good for him.

Costumes. He loves disguises and will borrow grownups' hats and shoes. Set aside some old clothing that doesn't matter if it gets dirty.

Toilet training

Toilet training usually begins at about 2 years old. Most children are fully toilet trained through the day between 2 and 4 years old.

Girls usually learn this a bit earlier than boys. Toilet training usually takes from 3 to 6 months. We recommend that you do not set a timetable. There is no use forcing a child who isn't ready.

Night-time bladder control may take several months or even several years.

A child is capable of toilet training somewhere between 18 months and 3 years of age. Here are a few signs that your child might be ready for this new experience:

- Your child can walk to his potty.
- He is starting to undress (he can pull down his pants).
- His diaper stays dry for several hours.

Photo: Martine Rheault

The age of toilet training varies greatly from one child to another.

- He understands simple instructions, like "take this to Daddy."
- He can express his needs with words like "want milk" and he will soon be able to say "need to pee!"
- He is proud he can do things by himself.

Here are some ways to make toilet training easier:

- Get him ready a bit at a time by teaching him the words and gestures of elimination – "poop", "pee", "potty", "toilet".
- Ask him to imitate you. Your child will want to copy you in the bathroom the same way he copies your speech. Put the potty close to the toilet and urge your child to do the same thing you do. When he's ready, he'll want to be like mommy and daddy.
- Use the potty rather than the toilet during the first steps. Your child will feel safer and more stable.
- Ensure that he is well seated on the potty, feet on the floor. If he's too high, use a small footstool so he can relax.

- To begin with, ask your child to sit on the potty with his clothes on, and then again after the wet diaper has been removed.
- Later, have him sit on the potty at set times of the day (for example, after waking up, after eating and before naps, baths and bedtime) to establish a routine.
- Congratulate your child every time he shows interest in sitting on the potty.
- Start using training pants or cotton pants after your child has been using the potty regularly for a few days.
- Don't be discouraged by accidents. This is all part of learning.
- Encourage his efforts and avoid punishing your child.

One of these days your child will want to go in the potty. There's no rush, and it will be easier if there's no stress.

It's not a good idea to start toilet training during an unsettled time in your child's life, such as when you move, hire a new sitter or a new baby arrives.

It's important to go at your child's speed so this major new step in life is positive. Never try to force him to toilet train before he's physically and mentally ready. Trust him!

Reading and writing

Now that your child has learned to handle books, he's beginning to discover the written word. Long before he goes to school, you can use everyday events to help him take the first steps toward reading.

Your child watches you and wants to imitate you. Do some of your reading and writing while he's watching. Here are a few suggestions for activities:

- When your child begins to talk, you can write the first words in large letters and put them on the fridge. Point at them and read them out loud from time to time.

The more your child is exposed to writing, the better he'll be able to read and study in school.

- When he begins naming the people around him, you can write each person's name beside their photo. If he says "daddy" for example, you can write the name in big letters under a picture of daddy.
- When he brings you a drawing, write his name at the bottom of it.

Your child will make the connection between speech and writing a bit at a time. He will discover the purpose of writing and decide it is a good idea. To know more about learning to read and write, see the documents "De A à Z on s'aide"on the ministère de l'Éducation, du Loisir et du Sport Web site (French only) at: www.mels.gouv.qc.ca/DFGA/disciplines/alphabetisation/autres_productions/txt_az.html

Feeding your baby

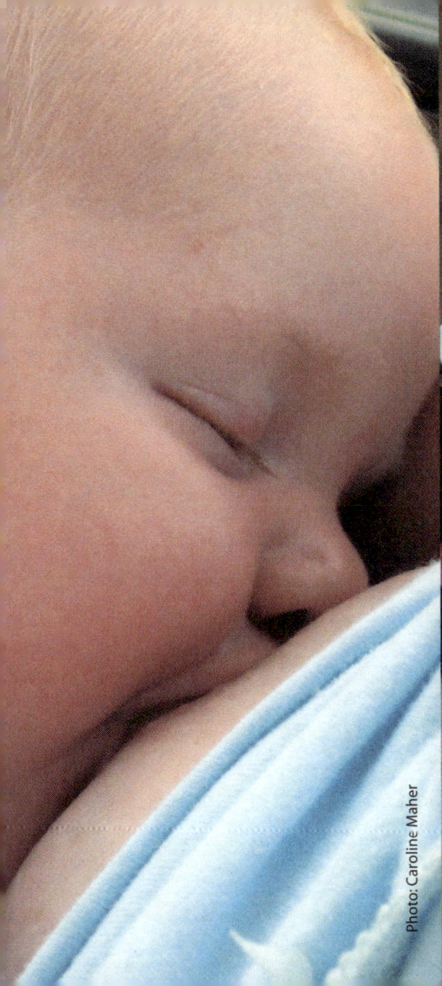

Photo: Caroline Maher

Photo: Marlen Laliberté

Photo: Nicolas Delaître

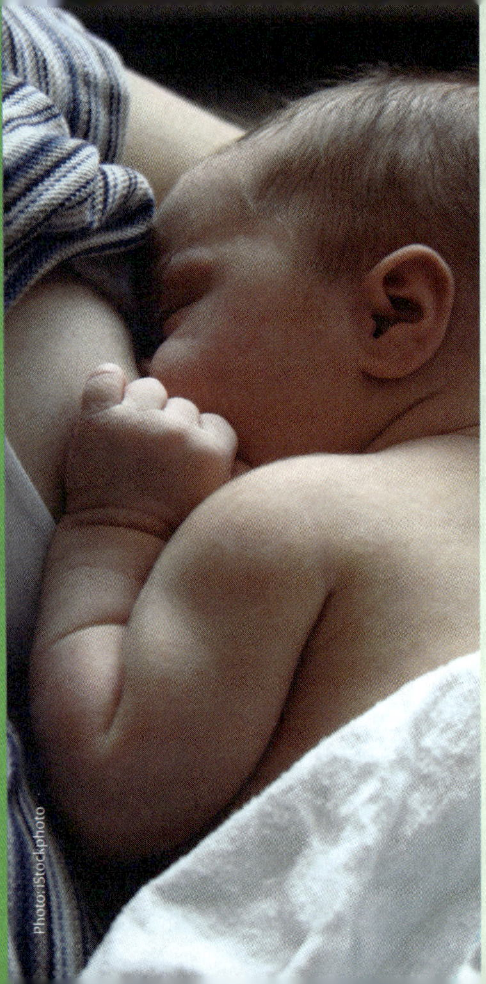

Photo: iStockphoto

Mother's milk

Breast-feeding is an intimate and enjoyable time. Skin-to-skin contact helps your infant feel warm and safe. Snuggled up to your breast after delivery, the first time he nurses will comfort him, and help stabilize his body temperature. Breast-feeding continues the physical and emotional relationship that started between you and your baby during pregnancy.

In Canada, as elsewhere in the world, health professionals (Canadian Paediatric Society, Dietitians of Canada and Health Canada) recommend breast-feeding only for babies during the first 6 months of life. Beyond that, breast-feeding can continue for up to 2 years with the help of complementary foods.

Today, almost 85% of Quebecers breast-feed their newborns and close to 50% continue to the age of 6 months or longer. Even a little bit of breast milk can make a difference. You may decide to breast-feed for a few hours, a few days, several months or more than 1 year. It's up to you. But be sure to enjoy this unique experience!

Breast-feeding is the most natural way to feed your baby, and it brings mother and baby closer together physically and emotionally.

Photo: Jasmine Kabuya Racine

Learning the art of breast-feeding

A baby arriving in your life brings an intense period of adaptation and learning. Breast-feeding, like giving birth, is totally natural. And, just as it's normal to get help during delivery, it's normal to need help with breast-feeding, especially at the beginning. The first days are an important time to learn to enjoy breast-feeding.

Breast-feeding is something we learn. Little by little you'll discover the pleasure of it. Give yourself time. Trust yourself. You can breast-feed!

10 things to make breast-feeding easier

- **Learn about breast-feeding and breast milk while you're pregnant.**
- **Skin-to-skin contact with your baby immediately after birth** awakens his senses and will give him the desire to nurse.
- **Letting your baby breast-feed as soon as he starts seeking out your breast,** ideally in the hour following his birth, will help breast-feeding start well.
- **Keep your baby close to you, both night and day.** Holding your infant close will allow you to get to know one another and to respond to his needs quickly.
- **Learn to recognize your baby's signs of hunger and satisfaction.**

- **Breast-feed on demand,** when your baby is hungry. Frequent nursing stimulates milk production and reassures your little one during this adaptation period.
- **Make sure your baby is latching on properly** and sucking effectively: this will help him drink well without causing you pain.
- **Don't skip feedings or offer your baby a pacifier or bottle before the age of 4-6 weeks.** Breast-feeding exclusively (without giving your baby other milk or complementary foods before the age of 6 months) promotes healthy milk production and will allow your baby to make the most of all the benefits breast milk has to offer.
- **Make sure you have support and avoid being isolated.** The support of your partner, someone close to you or a support group will often make a big difference.
- **Trust yourself** and enjoy the pleasures of parenthood!

The support and reassuring presence of the baby's father or someone close to you will often make a big difference.

Photo: Simiane Valentini

Breast size and care

Breast shape, size and colour vary from one woman to the next. The appearance and texture of the breast depends mainly on heredity. Like the rest of your body, breasts change over your lifetime. They will get bigger during pregnancy and at the start of breast-feeding. They'll gradually return to their normal size during breast-feeding and after weaning. Pregnancy will cause changes to many parts of your body but it won't deform your breasts or cause them to sag.

The breasts are often bigger and heavier during the first 6 weeks of breast-feeding. Whether or not you choose to wear a bra depends on your comfort. Nursing bras are usually more practical than regular bras but you don't have to wear one. Regardless of what you choose, it should be comfortable and large enough to avoid squeezing your breasts. Don't hesitate to sleep bare-breasted if you feel comfortable doing so.

If you use nursing pads, choose cotton or disposable ones without a plastic lining, and be sure to change them often.

A daily shower or bath is all you need to keep your breasts clean. Creams, ointments and other products are not recommended. You don't need to wash your breasts each time you nurse; this may irritate them. But washing your hands with soap and water is the best way to prevent infections.

Producing milk

Pregnancy hormones prepare your breasts for breast-feeding. Milk will begin to be secreted at the end of pregnancy. Some women will notice their breasts leaking during this time. Milk is available for your baby, regardless of the day he's born.

Colostrum, the milk you produce in the first few days, is thick and sweet. It's very rich in proteins, vitamins and minerals, and is the perfect nourishment for your newborn. Colostrum provides many white blood cells and antibodies that will help fight infections. It also cleans the intestines of residues that accumulated before birth.

Milk production will increase suddenly sometime between the 2nd and 5th day after birth. It becomes clearer and has a bluish or yellowish colour. This is when your milk "comes in." New hormones cause this change, which will happen even if your baby is not breast-fed. Frequent nursing during this period, including at night, will help the milk come in sooner and keep your breasts from becoming too engorged.

From then on, nursing will keep your breasts producing milk. The more often the breasts are emptied, the more milk they produce. This is why using your baby's needs as a guide is recommended, without limiting the number or length of feedings. Each breast produces milk independently. If only one breast is stimulated, after a few weeks, only that breast will produce milk.

Breast milk is complete and adapted to an infant's needs. Its composition will change during a feeding and over the course of the day. It also changes a bit over time to adapt to the needs of your growing child. This is why most breast-fed babies don't need any other food or liquid during the first 6 months. The gradual introduction of complementary foods after that will ensure the needs of your growing child are met. When a breast is stimulated regularly day and night, the mammary gland will produce enough milk for your baby for as long as you breast-feed.

Let-down reflex

Milk production and the let-down reflex are stimulated by your baby's sucking, which causes the secretion of the hormone ocytocin. This in turn causes contractions of the glandular alveoli in the breast – otherwise known as the let-down reflex. The let-down reflex can also be stimulated when you hear your baby cry or when you think about him. This way, milk is readily available when your baby begins to nurse.

When let-down happens during nursing, the milk flows more quickly and your baby will swallow faster for several minutes. Sometimes the let-down reflex happens several times during the same feeding, or so strongly that your baby has to let go of the breast to catch his breath. Some women get very thirsty when the let-down reflex happens. It may also cause a painless tingling sensation in the breast.

Ocytocin is also the reason for uterine contractions felt while nursing in the first few days after delivery. They are more intense after the birth of a second child. These uterine contractions prevent hemorrhaging in the mother.

First hours of breast-feeding

When your baby is born, ask that he be placed on your stomach with his skin against yours. This will let you both adapt and stay warm.

The sucking reflex starts in most newborns in the hour after birth. When your baby begins to move, he will instinctively seek out his mother's breast, explore and discover his sucking reflex. Help him as needed and offer him the breast as soon as he seems interested. Some babies don't want to nurse. If he doesn't nurse right away, hold him close to you until he wants to. Your baby will smell and recognize you; this will stimulate him to nurse.

The time between the first and second feedings will depend on your baby and how much he drank. Some babies will sleep for several hours after birth. Make the most of this time to rest as a family, keeping your baby near you. The first times you nurse are above all a time to learn and be in touch with your baby. Mother and child need to get to know each other and learn how to work together.

Some babies recover more slowly from birth and have a harder time nursing. If your infant takes a while reacting, squeeze a few drops of milk into his mouth. If he still doesn't want to nurse, don't insist. Offer him the breast a bit later when he shows signs of being hungry. Maintain skin-to-skin contact with your infant to stimulate his interest in nursing and to reassure him. You'll know when he's ready to nurse. Don't worry: some babies need more time than others. If need be, express your milk and give it to your baby using a small spoon or small cup. It's best to avoid giving him a bottle at this point. A nurse or midwife will be there to help if you need it.

At the hospital and at home, keep your baby close to you to get to know him and identify his needs. During the first few months, babies should stay in the same room as their parents, day and night (see Sleeping safely, page 247).

Caesarian section

There is nothing to prevent you from breast-feeding shortly after delivery. If you were under general anesthetic, you may breast-feed as soon as you are fully awake and feel comfortable. If you received an epidural (anesthesia injected into the lower back), you can breast-feed as soon as possible. Ideally, that would be in the hour after birth, even if you're still under the effect of the epidural. Many hospitals encourage the mother to nurse for the first time in the operating or recovery room.

Having your partner or another person you have chosen with you will allow you to keep your baby in your room. Staff will help you with nursing as needed. You will soon be able to care for the baby yourself. Many fathers take the opportunity to have their baby on their chest in skin-to-skin contact. Both father and baby enjoy the closeness and warmth.

First days (0 to 14 days)

Mother, father and baby are all learning. Sometimes you'll feel awkward and slow getting ready to nurse. This is normal when you're learning something new. At first it can be difficult to get your baby to nurse without help.

During the first few days, someone trained in breast-feeding (a nurse or midwife) will help make sure your baby is properly latched on and sucking well enough to get the milk he needs. The quality of the latch and sucking are more important than the number and length of feedings. A baby that nurses well will not hurt your nipples and will feed more quickly. Done properly, breast-feeding is not painful.

Trust yourself! With practice, you and your baby will soon be experts, and nursing will be easy and pleasant for both of you.

Breast-feeding a newborn – which involves nursing, frequent stimulation, burping and changing the diaper – can take from 45 to 90 minutes. If your baby often falls asleep while nursing, he needs to be stimulated. Some babies sleep so much they have to be woken up to nurse. Also, during the first days and weeks, babies have a tendency to fall asleep while nursing when the milk flow slows down, even if they haven't had enough milk.

If your baby falls asleep, stimulate him: tickle him, uncover him a bit, keep him close to you, talk or sing to him! Check that he's latching on properly. Stimulate your baby to nurse using the breast compression technique described on page 327.

Breast-feeding may seem to take a long time at first. Don't worry: when your baby becomes more alert and experienced, nursing will be faster.

Difficulty latching on

When your baby latches on correctly, his mouth will cover a large part of the areola, the coloured part of the breast that surrounds the nipple. For reasons we don't know, some newborns have a harder time latching on than others. A flat or inverted nipple may sometimes make it more difficult, but many babies adjust easily.

Your baby will learn to nurse regardless of the shape of your breasts. Patience, confidence and determination are key to success. You'll learn by trying several times a day for short periods of time. Have him nurse before he gets too hungry. If needed, start by giving him a little bit of breast milk using a small spoon or cup to calm him down. Try to make your breasts more supple if they're engorged.

If your baby is agitated, remove him from the breast for a few minutes until he calms down. If feeding isn't going well, don't insist; you can finish feeding him using expressed breast milk. It's best to avoid giving your baby a pacifier, bottle or nipple shield. If the situation doesn't improve after a few feedings, contact your midwife, a support group, CLSC nurse or Info-Santé.

Some newborns will easily latch on to one breast but refuse the other. Don't worry, this is common. Expressing milk from the breast he refuses will stimulate milk production. Continue offering this breast without forcing it – your baby will eventually take it.

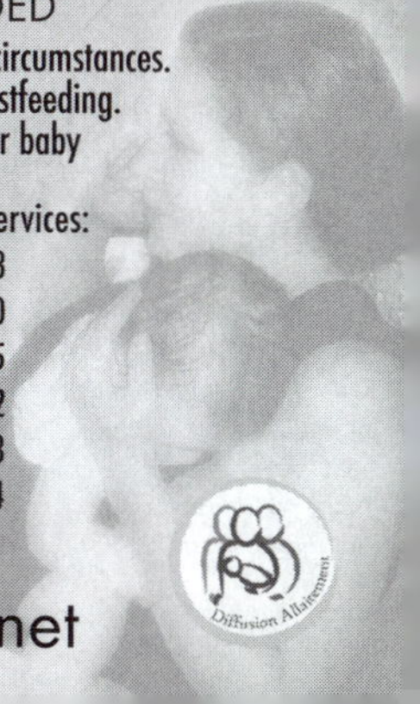

Nipple shield

A nipple shield is usually made of moulded silicone that adjusts to the breast's shape. Some people suggest using one when the baby will not take the breast or when your nipples become sore. It may seem like a quick solution but it will not teach your baby to nurse directly from your breast. Your baby will get used to it and then may refuse to nurse without it. Nipple shields decrease breast stimulation which may lower milk production.

A nipple shield should be used as a last resort, and rarely during the first few days. Other solutions almost always exist. If you decide to use a nipple shield, do so only until your baby is better at nursing. A lactation consultant or CLSC nurse can help if you have a hard time stopping afterwards.

Sensitive nipples

Sometimes, babies don't latch on properly when you're learning to breast-feed. Your nipples may then get sensitive and irritated. If the pain lasts more than 10 seconds and nursing is really uncomfortable, try to improve the latch, and ask for help. Don't wait; breast-feeding shouldn't be painful.

Before going home

Have someone check the way your baby sucks. Make sure you recognize the signs that your baby is nursing properly so that he is getting milk.

Ask someone to show you how to manually express your milk before you leave. You will then be able to soothe your breasts if they are too full, and you'll be able to give your baby breast milk without breast-feeding, when needed.

Your milk comes in

Having your milk come in is a normal stage of lactation. Hormonal changes mean that a new mother may often be close to tears during this period. Take care of yourself and allow others to spoil you. Milk production increases rapidly between the 2nd and 5th day after delivery. You'll probably notice an increase in the size of your breasts.

Some women experience discomfort when their breasts become full and hard. Effective, frequent (8 to 12 times in a 24-hour period) and regular (day and night) nursing will ease the discomfort, which normally lasts 24 to 48 hours. Most babies naturally want to drink more often during this stage, which will relieve the tension in your breasts and help your baby gain weight.

If your baby is having a hard time nursing because your breasts are too hard, you need to make them softer. To help the milk flow, place a washcloth soaked in hot water on each breast for 1 to 2 minutes before nursing. Then squeeze out enough milk so the areola (area surrounding the nipple) is softer. Your baby will then have an easier time latching on. It may also be a good idea to express milk after your baby nurses if he didn't drink much. Express enough to be comfortable without emptying your breasts.

Are your breasts really painful? Applying cold to your breasts for about 15 minutes every hour will help decrease pain and swelling. You can use a bag of crushed ice or a bag of frozen vegetables wrapped in a towel. Since cold reduces milk flow, you can put hot compresses on your breasts for 2 minutes before nursing. If needed, acetaminophen (e.g., Atasol™, Tylenol™) or ibuprofen (e.g., Advil™, Motrin™) reduces the pain and is not dangerous for the baby.

First few weeks (2 to 8 weeks)

The period of major change has come and gone, even if some days are still hard. You're gradually getting better at latching the baby on. You're beginning to feel more at ease and getting to know your baby. He wakes himself up to nurse and is alert for longer periods of time.

Around 4 to 6 weeks after delivery, many women feel tired by the lack of sleep and disrupted nights. You will have more energy if you eat well at mealtimes and have small snacks in between. It's normal to need a nap or rest time to recover. Getting outside and get-togethers with friends will also do you good!

If you doubt your abilities and are thinking about weaning your baby, you may need some encouragement or help. Don't go through this alone.

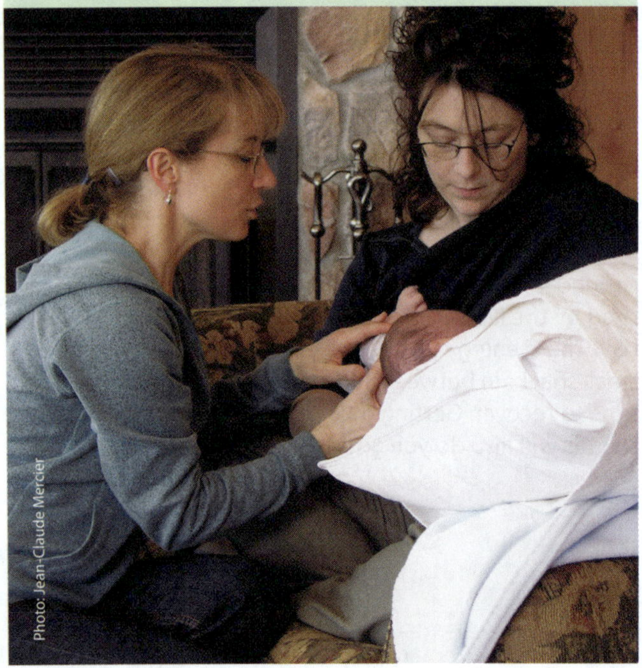

Photo: Jean-Claude Mercier

The support of your partner, a friend or someone who knows about breast-feeding can make all the difference. Breast-feeding support people and lactation consultants can help.

Some women experience crying spells after giving birth, whether or not they breast-feed. If crying makes you feel better, then go ahead. If the need to cry every day continues for a few weeks after birth or if you feel overwhelmed by everything that has happened, speak to a CLSC nurse, your midwife or doctor.

First few months (2 to 6 months)

Your baby is constantly growing and changing. Around the age of 2 months, a routine will begin to set in. Outings are easier and more interesting and fun for both you and your baby. Nursing takes less time. Now that your baby is older, he is able to make his needs known more clearly. When the milk flow slows, he may show that he needs to change breasts.

Around the 2nd month, your breasts become softer to the touch and decrease in size. Don't worry. You are producing at least as much milk as before; your mammary glands have adapted.

Around the age of 3 months, your baby takes more of an interest in what is going on around him. He's curious and sometimes interested in watching what's going on while he's nursing.

Around the age of 4 months, his appetite changes. Some babies nurse less often, while others want to nurse more often. His need for stimulation is increasing at the same time so it's not always easy to know whether your baby is hungry or wants more attention. Don't hesitate to nurse him. Try to vary his activities to respond to his curiosity.

Very few babies sleep through the night during the first few months of life. The age at which a baby will sleep for 6 hours in a row depends on his biological rhythm and temperament. It isn't unusual for a baby who has been sleeping through the night to start waking up again. This is part of his development.

Eating solid foods has little impact on a baby's sleep. A baby will not sleep through the night because you start feeding him cereal. Before the age of 6 months, breast milk is the most complete food to meet his growing needs.

Breast-feeding a toddler (6 months and up)

Breast-feeding an older baby is very different from breast-feeding a newborn. The breast-feeding rhythm changes little by little with the addition of solid foods around 6 months of age, and your baby adapts to the family routine. You and your baby continue to enjoy the benefits of breast-feeding, which will continue as long as you breast-feed.

As your baby gets older, he shows curiosity and initiative. This will also show up when he's breast-feeding. His autonomy may sometimes make you uncomfortable. He may sometimes ask to be nursed at times that don't suit you. Trust yourself. With breast-feeding, as with the rest of his education, you will learn to place limits on what you consider acceptable or not. Your baby will learn to wait a bit and can adapt to the way you nurse him.

Around the age of 1, babies normally nurse only a few times a day. Some nurse more often. The number of times a 1-year-old baby nurses varies from one day to the next, depending on his activities and mood.

In Québec, more and more women want to continue breast-feeding beyond the first few months. Mother and child may continue this privileged relationship, even if it's just for one feeding a day. For many people, breast-feeding in the evening is a pleasant part of the bedtime routine.

Support group volunteers know what it's like to breast-feed a toddler. Don't hesitate to speak to them.

Nursing: step by step

Babies have been breast-feeding for millions of years and each has his or her own way of doing it. Each mother and child will discover their own style. This section provides a step-by-step guide and explains the important points to help you make sure your baby is nursing properly and effectively. Someone familiar with breast-feeding can help you as needed.

The right time (signs of hunger)

A baby shows that he wants to nurse well before he cries. His breathing changes and he moves his eyes, mouth or face. He moves his arms and legs, stretches and brings his hands to his mouth or face. Then he starts sucking motions. There are many signs that your baby is hungry. This is the right time to offer to nurse him. You will both be calmer, and he will latch on more easily.

Don't wait too long to nurse once he shows signs of being hungry. He will be more patient and cooperate better if you have to remove him from the breast several times to get him properly latched on. It's hard to get an angry, crying baby to nurse. Changing the baby's diaper before nursing is a good idea to wake a sleepy baby but may be a bad idea if your baby is very hungry. Do what works best for you.

Position: for comfort and effective nursing

Nursing is a restful and enjoyable activity. Take the time to get comfortable. Choose a breast-feeding position that suits you. Several positions exist: cradle, cross-cradle, football, and lying down. Regardless of the position you choose, your baby's whole body must be turned towards the breast. His ear, shoulder and hip should form a straight line. He shouldn't have to turn his head to latch on. A support group can help you become familiar with the various positions.

Breast-feeding while lying down is enjoyable and promotes rest. When latching on is easy, mothers really enjoy this position. If you doze or sleep while nursing, the recommendations on pages 247 and 248 should be respected for your baby's safety.

A comfortable chair, music, cushions or pillows and a glass of juice or water will help you relax.

Photo: Anouk Jolin

Cross-cradle position

The most common position is the cross-cradle position, which has 2 advantages: it allows the mother to properly support her baby and to clearly see how he latches on.

In this position, the baby rests on his mother's arm opposite the breast on which he is nursing. If you are nursing from the left breast, you support your baby with your right arm. The palm of your right hand is under the nape of his neck, not behind his head. Your fingers, except the thumb, support his head while your forearm supports his back and bottom. The baby's bottom is held between your chest and forearm.

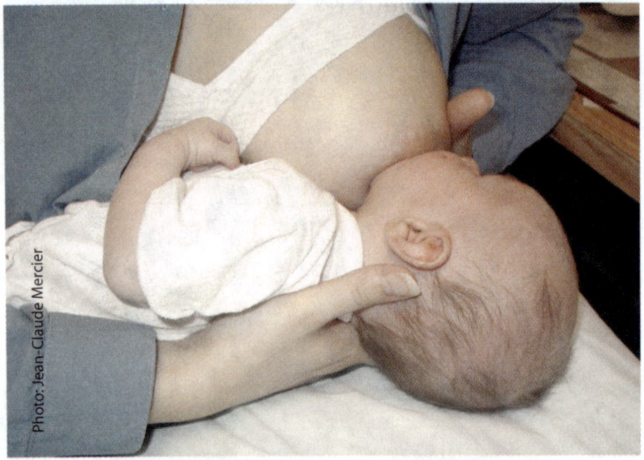

Photo: Jean-Claude Mercier

Hold your left breast with your left hand. Your thumb rests on the outer side of the breast with the other fingers on the inner side, far from the nipple and areola, to form a U.

Bringing baby to your breast

Regardless of the position you choose, and whether you are sitting or lying down, your baby must latch on properly.

- Wait until he opens his mouth very wide as though he was going to yawn or bite into a large apple. Stimulate him to latch on by brushing his upper lip with your nipple pointing towards his palate. This may take some time at the beginning. But with practice, he will learn and it will be easier.

- When his mouth is open, quickly bring him to your breast. Coordinate your movement with your baby's. It's the baby who latches onto the breast, but you must bring him close to it, especially during the first few weeks. Don't lean towards the baby because this will be uncomfortable for you. Instead, bring him close to you.
- Bring him close enough so his head is tilted just slightly towards the back. His chin should touch your breast first. The nipple will automatically point towards the baby's palate and not towards his tongue.

With your help, your baby will quickly learn what he needs to do to latch on and will soon be able to do it almost all by himself.

For the first few days, you may have to start over a few times to get your baby properly latched on. He may sometimes close his mouth either partially or fully before getting to the breast. His hands can also be a problem because they often end up in his mouth before the breast does! You'll be happy to have help from his father or someone else close to you. Be patient.

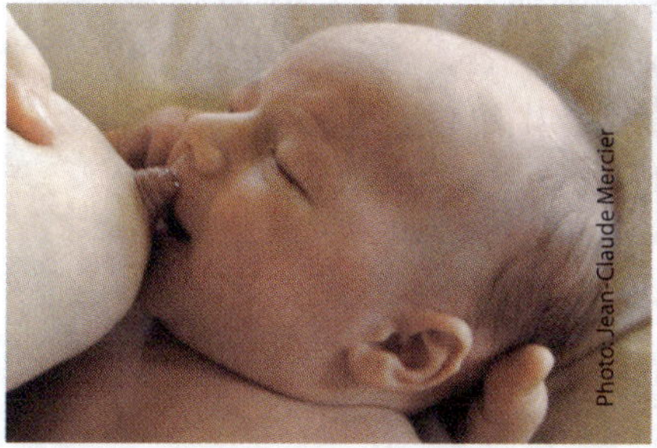

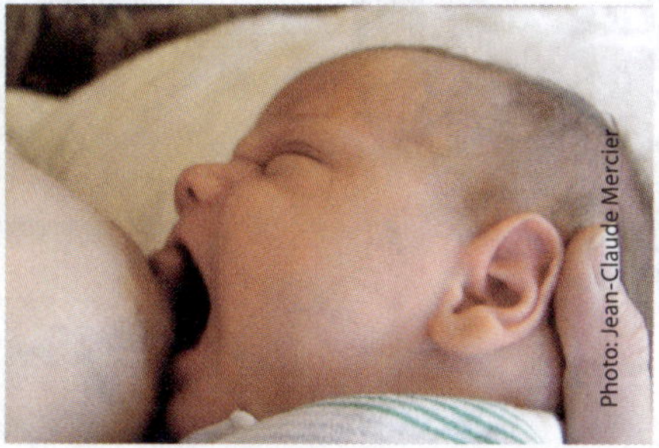

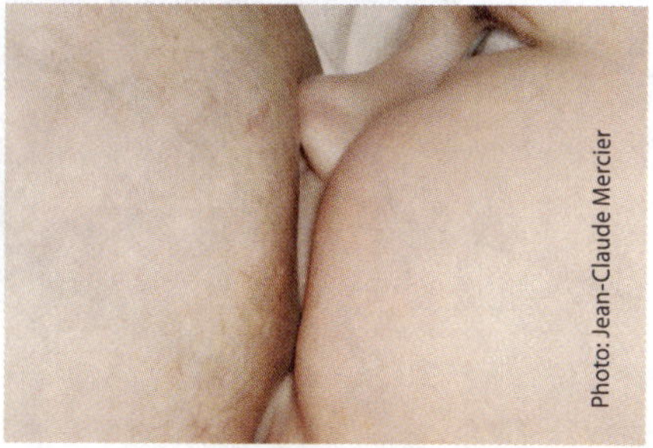

CROSS-CRADLE POSITION

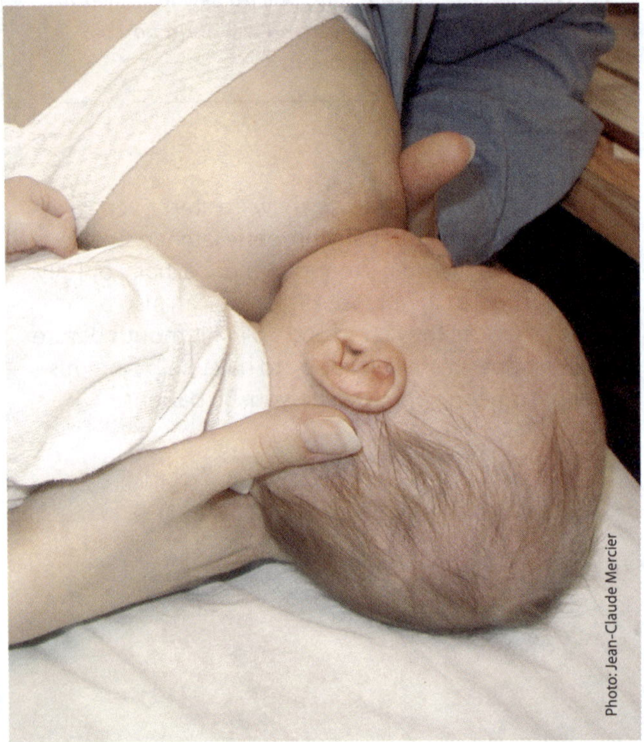

Photo: Jean-Claude Mercier

CRADLE POSITION

Photo: Jean-Claude Mercier

FOOTBALL POSITION

Photo: Jean-Claude Mercier

SIDE LYING POSITION

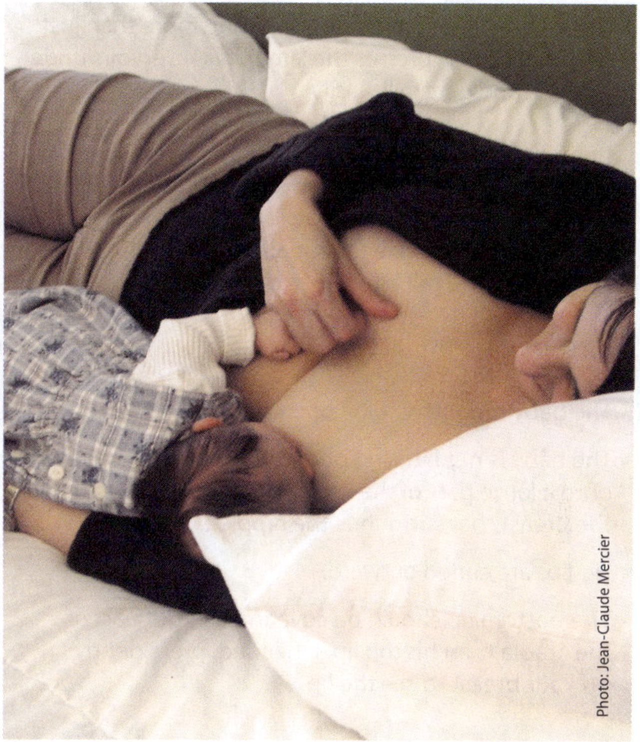

Photo: Jean-Claude Mercier

Latching on

When a baby latches on properly, taking more than just the nipple, he compresses the large milk reservoirs under the areola and gets milk easily.

When a baby doesn't latch on properly, he sucks mainly on the nipple. This may create painful cracks and the baby will get less milk. Some babies will then ask to nurse more often, which will irritate the nipples even more. Others will get tired and fall asleep before they're full.

Signs of a good latch

- The baby's mouth is wide open.
- The baby is not latching onto the nipple only but also onto a large part of the areola (the darkest part of the breast that surrounds the nipple).
- His lips are curled outward.
- The bottom lip should be covering a larger part of the areola than his top lip. If needed, press gently on your breast to see the lip.
- His chin is touching the breast and his nose is free.
- You can hear your baby swallow.
- Nursing is comfortable for the mother.

If you feel pain, try to improve the latch. Start by using your index finger to gently lower your baby's chin and curl his lower lip so that his mouth opens wider. It's not working and you're still experiencing pain? Contact someone who is trained in breast-feeding.

Effective sucking

Your baby's sucking motion can be seen in the jaw. When he starts to nurse, the movements are quick and light. When milk starts to flow, the movements become slower and deeper. You will see and hear your baby swallow.

If your baby's breathing is noisy during nursing, free up his nose by pressing his bottom against you to bring his chin closer to your breast. Don't worry, he won't suffocate. If he has trouble breathing he will release the breast. In some cases, you might need to press gently on your breast with your finger to free up his nose.

Breaking the suction

When you remove your baby from your breast, be sure to break the suction correctly to avoid hurting your nipples. Break the suction by putting your finger in the corner of your baby's mouth up to his gums, if needed. The nipple will release easily once the suction is correctly broken.

Frequency and length of feedings

If your baby latches on properly, nurses effectively and swallows the milk, he is breast-feeding well.

If your breasts hurt, improve the latch. A proper latch is the key to successful breast-feeding!

Photo: Jean-Claude Mercier

There's no such thing as "normal" nursing. Babies are like adults: each is different. Some babies have a regular schedule. Others are unpredictable and vary the frequency and length of nursing from one feeding to the next and from one day to another. This depends on the baby's sucking, his temperament, his appetite, his mood and the milk flow. A newborn will normally drink 8 to 12 times in 24 hours (see table on page 328). Some babies are very effective at nursing and will only nurse 6 times a day. As your baby gets older, feedings will be shorter and spaced further apart.

Does your baby seem satisfied after nursing but asks to nurse again 15 minutes later? This is normal, especially during the first few weeks. Don't hesitate to nurse him again so he gets his "dessert."

Focus on your baby instead of your watch. You won't avoid injury to your nipples by timing feedings, but you may deny your baby some of the milk and comforting warmth he needs. Watch for your baby's signs of hunger and satisfaction instead of the clock.

Cluster feeding

Nursing takes place more often at some times of the day than others. Evenings can be an intense time when most babies are sluggish and nurse a lot. They sleep a bit, cry a bit, nurse a bit and need comfort. Some babies may want to nurse almost non-stop for a few hours. Generally, they will then sleep for a longer period. This "cluster feeding" is normal. It can give the impression that you don't have enough milk because your breasts have less time to fill and are soft.

One breast or two? Or three?

Often a baby will release the breast because the milk flow has slowed down. Let your baby nurse from the first breast until he is satisfied, burp him, and then offer him the other breast, which he'll take if he's hungry. The milk reservoirs in the first breast will refill while the baby nurses from the second breast. If he still seems hungry, he can then nurse again from the first breast (the "third" breast).

If he still wants more, switch sides again to give him the "fourth" breast. Sometimes your baby will nurse from one breast, sometimes both, sometimes more. Follow his rhythm. Start the next feeding with the breast offered last or the one he nursed from least. If you don't remember, offer the breast that feels the heaviest.

Breast compression

Breast compression can help when a baby doesn't nurse efficiently enough to get the milk he needs. It increases the milk flow and keeps your baby nursing more actively. This is a useful technique when the baby:

- Quickly falls asleep when nursing;
- Is not gaining enough weight;
- Wants to nurse very often or for long periods;
- Seems dissatisfied.

It's a very good way to help your baby drink colostrum during the first few days of life.

The cross-cradle position is preferable. The hand forms a U at the base of the breast with the thumb on one side and the fingers on the other. The fingers should be positioned far away from the areola so they don't interfere with the baby's sucking. Squeeze the breast with your whole hand without moving your fingers. This should not be painful or stretch the areola.

Maintain pressure for 5 to 10 seconds or as long as your baby continues swallowing. Release the pressure as soon as he stops drinking. Repeat the process until he stops swallowing. Offer the other breast in the same way if your baby seems to want it. You can then return to the first breast and second one if needed. Stop using this technique when your baby nurses better.

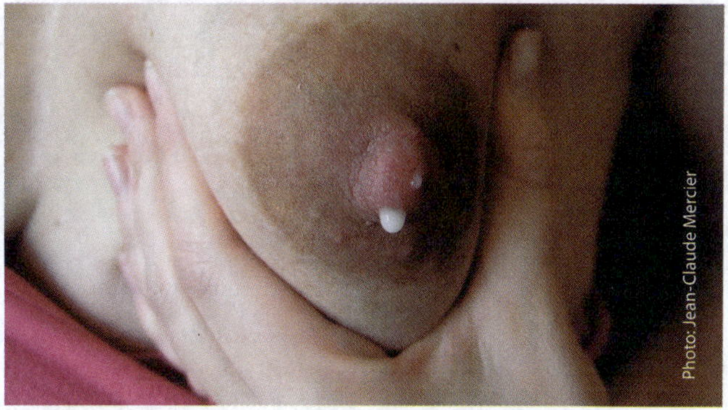

Photo: Jean-Claude Mercier

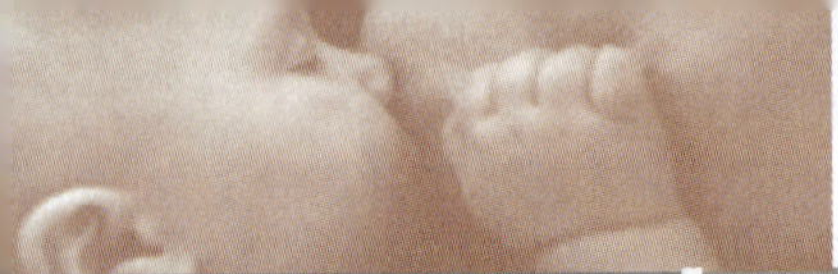

Breastfeeding Your Baby

GUIDELINES FOR NURSING MOTHERS

Your Baby's Age	WEEK 1: 1 DAY	2 DAYS	3 DAYS	4 DAYS	5 DAYS	6 DAYS	7 DAYS	2 WEEKS	3 WEEKS	4 WEEKS	5 WEEKS	6 WEEK: 6 MONT
Your Baby's Tummy Size Actual size is shown	Size of a cooked chick pea or hazelnut		Size of a cherry or medium grape						Size of a walnut or lichee			
How Much Milk Your Baby Needs Per day, on average over 24 hours	10 to 100 mL **or** 1 tablespoon to ⅓ cup		200 mL **or** almost 1 cup		400 to 600 mL **or** about 1 ½ to 2 ½ cups			700 to 800 mL per day **or** about 2 ½ to 3 ½				
How Often Should You Breastfeed? Per day, on average over 24 hours	In the first month 8 to 12 feeds per day (every 1 ½ to 3 hours)										By about two month at least 6 to 8 feeds per day	
Wet Diapers: How Many, How Wet Per day, on average over 24 hours	At least 1 WET	At least 2 WET	At least 3 WET	At least 4 WET	At least 6 HEAVY WET							
Soiled Diapers: Number and Colour of Stools	At least 1 to 2 per day BLACK OR DARK GREEN		At least 3 per day BROWN, GREEN, OR YELLOW		At least 3 large per day, soft and seedy YELLOW							At least 1 or more l every 1 to 7 YELLOW
Your Baby's Weight	Most babies lose about 5 to 7% of their birth weight in the first 3 to 4 days after birth. For example, a 3.2 kilogram or 7-pound baby will lose about 230 grams or ½ a pound.						Your baby should return to his or her birth weight by 10 to 14 days.		Your baby should gain about 112 to 224 grams a week for the first 3 months.			
Growth Spurts *	Babies often experience a sudden burst in growth—a growth 'spurt'—at certain times within their first few weeks. During these growth spurts your baby may want to nurse more than usual.							*	*			*

Breast Milk Is All the Food Your Baby Needs for the First Six Months

The World Health Organization (WHO) and UNICEF recommend that you feed your baby *nothing but breast milk* from birth to 6 months. At 6 months, begin adding solid foods while continuing to breastfeed your baby until age two or beyond.

Signs That Your Baby Is Getting Enough Milk

- Your baby is sucking strongly, slowly, and steadily.
- You can see your baby swallowing frequently.
- Your baby has a strong cry and moves actively.
- Your baby's mouth is moist.
- Your baby's eyes are bright and alert.
- Your baby comes off the breast looking relaxed and content.
- Your breasts feel softer and less full after breastfeeding.
- Your baby is growing, feels heavier and is gaining weight.

IF YOU NEED HELP:

Breastfeeding support is available in your community. Ask your doctor, nurse, or midwife for help.

Your health and social services centre can support you in your decision to breastfeed or direct you to breastfeeding resources.

Download our guide at:
www.msss.gouv.qc.ca/allaitement

Adapted with permission by the
Best Start Resource Centre

Santé et Services sociaux
Québec

How do I know if my baby drank enough milk?

There are several ways to tell whether your baby is getting enough milk:

- After the first week of your baby's life, he thoroughly wets 6 or 7 diapers a day. His urine is clear and odourless;
- His stools are liquid or very soft and frequent: 2 to 5 a day for the first 4 weeks. After that they are less frequent (e.g., 1 stool every 3 to 7 days) but very plentiful;
- He is gaining enough weight and gaining weight regularly;
- He wakes up on his own to nurse;
- He nurses well and often, 8 to 12 times in 24 hours.

What should I do if my baby is not drinking enough?

Here are a few tips to help your baby drink more milk:

- Check that he's latching on well and improve the latch if possible.
- Breast-feed more often, at least 8 times in 24 hours. Wake your baby up if necessary.
- Avoid using a soother, it doesn't provide milk and may hide signs of hunger.
- Stimulate your baby so that he nurses effectively and swallows regularly throughout the feeding.
- Use breast compression at each feeding (see Breast compression, page 327).
- Change breasts when your baby stops swallowing during nursing (see One breast or two? Or three?, page 326).
- Express milk between feedings and offer it to your baby, preferably from a spoon or small cup. Avoid using a bottle.

Contact someone with breast-feeding experience if the situation doesn't improve quickly or if you have concerns.

Growth spurts

Babies go through very rapid periods of growth during the first few months of life. Your child's appetite suddenly increases; he asks to nurse more often, sometimes every hour. Growth spurts last a few days and can occur at any time. Many babies have growth spurts often, regardless of their age. They occur most frequently around 7 to 10 days, 3 to 6 weeks and 3 to 4 months of age.

Milk production will adjust in a few days if your baby is allowed to nurse as often as he likes, both day and night. Help from those around you is very important during these intense periods.

Supplements

A breast-fed baby doesn't need water or sugared water. Breast milk provides all the water he needs.

Supplementing breast-feeding with commercial infant formula is rarely necessary. It can harm milk production if you use it regularly. If needed, contact someone with breast-feeding experience. She may be able to offer different suggestions to help you continue breast-feeding.

> Breast-feeding with your baby snuggled in your arms comforts him and may fulfill many of these needs.

Pacifier

The Canadian Paediatric Society makes the following recommendations:

- Never start using a pacifier until breast-feeding is fully established. Talk to your doctor or lactation specialist if you feel your baby needs to use one at this early stage. An exception is for premature or sick babies in the hospital. They may use one for comfort.
- Never give your baby a pacifier instead of feeding.
- Always see if your baby is hungry, tired or bored before giving him the pacifier. Try solving these things first.

A crying child is expressing himself: he needs food, sleep, comforting or contact. It's not always easy to know exactly which. Breast-feeding is not only a way to feed your baby. Don't worry; letting your baby nurse for comfort won't create a bad habit. In many cultures, nursing is used as much to calm a child as to feed him. The warmth of skin-to-skin contact with his father will also soothe your baby. Try rocking him or carrying him around in your arms.

Burping and gas

A baby that is calm during and after nursing probably doesn't need to burp. But if he seems in a bad mood or squirms while drinking, the first thing to try to calm him down is to burp him. One or two burps are usually enough, but a baby that drinks quickly may need to be burped more often.

Here's how to burp your baby: hold him in an upright position against your shoulder and rub or tap his back gently for a few minutes. After he burps, check to see if he's still hungry.

Don't insist if he doesn't burp; some babies won't burp. Let him be if he's asleep. He'll wake up if he needs to burp.

Hold him in an upright position against your shoulder and rub or tap his back gently for a few minutes.

Photo: iStockphoto

Most newborns have a lot of gas, and some babies are bothered by it. This is normal and isn't because of the milk. Hold your baby and comfort him as needed.

Breast-feeding in public

More and more women are breast-feeding in public. It's your right to breast-feed your child, regardless of the location. Breast-feed with confidence and ease. A large soft sweater or shirt will make things easier. Some places provide an area for breast-feeding and baby care for people who don't feel comfortable breast-feeding in public.

Who can help me and when should I get help?

Breast-feeding can sometimes be difficult. With experience you'll often find the solution. If you're thinking about stopping breast-feeding because you're having problems, call a CLSC nurse or a support group or contact a breast-feeding clinic. There are people available to help.

Consult someone if you experience any of the following:

- Difficulty latching on;
- Pain or lesions on the nipples or breasts;
- Lack of weight gain in your baby;
- Problems producing milk.

Support groups are very helpful in sharing information and general advice. They are made up of women who have breast-fed one or more children. They have up-to-date knowledge and offer their support free of charge in a straightforward and friendly way. Most support groups offer information sessions to prepare women for breast-feeding. Find out about the services offered by groups in your area. The contact information is available from your CLSC.

Various CLSC workers (nurses, dietitians/nutritionists, etc.) can help you. Nurses offer home visits after your baby's birth. These visits may be automatic or based on need, depending on the region where you live. The nurse can offer support as soon as you return home or later on. She can weigh your baby, check his general health and help you with nursing. Contact your CLSC nurse as needed.

Info-Santé offers a telephone consultation service 24 hours a day, 7 days a week throughout the province.

Specialized services exist in some regions. These include lactation consultants and breast-feeding clinics. These services are very helpful if you're having problems that regular services are unable to treat. Some specialized services are free; others are not.

Your doctor will examine your baby during regular checkups. This is the best person to evaluate your baby if you are concerned about his health. Your doctor should also be able to help if you have a breast or nipple infection.

Midwives provide follow-up for their clients for up to 6 weeks after delivery.

Breast-feeding problems and solutions

This new learning process between mother and baby goes well for most women. But problems can arise, especially during the first few weeks.

Difficulty nursing and refusing to nurse

Not all babies develop at the same pace. Some need more time before they're able to nurse. Others who have been nursing easily may suddenly have trouble. You can still give your baby your breast milk while waiting for things to get easier. Be patient; the trouble shouldn't last long.

You know your baby is hungry but he isn't able to latch on or is refusing to nurse altogether? There are many possible causes:

- Engorged breasts;
- Difficulty sucking;
- Premature baby;
- Stuffy nose or poor health;
- Preference for the bottle;
- No clear reason.

What should I do?

Regardless of the reason he's not nursing, it's important to continue feeding your baby and to maintain your milk production. You can feed him breast milk while waiting for him to start nursing again.

- Try to get your baby to nurse when he's calm and not overly hungry, over 10-minute periods.
- Don't force him to nurse; he may then completely refuse.
- Calm your baby before nursing by offering him a small amount of breast milk using a spoon or small cup.
- For infants, see Difficulty latching on, page 313.

Here are some tips for older babies:

- Nurse him just as he's waking up.
- Take a bath with your baby. Try nursing him once he's relaxed in the water.
- An older baby can easily go for a few hours without drinking.
- If the situation is not resolved after a few feedings, contact your midwife, a support group, a CLSC nurse or Info-Santé.

Sleepy baby

Your baby sleeps a lot and you wonder if you should wake him to nurse. It isn't always easy to know what to do. You can follow his rhythm and let him sleep if:

- He wakes up on his own to nurse 8 to 12 times in a 24-hour period (minimum of 6 times for babies that are very efficient at nursing);
- He is active while nursing and good at it;
- He dirties several diapers each day;
- He is calm and seems satisfied after nursing.

There is nothing to worry about. Each baby has his own rhythm that develops over time.

Some babies, especially during the first 2 or 3 weeks, sleep so much they skip some feedings. This means they have a hard time getting all the milk they need. You should stimulate your baby if he sleeps a lot and doesn't show the signs described above.

What should I do?

- Stimulate him: talk to him, massage his back, legs, arms, etc.
- Dress him in an undershirt or diaper: babies nurse less when they're hot.
- Check that he's latching on properly.
- Change breasts twice when feeding.
- Use the breast compression technique.
- Talk to a resource person if you're worried or if the situation doesn't improve in a few days.

Feeling like you don't have enough milk

Frequent crying and nursing often or for long periods may lead the mother to believe she doesn't have enough milk. This is not necessarily true. Your infant will cry for reasons that often have nothing to do with a lack of milk (see Temperament, page 261). His stomach is small and breast milk is digested quickly. During growth spurts, your baby will nurse more often to stimulate lactation.

What should I do?

If your baby nurses for a long time, make sure he's latching on properly. Stimulate him to maintain active sucking. He may get more milk in less time if he sucks more effectively. Breast compression can often help. You can also offer him each breast more than once.

Try not to be influenced by people's comments. Take the time to consider the situation before reaching the conclusion that you're lacking milk or that your milk isn't providing enough nourishment. Contact your midwife, a breast-feeding support group or a CLSC nurse if needed.

Milk flow

Your breasts may leak milk between feedings or at night. This is normal – it's a natural way for your breasts to relieve themselves. If it bothers you, protect your bed with a towel and wear nursing pads. There's no need to worry either if your breasts don't leak; this is also normal and doesn't mean that you're lacking milk.

Very quick milk flow (strong let-down reflex)

After nursing for a few minutes your baby swallows quickly and you can hear him swallow. Sometimes he might choke a little. He may also start crying and stop nursing when milk runs onto his face. Your baby is upset because the milk is flowing too quickly. This happens most often around the age of 1 month. When babies are older they adapt better.

What should I do?

Here are a few suggestions to make nursing more enjoyable. Try suggestion #1 first and then add the others one at a time to find the one that works best.

- Remove your baby from your breast for a few minutes if the milk starts flowing too quickly.
- Try different breast-feeding positions to see if another one suits you more. If you have a lot of milk, try offering one breast per feeding; this may be enough to satisfy your baby. Remove just enough milk from the other breast so that you're comfortable.
- If your breast is very full before nursing, express about 15 ml (1 tablespoon) of milk to trigger the first let-down reflex and slow the flow of milk at the beginning.

Painful nipples

Breast-feeding is a pleasant experience and should not hurt. During the first week, the nipples are often sensitive, especially at the beginning of a feeding. The baby and mother are both learning. Breast-feeding should not be painful after this period. Find out the cause of any pain that lasts after the first 30 seconds of a feeding or that makes you fearful of nursing. Pain that continues or cracks are often the cause of mothers weaning their babies too early. The pain will quickly decrease once the main cause of the injury is corrected. Don't suffer in silence.

Painful and cracked nipples can be caused by many things: (1) a poor latch, (2) thrush, (3) eczema, (4) vasospasm. Treatment will depend on the problem.

(1) Poor latch

The most common cause of nipple pain is a poor latch. The pain is normally the greatest at the beginning of the feeding. It is caused by pressure on the nipple between the baby's tongue and palate when he hasn't taken enough of the areola into his mouth. A deformed, flat or pinched nipple when the baby releases the breast is an indication of a poor latch.

What should I do?

Work at improving the latch so that it looks like the photo on page 325. You should feel a difference as soon as the baby improves the latch. If it's too difficult, promptly ask for help from someone with breast-feeding experience. It's easier to correct the problem early on. Here are a few tips that can help while waiting for the baby to improve the latch.

- Begin nursing with the less sensitive breast.
- Vary breast-feeding positions.
- Squeeze a few drops of breast milk onto the nipple at the end of a feeding.
- Over-the-counter ointments and creams don't correct the problem.
- An analgesic such as acetaminophen (e.g., Atasol™, Tylenol™) can help.

If pain prevents you from nursing your baby, it is important to express your milk to prevent engorgement and maintain your milk production.

(2) Thrush

A fungal infection called thrush can appear in the mouths of newborns (see Thrush in the mouth, page 477). This infection can also cause **diaper rash**.

When a breast-feeding mother has thrush it can cause pain on the nipple or within the breast. Sudden unexplained pain that occurs during nursing when everything was previously going well may be the result of a fungal infection. The pain may also come on gradually or add to existing pain.

The feeling is usually a burning sensation and often more intense at the end of nursing. The nipples may appear cracked or redder than normal. The areola may be red, smooth or shiny.

The mother may have thrush on her nipples even if the baby doesn't have any visible thrush in his mouth.

▶ **Diaper rash:** Skin irritation and redness in the area covered by the baby's diaper.

What should I do?

When the infection is limited to the nipple and areola, an ointment is often the only treatment required. Apply a thin layer after each feeding. You don't need to remove it before nursing. Nystatin ointments (e.g., Nilstat™, Nyaderme™, Mycostatin™) and miconazole (e.g., Micatin™, Monistat Derm™) are good choices: they are available without a prescription. Continue treatment for a few days after the pain goes away. If there is no improvement after 5 days or if you have breast pain, gentian violet may help (see Fungal infection in the breast, page 345).

(3) Eczema

The nipples or areolas can get eczema or contact dermatitis, where the skin is pinkish or very red and there is a burning sensation.

What should I do?

Stop applying any kind of cream, lotion, lanolin or other product to your breasts. You may need a medicated ointment prescribed by your doctor.

(4) Vasospasm

Vasospasm in the nipple is caused by a spasm or contraction of the blood vessels. It is a common but little known cause of nipple pain. It is brought on by contact with cold air on the nipple when the baby releases the breast. The end of the nipple becomes white and women often describe the pain as a burning sensation throughout the breast. After a period of time ranging from a few seconds to several minutes, the nipple returns to its original colour. It may become white again and then change colour several times. Many women also experience this pain when coming into contact with cold wind or when getting out of the shower.

A poor latch is the main cause of vasospasm. Nicotine and caffeine may increase the problem.

What should I do?

Vasospasm isn't dangerous and doesn't require treatment if you aren't experiencing pain. Check that your baby is properly latched on and correct the latch as needed.

Applying dry heat (palm of your hand, magic bag or clothing) to the nipple immediately after nursing may prevent or reduce the reaction. It may also help to keep your body warm.

If required, vitamin B_6 may provide relief. The dose is 150 mg/day for 4 days, followed by 25 mg per day until the pain disappears. Discontinue use if there is no improvement after a few days. Prescription medication may also help; consult a doctor if needed.

Breast pain

Breast pain is less common than nipple pain. Often the pain is accompanied by a hard area on the breast. Breast pain is not normal. You should treat the problem or consult someone about it. There are several possible causes for the pain, including: (1) engorgement; (2) a blocked milk duct; (3) a milk blister; (4) mastitis; (5) fungal infection in the breast.

(1) Engorgement

In general, milk production adjusts well to your baby's demand. But sometimes production can be excessive and cause the breasts to become engorged. The breasts feel heavy and tight. This can occur at any time during breast-feeding and can affect one or both breasts. Engorgement can be caused by the following:

- Your baby drinks less than usual.
- A feeding is delayed or skipped.

What should I do?

Extract enough milk to soften the breast and eliminate the tension and discomfort. Avoid staying engorged for several hours since this will increase the risk of a blocked duct or mastitis, as well as making you uncomfortable for longer.

(2) Blocked milk duct

When a duct is blocked, the milk from this duct no longer flows to the nipple. If you touch the breast after nursing, you will feel a hard and painful area that is sometimes red.

This blockage can have different causes: the breast may have been full for too long or it may have been pinched by your bra or an infant carrier.

Normally, the discomfort is felt only in one breast. You don't feel sick, but if the milk stays blocked for too long you may get an infection.

What should I do?

- Nurse your baby 8 to 12 times a day.
- Start with the sore breast and vary the positions so that milk flows easily. If possible, direct the baby's chin or nose so that it points to the hard area when he nurses.
- Gently massage the affected area during nursing.
- Apply ice for 10-15 minutes every 1-2 hours between feedings.
- Apply wet heat just before nursing. Use a wet washcloth, or better yet, massage the affected area while having a long hot bath.
- Avoid wearing an overly tight bra.
- Take the time to rest.

- Acetaminophen (e.g., Atasol™, Tylenol™) or ibuprofen (e.g., Advil™, Motrin™) can soothe the pain as needed.

Contact someone experienced at breast-feeding if the hard spot remains 24 hours after you started treating it.

(3) Milk blister

A small white blister can form on the nipple. It often causes intense pain throughout the breast, especially at the beginning of a feeding. There may also be a lump or hard area in the breast.

What should I do?

Take a long hot bath to soften the skin on the nipple. You may be able to open the blister by nursing your baby right after your bath. If this doesn't work, contact a lactation consultant.

(4) Mastitis

Mastitis is a breast infection caused by bacteria. Breast-feeding allows for quicker recovery because a well emptied breast promotes recovery. Your breast milk in the affected breast is still good. Continue to breast-feed on both sides.

The cause of mastitis is unknown. Fatigue, poorly drained breasts or cracks increase the risk of mastitis. Always make sure your baby latches on properly and avoid staying engorged.

The following are symptoms of mastitis:

- A hard, red, swollen and painful area on one breast;
- Aches, shivers, fatigue;
- Possible fever: more than 38.3°C (101°F).

In rare cases, mastitis may turn into an abscess.

What should I do?

If you have cracked nipples or redness on your breast that rapidly gets bigger, see a doctor as you may need antibiotics.

Empty the painful breast as much as possible. Have your baby nurse very often from the painful breast, including at night time. If nursing is very uncomfortable, start on the other side first and then change breasts as soon as milk is flowing freely from the painful breast. Change your baby's position during nursing so that his chin is pointing towards the affected area. If the baby doesn't drink from the affected breast, express the milk. The breast needs to become more supple. Apply ice for 10-15 minutes every 1-2 hours between feedings. Take acetaminophen (e.g., Atasol™, Tylenol™) or ibuprofen (e.g., Advil™, Motrin™) to soothe the pain and reduce fever.

If the symptoms start to decrease within 12 hours, antibiotics will probably not be necessary. If it takes longer, antibiotics may be needed. Whether or not you take antibiotics, the situation needs to improve: see a doctor if your condition suddenly gets worse or improvement stops for more than 24 hours. If you're prescribed an antibiotic, you need to take it for the whole period it was prescribed (normally 10 days) to prevent a relapse. Effective, risk-free antibiotics are available for breast-feeding mothers. Talk to your doctor and pharmacist.

It will take between 2 and 5 days for mastitis to clear up. The fever generally disappears within 24 hours, the pain and redness decrease in less than 48 hours and the hardened area within a few days. Sensitivity in the breast may last longer.

(5) Fungal infection in the breast

A fungal infection (thrush) may occur in the breast. It generally produces pain during or between feedings. Sometimes the pain comes gradually or in addition to existing pain. Mothers often describe it as a burning sensation or pins and needles going through the breast. The pain may wake you at night. It is generally felt in one breast only and there is no hardened area. The nipple or areola may not have any unusual redness.

Fungal infection can occur even if your baby doesn't have thrush in his mouth. The use of antibiotics by the mother increases the risk of fungal infection.

What should I do?

A visit to the doctor is needed to be sure of what you have. Both mother and child must be treated. Gentian violet in water (0.5% to 1%) is the remedy of choice and is available without a prescription. It treats mother and baby at the same time.

To apply it:

- Swab your baby's mouth with a cotton swab dipped in gentian violet.
- Have your baby nurse from both breasts in order to colour them; add gentian violet to the nipples and areolas if they are not completely coloured.
- Use this treatment once a day.

Treatment varies from 4 to 7 days.

If after 4 days:

- The pain has completely disappeared, stop using gentian violet.
- There is no improvement, stop using gentian violet.
- The pain has decreased but isn't completely gone, continue using gentian violet for 3 more days (7 days in all).

Gentian violet can sometimes cause small ulcers under your baby's tongue. This is why treatment shouldn't last longer than 7 days in a row. See a doctor if the gentian violet is not working or if you have to stop using it before the end of the treatment period. Your doctor can prescribe another treatment.

Watch out: it stains! It's best to apply the treatment at bedtime and use an old towel to cover your bed. Your baby's mouth will remain coloured for a few days.

An oral treatment may be prescribed to the mother in the case of a severe infection.

You can also use an ointment if your nipple or areola is irritated. Apply a thin layer after each feeding, but not after the feeding when gentian violet is applied. You don't need to remove the ointment before the next feeding.

You can breast-feed even if your baby was born before the 37th week of pregnancy.

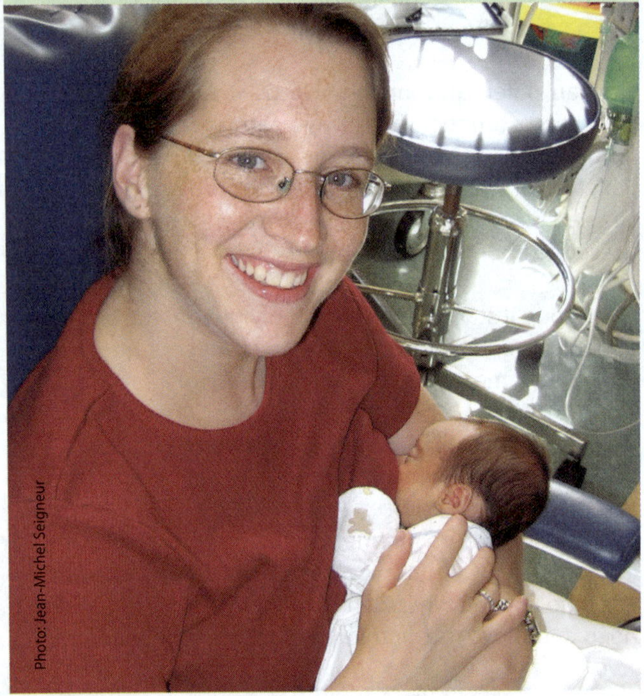
Photo: Jean-Michel Seigneur

Specific situations

Premature baby

Your milk is the best thing for your baby because it's adapted to his specific needs. You are the only one who can offer him this precious food!

You may need extra patience and perseverance, depending on the number of weeks your baby was in the womb. While he is in hospital you should establish and maintain your milk production by expressing milk with an electric breast pump 6 to 8 times every 24 hours. The hospital can provide a pump or you can rent one. You can ask for help from a hospital staff member trained in breast-feeding. A professional specializing in breast-feeding or a lactation consultant will be very helpful and will provide encouragement.

When your baby's health allows, hold him often and for long periods of time with his skin against yours. He will get used to you, recognize your smell and it will be easier to get him to nurse when he's ready. This intimate contact has been shown to benefit both the baby and his parents. The contact is as valuable as food.

At first, nurses will give your baby milk using a very thin tube. You can nurse him as soon as he's able to suck.

Be patient; premature babies need time to learn how to breast-feed. The Association des parents d'enfants prématurés du Québec can provide support.

Twins

The more you stimulate your breasts, the more milk they produce. Early on, mothers will appreciate being helped with the details of breast-feeding and care between feedings. It is very demanding looking after two newborns at once, but you will succeed – especially with the help of the father or someone close to you!

Ideally, you should feed both babies breast milk only. If your twins were premature, they will benefit even more from your milk. One of the babies is often ready to nurse before the other. You can express your milk while waiting for both babies to be able to nurse.

Some women prefer to nurse each baby separately while others find it more practical to breast-feed both at the same time. Most women will combine these two approaches. Generally, each baby will nurse from a single breast at each feeding then change to the other breast the next time. Since the babies' appetites and sucking will differ, this allows both breasts to be equally stimulated.

You can breast-feed twins.

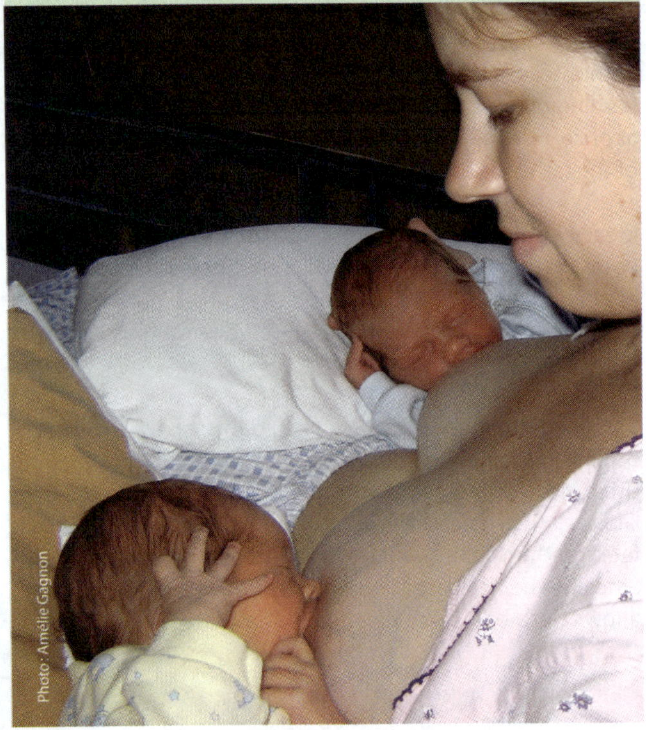
Photo : Amélie Gagnon

You can also try part-time breast-feeding, alternating between breast milk and iron-enriched commercial infant formula. Other approaches may be preferred depending on your situation.

The Association de parents de jumeaux et de triplés de la région de Montréal can offer support regardless of where you live. A breast-feeding support group can also put you in contact with another mother who has breast-fed twins. We recommend you read the brochure *"Allaiter en double ou en triple"* produced by the Association de parents de jumeaux et de triplés de la région de Montréal.

Association des parents de jumeaux et triplés de la région de Montréal
514 990-6165
www.apjtm.com

Association des parents de jumeaux et plus de la région de Québec inc.
418 653-9607
apjq@apjq.net
www. apjq.net

Breast surgery

Many women who have undergone breast reduction surgery are able to enjoy breast-feeding. Some mothers have enough milk to meet their baby's needs. Others do not and need to use infant formula to add to their natural milk.

Prenatal preparation, support during the first few days and regular follow-up will give you the best possible chance of breast-feeding and enjoying your experience.

Breast augmentation appears to have less of an impact on breast-feeding.

Deciding to breast-feed sometime after your baby's birth

You may not have breast-fed your baby after birth, but would like to now, after finding he doesn't tolerate commercial infant formula.

It's not too late. With determination and help from someone trained in breast-feeding, you can re-establish lactation, even if you never breast-fed your baby. You can also breast-feed an adopted baby. Don't hesitate to contact a lactation consultant or an experienced resource to help re-establish milk production.

Alcohol and Tobacco

Some of the alcohol a breast-feeding mother consumes ends up in her breast milk, so its consumption should be limited. Avoid drinking alcohol regularly.

However, occasionally consuming small amounts of wine and beer does not appear to be harmful to your baby.

Tobacco is harmful to both you and your baby, just as it was during pregnancy. But even if you smoke, breast-feeding offers many benefits to both you and your baby, including protecting him against respiratory infections. Tobacco can hamper milk production. Try not to smoke just before breast-feeding. Nicotine patches to help you stop smoking can be used when you are breast-feeding.

Cannabis and other drugs

Is the occasional use of cannabis (marijuana and other cannabis derivatives) harmful to a breast-fed baby? The long-term effects on babies are unknown but cannabis does enter breast milk so avoid occasional or regular use.

Other drugs like amphetamines, cocaine, heroin, LSD, and PCPs are dangerous for your baby.

Medication

Most medication enters breast milk, but in very small quantities. Some medication is better than others because it enters the milk less. In other cases, we know more about its effect because it has been in use longer.

Several drugs can be used safely and without any specific precaution during breast-feeding. These include acetaminophen (e.g., Atasol™, Tylenol™), ibuprofen (e.g., Advil™, Motrin™) and most antibiotics.

It's very rare to have to stop breast-feeding for the length of a treatment. If your doctor recommends you stop breast-feeding to take medication, consider the following:

- Don't hesitate to tell the doctor that breast-feeding is important to you and your baby.
- Ask your doctor to make sure his or her recommendation is based on reliable sources. These sources could be a pharmacist or professional specializing in breast-feeding.
- Ask your doctor to prescribe another medication that can be taken while breast-feeding. It's often easy to find another one to treat the most common illnesses.

Talk to a health professional before taking any medication or natural product. Some of these are very strong. Stick to medication that you really need.

Breast-feeding during pregnancy

Are you breast-feeding and have become pregnant again? You can continue to breast-feed without any danger to the fetus or the child you're nursing. Hormonal changes that occur during pregnancy can decrease milk production. Watch your child's growth, especially if he is less than 6 months old and is getting breast milk only.

Some mothers breast-feed their newborn while continuing to nurse their older child.

A breast-feeding support group can put you in touch with mothers who have had this experience.

Expressing your milk

Your baby can benefit from your milk even when he's not nursing: when you're away, or in the case of a premature or sick baby. Expressing milk keeps your body producing for your child. It's also helpful to soothe an engorged breast.

Breast milk can be expressed in several different ways. You'll find one that works for you according to your situation. It's important to handle your breasts gently and wash your hands before expressing milk.

How much?

If your baby breast-feeds, your production has adapted to his demand. When you express milk between two feedings you'll probably get only a little milk. You can get more if you express from one breast when your baby has nursed from the other only. Be patient; it's common to get only a few drops the first few times.

Stimulating the let-down reflex is important for expressing a decent amount of milk. This is easy when your baby is nursing, but may be harder on your own the first few times.

The following methods are often effective – see what you like best:

- relax;
- massage the breasts;
- apply hot compresses;
- visualize: imagine your baby is nursing;
- think about your baby or about something else (for example, watch television).

When?

There is no perfect time for expressing milk. The best time is when it's convenient for you. Try expressing at different times:

- when your baby has nursed from one side only;
- in the morning;
- when your breasts are engorged;
- between two feedings;
- while nursing.

The length of time will vary. Change breasts when the milk stops flowing. Take a break for a few minutes – like your baby does – and then continue.

Manual expression

Manual expression is a technique every mother should know. It can be used to soothe a very full breast, anytime and anywhere. It also allows your baby to have breast milk without nursing. And it's free.

This is the most effective technique for expressing colostrum. A nurse, doctor or midwife should have shown you how before you returned home. If not, ask a CLSC nurse or breast-feeding support group to show you. Don't worry; it's easier than it sounds.

- Wash your hands.
- Use a clean, large container (for example, a measuring cup).
- Encourage the let-down reflex by gently massaging your breast and rolling your nipple between your fingers.
- Lean forward slightly so the milk drips into the container.

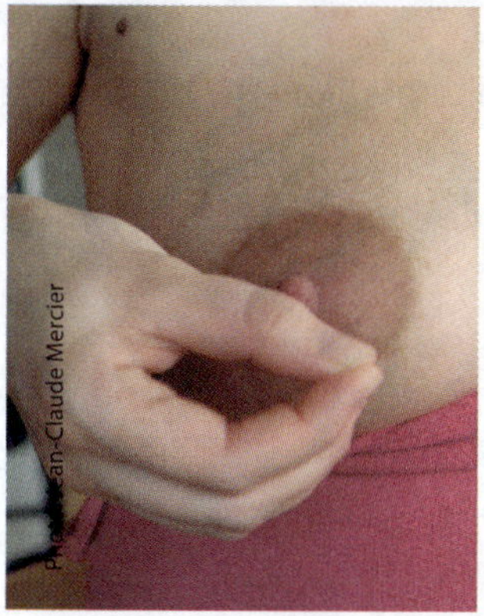

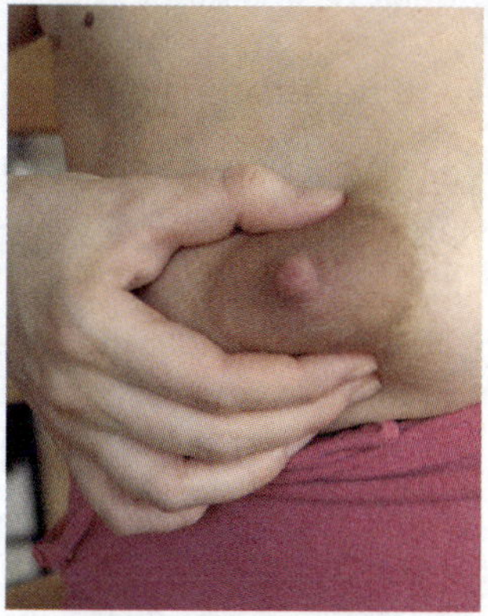

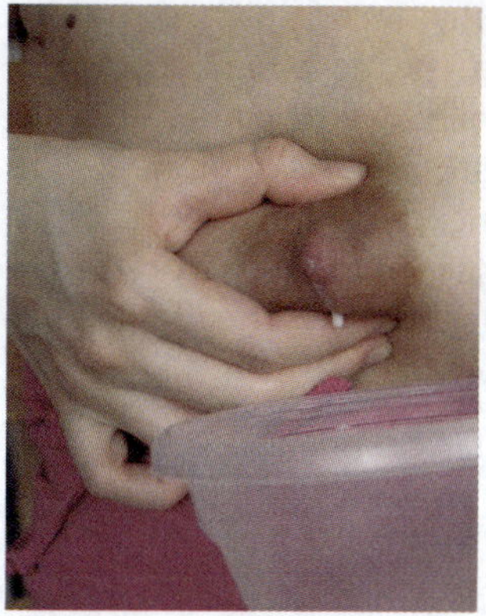

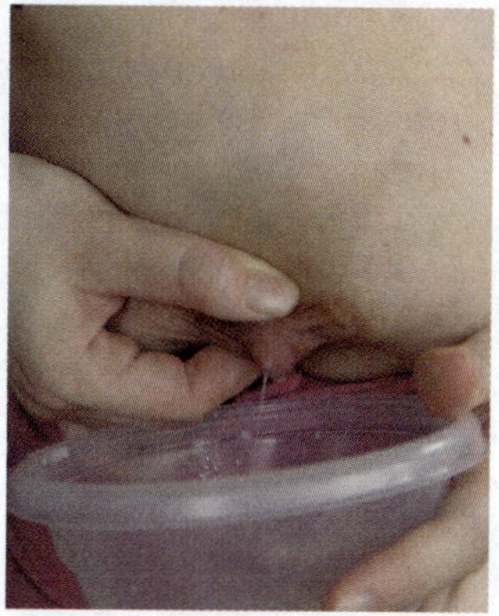

- Use your thumb and index finger to form a C. The ends of the thumb and finger should face each other like a pair of pliers.
- Place the thumb and index finger about 2 to 5 cm (1 to 2 inches) on either side of the nipple. You'll find the best distance with practice.
- Push your fingers into the breast horizontally towards the ribs.
- Bring the thumb and index finger closer together as if you were closing a pair of pliers, while keeping the fingers pressed into the breast. Repeat this pinching movement several times in a rhythmic fashion, the way your baby does when nursing. The movement should reproduce the baby's movement when he nurses. The milk will flow a drop at a time at the beginning and then in a stream over time. Be careful not to slide your fingers over your skin. Keep your fingers pressed firmly into the breast without stretching the nipple, which is painful and not very effective.
- With practice, you'll become faster and more effective.

You don't need to press hard. The movement shouldn't leave any mark on your breast or be painful. It takes a bit of practice to get your fingers properly positioned.

Work your way around the breast by moving your fingers to empty it.

Breast massage

This technique massages your breast before starting to express milk. It helps collect more milk. The main idea is to stimulate the breast using your knuckles, in a process similar to kneading.

- Make a fist and keep it closed throughout the massage.
- Press the knuckle of your index finger into the top of your chest and roll one knuckle after the other down towards the nipple.
- To massage under the breast, start by pressing the knuckle of your little finger into your ribs and roll one knuckle after the other going up towards the nipple.
- Move your fist to repeat the rolling motion all around your breast.

- Work your way around the breast once or twice and then start to express milk.

The massage shouldn't be painful and only the knuckles should be touching the breast. You can repeat the massage once or twice during a session of expressing milk.

Breast pump

Are you expressing milk several times a week but would prefer a different technique than manual expression? A manual breast pump may be a good option.

Electric breast pumps also exist. They are effective and very practical when the mother must express her milk over a long period. You can rent or buy electric pumps.

Several electric and manual breast pumps that are available for sale are of very poor quality, are ineffective and can hurt you. Before buying a breast pump, find out more from a support group or CLSC nurse. They can advise you on the best model in terms of quality and price, based on your situation.

Handling milk

Preserving breast milk

Mother's milk is best when it's fresh, straight from the breast; but it refrigerates and freezes well.

You can keep breast milk at room temperature if it will be used within 4 hours of being expressed. If it is to be used in the following few days, keep it in the refrigerator rather than the freezer.

If breast milk is to be kept longer than 8 days, freeze it immediately. You can store all containers of frozen breast milk inside a second container that closes tight. Note that frozen breast milk will lose a small amount of its nutritional value over time, but it is still better than any other type of milk.

Handling breast milk

- Wash your hands and the milk containers.
- Fill containers 2/3 full. The milk will expand when it freezes.
- Freeze various amounts (30 to 90 millilitres) to avoid wasting any.
- Close the container tight and mark the date on it.
- Put it in the refrigerator to cool.
- Store the cooled milk inside the designated milk container in the freezer.
- Use the oldest milk first.

Note that milk may acquire a distinctive taste, smell and appearance after it has been stored for a period of time. Don't worry; if the storage temperatures and times shown above are followed, the milk will still be good. Don't throw it out. If your baby refuses it, contact a breast-feeding specialist.

Choosing containers

Mother's milk can be stored in glass and rigid plastic bottles, or in specially made breast-milk bags for baby bottles. The regular bags are too thin for freezing and must be used one inside another. Keep several portions of breast milk handy.

	Room temperature	Refrigerator	Freezer*
Fresh breast milk	4 hours at 25°C (77°F) 24 hours at 15°C (59°F) (cooler with an ice pack)	8 days at 4°C (39°F)	6 months (refrigerator freezer compartment) 12 months (chest freezer) Do not put it on the door
Thawed breast milk	1 hour	24 hours	Do not re-freeze

* The temperature of the freezer must be cold enough to keep ice cream hard (-18°C or 0°F).

!

Caution

- Safe storage times cannot be combined. For example, don't keep milk 4 hours at room temperature, then refrigerate it for 8 days, then freeze it!
- Don't use these storage times with babies in hospital. Follow the staff's advice.
- Good hygiene is essential. Wash your hands and be sure all containers are clean. Human milk can vary in colour, having a blue, yellow or brown tint. It's also natural for the taste and smell to change depending on the mother's diet. Since breast milk is not homogenized, the fat separates. Shake well before use.

See page 367 to find out more about using bottles and nipple shields.

Breast-feeding and mother-child separation

One of the great things about breast-feeding is that it makes family outings easier. But other personal and professional activities may take you away from your child.

You can keep on breast-feeding even if your baby isn't always with you. But first consider:

- Your child's age;
- His preferences and yours;
- The length and frequency of separations.

Beginning at about 6 months, your baby may not need to drink from a bottle when you're apart. He can learn to drink from a cup to quench his thirst.

A local support group can help you with the different possibilities.

Occasional separations

Going out for a few hours? If you breast-feed before leaving and when you get back, your baby may not need to be fed while you're away.

Many mothers produce milk to save for an occasional separation. Depending on age and ability, the baby can drink it from a baby bottle or a cup. He may not want much milk. Don't worry; he'll probably fill right up when you come back.

While you're away you may or may not feel the need to soothe your breasts by releasing milk. You can bring along what you need to keep it cold until you get home.

Regular separation

Returning to work or school will cause regular separation, usually for many hours at a time. Many mothers in this situation continue breast-feeding.

You can express your milk, chill it or freeze it to be given to your baby while you're away, in a baby bottle or cup depending on his age and skills. When you're with your baby, offer him your breast. In this way, you'll continue to provide your child with excellent food for his health and growth, whether or not you're there all the time.

At about 6 months, some babies will be happy with complementary foods until mother comes home for breast-feeding. Babies may drink less during separations, but they make up for it by drinking more the rest of the time.

Another possibility is to breast-feed when you're with your child but give him another type of milk, depending on his age, while you're away. Your milk production will adjust to this mixed feeding. You can continue this relationship as long as you and your baby both want.

Many mothers tell of the pleasure they share with their babies while feeding before and after a separation.

Dangerous working conditions

At work you may have to change jobs or take progressive reassignment if you're exposed to various contaminants, such as solvents, inks, dies, etc., which could be dangerous while breast-feeding. Find out more from your doctor or the CLSC nurse.

Weaning

Like all steps in child development, weaning age varies from one child to another. Whether it's the mother or child who begins the process, various factors affect weaning: the child's age and temperament, the mother's feelings and the approach used.

Give yourself the time it takes. Pay attention to your child and stay flexible. If possible, it's better to delay weaning a sick child. He needs his mother's milk and the comfort that comes from breast-feeding.

You want to cut down the number of feedings but not yet wean your child? This can be done, but remember that some children lose interest in the breast and wean themselves more quickly than their mothers want. This is more common if you use a baby bottle regularly.

Weaning babies less than 9 months old

Milk production declines gradually as stimulation of the breast is reduced. Gradual weaning allows you to avoid swelling and reduces the possibility of mastitis. The time it takes to stop producing milk varies from one woman to another. Four weeks seems enough time to stop completely, and gives your child time to adapt calmly. Weaning faster may be hard on both you and your baby.

Start by replacing one daily breast-feeding with a commercial infant formula enriched with iron and served in a baby bottle or cup. Between breast-feedings you can soothe your breasts by expressing some milk or by emptying them under a hot shower.

Once you no longer feel overfilled, replace a second feeding when you're ready. At first, don't skip two consecutive breast-feedings. You will gradually replace as many breast-feedings as you want. Many mothers continue the main feedings, such as at bedtime and in the morning.

Some mothers feel engorged with milk for a few days after the last breast-feeding. Don't hesitate to express milk to make yourself comfortable. You can also put the baby to your breast for a few minutes.

Your baby will start drinking from a cup at about 6 months. At first, he will usually only take a small amount of milk. Finish up with a baby bottle if needed. Offer him the cup often, and make sure he's getting enough milk – it will remain his basic food until he's a year old, providing the calcium and protein needed to grow.

Some babies won't like the bottle at any age. That's normal because a bottle doesn't seem much like a breast. Be patient and don't push. In any case, he isn't likely to accept something new when he's angry.

Here are a few suggestions to help the transition:

- Begin the change while your child is well and not too hungry.
- Introduce the baby bottle or cup for a snack of milk. Your baby probably won't take much at first.
- Put the father to work. Quietly find yourself out of the way at feeding time.
- Put breast milk in the baby bottle or cup at first, then try another type of milk.
- Present the bottle or cup in a different way than the breast. Change the routine.
- Be patient. Wait a few days and try again.
- You can always change your mind while weaning and return to breast-feeding.
- Consult a local help group if needed.

Weaning babies older than 9 months

As your child gets older, you may decide to guide him more or less quickly toward weaning. You can gradually encourage him to develop other ways to satisfy his need for nutrition and contact. Many children lose interest in the breast when they lose the need to suck.

For older babies breast-feeding is a moment of comfort and contact. At this age, offering him a baby bottle instead of the breast is not likely to fulfill his needs. First include other moments of reassuring contact – rocking, massage, back-scratching and so on. Little by little, you'll be able to stop breast-feeding. He will eventually start going days at a time without asking to be fed.

Starting at about 9 months, your baby will be able to drink homogenized 3.25% MF milk instead of mother's milk.

Here are a few suggestions to help the transition:

- While not refusing to give your breast, you can stop offering it to him.
- Delay feedings if he is not too impatient. This will help space feedings out and reduce the number of them.
- Offer him a nutritional snack.
- Use distractions: suggest a game or other stimulating activity.
- Reduce the length of feedings.
- Change your daily habits. For example, don't sit in the feeding chair the baby associates with breast-feeding.
- You can always change your mind while weaning and return to breast-feeding.
- Consult a local help group if needed.

Mother's milk: the best one

Ingredient	Function	Present in breast milk?	Present in commercial infant formulas?
Water	Hydrates the child	✔	✔
Proteins	Provide energy and construction materials and regulates the organism's functions	✔	✔
Glucides	Provide the main energy source for all cells	✔	✔
Fat	Stores energy for future use	✔	✔
Minerals	Help cells and bones to grow	✔	✔
Vitamins	Aid in cell and bone growth	✔	✔
Active enzymes • Amylases • Lipases • Lysozymes	Aid in food digestion	✔	
Hormones • cortisol • insulin • thyroxin • prostaglandins	Regulate metabolism and promotes maturation of the immune system	✔	

Ingredient	Function	Present in breast milk?	Present in commercial infant formulas?
Growth factors • Human growth factors • EGF and others	Promote growth and development of the intestines	✔	
Antibacterial factors • SIgA, IgM, IgD • Bifidobacterium • Lactoferrin • Oligosaccharides • Lysozymes • Casein • Living cells in human milk (macrophages, T cells and B cells)	Protect against infections (*E. coli, S. pneumonia, V. cholera,* etc.)	✔	
Antiviral factors • SIgA, IgM, IgG • Living cells in human milk (macrophages, T cells and B cells)	Protect against viruses	✔	
Antiparasitic factors • IgA	Protect against viruses	✔	

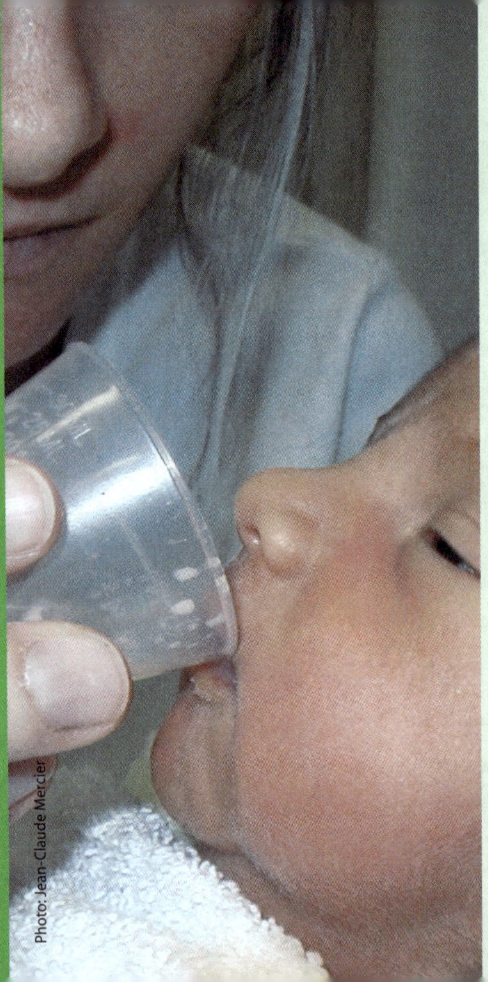

Photo: Jean-Claude Mercier

Other types of milk

Industry today converts cow's milk and soy protein so their nutritional components resemble something closer to human mother's milk. Commercial baby formula is not the same as breast milk. It does not contain antibodies, immune factors, growth hormones or white blood cells.

Commercial infant formula (commercial milk)

For babies not feeding on breast milk, the Canadian Paediatric Society, Dieticians of Canada and Health Canada recommend feeding a commercial baby formula enriched with iron until the age of 9 to 12 months. These products are better adapted to the infant's basic needs than ordinary cow's or goat's milk or soy drinks. They are a safe replacement that can meet your child's nutritional needs.

Commercial infant formula costs about $30 to $40 a week. Special preparations for babies with particular problems are more expensive. This expense must be included in the budget for the child's first 9 to 12 months and represents an amount of more than $1000.

Commercial infant formula is sold in three forms:

- Liquid concentrate;
- Ready to serve;
- Powder.

Liquid concentrates are sterile, easier to use, safer and about the same price as powders.

The ready-to-serve formulas are also sterile. They don't need to be diluted but are very expensive.

Commercial infant formula is not recommended for premature babies. The risk of contamination is greater with powders than with preserved milk. Powders require more precautions during preparation. If you decide on this type of milk, be sure to follow the recommendations on page 372.

Read the label to help choose the right product. Check the expiry date and don't use milk after that date. Return any damaged, bulging or suspect cans to the store.

What to buy?

A child born at full term and fed commercial infant formula will use up his reserves of iron in about 4 months. To prevent anemia, we recommend formulas enriched with iron starting at birth. They are usually tolerated as well as other formulas.

The commercial baby formulas supplied by various makers are equivalent. Some additives and special mentions are intended to increase sales, without providing any advantage to the child. The wording can often be confusing.

! So-called "transition" foods are not suitable for babies less than 6 months old. They contain more calcium than other current preparations, but less than cow's milk. They can be used as a transition between two types of milk but are not needed.

Special formulas

If your baby seems not to tolerate his milk, discuss it with a health professional. He may recommend a more suitable formula. In these circumstances, some mothers decide to return to breast-feeding. You may need help succeeding in this.

The doctor can also prescribe a special formula for your baby. These products are always iron-enriched and are intended for babies with particular problems.

Soy-protein based commercial infant formulas are suitable for babies in vegan families where dairy products are excluded. They are not recommended for babies who suffer from colic.

Medication insurance programs refund the cost of some special formulas when prescribed.

Baby bottles and nipples

Feeding schedule

Be sure to feed your baby on demand and not according to the clock.

Babies show signs of hunger long before they start to cry. Their breathing changes, their eyes, mouth and face begin to move, their limbs and body become tense and restless, legs waving, hands touching their face and mouth. Next comes sucking action. These are all signs that your baby is hungry. It's a good time for the bottle. You will both relax and feeding will go easily.

Daily feeding schedules vary widely from one baby to the next. Like adults, babies are all different. Some have regular schedules while others are unpredictable, feeding more or less often and at different times of day. This depends on your child's sucking ability, temperament, appetite, mood and the volume flowing through the nipple. Newborns usually feed 8 to 12 times every 24 hours. Some very efficient babies need only 6 feedings a day. Feeding will become quicker and less frequent as your baby grows older.

How much milk?

The amount of milk consumed varies widely from one baby to the next and from one day to another. At first your baby will drink a small amount because his stomach is still very small. The amount will increase gradually.

Your child may be less hungry in the evening than the morning. The best thing is to watch for signs of hunger and satisfaction and let him control his own intake of milk. Pay attention to your child's appetite!

Babies also cry for other reasons than hunger. Babies who drink quickly at the nipple may briefly need a pacifier because their hunger is satisfied before their need to suck. Boredom, discomfort and the need for warmth and security can also make a baby cry. Respond quickly to his needs.

Until your baby is about 6 months, milk supplies his needs better than cereals. It's the only food with the calcium and protein that are absolutely essential during the first year of life. At some points, during growth spurts for example, your child will need to drink huge amounts. Be sure he's ready before introducing complementary foods.

Warming the milk

There is no nutritional reason to heat milk, but most babies prefer it lukewarm. Children usually begin drinking fruit juice at 10 to 12 months, but if your child doesn't like cold milk, you can continue warming it up.

Put the container of milk in a pot of warm water for a few minutes, until it is lukewarm. Stir it gently. Throwaway bags heat more quickly than bottles.

To check the temperature, sprinkle a few drops on the inside of your wrist or the back of your hand. It should feel neither hot nor cold.

To reheat frozen breast milk, first pour cold water over the container, gradually adding small amounts of hot water until the milk becomes lukewarm. You can also put frozen breast milk in the refrigerator for 10 to 12 hours and then warm it in hot water. Stir it, check the temperature and give it to your baby.

We do not recommend warming milk in microwave ovens, which heat unevenly and create dangerous hot spots.

Some babies have been accidentally burnt this way. Bottles and bags can burst. Also, don't boil a bottle or bag of milk. All solid and liquid foods lose some of their nutritional value when overheated. Breast milk also loses some of its vitamins and antibodies when heated in a microwave oven.

Don't leave milk (except fresh breast milk) out at room temperature for more than an hour. Throw it away after that because bacteria can multiply quickly and cause diarrhea.

Bottle-feeding your baby

Get comfortable in a relaxed position and slide a pillow under the arm holding your baby. Lean back and put your feet up. Hold the bottle tilted to keep the neck full of milk so your baby doesn't swallow air. Change positions between feedings, moving your baby from one side to the other. This will help his vision to develop. It's sometimes a good idea to take a break or two while feeding, especially in the early months.

> Experience the love and magic of skin-to-skin contact!

Don't let your baby hold the bottle by himself in bed or the baby chair. The time you take to relax while feeding your baby in your arms is good for both of you. Feeding time is a regular occasion to form a good, comfortable relationship.

Cleaning bottles and nipples

Using baby bottles for breast milk or commercial formula calls for strict hygiene. Be sure to carefully wash bottles, nipples and other articles used for feeding. This will help prevent gastroenteritis and the growth of fungus in the mouth.

Immediately after feeding, rinse the bottle, nipple and cap in cold water. Be sure to run water through the hole in the nipple to clean it out.

Use nipple and bottle brushes and hot, soapy water for washing. Rinse in boiling water, drain and cover. You can use the dishwasher but some manufacturers don't recommend it for their nipples.

Don't regularly boil nipples because the rubber in them will break down. Examine them often – they will wear out in time from suction, heat, sunlight and contact with milk. Throw them out when they become soft or sticky and don't wait until they leak or tear.

Don't re-use fragile throwaway bags or pour hot milk into them – they may burst.

Handling commercial infant formula

Pay close attention and be very careful to avoid mistakes when diluting commercial formula, especially in powdered form. Closely follow all the instructions on the box and measure the powder with the spoon supplied, which differs from brand to brand. Be sure to wash the spoon, which can easily become contaminated.

Some parents save time by preparing the day's bottles all at once. Others prefer to do one at a time. It's up to you.

During the baby's first 4 months, always dilute the formula with water that has been boiled for one minute.

Photo: iStockphoto

Preparing canned concentrated milk

- Begin by washing your hands thoroughly.
- Assemble everything you need.
- Clean the can in hot water before opening with a clean can opener.
- Carefully follow the manufacturer's instructions for diluting the formula.
- Pour the milk into baby bottles and quickly cover them with nipples and caps.
- Refrigerate immediately.

If an open can of concentrated milk is left over in the refrigerator at the end of the day, you can use it tomorrow.

> **!** Never use hot tap water – it may contain lead and germs.

Extra precautions for mixing powdered formula

- Sterilize all utensils and objects that will be used to prepare the formula.
- Boil the water until it is at a full rolling boil if using a pot or until the kettle shuts off if using an automatic kettle.
- Put water in the bottle and allow it to cool (use it within 30 minutes; the water temperature should be at least 70°C).
- Add the required amount of powder to the warm water.
- Shake the bottle to mix the contents.
- Cool the bottle quickly using cold water before giving it to your baby or put it in the fridge to use later.

> **!** Caution! To prevent bacteria, always throw out any milk or formula left over after feeding.

Storing commercial formula

Prepared formula can be kept 1 hour at room temperature and 24 hours in the refrigerator. It does not freeze.

Well-covered open cans of concentrated or ready-to-serve formula can be kept in the refrigerator for up to 48 hours.

Open cans of powdered formula can be stored for 1 month if kept dry.

Pasteurized milk

Pasteurized cow's milk (3.25% MF)

Cow's milk contains three times too much protein and mineral salts, which can overload a baby's kidneys. It contains only half the lactose of mother's milk and one-third the linoleic acid – a fatty acid needed for growth of the brain and nervous system. It lacks vitamins A, B_1, B_6, C, D and E, copper, manganese and iron. It deprives the child of major protein elements such as taurine, cysteine and alpha-lactalbumin, and the immune protection contained in breast milk.

Before the age of 9 months

Before 9 months, cow's milk can cause anemia because of its low iron content and the blood loss it causes in the intestines. This bleeding is often invisible to the naked eye.

If you plan to feed your baby cow's milk before the age of 9 months for financial reasons, contact your CLSC to find out about the support you can obtain.

Cow's milk fails to meet the needs of a baby less than 9 months old.

After the age of 9 months

After 9 months, you can begin giving your child cow's milk, but not more than 900 millilitres (30 ounces) a day. Buy pasteurized whole cow's milk (3.25% MF).

Pasteurized goat's milk

Goat's milk has the same shortcomings as cow's milk. It contains little folic acid and vitamin D. Grocery stores sell goat's milk enriched with folic acid (vitamin B9) and vitamin D. Beginning at 9 to 12 months, you can give your child goat's milk in the same way as cow's milk. Buy pasteurized, enriched whole goat's milk (3.25% MF).

Some people recommend goat's milk to prevent or treat the allergy to cow's milk protein. Unfortunately, many people are intolerant to goat's milk. Some 80% of children allergic to cow's milk will also be allergic to goat's milk.

Milk to avoid

No raw milk

Milk from animals must be pasteurized. The retail sale of unpasteurized milk is illegal in Canada. Diseases spread by unpasteurized milk include poliomyelitis, typhoid fever, encephalitis, tuberculosis, diarrhea, salmonella poisoning, and brucellosis. We recommend you not give your children unpasteurized milk even if it comes from a herd in perfect health. The pasteurized milk sold in stores is just as nutritional and poses no health risk.

Industrial pasteurization consists of heating milk quickly to a very high temperature, then cooling it just as fast. The whole process takes only a few seconds. Dangerous organisms are destroyed and food value stays the same.

We do not recommend pasteurizing at home. It is too slow and inefficient and also causes heavy losses of milk's natural vitamins – A, B_1, B_2, B_6, B_{12}, C, D and folic acid.

Drinks made from soy, rice and almonds

Natural food stores and some other grocery stores sell drinks made from soy, rice, almonds, etc. They are not suitable for infants. They are incomplete and not nourishing compared to breast milk and even commercial baby formula. Babies grow fast so they need full and balanced nutrition. These drinks will cause serious shortcomings in your baby's nutrition and interfere with his normal development. If you have special circumstances, talk to your doctor. These drinks are good food for adults.

Photo: Julie Ward

Water

When to give your baby water

Mother's milk will naturally satisfy your baby's thirst. He doesn't usually need to drink water. Mother's milk contains plenty of water at the beginning of every feeding. After a few minutes, the amount of fat and protein increases.

Babies that are fed commercial infant formula may become thirsty between bottles. They may cry because they want water. A baby needs more water in warm weather, or when he has diarrhea or a fever. In the first 4 to 6 months, it's better to encourage his appetite by not giving water in the hour before feeding.

Around 6 months of age, when your baby begins eating complementary foods, you can offer him water. Give him small amounts in a cup.

Photo: Julie Bellemare

A breast-fed baby doesn't need to drink water.
A bottle-fed baby may need to drink water.

Choosing the right water

An infant must be given only good water whether for drinking or for preparing infant formula or baby food. Some micro-organisms that are harmless to adults can cause diarrhea or other illnesses in young children. The water they drink must not contain high levels of mineral salts. You can safely give your baby any of the following:

- Municipal tap water – unless the public has been warned against using it for cooking or drinking;
- Water from any private well that meets the quality standards in the upcoming section of this guide "Private well water" on page 381;
- Commercial bottled or bulk-packaged water, spring water and water processed without added mineral salts;

We do not recommend carbonated water, mineral water or mineralized water.

Do not use water from lakes, rivers or natural springs unless it is tested regularly for quality. Open water is usually contaminated. Don't drink water just because it looks clear.

Don't give water to your child if you're not sure it's clean. Give him water from another clean well or water supply, or recommended bottled water.

Boiling is essential

This is how to prepare and store boiled water:

- Put water in two pots. One will be used to sterilize a container to store the water or prepare milk, the other to boil drinking water for the baby.
- Boil the water at a full rolling boil for at least 1 minute.
- Use tongs or another kitchen tool to sink the container into the boiling water and sterilize it.
- Place the pot containing the baby's water into cold water to cool it.
- Carefully pour the boiled water into the sterilized container.

All water for babies under 4 months **must be boiled at a full rolling boil for at least 1 minute**, whether it comes from a municipal system, private well, bulk container or bottle.

Photo: iStockphoto

You can also use a kettle, but be sure to boil the water for at least 1 minute.

Boiled water can be kept in a properly closed and sterilized container in the refrigerator for 2 or 3 days or at room temperature for 24 hours. From 4 months on, your baby can drink unboiled water from an acceptable water supply.

Municipal tap water

When a municipality supplies water to 20 people or more it must meet strict standards. The drinking water regulation passed by the Québec government in 2001 requires regular testing for bacteria and 19 inorganic chemicals such as metals. When a water system supplies more than 5,000 residents, testing also includes 42 organic substances. When water fails to respect microbiological quality standards, the municipality or the operator of the water system must inform the ministère du Développement durable, de l'Environnement et des Parcs (MDDEP) and the public health department in the region. The system operator must then warn the public in various ways, such as through local media, individual and public notices, etc.

Private well water

You can use water from a deep well (artesian well) if recent tests show that it meets proper quality standards. If it's a new well, the water must be tested for chemicals and bacteria by a lab accredited by the ministère du Développement durable, de l'Environnement et des Parcs. 1 800 561-1616 or www.ceaeq.gouv.qc.ca/accreditation/palae/lla03.htm.

Water from a surface well needs to be monitored more closely because it can be contaminated more easily by bacteria and nitrates. At least two tests should be done per year.

Well water must contain no fecal bacteria (fecal coliform, *E. coli* or *enterococcus*). When signs of fecal contamination are present, water must be boiled for at least 1 minute before use.

Whenever you use tap water, let it run until it's cold first. This gets rid of dangerous lead and copper build-up as well as some bacteria which may be found in pipes.

Use cold water for preparing your baby's bottle, drinking or cooking. Warm water may contain more lead, bacteria or other contamination. Babies are more sensitive to it.

Photo: iStockphoto

The presence of total coliform bacteria in well water is not dangerous in itself, but this water might be contaminated more easily. Be safe and boil your water for at least 1 minute before using it, until the water collection system is proven safe. Repeated testing must show the water contains no fecal bacteria.

Nitrates can be found in some wells. They often come from fields fertilized with chemicals, liquid or solid manure or defective or poorly maintained septic tanks. Nitrates are dangerous in high concentrations, especially for babies under the age of 6 months. Nitrates cannot be removed by boiling the water. The maximum allowable concentration of nitrates and nitrites is 10 mg/L.

Fluoride can occur naturally in ground water. Fluoride is necessary for the healthy growth of teeth, but in large quantities it can cause spots on the teeth of young children. The maximum allowable concentration of fluoride in drinking water is 1.5 mg/L. If the quantity of fluoride in your drinking water is over 0.7 mg/L, you should tell your pediatrician and avoid giving your child fluoride supplements.

In general, when the concentrations of chemical substances are too high, use another source of drinking water, like bottled water. If you don't know what your water needs to be tested for, contact the public health department in your area.

Well owners must have their water analyzed at their expense at least twice a year to detect *E. coli*, nitrites and nitrates. Ideally, these analyses should be done after the spring thaw and fall rains or during a dry period. Samples may be taken more often if you suspect contamination.

Bottled water and bulk containers

Only two types of bottled water are suitable for your baby: spring water and unmineralized treated water.

Only the two following types of bottled water are suitable for your baby. Never give him carbonated water. Carefully read the list of ingredients on the bottle.

- **Spring water** comes from an underground spring approved for drinking water and has low mineral content. It has been tested for quality twice – at the spring and at the bottling plant. Spring water can be called "natural" when it has not been treated or altered. Bottled water sold in Québec has generally been disinfected using ozone or ultraviolet light to protect against micro-organisms.

Photo: iStockphoto

- **Unmineralized treated water** is municipal tap water that is filtered and purified to resemble spring water. It contains no added mineral salts.

Remember that bulk-packaged water is most likely to become contaminated when the containers are being filled. Be sure to use a reliable and stable supplier. All containers used for packaged water must be washed in very hot soapy water and thoroughly rinsed.

If you use a water cooler, be sure to clean it regularly according to the manufacturer's recommendations. Also, be sure to keep the cooler's spout clean. Pets and children or adults with dirty hands can easily contaminate the tap.

Water-treatment equipment

Some people use home water-treatment appliances to improve the quality or taste of their water. Among others, products certified by the National Sanitation Foundation (NSF), when used according to instructions, meet the quality standards for which they were designed.

Unless you are advised otherwise by the public health department in your area, it is best not to give home-treated water to a baby younger than 6 months since there are no official standards for this equipment. Little is known about the safety and efficiency of home water-treatment systems. Here are a few of the known risks of some equipment:

- Water softeners connected to the tap or water inlet increase the amount of sodium (salt).
- Charcoal filters with or without silver can increase the silver content and the amount of some bacteria.
- Stills and reverse osmosis machines reduce the mineral content.

As well, these devices are hard to clean. For example, don't forget to change the filter or membrane regularly according to the manufacturer's instructions.

Solving problems

Water can change in colour, taste or smell. During spring thaw, road salt can be the cause. Some farm and industrial activities can also contaminate domestic water supplies.

- If there is a problem with your municipal water supply, you should contact the municipality or waterworks operator.
- If it is a private well, you must consult a laboratory accredited by the ministère du Développement durable, de l'Environnement et des Parcs. 1 800 561-1616 or www.mddep.gouv.qc.ca/eau/potable/depliant/index-en.htm.
- If you have doubts or if water quality standards are not being met, you must consult the ministère du Développement durable, de l'Environnement et des Parcs or the public health department in your region.

Feeding your baby

Photo: François Gervais

Complementary foods

Complementary foods are everything other than mother's milk and commercial infant formula. They are often purées or soft foods and include fruit juice, so we call them "complementary" rather than "solid" foods. For practical reasons, the introduction of cow's milk is included in this chapter.

Your baby will take some time getting used to complementary foods. The first mouthfuls will be a discovery for her. Between 6 and 9 months, she will develop a taste for various foods and textures. From 9 to 12 months, she will begin eating on her own. Finally at about 1 year, she will be eating the same food as the rest of the family.

The advice in this chapter applies to most breast-fed or bottle-fed babies. Remember that throughout your child's first year, mother's milk and/or infant formula will be her basic food. As the name indicates, complementary foods are meant to be an addition to milk and not to replace it. For this reason, we strongly recommend that you give your child complementary foods at her own pace and according to her needs.

Between 6 and 9 months, she will develop a taste for various foods and textures. From 9 to 12 months, she will begin eating on her own. Finally at about 1 year, she will be eating the same food as the rest of the family.

But there is no advantage to a baby starting early on complementary foods, which are less nutritional than mother's milk and infant formula. If started too soon, complementary foods replace milk instead of adding to it.

Introducing complementary foods at about 6 months

Experts agree that most babies don't need complementary foods before 6 months. There is no advantage to a baby starting early on complementary foods, which are less nutritional than mother's milk and infant formula. If started too soon, complementary foods replace milk instead of adding to it. Your baby won't start sleeping through the night just because she's eating cereal at suppertime. There is no connection. Sleeping time depends on your baby's biological rhythm and temperament.

At about 6 months, a baby's food needs change, and complementary foods are important. A baby is usually ready to start eating complementary foods at about 6 months because:

- She is producing enough saliva;
- She has enough food-digesting enzymes;
- Her kidneys are more mature and can absorb more protein;
- Her immune system is stronger and there is less chance of developing allergies.

Don't wait until your baby is 7 months old.

When will your baby be ready?

It's sometimes hard to know the right time to begin adding complementary foods to an infant's diet. It can vary, and since they can't talk at this age you'll have to watch for the signs showing that you can start to give your baby complementary foods:

- She is about 6 months old;
- She can sit up in her chair without support;
- She can fully control her neck muscles, for example by turning her head to refuse something;
- She drinks according to her needs. The number of feedings has increased over the past 5 or more days, but she seems unsatisfied and cries after feeding;
- She can close her lips tight over a spoon and push food to the back of her mouth with her tongue.

You can continue breast-feeding as often as she wants, or give her at least 750 ml (25 ounces) of commercial infant formula per day.

Remember that a baby who drinks more often for a few days is not necessarily ready for complementary foods. This may just indicate a growth spurt or a brief need for more milk.

The main thing is to watch your baby closely. In general, babies are ready to begin the switch at about 6 months. At this age, food can be introduced quite quickly. The order in which you introduce foods does not matter much. Babies with good appetites can begin a few weeks before 6 months, starting with cereals, fruits and vegetables at first, and waiting until after 6 months for other foods.

Babies' interest in food can vary. Some need a bit of encouragement to begin, with various types of food textures offered, for example. Others like complementary foods so much they lose their taste for milk.

When your baby starts to eat, she will continue drinking as much milk as before, but this will decrease before long.

Premature babies

Complementary foods are introduced to premature babies in the same way as for full-term babies. Be sure to use your child's corrected age, based on her predicted birth date.

How to introduce complementary foods

The usual order

The order for introducing complementary foods is not very important, especially if your baby begins eating at about 6 months. Eating habits depend on your family's culture and customs.

Serve your baby one new food at a time; don't mix foods, and choose a variety of healthy foods.

In Québec, infants usually begin by eating baby cereals. They are enriched with iron, an element that can be lacking in milk. The next foods to introduce are vegetables, then fruits. High-protein foods such as meat, egg yolk, cheese and yogurt come last because they can overload an infant's kidneys.

Photo: Nicolas Delaitre

Little by little and by 9 months at the latest, you will be able to give your baby soft foods in small morsels or mashed with a fork.

Texture

At first, offer your baby thin purées, thickening them as she learns to eat and as you feel she is ready for them.

The first meal

To make it easier, choose an occasion when your baby is in a good mood. Begin by feeding her some milk. Then put her in the high chair, which will help her digestion.

> Your baby's first meal can be a surprising event. But remember to go at her pace so this new experience is a happy one.

Your baby will slowly learn to eat. Don't forget she is learning very different movements than those she uses for nursing. For this reason, don't use a baby bottle for complementary foods.

New foods

These are a few tips for introducing new foods more easily:

- Serve **only one** food at a time.
- Choose a time when your baby is relaxed and in good shape; otherwise she may frown on the new dish.
- If she rejects a new food for a few days, don't insist.
- Wait about 3 days before adding another food to the menu. If she shows signs of an allergy, it will be easier to trace.

It takes time to accept change, so be sure to respect your baby's pace and her preferences. Taste will develop by trying various foods over many weeks.

Photo: iStockphoto

A changing appetite

It's normal for your baby to eat less sometimes. She may not enjoy certain foods and textures. Like an adult, a baby's appetite may vary from day to day.

You can learn to satisfy your baby's appetite by watching for signs of hunger or contentment. If she's interested in the food you give her, she is still hungry. But if she closes her mouth, sulks, pushes away the spoon, turns her head, cries or plays with her food, she's had enough to eat.

Suggested schedule for introducing complementary food

At about 6 months – Step 1	Step 2	Step 3
Breast milk or commercial infant formula	Breast milk or commercial infant formula	Breast milk or commercial infant formula
Baby cereal • Rice • Barley	Baby cereal	Baby cereal
	Cooked vegetables in a thin purée Fruit in a thin purée	Cooked vegetables in a thin purée Fruit in a thin purée
		Meat in a thin purée Poultry in a thin purée

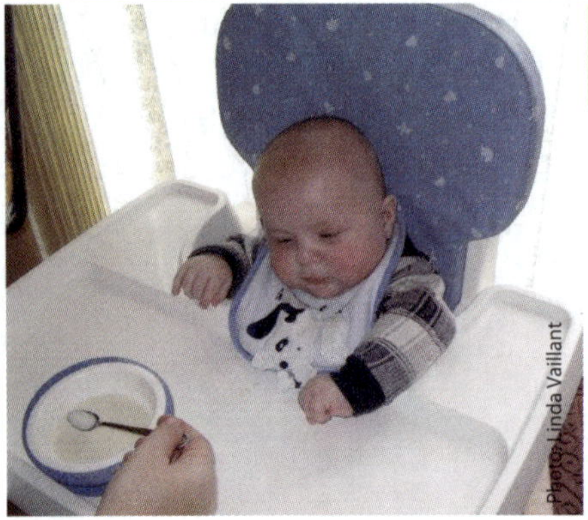

From 7 to 9 months	From 9 to 12 months	From 1 to 2 years
Breast milk or commercial infant formula	Breast milk or commercial infant formula	Breast milk
Baby cereal • Oats • Soy • Blends	Baby cereal Bread Pasta	Baby cereal Bread Pasta Cereal with little sugar
Mashed cooked vegetables Mashed fruit	Soft cooked vegetables Soft peeled fruit	Cooked or raw tender vegetables Peeled fruit pieces
Meat Poultry Egg yolk Fish*	Meat Poultry Egg yolk Fish* Legumes Tofu	Meat Poultry Egg yolk, egg white Fish* Legumes Tofu Peanut, almond or other smooth nut butters Seafood
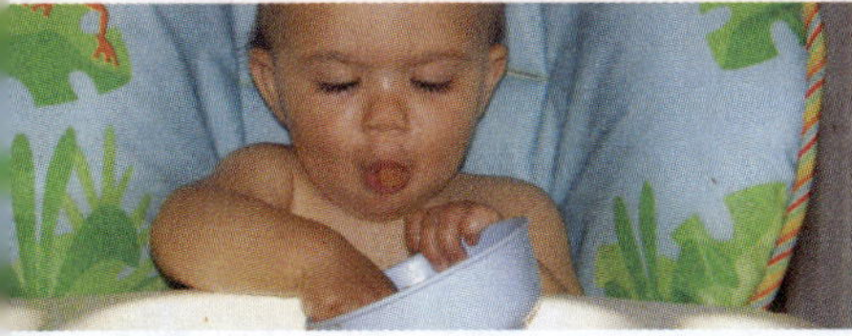 Photo: Nicolas Delaitre	3.25% M.F. dairy milk Yogurt Cheese	3.25% M.F. dairy milk Yogurt Cheese Ice cream or frozen yogurt Milk pudding

* See What type to choose?, page 416.

Honey and botulism

To be safe, never give honey to children under 1 year old. Whether pasteurized or not, honey can contain botulism spores, the reproductive cells of this deadly disease. If they enter a baby's system, they can cause infantile botulism, a rare but often fatal sickness.

Don't use honey for cooking. Use ordinary white sugar, or fructose. Fructose tastes stronger, so use only half as much.

Choking

Some foods can get caught in the throat or block the airways. Each year, many children choke as a result. Smaller bits of food caught in the airways can cause infection. See page 549 to find out what to do about a choking baby.

Until the age of about 4, don't give children food that can cause choking: nuts, peanuts, seeds, hard candy, cough drops, popcorn, chewing gum, whole grapes, raisins, sliced sausage, raw carrots or celery, food on toothpicks or brochettes, popsicles, etc.

Rules to prevent choking

- An adult should supervise children eating.
- Sit your child at the table or in a high chair.
- Don't let a child walk or run with food in her mouth.
- No eating in the car.
- Keep dangerous foods out of reach.
- Ask older children to follow these rules.

Starting at about 1 year, a child can eat raw tender vegetables: mushrooms, cucumber, zucchini, tomatoes, etc. Grated carrots can also be served. Raw apples should be peeled and cut into small pieces.

At 2 years, she can eat raw vegetables cut into strips, whole peeled apples, and whole small fruit except grapes.

These tips will also help prevent choking:

- Remove bones from meat and fish.
- Cut sausage into sticks and then small chunks.
- Cut grapes into quarters.
- Remove the cores and stones from fruit.

Photo: Nathalie Gignac

Cereal at about 6 months (Step 1)

Iron-enriched baby cereals provide extra calories, starch, some vitamins, and minerals including iron, which helps prevent anemia. They are a preferred food until 24 months.

What cereals to choose

Start your baby off with simple cereals: a single grain such as rice or barley, without fruits or vegetables to limit the risk of allergy. Since oat cereals usually contain barley, serve them after rice and barley. Be sure to read the list of ingredients on the package to see what your baby's food contains.

Give your baby a few days to get used to eating cereal. Once she's eating several simple cereals, you can start with blends. To prevent allergies introduce soy last.

Preparing cereals

Start by making a thin paste using about half as much dry cereal as breast milk or infant formula. The mixture must be fluid enough to go into your baby's mouth but thick enough that she doesn't try to suck it down. With cereal blends containing powdered milk, add only water as instructed.

If your baby won't eat cereal

Don't insist if she doesn't seem to want the cereal. Try again at later meals for a day or two.

If she continues to refuse, try to understand why. She may not yet be ready for complementary foods. She may also not like the food you are serving or may be allergic to it. If you think she is ready, try another kind of cereal. If you aren't sure, have another look at page 388 for the signs of when a baby is ready for solid food.

Don't add sugar to cereal. Too much sugar is unhealthy and causes tooth decay. To know what your baby's cereal contains, read carefully the list of ingredients on the package. Sugar hides behind many names: dextrose, maltose, sucrose, inverted sugar, glucose polymers, fructose, syrup, honey, etc.

How much to serve?

Start by giving your baby 3 to 5 ml (½ to 1 teaspoon) of cereal after nursing, once or twice a day.

If she accepts, gradually increase the portion from 5 to 15 ml (1 to 3 teaspoons) at a time, until she's satisfied. Don't forget, she's already had her milk.

The amount of dry cereal should reach 125 to 175 ml (½ to ¾ cup) per day toward the end of the first year. This will provide all the iron your child needs.

Homemade baby food

Homemade baby food provides excellent nutritional value. It is fresher, provides more variety, tastes better and costs less than commercial baby food. It also has only the ingredients you want. It may take a bit of time to make, but you'll soon see how easy it is.

It's best not to give a baby salted, sweetened or seasoned food. Also remember that she will digest well-cooked food better, although over-cooked food loses vitamins and minerals.

Buying products

Buy the freshest possible fruits and vegetables. Frozen products must not contain salt, sugar, sauce or seasoning. Meat must be lean and of good quality. It is best not to buy preserved vegetables, meat or fish that has been salted. You can use preserved fruit if it is packed in real fruit juice.

Hygiene

It's important to wash your hands and carefully clean kitchen utensils before starting to cook baby food, and every time you change foods.

> If you know other parents with a baby the same age as yours, think about cooking baby food together to make it more fun. Local groups also operate community kitchens. Your CLSC may have details.

Photo: iStockphoto

Photo: iStockphoto

Photo: Nathalie Gignac

Preparing fruit and vegetable purées

Preparing fruit and vegetable purées is quite easy.

- Wash all fruits and vegetables before cooking.
- Remove the skin and anything else that should not go into the baby food: cores, stones, pips and seeds.
- Cut them into pieces.
- Except for bananas, cook fruits and vegetables in a bit of boiling water, a steamer or microwave oven.
- Check that they're done – when a fork penetrates easily.
- Run the food through a mixer or food processor in small amounts.
- Purée the food while gradually adding enough liquid for the desired thickness.
- If possible, use the cooking water as your liquid.
- For carrots, use fresh water, not the cooking water.
- Add liquid to fruits only as needed.
- Don't add sugar, salt, butter or other seasonings during or after cooking.

Preparing meat purées

Special care is required when cooking meat for baby-food purées.

- Remove the skin from poultry and any visible fat from meat.
- Cut the poultry or meat into pieces.
- Cook it in plenty of water. Meat is cooked enough when it can be cut with the edge of a fork.
- For extra flavour, add vegetables (onions, celery or carrots) halfway through cooking.
- Put the meat or poultry through a blender without the vegetables.
- Purée the meat or poultry while adding enough cooking liquid for the desired thickness.
- Don't add salt or other seasonings during or after cooking.

Salt and other seasonings are not recommended during or after cooking. Salt can contribute to high blood pressure and can overload your child's kidneys, increasing the danger of dehydration.

Freezing homemade baby food

If possible, freeze the food immediately after cooking.

- Pour the lukewarm purée into ice-cube moulds.
- Cover and cool in the refrigerator.
- Put the moulds in the freezer for 8 to 12 hours.
- Remove purée cubes from the moulds and put them in a plastic freezer bag.
- Squeeze out the air.
- Write the type of food and date on the bag and put it back in the freezer.

Preserving homemade baby food

Type of food	Refrigerator	Freezer
Fruits, vegetables	2 - 3 days	6 - 8 months
Meat, poultry, fish	1 - 2 days	1 - 2 months
Meat with vegetables	1 - 2 days	1 - 2 months

▶ **Note:** Do not refreeze thawed food.

Commercial baby food

Commercial baby food, frozen or in jars, has good nutritional value. It is handy and always ready to serve, but costs much more than homemade purées. Commercial baby food may also have needless ingredients such as starch, sugar, flour, tapioca, cream, etc. Read the ingredient list on the package to help choose simple foods without needless additives.

- **Meat-vegetable blends** are sometimes practical, although they usually contain little meat, especially those in small jars. Frozen products have more meat. Choose simple baby foods to control the amount of meat your baby eats, and give her the vegetables you want.
- **"Junior" foods** are purées containing small chunks to help in the transition from baby food to the family menu. As soon as she is ready, serve your baby some foods in chunks or mashed with a fork, so she can learn to chew.
- **Ready-to-serve meals** contain salt and must not be given to children under 12 months old. By then they are of little use because your child can share the family menu.

Mother hen
A COMPLETE LINE OF NATURAL & ORGANIC BABY FOOD
27 VARIETIES OF PUREES FOR BEGINNERS AND JUNIORS
JUST LIKE YOU,
MOTHER HEN WANTS THE BEST FOR YOUR CHILD
HOMESTYLE
• PREPARED FROM HOMESTYLE RECIPES
• NATURAL & ORGANIC INGREDIENTS
• NO PRESERVATIVES
QUICK-FROZEN
• PRESERVES FOOD TEXTURE
• KEEPS ITS FLAVOR AND NUTRIENTS
PRACTICAL
• COMPLETE LINE OF PUREES AND TODDLER MEALS
• EASY TO HEAT AND SERVE
• AVAILABLE IN DRUGSTORES AND SUPERMARKETS
No added sugar
Homestyle Recipe
No added salt
Beginner
Junior
1 866 852-5858 • www.motherhen.ca

Handling commercial baby food

Here are some steps to prevent any chance of food poisoning with commercial baby food.

- Throw out or take back to the store any jars with rusted lids, chipped glass or that don't "pop" when opened.
- Store unopened jars in order of best-before date and use the oldest ones first.
- Check the colour code or other manufacturer's indicators, but keep in mind that they do not always meet current recommendations or your baby's individual needs.
- Don't feed your baby right from the jar.

Put the amount you will use in a little bowl and put the rest back in the refrigerator right away. Commercial baby food can be kept in the refrigerator for 3 days. Some of it can be frozen.

Fresh or refrigerated purées

Serve fresh or refrigerated purées as follows:

- Put the purée in a small pot or double boiler.
- Heat the purée over low on the stove.
- Put a small amount of purée in a glass bowl and let it warm slowly in hot water.

Warming up baby food

Whenever possible, don't heat any more baby food than you need. Before giving it to your baby, always test the temperature on the inside of your wrist or the back of your hand. To prevent contamination, never keep leftover heated baby food.

Frozen baby food

You can heat cubes of frozen purée for a few minutes in the double boiler.

Explain the procedure to other family members and babysitters, or suggest another way to heat your baby's food.

! Using the microwave oven

Beware of the microwave oven. It heats unevenly so food may be cold in some places and burning hot in others. To use it safely, take the following precautions.

- Heat the purée on a small plate and not in the glass jar, which might explode.
- Heat normal portions because all small portions become burning hot in a few seconds.
- Stir the food after it has been warmed.
- Wait 30 seconds.
- Test the temperature on the inside of your wrist or the back of your hand before feeding.

Fruits and vegetables at about 6 months (Step 2)

You can start serving vegetables to your baby a few days after giving her cereal. Start on fruit next.

As well as adding many new taste sensations to her menu, fruits and vegetables provide calories, vitamins, minerals and fibre. These foods are essential to good health and help regular bowel movements. Serve some every day.

Introduce your baby to vegetables one at a time. Wait about 3 days before trying another. Your baby must eat several vegetables separately before taking them in combination.

Photo: iStockphoto

Which vegetables to choose?

Start with the following: carrots, squash, zucchini, yellow and green beans and sweet potatoes. At this age, it's important to serve your baby's vegetables cooked and blended to a thin purée.

How much to give?

You can start by giving your baby 3 to 5 ml (½ - 1 teaspoon) of vegetable per meal, at lunch and supper. Gradually increase the amount to 5 to 15 ml (1 - 3 teaspoons), until she seems to be eating all she wants.

Nitrates in vegetables

Nitrates exist naturally in water and the earth. Some vegetables, such as carrots, beets, turnips and especially spinach, contain more than others. Consumed in normal amounts, nitrates in food and water don't cause health problems. But in certain conditions they change into nitrites, which can hamper the movement of oxygen through the blood. This change is more common in babies younger than 1 year and still more so before the age of 6 months.

If your baby has a varied diet, the vegetables she eats won't contain enough nitrates to cause health problems. It's better to be careful and wait until your baby is 9 months old before serving her vegetables that are high in nitrates, like beets, turnips and spinach. Babies love carrots and you can include them among the first vegetables you give. However, until 9 months it's better to throw away the carrot cooking water and blend the purée using fresh tap water.

Which fruits to choose?

You can start your baby on an apple, a pear, a peach or a banana. They can be served cooked and blended, except for bananas, which are served fully ripe and mashed with a fork. Don't add sugar when preparing fruit.

Introduce your baby to fruits one at a time. Wait about 3 days before trying another. Your baby should eat several fruits separately before taking them in combination.

How much to feed?

Start your baby with 3 to 5 ml (½ - 1 teaspoon) of puréed fruit after the cereal and vegetables at lunch or supper. Gradually increase the fruit portion from 5 to 15 ml (1 - 3 teaspoons) until she's no longer hungry.

Some very helpful advice

- Don't buy fruit and vegetable purées containing tapioca, corn starch, flour or sugar because they have less food value.

- Don't add salt or sugar to your baby's food.
- Give her water to help digestion and hydration.

Fruit juice

Like the fruit itself, fruit juice provides calories, vitamins and minerals. But juice has very little fibre. Introduce fruit juice to your baby's diet when she can drink from a glass or cup and is already eating fruit.

Recommended by the Canadian Paediatric Society

Never give your baby juice in a baby bottle or over a long period even in a cup because of the sugar it contains. This habit can cause serious tooth decay in early childhood.

Too much fruit juice can cause diarrhea. It should be served at room temperature in moderate amounts. It must never take the place of milk and other foods needed for a baby to grow and be healthy.

In the hour before mealtime, juice can spoil your child's appetite.

Fruit juice is not essential. Water is better for quenching your child's thirst between feedings.

Apple juice and grape juice are usually easy to digest. Wait until later for blended juice.

Photo: iStockphoto

Which fruit juice?

Buy 100% pure pasteurized fruit juice with no added sugar. You don't need to buy special "baby" fruit juice products, which are exactly the same as regular fruit juice but cost more money.

Don't buy drinks, beverages, cocktails, punch or fruit-flavoured crystals. They are not real juice. They have little food value and are made with sugar. Look for the words 'pure juice' on the label.

How much to give?

At about 7 months, a child can drink 60 to 90 ml (2 - 3 ounces) of juice daily at the most. During the first weeks, cut the juice half-and-half with water. A child about 2 years old can drink up to 125 ml (4 ounces) of juice daily.

Freshly squeezed juice bought directly from a grower and some refrigerated juices sold in grocery stores are not pasteurized and may contain harmful bacteria. Young children are very sensitive to these bacteria.

Meat at about 6 months (Step 3)

As with milk, meat provides protein along with certain vitamins and minerals, particularly iron and zinc. The body easily absorbs iron from meat. Your baby needs a small amount of meat in her first year.

A well-balanced vegetarian diet may be adequate for a baby but there is a chance of deficiencies, especially if the diet is strict. It's best to see a dietitian or nutritionist about this.

To help digestion and hydration, give your baby water after meals.

From 6 to 7 months is the time to start putting meat on your baby's menu.

How much to give?

Start by serving your child 3 to 5 ml (½ - 1 teaspoon) of meat at lunchtime for a few days. Then gradually increase the portion from 5 to 15 ml (1 - 3 teaspoons) at a time, taking into account her taste and appetite.

What meat to choose?

At first you can give your baby lamb, chicken and turkey. Then at about 7 months, try veal, beef and pork. At that age, you can put liver on the menu once a week. It's best to serve meat as a thin purée until about 9 months; otherwise she'll have trouble chewing it.

Spiced meats, raw or smoked sausage, ham and salami must be kept off your baby's diet. They contain lots of fat, salt, spices, nitrates and other harmful ingredients. Eating sausage can also cause your baby to choke.

At about 7 months, you can serve her well-cooked game meat. Be sure that the carcass was handled properly on site and that all lead shot was removed, along with any meat that touched it. However, the organs of game animals are not recommended, as they are often contaminated.

Flavours and textures between 7 and 9 months

Now that your baby has tasted food from all of the food groups, learning about the flavours and textures will be an important part of mealtime.

Beginning at 7 months, if your baby doesn't tend to choke, she can eat thicker, lumpier purées made quickly in the blender or mashed with a fork.

Babies love to chew. Be careful though since some foods can cause her to choke.

Milk

During a baby's first year, breast milk or commercial infant formula is the most important part of her diet. After 7 months, daily milk consumption will decrease gradually in favour of complementary foods. For breast-fed babies this decrease happens naturally.

Once all food groups have been introduced, milk can be offered before or after complementary food. Most importantly, give your baby everything she needs in terms of food value. Some parents split the milk in two. They give milk first, followed by complementary food. Then they wait a little before finishing the meal with the rest of the milk.

> *You know your baby well, so choose what works best for her and allows her to get the amount of milk she needs.*

Cereal

At this age, you should give your child iron-enriched baby cereal each day. You can also serve her soy and mixed cereals.

Around 9 months of age, she should eat enough cereal in the morning, about 125 ml (½ cup), to satisfy her daily needs. You no longer have to feed her cereal at supper.

Vegetables

Your baby already eats some vegetables. You can now add new vegetables to her diet: cauliflower, broccoli, asparagus, peas, potatoes, corn, Brussel sprouts, avocado, etc.

Go ahead and make thicker purées. For variety, mix vegetables that she's already tried.

Around 8 or 9 months, you can cut the vegetables prepared for the rest of the family into small pieces and serve them to her, as long as they have been cooked without salt. Wait until your baby is 9 months old before serving her spinach, turnips and beets.

At 8 or 9 months of age, you can encourage her to eat small pieces of soft foods with her hands, like well-cooked vegetables or ripe or canned fruit. No need to wait until she has teeth; she can chew with her gums.

Photo: Mireille Simard

Fruits and juice

At this age, your baby is already eating fruit. You can introduce new fruits: plums, apricots, nectarines and pineapple. Mix together the ones she likes.

Gradually feed her fruit that's been mashed with a fork. Ripe fruits can be cut into pieces and eaten with her hands.

Berries like strawberries, blueberries, raspberries, blackberries and gooseberries should always be puréed and strained to remove the skins and seeds. Pre-strained purées are available in jars but they contain needless ingredients like sugar and starch.

To avoid spoiling your baby's appetite, do not give her more than 60 to 90 ml (2 - 3 ounces) of juice per day in a glass or cup. If she's thirsty at bedtime, offer her water.

Egg yolk

You can give your baby egg yolk at this age if she's already eating meat. It must be fully cooked, never raw or runny. Hard boil the egg to easily separate the yolk from the white.

Legumes and tofu

To replace meat, you can start giving your baby legumes or tofu. Red and orange lentils are the easiest to purée. Soft tofu can be puréed and mixed with puréed vegetables.

How much to give?

You can begin by giving your baby 5 ml (1 teaspoon) of egg yolk mixed with a bit of milk or added to cereal or vegetables. Increase the quantity to about 3 egg yolks per week. **Wait until your baby is 12 months old before offering her a whole egg**, since egg whites are more likely to cause allergies than the yolks.

Photo: iStockphoto

Fish

Fish is a healthy food. It contains proteins and essential fats. Unless fish is not recommended for your baby, you can start serving it to her a few weeks after introducing meat.

Recommended by the Canadian Paediatric Society

Shellfish (shrimp, crab, lobster) present a high allergy risk. Avoid them until your child is at least 1 year old.

What type to choose?

When your baby is 7 months old, you can offer her new species of fish:

- Commercial fish: haddock, pollock, cod, halibut (turbot), plaice (sole) and salmon;
- Game fish: shad, lake whitefish, brook and other trout, American (rainbow) smelt, salmon and tomcod.

You can buy fresh or frozen fish. It is best not to serve your baby canned fish as it is usually very salty. Unsalted canned tuna and salmon are available. You can serve them occasionally.

Some species of fish may contain pollutants. For this reason you should:

- choose light canned tuna over white canned tuna;
- only eat swordfish, shark and tuna once a month, regardless of whether it is fresh or frozen;
- only eat bass, pike, wall-eyed pike, muskellunge or lake trout (grey trout) occasionally. If you eat game fish regularly, you should find out about the contamination level of the fish based on where they were fished as well as the recommended frequency for eating them. Consult the Guide de consommation du poisson de pêche sportive en eau douce (www.mddep.gouv.qc.ca/eau/guide) or call the ministère du Développement durable, de l'Environnement et des Parcs at 418 521-3830 or 1 800 561-1616.

Preparing fish

Fish is not sold puréed so you will have to take a few precautions while preparing it yourself.

- Cook the fish in a court-bouillon, poach it in milk or cook it in the microwave, without adding salt.
- Carefully remove all bones.
- Break up the fish with a fork or purée it with the cooking liquid.

! Avoid raw fish since young children are more sensitive to the parasites they may contain.

Less sugar,
just as yummy yummy.
Yoplait
Minigo
FRAISES - BANANES
STRAWBERRY - BANANA
NOW
25%
LESS
SUGAR

SOURCE OF
CALCIUM
GOOD SOURCE OF
VITAMIN D
GOOD SOURCE OF
PROTEIN
NO PRESERVATIVES
NOW 25% LESS SUGAR
Yoplait
Minigo
FRAISES - BANANES
STRAWBERRY - BANANA
Now
every Minigo
contains
25% less sugar
for 100%
deliciousness.
Yoplait
Minigo
yoplait.ca

Independence from 9 to 12 months

Your baby is eating with her fingers. Encourage her – she's learning to feed herself. And she's becoming more independent!

It's a good idea to serve part of her meals in small pieces. Of course, it's messier and will take her longer to eat but this phase will last only a few months.

While keeping an eye on her, let her eat dry foods like toast, rusks and breadsticks. Don't give her raw, hard foods like carrots and celery because she could choke. If she's teething and needs to chew, give her a teething ring.

It's possible that at this stage when she's starting to feed herself, she will eat less. Don't insist. Mealtime will be more pleasant for the whole family, and your child will learn to be guided by her appetite. Trust her, she knows when she's full.

The importance of milk

At this age, milk is still the most important part of her diet. Breast milk is the best choice. You can continue to breast-feed her as often as you like. If she drinks commercial infant formula, make sure she gets enough to satisfy her needs, about 750 ml (25 ounces) each day. Whenever possible, hold your baby when she is drinking to offer her warm, reassuring contact. She should never fall asleep with her bottle, as this promotes cavities.

Photo: iStockphoto

Because cow's milk contains many proteins and minerals, you shouldn't give your baby more than **900 ml (30 ounces)** a day.

Cow's milk at 9 or 12 months?

Your baby can begin to drink cow's milk at the age of 9 months, provided that her diet is varied. She should now be eating:

- vegetables, fruits and meat every day;
- at least 125 ml (½ cup) of iron-enriched baby cereal;
- foods prepared with a bit of oil or non-hydrogenated margarine to satisfy her need for essential fatty acids. If she's not yet eating all these foods, wait until she is 12 months old before giving her cow's milk.

At this age, 3.25% M.F. whole cow's milk is recommended for your baby, either:

- regular, vitamin-D enriched homogenized milk; or
- unsweetened, canned evaporated milk, enriched with vitamins C and D, which must be diluted with an equal amount of water.

Cow's milk should be introduced gradually over a period of about 2 weeks. You can begin by replacing some breast milk or commercial infant formula with cow's milk. Gradually increase the proportion of new milk at each feeding.

Do not use 2% or skim milk

Young children need fat for their growth and the development of their brains. It's best not to give them 2% milk before the age of 2. You should avoid giving your baby 1% and skim milk.

You can continue to give your child 3.25% milk right up until she goes to school. Never give your baby sweetened condensed milk.

Yogurt

When your baby is eating from all food groups, around the age of 9 or 10 months, you can add yogurt to her diet. At this age, a serving is about 75 ml (1/3 cup).

It's best to choose plain yogurt and then add puréed fruit or pieces of fresh fruit. It will taste better than fruit yogurts that have added sugar.

Avoid feeding your baby low-fat or fat-free yogurt; she needs fat to grow and for her brain to develop. If you make your own yogurt, use whole milk (3.25% M.F.). Homemade yogurt is rich in vitamin D, since the milk it's made from contains this vitamin.

Unripened cheese with fruit (e.g., Minigo™ and Petit Danone™) is not yogurt. It contains more protein and calcium than plain yogurt and puréed, sweetened fruit. You can give it to your baby when she is 12 months old.

Cheese

Children usually like cheese. Around the age of 9 or 10 months, you can start serving your baby cheese that can be eaten off a spoon, like cottage cheese, quark or ricotta. One serving is 30 to 60 ml (2 - 4 tablespoons). Next give her hard cheese (mild and white, grated or thinly sliced). One serving is equivalent to 15 g (½ ounce).

Some people believe that cheese causes constipation. It will not be a problem for a child who eats a reasonable amount of cheese and who has a balanced diet.

Meat and alternatives

Your child needs a small serving of meat or an alternative at lunch and supper. A serving of 15 to 30 ml (1 - 2 tablespoons) is enough.

If she doesn't like meat, you can serve her poultry or fish more often or replace the meat with an egg, legumes or tofu.

At 9 months, she can begin to eat finely ground meat. Later she will be able to eat small mouthfuls. You can begin with chicken, which is more tender, and then try red meat.

Legumes and tofu

Like tofu, legumes (chick peas, lentils and dried beans of all kinds) are nutritious and inexpensive. They can replace meat from time to time. They need to be well cooked, puréed or mashed with a fork. One serving is 30 to 60 ml (2 - 4 tablespoons).

Tofu can also replace meat. Purée soft tofu and crumble or dice firm tofu. Tofu can be mixed with vegetables to give it more flavour. A serving is about 30 g (1 ounce).

Whole eggs

When your baby is about 12 months old, she can begin to eat whole egg. Serve eggs hard-boiled, poached, scrambled or as an omelette. Eggs are a practical food and easily digested.

Your child can eat 3 eggs a week, or even more if she's not eating much meat.

Fruits and vegetables

You should serve your child a variety of well-cooked, unsalted vegetables cut into small pieces at both lunch and supper. She can now try spinach, beets and turnips. You can also add cooked tomatoes and onions to her diet.

At this age, it's recommended that you serve fruit in pieces at least twice a day, at dessert or as a snack: grapes cut in 4; pieces of orange, grapefruit or clementine; grated or slightly cooked apples. You can give your baby fruit juices rich in vitamin C, but not more than 60 to 90 ml (2 - 3 ounces) each day.

A variety of grain products

Once your child begins eating with her hands, you can offer her toast with butter or other spreads, pita bread or chapati, tortillas, breadsticks, unsalted crackers and all kinds of pasta, either plain or with a bit of sauce. Be careful with rice, because your child can choke on it. It's best to start with sticky, short-grain rice and to mash it with a fork.

Serving grain products at lunch and supper is recommended. One serving is equivalent to ¼ - ½ slice of bread or 30 to 50 ml (2 tablespoons to ¼ cup) of rice or pasta.

Continue giving your child baby cereal for breakfast until she is 24 months old. She needs it for the iron. If she doesn't like it very much, add fruit, make it with fruit juice instead of milk or try different flavours. If your child eats well in the morning, she can finish breakfast with ½ piece of toast or a few handfuls of iron-enriched, unsweetened ready-to-serve cereal (e.g., Nutrios™).

You don't need to give your child baby biscuits or teething biscuits; they're sweetened.

Snacks

At this age, your child may need a small, nutritious snack.

Don't give your baby coffee, tea or soft drinks. Never give her alcohol.

Your baby doesn't need chocolate, candy or chips and she doesn't need soft drinks. These foods have little nutritional value and some of them promote cavities.

★ You can give your child a snack about 2 hours before a meal: pieces of fruit, cheese, yogurt or Melba toast. If she seems thirsty, offer her water.

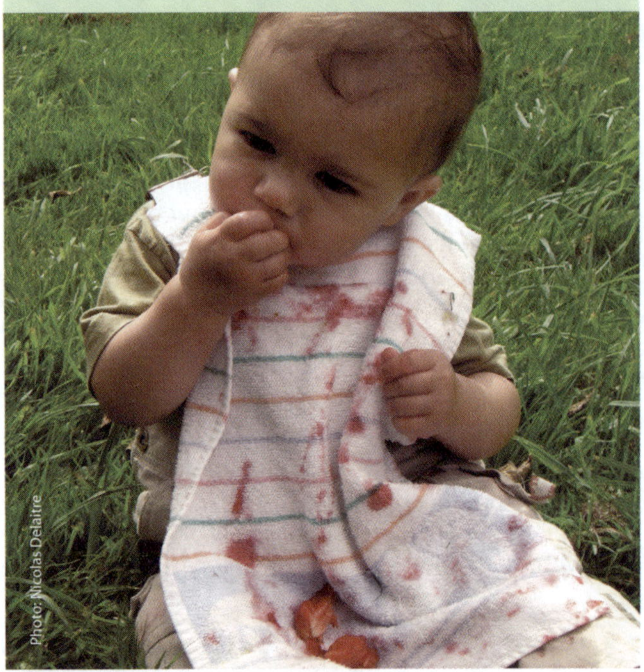

Family menu from age 1 to 2

Your baby's menu is now quite varied and includes almost all the foods your family eats. She eats her 3 meals with you and probably needs 1 or 2 snacks a day. You can start to give her foods cooked with a bit of salt.

By the time your baby is 1, her birth weight will have tripled. Her growth rate will now slow down a bit and her appetite will drop until the age of 5. She's interested in different games and her attention may be focused on them instead of food.

This change can worry some parents. If your child is healthy and happy, having fun and developing normally then there's no need to worry. But if you notice she's less active than usual, often sick or small for her age, you should see a health professional.

Making family meals easier

If your child is interested in the spoon you're using to feed her, give her another one to play with. Little by little, she'll learn how to use it. Encourage her to eat on her own and at her own pace, either with her fingers or a spoon.

Around the age of 18 months, she'll drink well from a cup but may tip it over when putting it down. Give her a little at a time to drink from the cup without major spills.

During mealtime, it's best not to expose your child to loud noises like the television or radio. They may distract her while she's eating. Present the food attractively, as babies love colour. Give her small portions so she doesn't get discouraged.

It's best to wait until your baby has finished her main course before serving dessert to the rest of the family. It will be easier to keep her interested in her meal, which is essential to her health. But don't force your child to eat everything on her plate. Her appetite will vary from day to day. Respect her appetite, tastes and preferences. You can adjust the dessert portion accordingly.

At age 2, your child will be more skilful: she'll be able to eat well with a spoon and hold a small glass in one hand.

Encouraging good habits

When possible, get your baby used to eating the same menu as the rest of the family. It's best to follow Canada's Food Guide (see p. 428). Your meals should include the 4 food groups: vegetables and fruits, grain products, milk and alternatives, meat and alternatives.

Some ingredients harm the health of both children and other family members. They are:

- salt;
- all forms of sugar (sucrose, glucose, fructose, etc.);
- fats and oils (shortening, hydrogenated oils, coconut oil, palm oil or palm kernel oil) that contain harmful fats.

Buy simple, minimally processed foods. Food labels can help you choose.

Breast milk is still an excellent food for children between the ages of 1 and 2. Don't hesitate to breast-feed your baby as often as you and she want.

Milk and alternatives

If your baby has been fed commercial infant formula, she can now drink cow's milk. Until the age of 2, she should have 3.25% M.F. homogenized whole cow's milk. Your baby should drink between 600 and 720 ml (20 - 24 ounces) each day. Part of the milk can be replaced with dairy products. A 125 g (½ cup) serving of yogurt or 30 g (1 ounce) of firm cheese replace 150 ml (5 ounces) of milk. Don't offer her more than 900 ml (30 ounces) of milk products a day because she needs to have an appetite for other foods.

Chocolate milk is a good alternative for children who drink little plain milk, but it has a lot of sugar. Ice cream, frozen yogurt and unripened cheese with added fruit are good desserts, even though they contain some sugar.

★ To meet her need for vitamin D, your child should have 500 ml (16 ounces) of milk per day.

Grain products

You can serve your child grain products at each meal, preferably those that contain whole grains: bread, pita, chapati, macaroni, spaghetti, pizza crust, crackers, rice, etc. Between the ages of I and 2, one serving is equivalent to 50 ml (¼ cup) of pasta or ½ a slice of bread.

Keep giving a 125- to 175-ml (½ - ¾-cup) serving of baby cereal at breakfast; it provides iron. Ready-to-serve whole grain breakfast cereals that contain little sugar can be offered occasionally for breakfast or as a snack.

Every day you should serve your child at least 2 portions of cooked or raw vegetables. At this age, a portion is equivalent to 15 to 30 ml (1 to 2 tablespoons). The most tender vegetables are tomatoes, cucumbers, mushrooms and avocado.

Now is also the time to give her ripe fruit cut into pieces. Be sure to remove the peel, pit and seeds. Try pear, peach, melon, banana, mango, kiwi or papaya; orange or clementine sections; strawberries or grapes cut in 4; peeled and thinly sliced apples; and puréed dates or figs.

Photo: Nathalie Gignac

Vegetables

Your child can now eat potatoes, which are a healthy food. She's also ready to try raw vegetables. Around the age of 2, offer her firmer vegetables cut into thin strips. You can serve the vegetables with a bit of dip made with yogurt or mayonnaise.

Fruit

It's a good idea to serve your child at least 2 portions of fruit every day. One portion equals ¼ to ½ a fruit or 30 to 50 ml (2 tablespoons to ¼ cup) of fruit pieces. You can offer her up to 125 ml (½ cup) of juice.

Meat, poultry, fish and alternatives

Some children already like meat cut into pieces but others prefer it finely chopped or even puréed. To help your child get used to eating pieces of meat, give her small tender and juicy pieces or, if you like, add a bit of gravy or sauce.

Your child will probably like poultry and fish – most children do. It's a good idea to offer liver from time to time, preferably chicken or veal liver.

It's best to avoid serving cold cuts (sausages, smoked meats, pâtés, salami, etc.) because they contain harmful nitrates and nitrites that are not recommended for your health. If you do serve them, choose the leanest, least salty, least spicy types. Some kinds of turkey breast are available without nitrites.

Peanut butter, peanuts and nuts

Peanut butter is a practical and healthy food. But more and more children suffer from a serious, permanent allergy to peanuts. When you give peanut butter to your child for the first time, pay particular attention to food allergy symptoms (see How do I recognize an allergy?, page 435).

To avoid choking, give creamy peanut butter only, spread thinly on warm toast.

Between the ages of 1 and 2, your child should eat 2 portions of meat or alternatives each day. One serving is equivalent to:

- 15 to 30 ml (1 to 2 tablespoons) of meat, poultry or fish; or
- 1 egg;
- 50 ml (¼ cup) of cooked legumes;
- 30 g of tofu.

Avoid giving your child peanuts, nuts or crunchy peanut butter before age 4, to prevent choking.

Healthy food guide for the whole family

Canada's Food Guide is a valuable tool. It will help you serve wholesome meals to your family by choosing a wide variety of foods from the 4 food groups. The new edition recommends the number of servings of each food group, beginning with children between the ages of 2 and 3. But it is meant as a guide. It's important that you adapt the quantity of food to the needs of your children.

You can order it for free by calling 1 866 225-0709.

Vegetables and fruits

4 servings

- 125 ml (½ cup) fresh, frozen or canned vegetables
- 1 fruit or 125 ml (½ cup) of fresh, frozen or canned fruit
- 250 ml (1 cup) of raw leafy vegetables or 125 ml (½ cup) of cooked vegetables
- 125 ml (½ cup) of 100% pure juice

Daily servings for children aged 2 to 3 as recommended by Canada's Food Guide		
Grain products 3 servings	**Milk and alternatives** Breast milk or 500 ml (2 cups) of milk (2 servings)	**Meat and alternatives** 1 serving
• 1 slice of bread • ½ bagel • ½ flatbread (pita or tortilla, etc.) • 125 ml (½ cup) of cooked rice, bulgur or quinoa • 30 g of cold, ready-to-serve cereal • 175 ml (¾ cup) of hot cereal • 125 ml (½ cup) of cooked pasta or couscous	• 250 ml (1 cup) milk • 250 ml (1 cup) of enriched soy beverage • 175 g (¾ cup) yogurt • 175 g (¾ cup) Kefir • 50 g (1½ ounces) of cheese	• 75 g (2½ ounces) or 125 ml (½ cup) of cooked fish, poultry or meat • 175 ml (¾ cup) of cooked legumes • 150 g or 175 ml (¾ cup) tofu • 2 eggs • 30 ml (2 tablespoons) creamy peanut butter or nut butter

Photo: Pascale Turcotte

Food-related problems

Colic

When a healthy baby cries very hard it may be colic. Colic is usually part of your child adapting to his environment (see Colic or excessive crying, page 227). But in some cases, colic is a sign of allergy or food intolerance.

Any baby may have colic. There are several possible causes for breast-fed babies:

- Some women have such a strong let-down reflex that the baby chokes while nursing and starts to cry, which causes him to swallow air.
- Most breast-feeding mothers can eat whatever they like. Babies aren't allergic to breast milk because it's perfectly adapted to their immature intestines. In rare cases, some sensitive babies may be allergic to food eaten by the mother that has "entered her milk." This may happen with a variety of foods, including dairy products. To check if this is causing the problem, the mother should avoid the foods in question for about 1 week, and then re-introduce them into her diet. The baby's colic may decrease a lot and then start up again when the mother begins eating the foods causing the problem. If this situation repeats itself, this means that your baby doesn't tolerate these foods. But if your baby's condition doesn't improve after 1 week, the mother can resume a normal diet. This means that her diet is not causing the colic. If your baby is allergic to milk and dairy products, it's a good idea to consult a dietitian or nutritionist to balance his diet.
- The caffeine found in coffee, tea and cola and substances in tobacco enter breast milk and can irritate your baby.

If your baby drinks commercial infant formula and has colic, it may be a sign of intolerance to the formula. But you should seek professional advice before changing the formula. Frequent brand changes are bad for your baby. Talk to your doctor or another health professional in case of this problem.

If your baby is intolerant to commercial infant formula, a lactation consultant can guide you through the process of resuming breast-feeding.

Regurgitation

Is your baby spitting up fresh milk mixed with saliva? This is normal. The valve that prevents food from flowing back into the mouth is not completely developed. The amount regurgitated may seem like a lot when it soaks up a cloth, but it's actually only a small amount of milk (5 to 15 ml or 1 to 3 teaspoons). Regurgitated breast milk is odourless. Regurgitation is a nuisance for parents, but normal for babies.

> Most babies regurgitate, some more than others. If your baby is happy and is gaining weight, there's no need to worry. He will probably stop regurgitating around the age of 1 when he's standing up more often.

What should I do?

Generally, if your baby regurgitates small quantities of milk, is cheerful and is gaining weight, there's no reason to worry. Sometimes when a baby drinks too much or is active, he may regurgitate. You can try to slightly decrease the amount of time he breast-feeds or the quantity of milk in his bottle, or limit his activities right after he drinks. The flow of the milk from the nipple of the bottle may also be the cause. If milk flows too quickly from the bottle, your baby will drink too much milk while trying to satisfy his need to suck.

If your baby has discomfort, is not gaining enough weight or regurgitates more than 15 ml of milk, it's best to see a doctor who can help you find the cause of the regurgitation.

Stools and solid food

A baby who eats solid food will have stools that vary in colour and consistency based on what he eats. A new food, vegetable or fruit may make his stools soft for a few days if the food is not completely digested. His bowel movements may also change colour. For example, a baby that eats green vegetables may produce green stools. Don't worry if your baby's diaper contains bits of vegetables and fruit. This is common and normal most of the time. You can help him out by mashing his food or chopping it up more finely.

Constipation

It's not absolutely necessary for a baby to have a bowel movement every 24 hours. After the age of 6 weeks, a breast-fed baby may only produce a stool every few days. Does your baby strain and turn red when having a bowel movement? If his stools look normal then there's no need to worry. But if your baby experiences pain and the stools are small, hard and dry, he's probably constipated. A hard stool can cause anal fissures, which will complicate the problem.

What should I do?

If your child doesn't have a bowel movement every day but his stools are soft, this is normal and you don't need to do anything.

If he is fine and doesn't experience any pain, even if his stools are hard, you don't need to do anything. But if he is suffering, a treatment may help.

In the case of constipation, increasing liquids for a baby and increasing fibre for older children is recommended.

For babies that don't eat yet

- Breast-fed infants are rarely constipated. If your baby is constipated, make sure he's drinking enough milk and see a doctor if in doubt.
- For babies that eat commercial infant formula, you can give about 15 ml (1 tablespoon) of cooled boiled water between feedings. If your baby is over 3 months of age, you can add 15 ml (1 tablespoon) of prune, apple or pear juice to the water. See a doctor if your baby is having trouble eliminating a hard stool.

For babies 6 months or older

- It's important to give your baby water.
- You should offer him more vegetables and puréed prunes, alone or mixed with other fruit. You can add about 5 ml (1 teaspoon) of wheat bran to his cereal.
- Around the age of 7 or 8 months, you can serve him mashed fruits and vegetables, and, later on, fruits and vegetables that have been cut into pieces. You can also give him whole-wheat bread.
- Around the age of 9 months, give him mashed legumes. However, don't give him too much fibre and make sure that he drinks enough. Don't deprive him of rice cereal, carrots and bananas: there's no proof that they cause constipation.

See a doctor if the constipation continues, if your baby vomits or is growing too slowly. Never give your baby a laxative without medical advice.

Helpful tips

- *Gently move your baby's legs in a pedalling motion.*
- *Massage your baby's tummy very gently in a clockwise motion, 3 or 4 times each day.*
- *An overly tight diaper can be harmful. Undo the diaper on one side and lay your baby on his back. He will expel gas and probably have a bowel movement.*

Food allergies

A child suffers from food allergies when his immune system reacts to a particular food that he eats. Some allergies are permanent and very serious. Your child is not being temperamental. A child with a known allergy to a particular food must never eat that food.

A newborn may be sensitive to foreign proteins like those in cow's milk (found in most commercial infant formulas) or to goat's milk or soy milk. Generally, babies become less sensitive as they grow. Allergies in babies usually disappear between the ages of 1 and 2 years.

How do I recognize an allergy?

An allergic reaction may be immediate, i.e. within 2 hours after having eaten the allergy-causing food, or delayed. Reactions that take longer are harder to diagnose. Check for the following symptoms:

- crying, repeated diarrhea, persistent constipation, black stools (blood in the stool);
- projectile vomiting;
- eczema, hives, red swollen patches;
- asthma, trouble breathing, swelling of the lips, tongue and throat;
- inadequate weight gain, anemia;
- trouble sleeping, irritability, rapid changes in overall condition.

Any child can experience these symptoms at times, but they last longer for a child with allergies.

Allergies to cow's milk

Up to 5% of babies react poorly to the proteins in cow's milk. These proteins are found in most commercial infant formulas. They may also be found in small quantities in breast milk if the mother consumes dairy products.

What should I do?

If your breast-fed baby is allergic to the proteins in cow's milk, it's best for the mother not to eat dairy products and to see a dietitian or nutritionist for help getting a balanced diet. If your baby is fed commercial infant formula, your doctor can prescribe a special formula. Your prescription drug insurance plan may reimburse you for the formula prescribed. Most children overcome an allergy to cow's milk between the ages of 1 and 2 years.

Soy allergy

Soy allergies are more troublesome since soy is used in many commercial products, including some baby cereals. To prevent soy allergies, introduce soy cereals after all other cereals in your baby's diet.

Allergies after 6 months

See a doctor if your baby shows signs of allergies after complementary foods are introduced. If needed, your doctor will perform tests to see which food is causing the problem.

If a food allergy is diagnosed, you must eliminate the food causing it. Consult a pediatric dietitian or nutritionist in a hospital or CSSS, who can develop a balanced diet for your child.

If you're breast-feeding, avoid eating the food causing your baby's allergy, only if he reacts to this food when you eat it. You can probably reintroduce the allergy-causing food to your diet later on. Your doctor will tell you whether your child has overcome his allergy.

Be very careful if your child suffers from a severe allergy. Carefully read the labels of prepared foods to ensure they do not contain the ingredient causing the allergy. At restaurants, ask for a list of ingredients.

For more information contact the Association québécoise des allergies alimentaires at: 514 990-2575 or: www.aqaa.qc.ca (in French only).

Preventing allergies

To reduce the risk of developing food allergies, give your baby only breast milk for the first 6 months of his life.

> ★ You might need an epinephrine injector (e.g., EpiPen™ or Twinject™) on hand for your child in case of emergency. The doctor can show you how to use it. Make sure that babysitters know how to use it. Have your child carry a card or wear a bracelet (e.g., MedicAlert™) indicating his allergy.

Is your child at risk of having food allergies?

Your child is at greater risk of developing food allergies if a parent, brother or sister suffers from them.

If your child is at greater risk, follow the normal order for introducing complementary foods while paying particular attention to the appearance of allergy symptoms. It is also recommended that you:

- continue breast-feeding beyond the age of 1 year.
- if you wean him earlier, give him commercial infant formula recommended by your doctor.

Lactose intolerance

Intolerance occurs when a food disagrees with a baby but does not affect the immune system. Lactose is a useful sugar that helps the baby's nervous system develop and promotes calcium absorption. When it disagrees with a baby, this is called lactose intolerance. Symptoms include stomach ache, gas and explosive liquid stools. Lactose intolerance sometimes follows a bout of gastroenteritis (stomach flu). It's rare among children and normally doesn't last long.

What should I do?

Breast-fed babies rarely experience lactose intolerance. If you're breast-feeding, you can continue to drink milk as it won't affect the lactose in your breast milk. If your baby is drinking commercial infant formula, see a doctor, who may prescribe a lactose-free formula to help your baby's intestines heal. Once your baby is better, he can continue to drink regular formula.

Anemia

Anemia is a fairly common problem among babies between the ages of 6 and 24 months. It needs to be treated since it can be harmful to your baby's health and growth. A child who suffers from anemia has trouble learning, sometimes until he reaches school age. Anemia can be prevented by having an iron-rich diet. No iron supplements are needed, except in the case of premature babies.

A baby's lack of iron may show itself in different ways. He may have little energy and a poor appetite, be irritable, have trouble paying attention, not be gaining enough weight or have repeated infections. These symptoms can also be a sign of another health problem, though. When in doubt, see a doctor.

Beware of cow's milk (3.25% M.F.)

A baby fed cow's milk before the age of 9 months risks becoming anemic because this milk:

- can cause blood loss in an infant's fragile intestines;
- contains little iron that is not well absorbed by the baby.

When your baby is over 9 months and eats a variety of foods, he can drink cow's milk without risking anemia. **He should not have more than 900 ml (30 ounces) of cow's milk each day.**

Preventing anemia

A full-term baby who breast-feeds only has iron reserves up to the age of 6 months. After that, he needs to eat foods that contain iron. If you wean your baby before 9 months of age, give him iron-enriched commercial infant formula.

A baby who is fed commercial infant formula will exhaust his iron reserves around the age of 4 months. To prevent anemia, it is strongly recommended that you feed him **iron-enriched formula** from birth until he is 9 to 12 months old. Other foods will provide additional iron.

A premature baby has not had time to store iron. Beginning at 2 months, you should give him a liquid iron supplement prescribed by your doctor.

Iron-rich foods

Your baby's diet should include good sources of iron every day. In addition to breast milk, the best sources of iron are:

- iron-enriched baby cereals (keep serving them until your baby is 2 years old);
- liver (offer it once a week only);
- meat (lamb, chicken, turkey, veal, beef, pork);
- tofu;
- legumes;
- egg yolk;
- dark green vegetables.

Vitamin C doubles the iron absorption of some foods. It's a good idea to eat foods that are rich in vitamin C at meals with or without meat. The following foods are good sources of vitamin C:

- citrus fruits and juices (orange, grapefruit, clementine, tangerine, mandarine, etc.);
- strawberries, cantaloupe, melons, mango, kiwi;
- cabbage, cauliflower, broccoli, Brussel sprouts, pepper (green, red or yellow).

If your child refuses to eat baby cereal, you can try different varieties or add fruit. If you can't change his mind, serve him cereal Os for children (Nutrios™) or iron-enriched biscuits (Farley's™). You can also add baby cereal to recipes (pancakes, muffins, biscuits, etc.) by replacing half of the flour with double the amount of dry cereal. The following recipe is an example.

Cereal-based cookies for babies

- 125 ml (½ cup) butter, margarine or oil
- 125 ml (½ cup) sugar or fruit purée (e.g., apple, date, banana)
- 10 ml (2 teaspoons) vanilla
- 1 egg, beaten (or 2 egg yolks, for babies under 1 year)
- 150 ml (⅔ cup) white or whole-wheat flour
- 150 ml (⅔ cup) baby cereal
- 5 ml (1 teaspoon) baking soda
- 1 small pinch of salt
- 30 ml (2 tablespoons) cocoa powder (optional)

Preheat the oven to 190°C (375°F).
Grease 2 cookie sheets. Cream the fat with the sugar or fruit purée. Gradually add the vanilla and beaten egg. Mix the other ingredients together in another bowl.
Carefully add the dry ingredients to the wet.
Shape into 24 balls. Place on the cookie sheets and flatten.
Bake for 10 minutes.

Poor appetite

Children, like adults, sometimes lose their appetite. This can be caused by illness, like a sore throat, teething, or the effect of medication. Loss of appetite can be caused by excitement, thrilling discoveries, fatigue or a slowdown in growth. Children aged 18 to 24 months will often lose their appetite.

True diet-related problems are rare. If your child is growing normally, he is eating enough to satisfy his needs. It's more important to make mealtimes enjoyable than to make your child eat a specific amount of food.

What should I do?

Take the time to see what's going on in your child's life and environment. As he grows, he wants to do more and more things on his own. Accept his clumsiness and a bit of wasted and lost time without scolding him.

Give your child small servings of healthy food suited to his age. Make sure to let him eat the way he wants, the amount he wants and in the order he wants. If he hasn't eaten anything after 20 minutes, simply remove his plate without scolding him or making a big issue of it, and let him play. Serve milk at the end of the meal.

Offer snacks between meals, but keep them small to avoid spoiling his appetite for the next meal. Serve your baby fruits, vegetables, cheese and water. Avoid giving your baby too much juice or milk between meals.

In some cases, a vitamin or mineral supplement may be a good idea. When in doubt, talk to your doctor or a dietitian or nutritionist to see whether your child's nutritional needs are being met.

Underweight babies

Do you feel like your baby, who is over the age of 6 months, is not gaining enough weight? He may not be eating enough for one of the following reasons:

- lack of appetite;
- illness;
- trouble swallowing.

He may be absorbing food poorly. A premature baby's growth should be assessed according to his adjusted age. You can check your baby's growth based on the growth curve on pages 454 and 455 and discuss it with your doctor.

What should I do?

A doctor should check to see if your baby is sick. His diet should also be studied. A dietitian or nutritionist that works in a hospital or CLSC can help. Remember that no vitamin or mineral supplement can correct a growth retardation.

Chubby babies

There is no evidence to suggest that a plump baby will become an obese adult. Most of the time, baby fat will disappear as your child grows. Don't worry if your breast-fed baby seems chubby during the first few months; it won't last. In fact, breast-feeding decreases the risk of obesity in children. Continue breast-feeding as long as you like.

Take the time to observe your child as he grows. Pay close attention. See whether food seems to stimulate, console or reward your baby. It's important to find out what he really needs and try to respond to it. Often his need is an emotional one. Try not to use only food to reward or punish your baby.

Tips

- Resist social pressure.
- Never impose a weight-loss diet on your baby, regardless of his age.
- Don't give low-fat or low-calorie foods to a baby under the age of 2.
- Help your child adopt healthy eating habits beginning at a young age.
- Encourage your child to do physical activity – get active with your children.
- Set a schedule for meals and snacks.
- Respect your child's appetite.
- Discourage nibbling between meals and instead offer water.
- Sit down as a family for meals.
- Don't rush meals and wait until everyone is finished before serving dessert.
- Avoid offering fatty and very sweet foods regularly.
- Choose special occasions to offer treats (e.g., a party) instead of denying them altogether.

Photo: Alain Ouellet

Photo: Marie-Andrée Lusignan

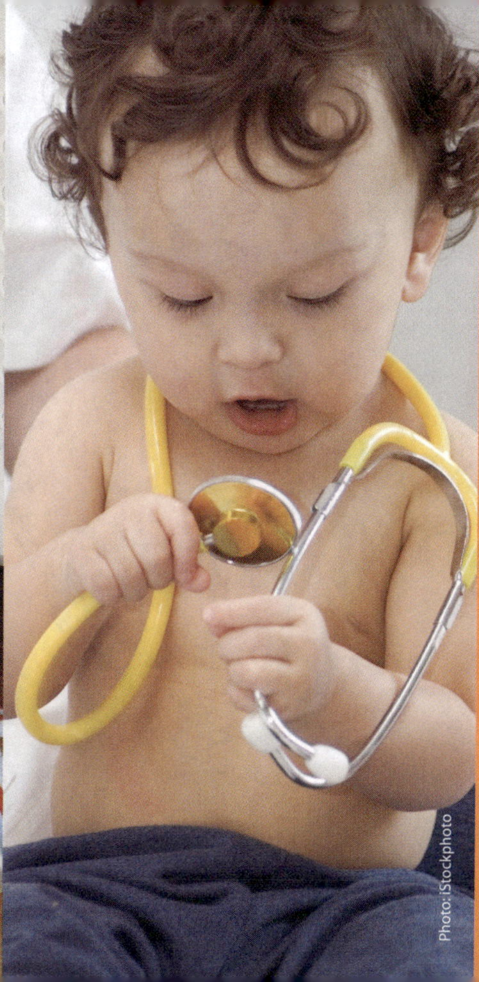
Photo: iStockphoto

Health

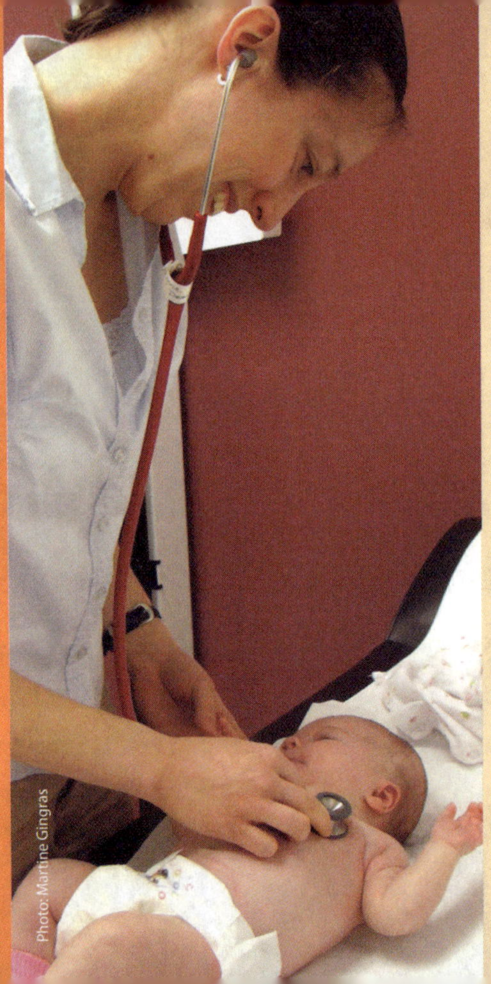

Monitoring your baby's health

Your baby's health is your responsibility

To grow up strong and healthy, your baby needs her parents first of all. You will usually know how to heal her little hurts.

But sometimes you'll need help from professionals. They can assist with health care and give you support and advice.

Who can help your baby?

You will meet different health professionals during your baby's early years. Family doctors, pediatricians, nurses, pharmacists and other specialists know a lot about different aspects of infant health and can be very helpful.

Health professionals are available to help you.

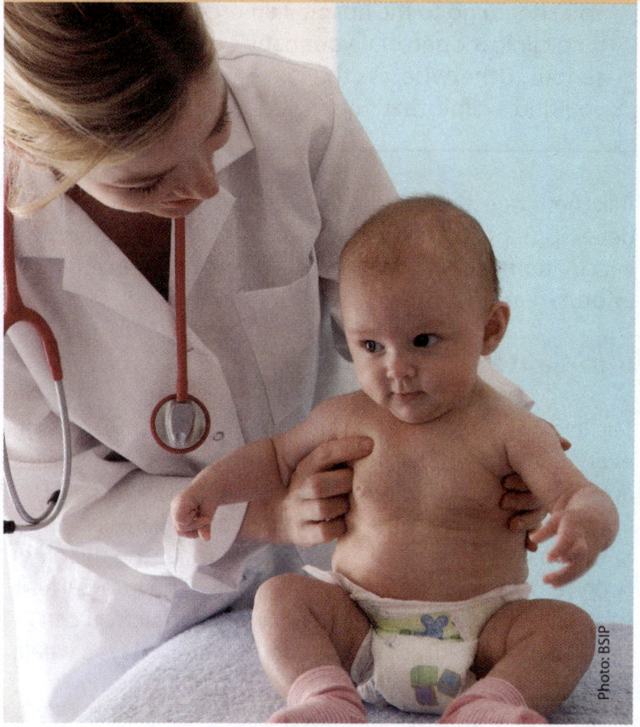

Photo: BSIP

Emergency – for emergencies only!
You should go to the hospital emergency ward only if no clinic is open or if your baby's condition is very serious. Otherwise, ask the Info-Santé nurse to help you find a clinic that's open.

Ask them questions about your baby's growth and development, nutrition, safety and health, including vaccinations. They will be glad to answer with useful information.

Info-Santé

The Info-Santé service is available through the CLSC network everywhere in Québec. To contact the Info-Santé service anywhere across Québec except for one region, dial 811. For the far north region (Terres-Cries-de-la-Baie-James and Nunavik), look in the phone book under the heading "Centre de santé et de services sociaux." The Info-Santé telephone help service is free and very handy. You can talk to an experienced nurse 24 hours a day, 7 days a week.

Depending on your situation, you will then decide whether to:

- See a nurse or doctor at the CLSC;
- Go to a clinic with or without an appointment;
- Go to the hospital emergency ward.

Family doctor

Your family doctor can monitor your baby's health with you unless there is a major problem. He or she will ask lots of questions during the baby's first examination to complete her file and get to know her better. Feel free to tell the doctor about any worries you have, and ask all your questions. The doctor's job is also to give you information and support. At every appointment, he or she will examine your baby and check her health. It's important to discuss your child's growth, development, nutrition, safety and health, including vaccinations. Your baby's health will be easier and better monitored if you always go to the same clinic. If your doctor isn't available, his or her replacement will always have the baby's complete file. You can also write down important notes in your child's vaccination booklet.

The CLSC nurse

At one time or another during pregnancy, most new parents spend time with nurses because they are involved in prenatal, birthing and postnatal care.

Nurses help in many different ways (see Services provided at CLSCs, page 72). For example, during the baby's early years, a nurse at a vaccination clinic or family medicine group can give her all the inoculations recommended in her immunization schedule. Nurses can tell you about the different types of vaccine, how they're given, what they're intended for, side effects and more. At the same time, the nurse will be examining your baby's health and providing any needed care. If necessary, he or she will provide support with breast-feeding, asking about your condition and referring you to the proper help, if needed. You can also talk to a nurse at any time, 24 hours a day, 7 days a week on the Info-Santé line.

Lactation consultant (IBCLC)

Only a few unusual situations call for breast-feeding to be discouraged or stopped. With the right help, breast-feeding can continue, benefiting both mother and child. Lactation consultants can help you overcome any problems you may have with breast-feeding. The IBCLC designation (International Board Certified Lactation Consultant) certifies that she has the required skills to work in this field.

Some health institutions offer the services of a lactation consultant. Many consultants work in the private sector, from home or in an office. To find out more or to obtain the address of the IBCLC nearest you, call the AQC (Association québécoise des consultantes en lactation diplômées de l'IBLCE) at 514 990-0262 or consult the Web site: www.ibclc.qc.ca.

Midwife

Your midwife can monitor your baby's health for the first 6 weeks. After that, you should choose another professional to examine and vaccinate her.

Pediatrician

Children with serious health problems should be followed by a pediatrician. If needed, the pediatrician who examined your baby at birth will give you an appointment or refer you to another paediatrician. If problems arise later, your family doctor will suggest who to see.

Dentist and dental hygienist

The dentist and dental hygienist can help your baby have a healthy smile at any age.

Optometrist

You should take your baby to an optometrist at about 6 months old to check her eyes and vision, then at 3 and 5 years old unless a problem arises. Optometrists are on the front line of care; they can diagnose troubles and prescribe treatment. Visits are by appointment but emergencies will be seen right away.

For more information, contact: Ordre des optométristes du Québec, 514 499-0524; Association des optométristes du Québec, 1 888 SOS-OPTO or see the Web site www.aoqnet.qc.ca/public/informations/laVisionDeVotreEnfant.php.

Specialists

If you think your child needs specialized care, ask your doctor for advice. Don't be shy. Every child is different and has his or her own particular needs. Specialists are available for you and your baby at the hospital or a private clinic.

Some children need the help of a speech therapist to learn to speak properly, while others may need to see a special-education teacher, dietitian-nutritionist, physiotherapist or occupational therapist, for example.

How to choose your child's doctor?

Ask parents and friends, and find out about health professionals. Pay attention to the doctor; how you feel about his or her care is important.

- Does she listen to your concerns?
- Does he introduce himself to your child?
- Does she call your child by her name?
- Does he smile and talk to her?
- Does she get down to her eye level when examining her?
- Does he let you hold her yourself whenever possible?
- Is she calm and patient even when the child is not?

If you aren't comfortable with your doctor's attitude or surroundings, see another doctor instead.

Bring a favourite book, toy or teddy to comfort your baby in the waiting room and during the appointment.

Growth

Every baby grows at her own speed. Changes come in spurts. Premature babies grow more slowly, but catch up by about 5 years old.

A typical growth rate:

- 1 kg (2 lb.) per month from birth to 3 months;
- 500 g (1 lb.) per month from 4 to 6 months;
- 250 g (1/2 lb.) per month from 7 to 12 months;
- 1.8 to 2.3 kg (4 to 5 lb.) from 1 to 2 years.

Babies usually double their birth weight by 4 or 5 months and triple it by 12 months. Premature babies grow a bit differently.

Is your baby feeding enough?

Here are some ways to check whether your baby is feeding enough during the first 4 weeks:

Elimination: Count the diapers used. After the first week, your baby should urinate about 6 times every 24 hours.

Weight gain: During the first 4 weeks, your baby should be gaining 20 to 30 grams a day.

Growth: To learn if your child is growing normally, ask yourself these questions.

- Is she gaining weight?
- Does she seem well? Does she react when you speak to her?
- Is she energetic? Is she a healthy looking colour?
- Does she seem satisfied after feeding?

If you answered "no" to any of the questions, your baby may not be getting enough milk or may not be digesting it well. You should see a health professional.

Growth curves

Growth curves allow us to compare the baby's measurements (weight, height and head size) to standards for healthy babies the same age.

A normal child's growth curve is between the top and bottom lines and follows one of the corridors.

The growth curves of breast-fed and bottle-fed babies are not the same. Breast-fed babies grow more quickly in the first 3 months and bottle-fed babies from 3 to 6 months.

First teeth

Your baby's teeth begin to form during pregnancy. This is one reason mothers should eat well. At birth, the 20 baby teeth are still taking shape under the gums, and your baby's feeding is already having an effect on how her permanent adult teeth will grow.

The first teeth generally appear at about 6 months, beginning with the lower front teeth (central incisors). They can come sooner and some babies are even born with one or two teeth. Some teeth can come in much later or may not appear at all.

Teething may go unnoticed or may cause discomfort. Your baby will usually salivate a lot and need to bite. Fever and diarrhea may be caused by some other health problem, not by teething. If the discomfort seems serious, contact Info-Santé.

GROWTH CHART

Weight-for-age percentiles: Boys, birth to 36 months

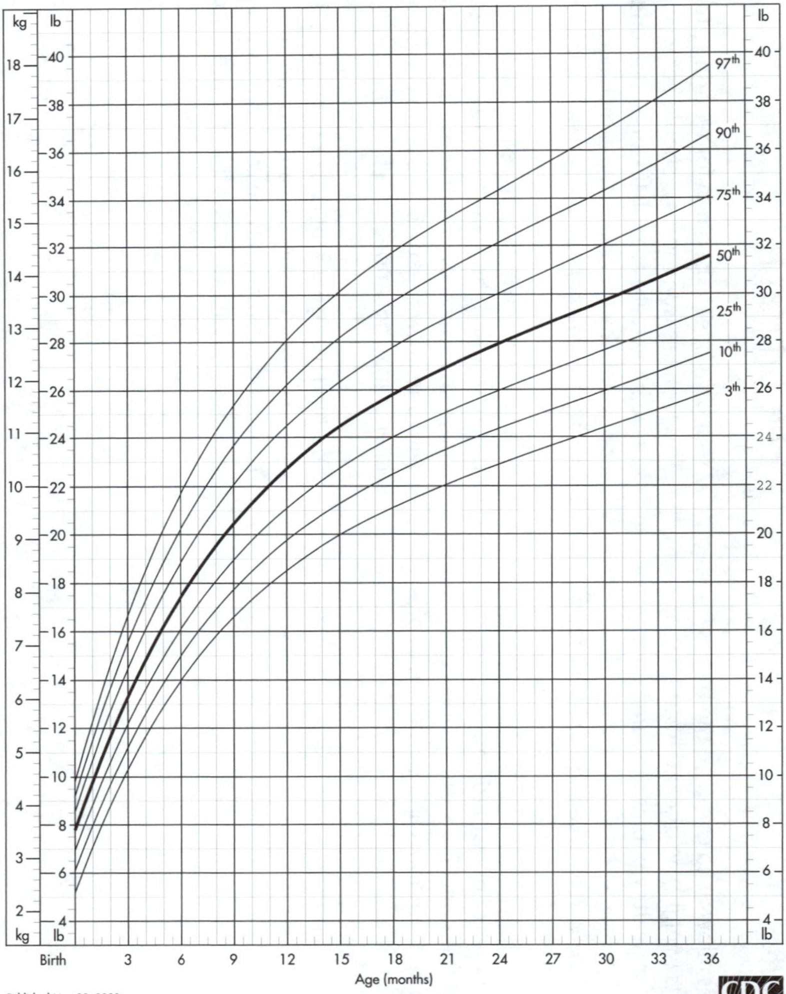

Published May 30, 2000.
SOURCE: Developed by the National Center for Health Statistics in collaboration with the National Center for Chronic Disease Prevention and Health Promotion (2000).

CDC SAFER • HEALTHIER • PEOPLE™

GROWTH CHART

Weight-for-age percentiles: Girls, birth to 36 months

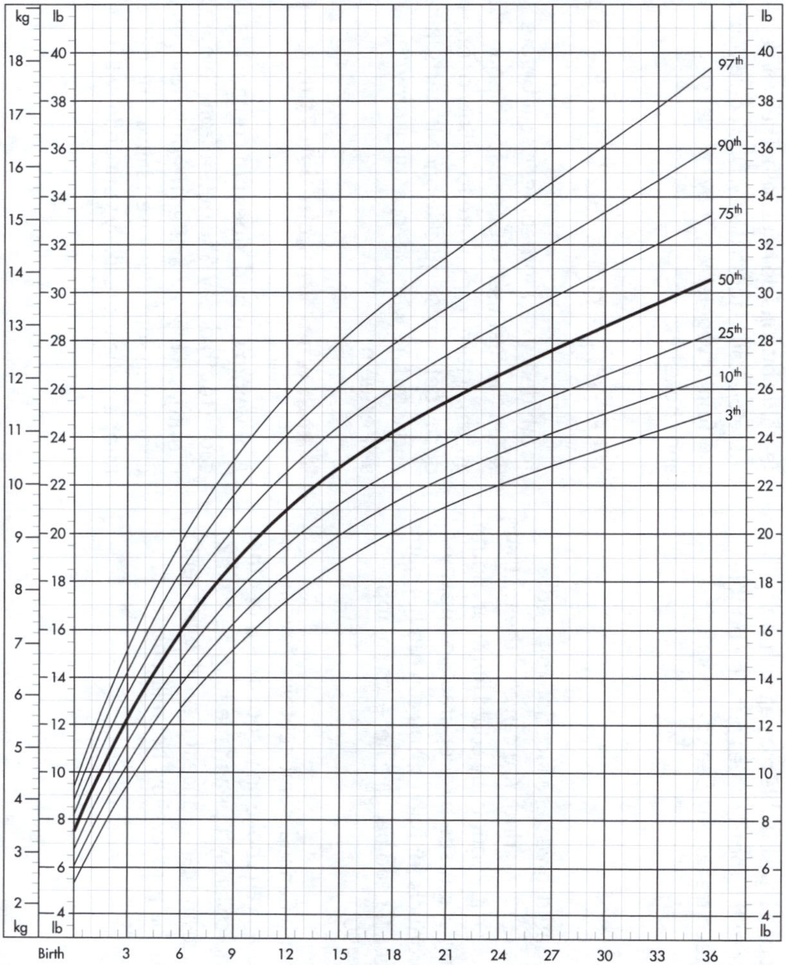

Published May 30, 2000.
SOURCE: Developed by the National Center for Health Statistics in collaboration with the National Center for Chronic Disease Prevention and Health Promotion (2000).

CDC
SAFER · HEALTHIER · PEOPLE™

An eruption cyst or a blue bubble may appear on the gum just before the tooth comes out. The bubble doesn't usually need treatment. See your dentist if necessary.

What should I do?

If your baby is irritated, give her a facecloth dipped in cold water or a teething ring. You can cool the teething ring but don't freeze it – your baby could hurt her mouth. Make sure the ring was made by a reputable company specializing in products for babies. You can rub her gums with a clean finger. If need be, give her acetaminophen (see Fever, page 490).

According to Health Canada, some teething toys are dangerous. Children can choke on wooden balls or other parts of a teething collar. Syrups and teething gels work only on the surface and can reduce the swallowing reflex, which allows your baby to swallow her milk and food.

Teething biscuits do not sooth. They contain sugar and can therefore cause tooth decay. Don't give your baby pieces of raw fruit or vegetables. They can get stuck in the throat and choke her.

Preventing tooth decay

Tooth decay can sometimes occur before 5 years of age, when the first teeth appear. Tooth enamel becomes dull and may turn from white to yellow or brown. Tooth decay gets worse quickly once it starts. It can be painful and interfere with sleep, eating, growth, language and self-esteem.

Watch what your child puts in her mouth

A newborn's mouth does not contain the bacteria that cause tooth decay. She gets it from things she puts in her mouth, such as a pacifier, utensils, toys, etc., and food containing someone else's saliva. The earlier these things happen, the more likely your child will have tooth decay.

Set an example

Take care of your teeth every day and see your dentist regularly. Parents' good dental hygiene will influence your child and reduce the risk of transmitting the bacteria that cause tooth decay.

Brush your baby's teeth twice a day

As soon as your baby's first teeth appear, you should start brushing them twice a day.

Use a very small amount of toothpaste with fluoride.

Photo: Nataly Lorin

A young child will be more likely to have tooth decay if:

- He drinks a lot of juice and eats a lot of sweet foods;
- His teeth are not well brushed every day;
- He lacks fluoride;
- Family members have lots of tooth decay.

The toothbrush

- Use a children's toothbrush with soft bristles.
- Rinse the toothbrush after every use.
- Let it air dry, head upward.
- To avoid spreading germs, don't let it touch other toothbrushes. Your child must have her own toothbrush and not share it with anyone.
- Change brushes as soon as the bristles start to bend.

Positions that may help in brushing your baby's teeth

- Sitting on a sofa or bed, or on the ground, keeping your child's head on your thighs;
- Standing up behind her in front of a mirror, her head leaning against you so you can see into her mouth;
- Lying your child down in a safe and comfortable place.

To brush:

- Push back the lip with your free hand;
- Hold her mouth open to reach the back teeth;
- Brush the upper teeth downward and the lower teeth upward, using a back-and-forth motion;
- Avoid sudden movements that can hurt the gums.

Your baby must learn – while you watch

Between 13 and 18 months, your child will become more independent. She may ask to brush her teeth by herself. Encourage her but keep watching. Children love to imitate you. Brush your teeth at the same time she does.

Before 6 years of age, a child will have trouble brushing her teeth. Parents must do the final brushing. Be sure to brush at bedtime.

Fluoride – excellent protection

Fluoride is a natural substance that protects well against tooth decay. For this reason, it's added to toothpaste and some drinking water, and is sold as drops and tablets.

Fluoride in water – Fluoridated water prevents tooth decay in all people, regardless of age. Some Québec municipalities add fluoride to their drinking water, and 8% of Québec residents use fluoridated water. Find out at your town hall or CLSC whether your water is fluoridated.

The amount of toothpaste – Put a very small amount of fluoridated toothpaste on a few bristles at the tip of the toothbrush by gently wiping it across the mouth of the tube.

Young children tend to swallow their toothpaste, and too much fluoride could cause white stains on the teeth. The amount used should be no bigger than a grain of rice.

A health professional may recommend you change the use of fluoridated toothpaste for children aged 2 and under, especially if your water supply is fluoridated.

Always keep toothpaste and fluoride supplements out of children's reach.

Fluoride drops and tablets – If your water is not fluoridated, ask your dentist, dental hygienist or doctor about fluoride supplements. If he or she thinks your child has a high risk of tooth decay, fluoride drops or tablets may be recommended, alone or with vitamins.

Beware of sugar

The more a child's teeth are in contact with sugar, the higher the risk of tooth decay. Be careful: sugar is often added to toddlers' food, drink and medicine. It also exists naturally in fruit, juice and milk.

In the baby bottle – Don't let your baby sleep or walk with a baby bottle or cup of milk, juice or other sweetened liquid. Don't use the baby bottle or cup to comfort your child. If your baby has gotten into this habit, gradually dilute the content until it is just water. One year old is a good age to finish with the baby bottle.

On the pacifier – Never dip a pacifier in honey, corn syrup or any other sweetened product.

In snacks – Serve cheese, fresh fruit and vegetables. Buy fruit juice with no added sugar. But be careful; all fruit juice contains natural sugar. Drinking a lot of juice could give your child tooth decay. Don't give your baby sweets between meals. Unsweetened snacks that don't stick to the teeth are best to prevent decay.

In medication – If your child takes medication, syrup or vitamins, clean her teeth or at least rinse her mouth well with water afterward.

As a reward – Don't use sweets, juice, fruit drinks or soft drinks to reward your child.

Look in her mouth often

Check the appearance of your child's teeth. Dull white, yellow or brownish stains near the gums may indicate the beginning of tooth decay. Ask your dentist or the dental hygienist at your CLSC.

Visit the dentist

Your child should first visit the dentist at about 1 year. The dental hygienist at your CLSC can also give you information.

The provincial health insurance board (Régie de l'assurance maladie du Québec) pays for dental examinations and some treatments for children under 10. A baby's tooth decay must be treated.

Vitamins and minerals

The only supplement breast-fed babies need is vitamin D. Mother's milk contains enough of the other vitamins and minerals needed for healthy growth.

Babies fed commercial baby formula don't need supplements. Don't give any to your bottle-fed baby even if you are given free samples. Commercial formula contains all the vitamins and minerals your baby needs.

If she eats a varied diet of healthy foods, your child will have everything she needs.

Vitamin and mineral supplements do not replace food – they can complement it. If supplements are necessary, buy only those the baby really needs. Don't give your child multi-vitamins without health professional advice.

If your child needs supplements, don't overdo it. Infants become intoxicated more quickly by vitamins and minerals than adults do. Read the label and don't give your baby too much. Measure carefully.

Vitamin D

Recommended by Health Canada

Health Canada recommends a vitamin D supplement for breast-fed babies.

The recommended dose of vitamin D for breast-fed babies is 400 IU per day (international units).

Babies fed commercial infant formula do not need a vitamin D supplement because the formula includes it.

Infants absorb a small amount of vitamin D from breast milk. So your baby should receive a supplement until her daily vitamin D intake from feeding reaches 400 IU or that she turns 1 year old. This amount is equivalent to about 1 litre (34 ounces) of cow's milk or commercial baby formula per day. Vitamin D is found mainly in enriched dairy products.

The best source of vitamin D is normal exposure of the skin to sunlight. Five to 30 minutes of sun a day will allow the body to produce enough. However, your baby should not be exposed directly to the sun. Moreover, winter sunlight appears to be too weak to promote the production of vitamin D.

Vitamin A

Breast-fed and formula-fed babies do not need a vitamin A supplement. Later on, milk, fruit and yellow, orange and dark-green vegetables will supply enough.

Vitamin C

Breast-fed and formula-fed babies do not need a vitamin C supplement. Once your baby is drinking cow's milk, which contains virtually no vitamin C, she will need a varied diet with plenty of fruit and vegetables to get her daily dose. For example, half an orange, 50 millilitres (¼ cup) of broccoli or 60 to 90 millilitres (2 to 3 ounces) of fruit juice rich in vitamin C will provide a day's supply.

Iron

Breast-fed and formula-fed babies do not need an iron supplement, but if your baby is fed another type of milk, she may need one. Premature babies also need an iron supplement; a health care professional can give you more information. Later on, a varied diet should be enough if it includes food with lots of iron (see Anemia, page 439).

Vitamin B_{12}

If a nursing mother is a vegan (she eats no animal products), her baby may be lacking in vitamin B_{12}. She should take a supplement to avoid this.

Fluoride

Fluoride is excellent protection against tooth decay. It is added to toothpaste and sometimes tap water, and is sold in drops and tablets. Ask your health professional before giving your child a fluoride supplement.

Vaccination is your child's best protection against some very serious diseases.

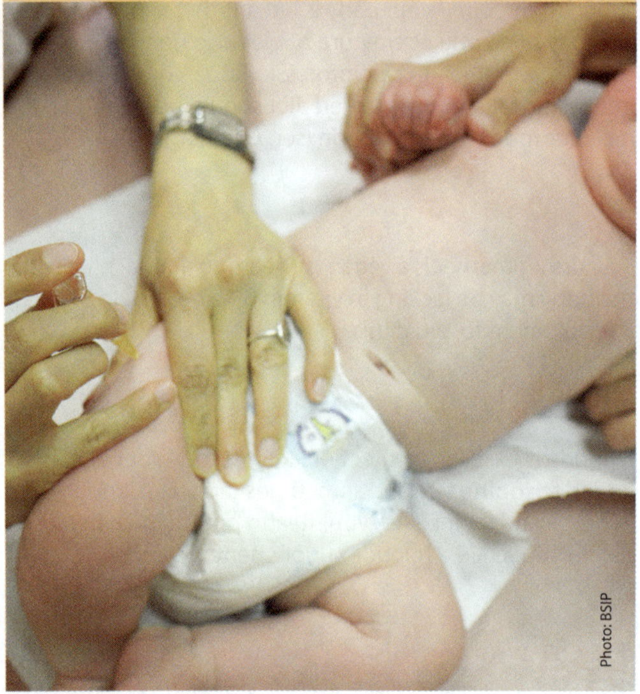
Photo: BSIP

Vaccination

All children should receive the recommended vaccines, even if they are healthy and eat properly. Breast-feeding protects against many infections but not against the diseases prevented by vaccination. These diseases are less common today, but they can still threaten your baby's health. Without vaccination programs, they would quickly come back.

Vaccination is safe and efficient. Millions of doses are given every year and there are very few serious side effects. It is better to vaccinate than to risk having your baby catch one of the diseases the vaccination can prevent.

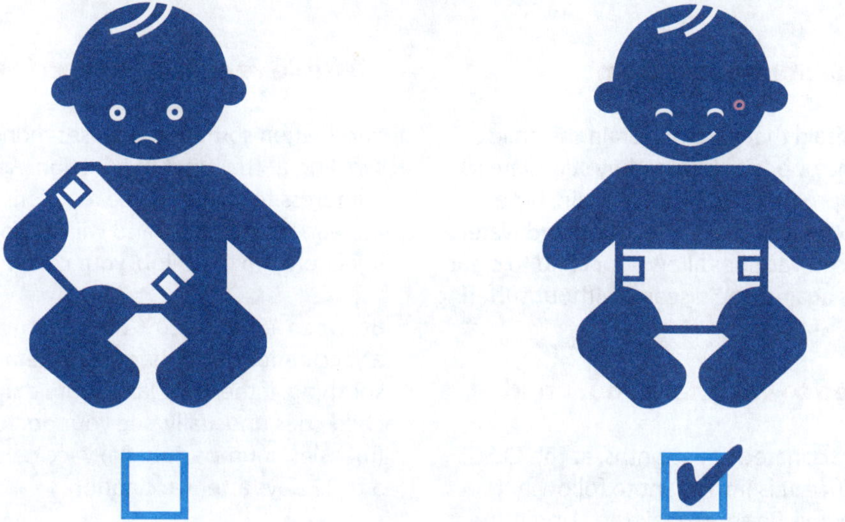

Vaccines and the immune system

Some parents are afraid that vaccines drain the child's immune system. The opposite is true: they stimulate it. The body naturally produces antibodies against the thousands of microbes found in the air, food and water and on many surfaces. Vaccines allow your child to create her own antibodies against the disease, without suffering from the disease itself.

Where and when to vaccinate your child

Your child can be vaccinated at 2 months, at the CLSC or your doctor's office. It is important to follow her immunization schedule. Be sure to take an appointment as early as possible in order to avoid any delays in her schedule. Your child must receive several inoculations to create enough of the antibody to prevent the disease. The best protection for your child is vaccination at the recommended age. If several injections are called for during the same visit, for the quickest protection against infection, they should all be given. This won't cause side effects to be more frequent or worse. It will also mean fewer visits to the doctor's office or CLSC.

Possible reactions to vaccines

Vaccination sometimes causes redness, sensitivity or swelling at the point of injection. Apply a cold-water compress to reduce these reactions. A small bump may appear. It is harmless and will last for a few weeks. If the injection is in the thigh, your child may limp for a while.

Between 15% and 20% of children have fever after a vaccination. If this happens, acetaminophen can be soothing. If the fever lasts more than 48 hours or your child cries unusually, see your doctor. The MMR II (measles, mumps, rubella) vaccine can cause fever 5 to 12 days after vaccination.

Serious allergic reactions are very rare. If your baby has an allergic reaction, it will begin within minutes of the vaccination, and the doctor or nurse can treat it right away.

For this reason you should wait for at least 15 minutes after the vaccination before leaving.

VACCINES

DTaP-Polio-Hib Combined vaccine	Pneumococcus	MMR Combined vaccine	Varicella Can be given combined with the MMR vaccine at 12 months	Meningococcus serogroup C	Hepatitis B and A Combined vaccine	Tdap Combined vaccine
Protection against						
• Diphtheria (D) • Tetanus (T) • Whooping cough (aP) • Poliomyelitis (Polio) • Hib infections (*Hæmophilus influenzæ* Type B)	Serious pneumococcus infections (meningitis, bacteremia, pneumonia)	• Measles(M) • Mumps (M) • Rubella (R)	Chicken pox (varicella)	Serious meningococcus C infections (meningitis, meningococcemia)	• Hepatitis B • Hepatitis A	• Diphtheria (d) • Tetanus (T) • Whooping cough (aP)
Recommended age for vaccination						
2 months 4 months 6 months 18 months 4 to 6 years (without Hib)	2 months 4 months 12 months	12 months 18 months	12 months	12 months	Grade 4 (2 doses)	Between 14 and 16 years. Afterward, back every 10 years for diphtheria and tetanus shots (d_2T_5)

Influenza vaccine – during influenza season. Children between 6 and 23 months.
Human Papillomavirus vaccine (HPV) responsible for the cervical cancer: given to all girls in 4th grade and 3rd year of secondary school.

Why not vaccinate

There are few reasons to prevent a child from being vaccinated. If you have any doubts, you should talk about them with your doctor or the CLSC nurse.

If your child seems sick to the extent she is cranky and cries a lot, postpone your appointment. Vaccinating the child at this time might give the false impression that she is reacting to the vaccine.

A child with a cold can be vaccinated right away. Ear infections, runny nose or taking antibiotics should not delay a vaccination.

Premature babies

The premature baby should have her first vaccination at 2 months old regardless of her birth weight or the number of weeks of pregnancy.

Vaccination booklet

This important document keeps track of your child's vaccinations. Bring it with you to record the dose and date when she receives a vaccination. It's handy to have with you for appointments with health professionals. You can also record your baby's measurements (weight gain, growth) and other information about the vaccination and your child's health. Take good care of this booklet; it will be important all your child's life.

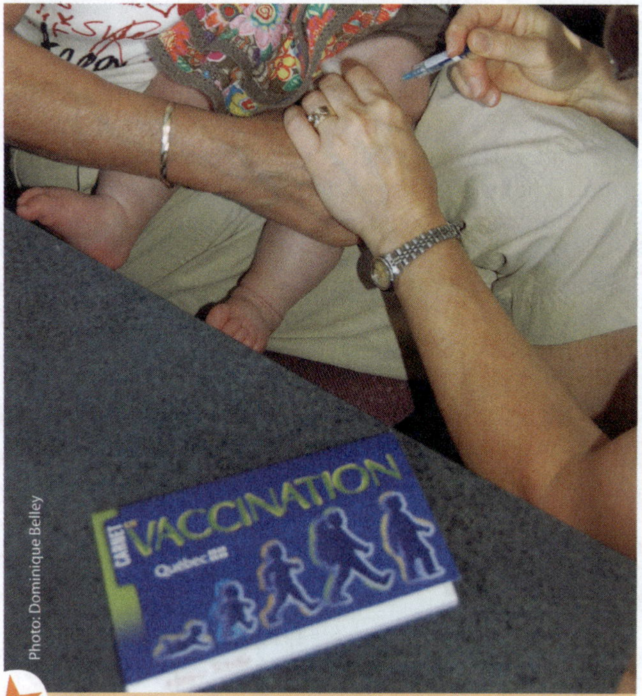

Photo: Dominique Belley

Bring your child's vaccination booklet to all medical appointments.

Contagious diseases

Contagious diseases are caused by microbes – viruses, bacteria, parasites and funguses. Vaccination is the best way to protect your child from many serious infections, especially in the first year. Vaccination has made measles, mumps and rubella very rare in Canada. These days, the most common childhood diseases are whooping cough, chicken pox, roseola (sixth disease) and scarlet fever.

There are several reasons that infectious diseases continue to exist:

- We have not yet found vaccines against some of them;
- Parents refuse vaccination, neglect it or leave their child's vaccination incomplete;
- Vaccines are not 100% effective.

If your child has symptoms of a contagious disease, in most cases you should see a doctor. He or she will make the correct diagnosis and prescribe any treatment needed.

This section deals only with some infectious diseases that children can catch in their first 2 years. They are listed here in alphabetical order.

Whooping cough

Whooping cough begins like a cold: a mild fever of about 38°C (100.4°F) and continual heavy coughing. After coughing, your child may have trouble catching her breath for a few seconds and then may produce a sound like a rooster crowing. The cough can cause vomiting and may last 6 to 10 weeks.

Whooping cough is a contagious disease caused by bacteria. It is very serious in children under 1 year. It is transmitted by direct contact with secretions from an infected person's nose or throat. Once a child is cured, she will be protected from it for a long time. There is a vaccine to prevent whooping cough but it is not 100% effective.

The incubation period is 7 to 10 days.

People with whooping cough become contagious a few days before the fever starts and stay contagious up to 5 days after treatment with antibiotics begins. If whooping cough is not treated, contagion can last up to 3 weeks after coughing fits begin.

Whooping cough can last from 1 to 3 months.

What should I do?

A doctor will prescribe antibiotics that, if administered early, can reduce the seriousness of the disease and its contagiousness. Have your child drink plenty of liquids. Keep your child away from smoke from cigarettes or any other source, such as a fireplace or wood stove. Talk to the doctor again if your child has difficulty breathing.

Keep your child out of daycare until five days after antibiotic treatment begins.

Meningitis

The symptoms of meningitis are:

- Fever,
- Fatigue,
- Stiff neck,
- Loss of appetite,
- Vomiting,
- Grouchy mood.

See your doctor right away if your child shows these symptoms.

Meningitis is caused by different viruses and bacteria.

In Québec, children are vaccinated against ***Haemophilus influenzae*** **bacterial meningitis** Type-b (Hib) at the age of 2 months. This type of meningitis is transmitted by an infected person coughing and sneezing, and by touching hands and objects that have been contaminated by secretions. Hib meningitis mainly targets children under 3 years old, but it has almost disappeared since Hib vaccine has been in use, and is included in DTaP-Polio-Hib vaccine.

Meningococcus bacterial meningitis was the target of a Québec-wide vaccination campaign in 1992, 1993 and 2001. Since 2002, the vaccine against this type of meningitis has been included in the vaccination schedule; it is given at 12 months old.

Another cause of **bacterial meningitis** in children is **pneumococcus bacteria**, which react well to antibiotics given at the very onset of the disease. Pneumococcus can be prevented by a vaccine, which is provided free in Québec for children between 2 months and 5 years old.

Viral meningitis is caused by different viruses. There is no specific treatment. It is not dangerous and normally has no after-effects.

Other forms of meningitis are also caused by bacteria. They show the same symptoms as viral meningitis but they can be treated effectively with antibiotics.

Roseola

Roseola triggers a high fever that lasts 3 to 5 days, then breaks. Small red spots then cover the face, neck and trunk. This contagious disease is caused by a virus. It is common in children from 3 to 24 months old.

We don't know how roseola is transmitted. There is no vaccine to prevent the disease but it is not very contagious. Once your baby has roseola, she will probably be immune for life.

The incubation period is 5 to 15 days.

Contagion probably lasts four days from the beginning of the fever.

Once the spots break out, your child is almost cured. In most cases, general health remains good.

Roseola lasts about a week.

What should I do?

There is no treatment. Give your child lots of fluids and use acetaminophen (Tempra™, Tylenol™, etc.) to reduce fever.

Measles, mumps and rubella

These three contagious diseases are quite rare in Canada and Québec thanks to a two-dose vaccine given at 12 months and 18 months.

Scarlet fever

Scarlet fever is an acute infectious disease cause by streptococcus bacteria, which produce a toxic substance. The first sign of scarlet fever is usually a streptococcus throat infection. Your child's temperature then climbs to 40°C (104°F). The skin is hot and bright red, and finger pressure leaves white marks that look like goose bumps on a pink background.

People can catch scarlet fever more than once. It spreads through droplets from the nose and throat of someone who is infected. There is no vaccine for scarlet fever.

The incubation period is 1 to 5 days, the shortest of all infectious diseases.

When a child has scarlet fever, she has a sore throat and trouble swallowing. Her tongue becomes the colour of a raspberry. Her temperature climbs to 40°C (104°F), and a rash appears on the neck and in the body's creases (at joints, such as behind the knees).

Scarlet fever is contagious for less than 24 hours after antibiotic treatment begins. Without treatment, it can last up to 21 days and cause serious complications. It's essential to consult your doctor or CLSC nurse right away.

Scarlet fever lasts for about 1 week. The skin will then peel.

What should I do?

See the doctor to check the diagnosis and prescribe antibiotics. Give your child acetaminophen (Tempra™, Tylenol™, etc.) to reduce the fever, and plenty to drink.

When a child has chicken pox, her temperature rises to 38°C (100.4°F). Red spots appear on the skin and turn into blisters full of clear liquid. These "pox" burst and dry to form a crust. New pimples appear for 3 or 4 days and become encrusted on about the 7th day.

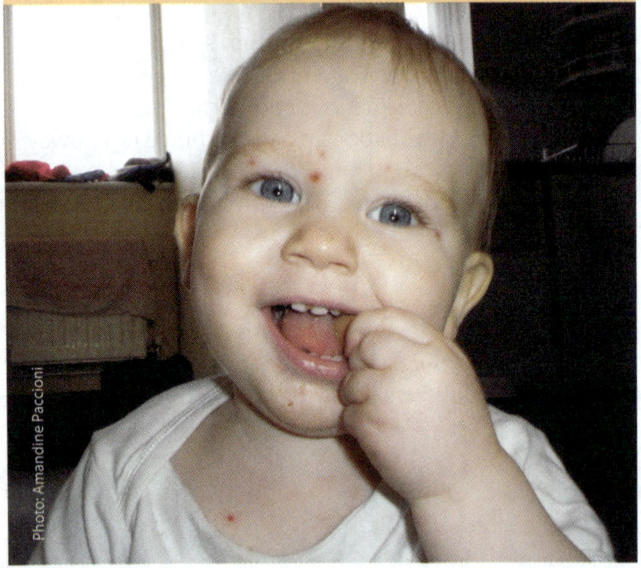
Photo: Amandine Paccioni

Chicken pox

Chicken pox is very common and very contagious but most people catch it only once. Catching it provides long-term protection. It's caused by a virus and is transmitted directly from person to person. The disease is rare in infants younger than 6 months. Except for newborns, childhood chicken pox is usually harmless. It's more serious in adolescents and adults. After chicken pox, streptococcus sometimes causes skin infection.

Beginning at 1 year of age, children can be given a vaccine against chicken pox, which is free in Québec.

The incubation period for chicken pox ranges from 10 to 21 days, averaging 4 to 16 days.

It is contagious from 1 or 2 days before the first blisters appear until up to 5 days later, or until all the blisters are encrusted.

The illness usually lasts 7 to 10 days.

Whatever the condition of the blisters, a child with mild chicken pox can return to daycare or school as soon as she is well enough to participate normally.

What should I do?

- If your child scratches herself a lot, you can put mittens on her and keep her fingernails short.
- Give your child lots of baths to sooth her. You can add colloidal oat flour (Aveeno™) or 50 to 60 millilitres (3 or 4 tablespoons) of baking soda to the bathwater.
- Acetaminophen will reduce the fever. Don't give her aspirin (ASA) or ibuprofen (Advil, etc.).
- Give her plenty of liquid: water, milk and fruit juice.

! Since chicken pox can sometimes cause complications, you should talk to your doctor if any of the following situations occur:

- The child's temperature stays above 38.5°C (101.3°F) for more than 2 days;
- A new fever develops a few days (the 4th) after the onset of chicken pox;
- A pimple grows, reddens or becomes painful;
- Growing redness around sores (possible cellulitis);
- Your child seems very sick;
- She coughs or has trouble breathing (possible pneumonia).

Health

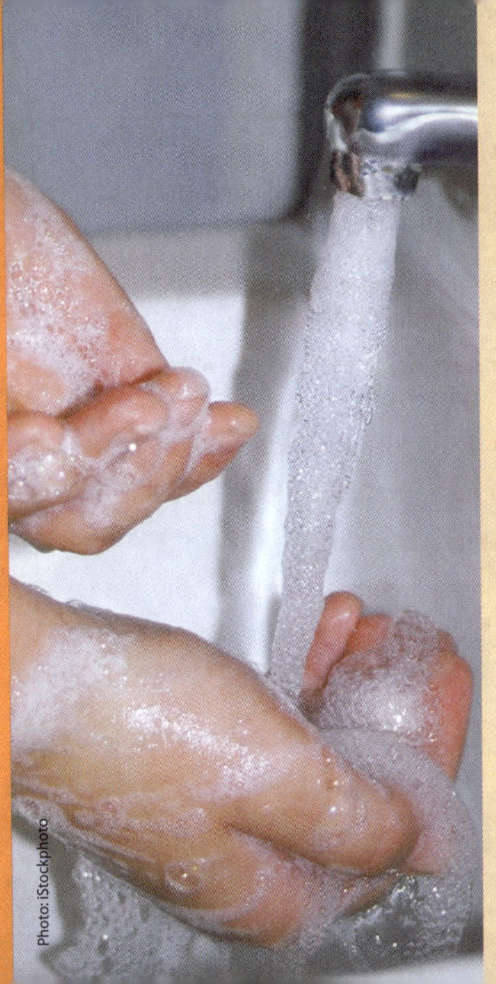

Photo: iStockphoto

Health Care

Thrush in the mouth

White spots, like curdled milk, appear in the mouth, on the tongue, lips, palate and inside the lips and cheeks. If the spots stay after rubbing them, they're symptoms of thrush.

What should I do?

Using a cotton swab, daub your child's mouth with medication prescribed by your doctor, nystatin, 4 times a day for 7 to 14 days. Gentian violet is also used for nursing babies. For details on this treatment, see page 345.

Thrush is caused by a fungus that can be prevented as follows:

- Each day, wash in boiling water all items that are in regular contact with your child's mouth: nipples from baby bottles, pacifiers (soothers), rattles.
- Buy new nipples and pacifiers when they start to be sticky.
- Avoid putting the pacifier in your mouth to clean it if it falls on the ground.

Cradle cap (seborrhea)

Many babies will have yellowish crusts or peeling scales on the scalp. This is due to an excess of oily secretions, sebum, or repeated poorly rinsed hair washing. Generally there's no problem, but sometimes they cause itching.

What should I do?

A basic shampooing can get rid of the crusts. Apply shampoo, rub it in and let it work for 10 to 15 minutes to soften the crusts. Rinse very well with warm water. If this doesn't get rid of them, apply olive or baby oil to your child's scalp. After a few hours, use a soft brush to remove the crusts, even on the fontanel. Shampoo with warm water, rinse and dry. Repeat the treatment if needed.

If there's no change and your child seems uncomfortable, a health professional can suggest a medicated shampoo.

Skin care

Newborns sometimes experience skin irritations, which have several causes.

Milium (white heads)

These are small white pimple-like bumps on the forehead, nose or cheeks. They're about the size of a pinhead, appearing after birth due to an excess of oily secretions being stuck in the skin's pores.

What should I do?

Don't apply oil, Vaseline, lotion or antibiotics.

Prickly heat

Prickly heat is a small, roundish, sometimes raised rash on the forehead, around the neck and in the fold's of the baby's skin. This is a normal reaction that happens when it's hot and humid and when babies have a fever.

What should I do?

Don't cover your baby too much if the temperature is hot. He shouldn't sweat. The heat rash will go away when the temperature cools down.

Intertrigo (redness in the skin folds)

This irritation can happen when two skin surfaces touch each other: underneath the chin, around the neck, under the arms, on the thighs or underneath the scrotum, for example. Wash and dry these areas well. The rash will appear in areas that are moist due to sweat, stools or milk, which encourages the growth of germs.

What should I do?

There's only one solution: cleanliness.

Wash the affected areas and dry well.

Diaper rash

The baby's bottom becomes bright red and stings when he pees. The rash is hot and painful… baby's not happy! The rash may reach the thighs, vulva or scrotum. Ammonia in the urine becomes acidic on contact with stools. Diaper rash is less common in breast-fed babies.

Diapers may cause the rash. Cotton diapers can be irritating if poorly rinsed or not changed often enough. Some scented disposal diapers are more irritating. You can sometimes solve the problem by changing the type of diapers.

Vaseline helps protect your baby's bottom, and non-scented zinc-based cream can help the rash go away.

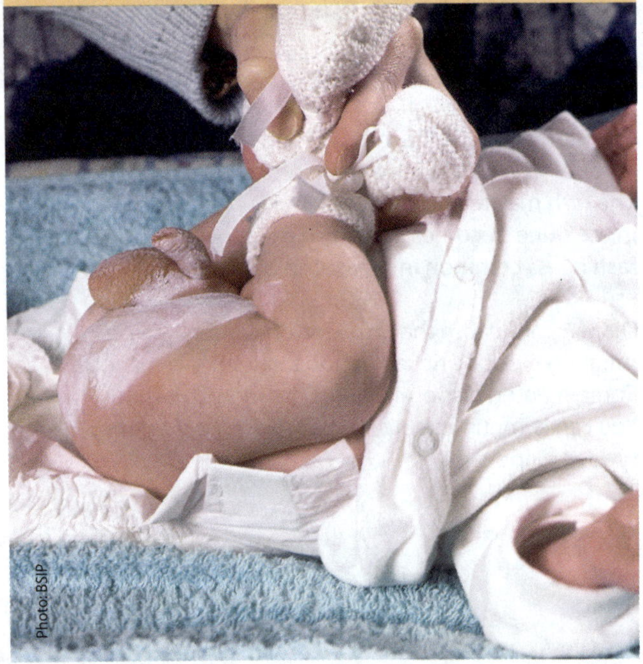

What should I do?

Change your baby's diaper as soon as it's wet or dirty. Wash his bottom with warm water that has a drop of olive oil in it. Pat dry; don't rub. Repeat three or four times a day.

Avoid diapers that are too tight and plastic pants; they keep moisture in and stop air from circulating. Use disposable diaper liners.

Let him go bare bottom for a while.

Wet wipes sold at the pharmacy are irritating and should be used only when needed.

If the rash doesn't go away after 3 or 4 days of putting cream on your baby's bottom, see a doctor. A fungal infection may be causing the diaper rash, especially if your baby has thrush in the mouth.

Dry skin

Your baby's skin may become very dry, to the point of peeling or cracking.

What should I do?

Use unscented soap to wash his hands and bottom only. He doesn't need soap for the rest of his body. Use an unscented moisturizing cream on his skin. Avoid foaming bath products. If the problem continues, see a health professional.

Hives

Very itchy, puffy, raised red welts appear on the body. Hives are an allergic reaction to a food, virus or bacterium, and very rarely, to a vaccine.

What should I do?

See your doctor, who can try to find the cause and suggest a remedy.

Eczema

The skin becomes red, rough and itchy, causing your child to scratch and become irritable. Eczema affects 2% to 8% of children. It causes sores that can reappear after being treated.

In young children, the sores appear on the face, head, chest, back of the arms and front of the legs. They sometimes reach the folds of skin at the elbow and knee. Children with eczema seem more likely to become asthmatic.

What should I do?

See your doctor for a proper diagnosis. He or she can suggest the right treatment, such as a lotion, cream or moisturizing ointment (Glaxal Base, for example), a bath with colloidal oatmeal (Aveeno™), or an anti-inflammatory cream or ointment with or without cortisone.

The skin of a child with eczema becomes red and rough.

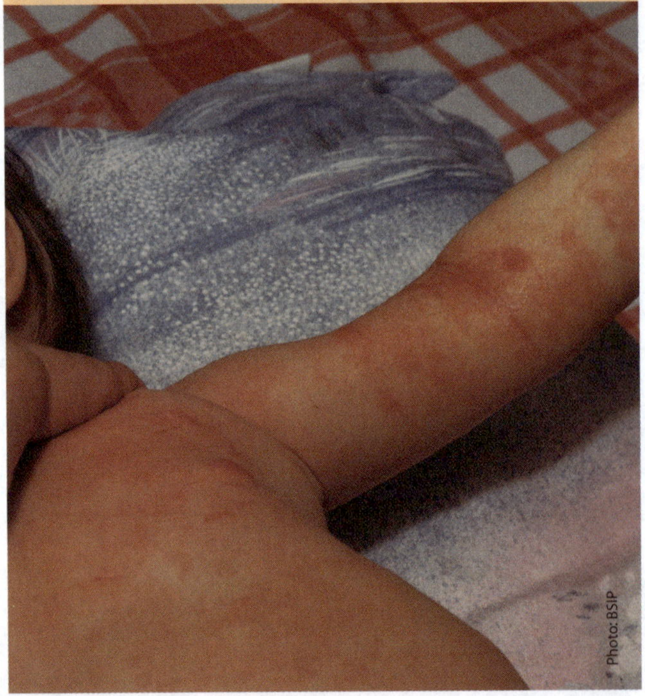

Photo: BSIP

Allergies

Allergies are a form of extra sensitivity to normally harmless or toxic substances, called allergens.

Allergenic substances come from different sources:

- Food;
- Tree and plant pollen;
- Animal hair;
- Mould;
- Dust and mites;
- Pollutants, irritants, cigarette and wood smoke;
- Medication, penicillin.

Allergic reactions usually affect the skin, breathing, digestion and eyes. The symptoms vary:

- Hives, eczema;
- Sneezing, runny nose, asthma;
- Vomiting, diarrhea;
- Red and teary eyes.

What should I do?

You should see a doctor if any of these symptoms appear. He or she will try to find the source of the allergy before suggesting a treatment. Anti-allergy vaccines are used only in severe cases.

Some children are more at risk because allergies are common in their family. In this case, avoid potential allergens as much as possible. Breast-feeding for as long as possible is strongly recommended. You can talk to your health professional to decide if some foods should be avoided, such as nuts, fish, seafood or peanuts (see Food allergies, page 435).

Prevention: hand-washing

The best way to avoid spreading infection is by washing your hands with soap several times a day.

You can't avoid germs. As soon as you finish washing your hands you start collecting them again: when you open a door, wipe faces, handle toys and change a diaper.

But you can lower the chance of infecting others by washing your hands before and after doing activities where infections are likely to be shared.

Parents

Wash your hands:

- BEFORE cooking, eating, breast-feeding, feeding your child or giving her medicine;
- AFTER going to the bathroom, taking your child to the bathroom or changing her diaper, taking care of someone who is sick, blowing your or your child's nose (if possible), touching pets, and cleaning an animal's cage or litter.

The best way

- Place your hands under running water.
- Rub them with soap – liquid or a bar – counting to 5.
- Rinse them under running water, counting to 5.
- Dry them with a clean towel.
- Use a moisturizing cream, if needed, to prevent chapping.

Children

Wash your children's hands as much as needed:

- BEFORE eating;
- AFTER a diaper change, going to the potty or toilet, playing outside, in the sand or with animals.

YOUR CHILD HAS BEAUTIFUL EYES…

BUT ARE THEY GOOD?

An eye health and vision examination by your optometrist will give you the answer.

This examination is recommended at the age of 3, or at any previous age if the child shows signs of vision problems or eye disease, or if there are hereditary issues in the family.

Eye health… It's important!

Association
DES
OPTOMÉTRISTES
DU
QUÉBEC

www.aoqnet.qc.ca

The best way

- First wash their hands with a clean towel, paper towel or cloth, with lots of warm water and soap.
- Rinse them well with another towel soaked in warm water.
- Dry well.

Eye health

In the first hours of her life, your baby will be given a dose of antibiotic ointment to protect her eyes. They may have been infected as she left the womb.

Her eyes may get infected in the following weeks despite this treatment. The symptoms to watch for are:

- Red or swollen eyelids;
- Yellowish secretions;
- Sticky eyelids;
- Trouble opening her eyes and looking at light.

Red, sticky or teary eyes

Nine times out of 10, when babies or young children have red or sticky eyes, it's the sign of an infection. You should see an optometrist or doctor, who can prescribe a treatment and medication, if needed. The infection may have been caused by bacteria: her eyelids are very swollen and there's a lot of pus and redness. A virus may also be the cause: there's a lot of tears and a bit of redness. Or it might be an allergy: her eyes are itchy, warm, teary and slightly to moderately red.

The infection may come with the flu, a cold or sore throat caused by a virus.

More than four out of one hundred people in Quebec suffer from amblyopic vision (lazy eye syndrome).

Amblyopic vision is a condition that stems from childhood and must be treated early to prevent serious consequences.

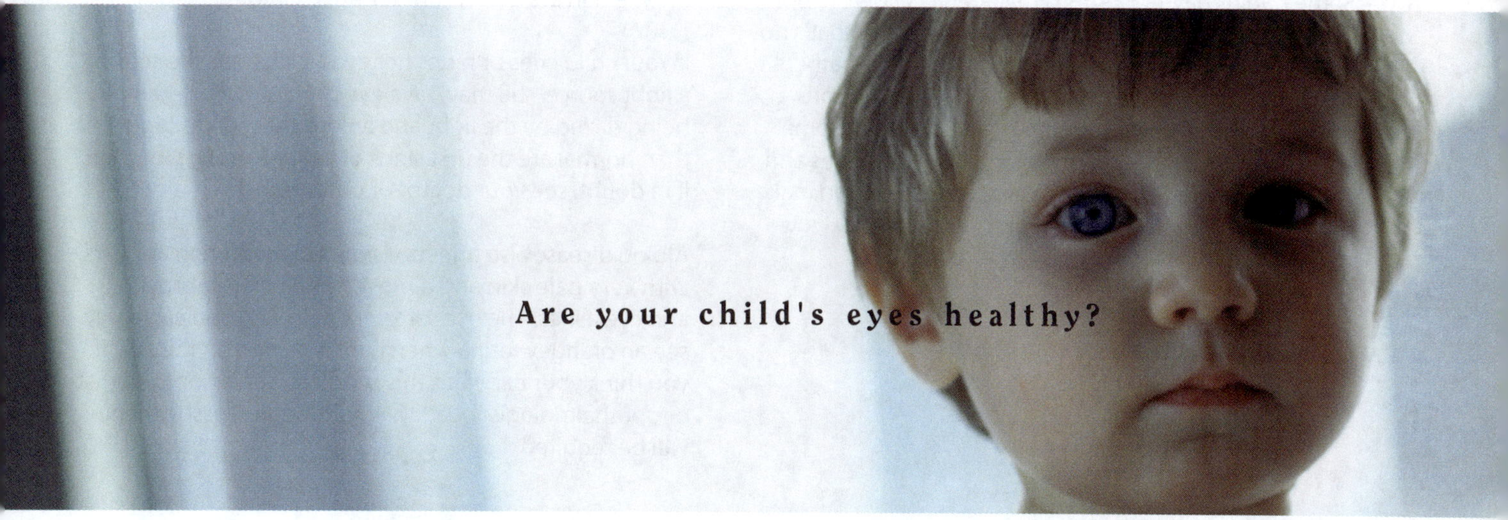

See your optometrist for a complete examination of your child's vision.
Optometrists are health professionals trained to detect, prevent and treat ocular and visual problems.

Seeing past the end of your nose

ordre des optométristes du québec

Don't give him medication prescribed for other members of the family. Many are not allowed to be given to babies under 1 year old.

Some babies have secretions that aren't yellowish, but look a bit like pus. This comes from an opening that's not working properly in a canal near the nose that gathers tears called the canthus. An accumulation of debris causes the secretions. The canal should open at some point during your baby's 1st year. Warm compresses and massaging the affected area 2 or 3 times a day can make your baby feel better. If the canal doesn't empty, you need to see a doctor or an optometrist.

Glare

Very young children can easily be blinded by light from the sun or another source. Those with light-coloured eyes or pale skin are even more sensitive to light.

If your child cries or hides her eyes each time she sees a light source, she may have eye problems. For example, being dazed by the light and an eye that seems bigger than normal are the first signs of **congenital glaucoma**. If in doubt, see your doctor or optometrist.

Albino disease also affects vision. This condition appears with very pale skin and almost white hair, eyebrows and eyelashes. The eyes are very pale, and you can easily see an orangey retina when light is shined on the eye. If you think your baby has this problem, see an optometrist or ophthalmologist quickly. A neurological assessment will be required.

▶ **Congenital glaucoma:** A rare disease caused by pressure inside the eye due to a malformation. The eye becomes bigger. The child must be treated to avoid loss of vision.

Herpes

The herpes simplex virus is very common in our society. Cold sores are the best known symptom. But herpes can also affect the eyes, and the first infection often happens in early childhood.

The signs and symptoms of herpes may go unnoticed, but most often you find:

- An irritated, itchy eye;
- More tears and secretions than usual;
- Red, leaky pimples along the eyelid and cheek;
- Difficulty looking at light;
- Swollen glands near the ear on the affected side of the face;
- Sometimes a fever;
- Only one side of the face affected;
- Short-term symptoms – lasting two or three days.

In most cases, this first infection by the virus goes unnoticed. But if your child complains, or signs of herpes show up, it's a good idea to see an optometrist or ophthalmologist. If sores appear on the cornea, your doctor will prescribe an anti-viral medication.

The virus then stays in the body for the rest of your child's life and may reappear occasionally. The most noticeable sores around the eyes appear when the virus flares up again, later; rarely during the first infection.

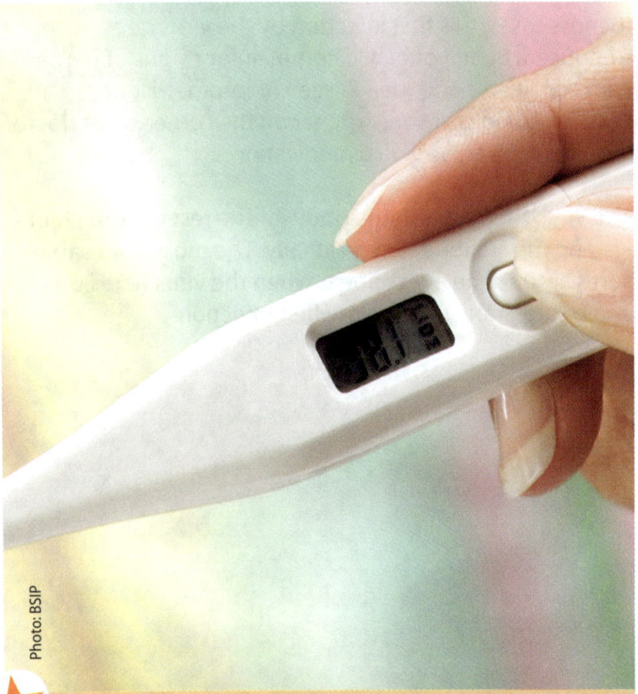

Photo: BSIP

A child has a fever if her rectal temperature is 38.1°C (100.5°F) or more.

Fever

In most cases, quiet time, love and liquids do the job. The fever will go away in two or three days.

Fever is the body's normal defence against infection by bacteria or virus. It is very common among young children. Fever in itself is not dangerous. In general it disappears within 72 hours (3 days).

Older children with a fever may be cared for at home, as long as they drink enough fluids and otherwise seem in good health. However, they should also be examined by a doctor if the fever lasts more than 72 hours.

When should I take my child's temperature?

If your child seems sick, hot, red, cranky, whiny or worn out, take her temperature. Write it down so you can tell Info-Santé or your doctor if needed.

What's the best way to take the temperature?

You can take your child's temperature several different ways:

Rectally

Taking the rectal temperature is the only reliable method to use for children ages 2 and under.

Under the arm

Taking the temperature under the arm is not as reliable but can be used to see whether or not your baby has a fever.

In the ear or mouth

Taking the temperature in the ear is quick but is not recommended because it is less accurate in young children.

Taking the temperature orally (mouth) is not recommended for children under the age of 5.

Thermometers

The best choice is the use of an electronic thermometer with digital display, made of unbreakable plastic and without glass or mercury, that is designed for rectal (bum), oral (mouth) or axillary (under the arm) use.

Mercury thermometers aren't recommended any more because if the thermometer breaks, mercury is a toxic substance for people and the environment.

How do I use it?

Rectally

- Wash the thermometer with cool water and soap; rinse well.
- Cover the tip with petroleum jelly (such as Vaseline).
- Put your baby on her back with her knees bent (see photo).
- Gently insert the thermometer about 1.5 cm (¾ inch) into the rectum.

Taking the rectal temperature is the only reliable method to use for children ages 2 and under.

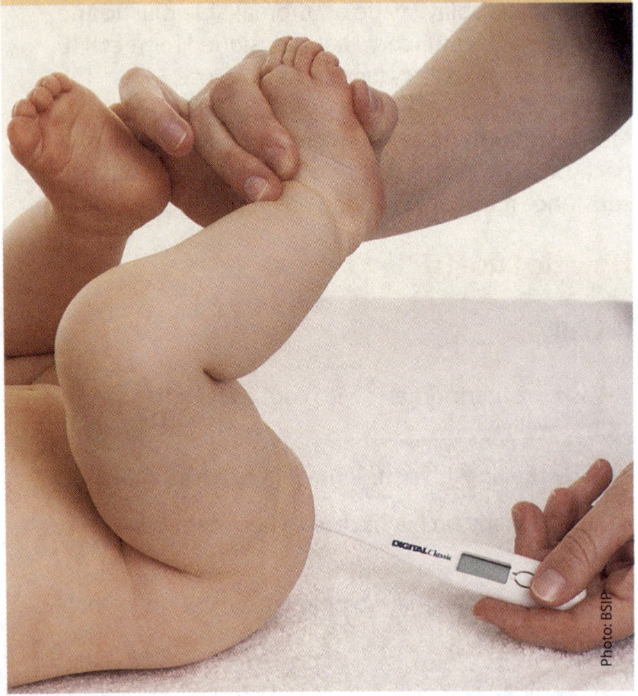

Photo: BSIP

- Keep the thermometer in place until you hear it beep. Remove the thermometer and write down the temperature.
- Wash the thermometer.

Under the arm

Axillary temperature (under the arm) is not as accurate as the rectal temperature. However, it does allow you to see whether or not your child has a fever.

If your child is under the age of 2 and you have determined that she has a fever (more than 37.3°C) when her temperature is taken under her arm, confirm your reading by taking her temperature rectally. If her taken temperature under her arm does not indicate that she has a fever but she seems hot and sick, check her temperature by taking it rectally.

- Use an electronic rectal or oral thermometer.
- Wash the thermometer with cool water and soap; rinse well.

- Place the tip of the thermometer in the middle of the armpit.
- Make sure your child's arm is held closely against her body.
- Keep the thermometer in place until you hear it beep. Remove the thermometer and write down the temperature.
- Wash the thermometer.

What is a child's normal temperature?

A child's normal temperature will vary depending on the method used to take the temperature:

Method used	Normal temperature variation
Axillary (under the arm)	From 34.7°C to 37.3°C (94.5°F to 99.1°F)
Rectal	From 36.6°C to 38.0°C (97.9°F to 100.4°F)

A child's temperature is lower in the morning and varies during the day, based on her activities. You don't need to take the temperature of a child who seems to be feeling well. When a child has an infection, her temperature will change easily: it can go up or down very quickly.

What should I do if my child has a fever?

The child's general condition is usually a better indicator of the severity of the illness than how high the fever is.

Dress your child lightly, in a t-shirt, diaper and socks. Lay her down for a nap and cover her with a sheet. Don't undress her completely because that may make her cold. Give her lots to drink to help avoid dehydration: milk, water or juice, depending on her age. The room temperature shouldn't be above 21°C (70°F).

Sponge baths are no longer recommended. The effect doesn't last long and it stresses a feverish child.

Fever medication

Medication is more helpful in improving a child's comfort than in reducing her fever. A feverish child does not necessarily need medicine if she doesn't seem sick and appears to be comfortable. However, if she is suffering or irritable, medication can help her feel better.

You can give your child either of the following medications, unless your doctor has a specific recommendation for your child. Don't give your child both medications at the same time.

Your child's dose will depend on her age and especially her weight. It is important to follow the manufacturer's instructions on the packaging.

Acetaminophen

Acetaminophen (Tempra™, Tylenol™, Panadol™, etc.) has been used for a long time and is a suitable choice. The manufacturer recommends giving a dose every 4 hours, without exceeding 5 doses in 24 hours.

Ibuprofen

Ibuprofen (Advil™, Motrin™) is also used to reduce fever. Its effect lasts longer, so you can give a dose every 6 to 8 hours, without exceeding 4 doses in 24 hours.

Don't give your child ibuprofen in the following situations:

- She is under 6 months old;
- Dehydration: severe stomach flu or a child that doesn't drink;
- Chicken pox;
- Asthma;
- Kidney failure;
- Immediately before or after an operation.

The two medications generally lower the fever in 30 to 60 minutes, but the effect does not last long. Usually, the temperature increases again after a certain amount of time and it may be necessary to give another dose. It is important not to exceed the recommended dose.

Never give your child aspirin.

The following table gives the main information about these two types of medication.

First choice: Acetaminophen	Second choice: Ibuprofen
Tempra™, Tylenol™, Atasol™, Pediaphen™, Pediatrix™ and others	Advil™, Motrin™ and others • Not recommended before the age of 6 months
Effects of both medications: • Lower fever without fighting the infection that causes it • Effective at the right dose • Start working in 30 to 60 minutes	
Dose:	
• Decide according to your child's weight • 15 mg per kilogram of weight • Repeat every 4 to 6 hours • Maximum of 5 doses in 24 hours	• Decide according to your child's weight • 10 mg per kilogram of weight • Repeat every 6 to 8 hours • Maximum of 4 doses in 24 hours
If you don't know or can't measure your child's weight, use her age to estimate the right dose. Talk to your pharmacist if needed.	
Form:	
• Drops, in suspension, pills	• Drops, in suspension, pills The amount of ibuprofen in the medication depends on the form it comes in.

Put medicine away in child-proof containers, which you can get at the pharmacy. Store them and the thermometer out of your children's reach in a cabinet that locks with a key or a safety lock.

What if your child throws up the dose?

If your child throws up her medication shortly after taking it – after less than 30 minutes – don't give another dose. Wait 1 hour and take her temperature again. If she still has a fever, give another dose. If she throws it up again, don't repeat the dose; see a doctor right away.

When should you see a health professional?

A high fever doesn't always mean serious illness. You should check your child's general condition, behaviour and other symptoms. A feverish child is clingier and less hungry; this is normal.

Contact an Info-Santé nurse or a doctor if your child has a fever and:

- Drinks very little;
- Throws up;
- Is difficult to comfort or is very cranky;
- Coughs a lot;
- A rash (red spots on the skin);
- Has had a fever for more than 72 hours for no apparent reason.

You can also contact an Info-Santé nurse or a doctor if you have concerns.

Febrile convulsion (seizure)

Between 2% and 4% of children between the ages of 6 months and 5 years have convulsions when they have a fever. They faint and shake in jerky movements. The seizure is very upsetting for parents, but generally not serious for the child. It normally lasts between 1 and 2 minutes, sometimes up to 15 minutes or longer, and most of the time stops on its own.

What should I do?

Stay calm if your child has a convulsion: turn her head to the side in case she throws up. Don't put anything in her mouth. Don't try to stop her movements. It's important to see a doctor quickly. An Info-Santé nurse can help you.

! See a doctor quickly if your child has a fever and shows one or more of the following symptoms or characteristics:

- Is less than 3 months and has a rectal temperature ≥ 38°C;
- Is between the ages of 3 and 6 months and has a rectal temperature ≥ 39°C;
- Throws up a lot;
- Cries non-stop;
- Is difficult to wake;
- Is pale or has an unhealthy colour;
- Reacts very little to others;
- Wheezes when she breathes;
- Has a fever over 41.1°C (106°F);

Respiratory infections

Upper respiratory tract infections – cold, flu, sore throat, earache and bronchiolitis – are common among children.

It appears as a stuffed up nose, cough and fever. As your child gets older, he has more contact with other people and his immune system is developing. This means that infections will be common.

Respiratory infections are caused by a virus that is mainly passed on by contact with an infected person: hand contact and exposure to sneezing and coughing by the infected person.

Preventing respiratory tract infections

For adults and older children:

- Wash hands often.
- Teach your child to cough or sneeze into the bend of his elbow and not into his hands. Set an example by doing the same; it's an excellent way to prevent infection.
- Wash toys and other items.
- Throw tissues away immediately after use.

Colds and flu

Colds and the flu are caused by viruses. Flu is a more severe illness caused by the influenza virus. A vaccine exists to prevent it. There is no vaccine to prevent a cold. A person can catch a cold several times in a year, but generally a person only gets the flu once a year.

The main symptoms of cold and flu and their differences are described here:

Symptoms	Cold	Flu
Fever	Mild 38-39°C (100.4-102.2°F)	38-40°C (100.4-104°F)
Headache	Rare	Significant
Chills	Significant	Significant
Muscle pain	Mild	Significant, may be sharp
Fatigue, weakness	Mild	Pronounced
Stuffy nose	Often	Occasionally
Runny nose	Significant	Occasionally
Sneezing	Significant	Occasionally
Sore throat	Significant	Occasionally
Cough	Mild to moderate	Heavy
Chest pain	Mild to moderate	Heavy

What should I do?

A child with a cold or flu may eat less. It is important that he drinks lots of liquids, especially if he has a fever.

Take your child's temperature every 4 to 6 hours. You can give him acetaminophen if he has a fever or is uncomfortable.

It is recommended that you air out your child's room regularly and keep the room temperature at 21°C (70°F), and no higher.

Other characteristics	Cold	Flu
Causes	Different respiratory viruses	Influenza virus
Incubation period	1 to 3 days	
Infectiousness	24 hours before and up to 5 days after symptoms appear	
Transmission	Through contact with secretions from the nose and throat, through sneezing, coughing, kissing and contaminated objects	
Duration	5 to 7 days	More than 7 days
Treatment	No treatment	If Type A flu or complications
Complications	Ear and sinus infections	Ear infection, bronchitis, pneumonia

Stuffy nose

If your child has a stuffed up nose and the secretions are thick, be sure to clean it out as often as needed and especially before he drinks and at bedtime. Using salt water to clean the nose is recommended. You can buy saline solution from a pharmacy in a small bottle with a dropper. When the bottle is empty you can prepare your own saline solution at home.

When your child has a cold or other infection, clean his nose 3 or 4 times a day.

Try not to give medication to a baby under the age of 1, unless advised by a doctor.

Saline solution for the nose

Add 2.5 ml (1/2 teaspoon) of salt, never more, to 240 ml (8 oz.) of cooled boiled water.

Measure the quantities accurately.

Cleaning your child's nose

- Lay your child on his back.
- Place a full dropper (1 ml) of salt water in each nostril.
- Clean inside the nostrils using a cotton swab (Q-tip).
- Apply another full dropper of salt water in each nostril.
- Wipe his nose while encouraging him to breathe out through his nose if possible.

Overuse of saline solution, as well as using a nasal aspirator to get rid of secretions, can irritate a toddler's delicate nose.

Taking a bath or long shower with your child can ease his congestion and irritated nose. You can also use a non-medicated ointment (Vaseline) on the irritated skin around the nose.

To teach your child to blow his nose, encourage him to blow bubbles through his nose in the bath.

Cough

Coughing is normally a way for the body to get rid of secretions. It may also be caused by an irritation due to an infection of the nose, throat and ears, but is most often caused by a virus.

What should I do?

Don't give your child cough syrup if he develops a cough. Coughing is a defense mechanism, and cough syrup can be dangerous during the first year of a child's life.

See a doctor if your child has a fever and doesn't look well or has trouble breathing.

Sore throat

A sore throat is a throat infection (pharyngitis or tonsillitis) accompanied by a fever, a red throat, swollen and sore **lymph nodes** in the neck, and occasionally nausea and vomiting. It's painful for your baby to swallow, so he will drink less.

Pharyngitis is most often caused by a virus (80-90% of the time), in which case there is no treatment. If it is a bacterial infection, normally streptococcus, an antibiotic will be prescribed. By taking a throat swab, doctors can tell whether the infection is caused by a virus or bacteria. When redness appears on the skin, it may be a manifestation of the virus or scarlet fever (see Scarlet fever, page 473).

▶ **Lymph nodes:** Situated in the neck and other parts of the body, they help fight disease.

Pharyngitis is passed on through direct contact with nasal and throat secretions from an infected person when he or she coughs and sneezes. Your child can get pharyngitis many times and there is no vaccine against it.

What should I do?

If your child has a sore throat you can give him acetaminophen to lessen the pain and reduce his temperature.

Ice cream or ice milk and popsicles will help his throat feel better. Have your child drink lots of liquids.

See a doctor if the fever persists or is very high.

Ear infection

Otitis is an infection of the ear that cannot be seen from the outside. Your child may have had a runny nose a few days before. Otitis is caused by a virus or bacteria, and particularly affects babies between the ages of 6 months and 2 years, usually in the fall and winter.

Your baby touches his ear, rolls his head on the pillow, cries, and doesn't eat. He may vomit and have diarrhea. He may or may not have a fever.

Otitis is not contagious; it cannot be transmitted like a cold.

What should I do?

See a doctor if your baby is crying a lot, you have the impression that he's in pain and he has a high fever. If he is diagnosed with otitis caused by a bacteria, an antibiotic is often needed. The antibiotic will prevent complications. Be sure to continue the antibiotics up until they're finished even if your child seems better. His body will be less likely to develop resistance to treatment, and it will be easier to treat future infections if all doses of medication are taken as prescribed.

After having otitis, make sure your child hears well. Watch his reactions to noise, music, and the sound of a small bell. Repeated and untreated ear infections can result in hearing problems. Tubes may need to be inserted into his ears.

Prevention

Don't put your baby to bed with a bottle; the liquid may run into his ear. Your baby should drink in your arms, with his head raised. Nasal hygiene is also very important.

If your child has an earache, you can ease the pain and bring down the fever with acetaminophen.

These are the recommended treatments:

- Give him something to drink often.
- Clean his nose with salt water.

See a doctor if your baby is crying a lot, is irritable or has a high fever.

Photo: BSIP

Other types of otitis

After a case of acute otitis media, a serum-like liquid may remain behind the eardrum. This is known as serous otitis media, which can decrease hearing and last for several weeks. Serous otitis generally goes away on its own.

Swimmer's otitis is an infection of the external auditory canal, which becomes swollen, red and painful. You must see a doctor.

Bronchiolitis

Bronchiolitis is an infection in the bronchioles, the small canals that allow air to circulate in the lungs. It's often caused by cold germs, and mainly affects children under the age of 1. It is one of the most common illnesses among children up to age 2.

The symptoms are usually wheezing, a cough, runny nose and mild fever. It's because the inside of the bronchi swells and produces secretions, causing the air not to flow properly and your baby to wheeze.

The bronchiolitis virus is very contagious and is caught through coughing and contact with infected secretions.

What should I do?

As with colds, there are few effective ways to treat bronchiolitis. But some treatments can help relieve your child. To free his nose of thick secretions, it's a good idea to wash the inside of his nostrils with salt water. To ease your child's breathing, raise the head of his bed by slipping a pillow under the mattress. Do not put your baby directly on the pillow.

Cough syrups are not recommended and may even be harmful.

See a doctor if your child's health gets worse, especially if he is less than 6 months old. Signs that he is getting worse are rapid breathing, difficulty eating, coughing and choking while drinking.

Just because your child has bronchiolitis does not mean he'll get asthma later on, even if the symptoms are similar. Talk to your doctor if you're concerned.

Intestinal problems

Your child doesn't look sick but has had liquid stools for the past day or two. Could this be an intestinal disorder?

What should I do?

Check whether your child is drinking too much juice or overly sweet liquids. Up to the age of 2, your child should drink only 60 to 125 ml (2 to 4 oz.) of juice a day. Avoid soft drinks and limit prune juice, which contain laxative substances. Lower the quantity of cold food that you give him: milk, juice, ice milk or cream, popsicles and slush.

If your child drinks a lot of cow's milk, give him whole milk (3.25% M.F.) and limit the quantity to 600 to 725 ml (20 to 25 oz.) a day.

A new food may be causing the problem. If so, stop giving it to him for a few weeks. Try again later since intolerance can disappear over time.

Intestinal sensitivity may be part of his nature. But talk to a health professional if you're still worried.

> If your child is eating enough, gaining weight and in good health, there's no reason to worry.

Stomach flu

A child has gastroenteritis, or stomach flu, when his stools are more frequent and liquid than usual; sometimes they contain blood. He may also throw up or have a fever. Your baby looks sick, cries more and doesn't eat very much. In most cases this is caused by a virus. The diarrhea will go away in several hours or a few (2 to 5) days.

Gastroenteritis is one of the most common illnesses in children. Almost every baby will get it at least once during his first year of life. Children at daycare centres are exposed more often. Babies that are breast-fed suffer less often because breast milk helps prevent and cure it.

The main risk of stomach flu is dehydration. This risk is greatest among babies that are under 1 year old. The concentration of electrolytes (minerals in the blood) can become unbalanced.

What should I do?

Have your child drink often to prevent dehydration (loss of large quantities of water).

Here are some examples of treatment based on the symptoms:

1st case: Your child has diarrhea but doesn't vomit, or only vomits a little.

For a baby that is breast-fed only, continue nursing as usual. The breast milk will speed up the healing process. If your baby is drinking less milk, nurse him often.

For a bottle-fed baby, offer the milk as usual and alternate it with an electrolyte solution from the pharmacy.

For a baby that is breast- or bottle-fed and that is eating solid food, use the same treatments as described above depending on the type of milk he drinks. Give him his regular food: cereal, fruit and vegetable purées, etc. Cooked, mashed rice seems to help lessen diarrhea.

2nd case: Your child has diarrhea and vomits a lot.

For a breast-fed baby, continue breast-feeding, but stop giving solid foods for about 4 hours. Offer shorter, more frequent feedings. If your baby does not want to nurse or is not breast-fed, give him a small quantity (5 to 10 ml, [1 to 2 teaspoons]) of electrolyte solution every 5 to 10 minutes, using a spoon or dropper.

The electrolyte solution will fix the balance of mineral salts lost during the vomiting and diarrhea.

For a bottle-fed baby, stop his regular food (milk and solid food) for about 4 hours. Give him a small quantity (5 to 10 ml, [1 to 2 teaspoons]) of electrolyte solution every 5 to 10 minutes using a spoon, dropper or bottle. Gradually increase the quantity of liquid when the vomiting decreases and your baby is doing better. Start giving him milk and his regular solid foods a little at a time.

For nine months you **kept your baby protected.**

Continue **to help protect your baby** with

RotaTeq®

(Rotavirus Vaccine, Live, Oral, Pentavalent)

HOW CAN I HELP PROTECT MY BABY AGAINST ROTAVIRUS GASTROENTERITIS?

- There is an oral vaccine available to help protect infants from rotavirus infection. It is called RotaTeq®.
- RotaTeq® offers protection against the most common types of rotavirus in Canada.
- RotaTeq® is a convenient oral vaccine. It is not an injection.
- Physicians can give RotaTeq® to your baby at the same time as the other childhood vaccines, at 2, 4 and 6 months of age.

The most common side effects reported with RotaTeq® were fever, diarrhea and vomiting. As with any vaccine, vaccination with RotaTeq® may not result in complete protection in all recipients.

Discuss RotaTeq® at one of your baby's **first visits to the doctor, such as 1 month!**

1 Month

MERCK FROSST
Discovering today for a better tomorrow.

Merck Frosst Canada Ltd., Kirkland, Quebec

To learn more about rotavirus, visit: www.rotavirus.ca
For more information about RotaTeq®, visit: www.rotateq-canada.ca

RTQ-06-CDN-84120225a-JA

Electrolyte solution

This liquid replaces the water and mineral salts lost through diarrhea and vomiting. Your pharmacy sells ready-made electrolyte solutions like Pedialyte™, or Pediatric Electrolyte™, as well as Gastrolyte™, a powder sold in packets to be dissolved in cooled boiled water.

Recommended by the Canadian Paediatric Society

The Canadian Paediatric Society recommends that parents keep an electrolyte solution on hand since diarrhea is common in young children.

If gastroenteritis starts during the night when your pharmacy is closed, and you don't have any electrolyte solution in the house, you can prepare a homemade rehydration solution for your child. But be careful! This solution should be used only in the following conditions:

- Only use the homemade solution while waiting for the pharmacy to open, and not for a period longer than 12 hours;
- Follow the recipe precisely to avoid making the dehydration worse and causing the concentration of mineral salts in the blood to become unbalanced.

Recommended by the Canadian Paediatric Society

The Canadian Paediatric Society does not recommend using a homemade rehydrating solution because of the problems that can happen when it's improperly made. As soon as the pharmacy opens, buy an electrolyte solution.

Homemade rehydration solution

Use a measuring spoon and a measuring cup to make sure the quantities are exact.

Mix the following ingredients together thoroughly:

- 360 ml (12 oz.) unsweetened, ready-to-drink orange juice
- 600 ml (20 oz.) cooled boiled water
- 2.5 ml (1/2 teaspoon) salt, never more.

How much do I give to hydrate my child?

The amount to give in a one-hour period depends on your child's age:

- Under 6 months: 30 to 90 ml (1 to 3 oz.)
- 6 to 24 months: 90 to 125 ml (3 to 4 oz.)
- Over 24 months: 125 to 250 ml (4 to 8 oz.).

If vomiting continues, decrease the amount you give. At the height of stomach flu, some babies will tolerate only 5 ml (1 tsp.) at a time.

When vomiting has stopped for 4 to 6 hours:
Your baby can start drinking commercial infant formula again. Stopping his formula for more than 12 hours is not recommended. You need to give your baby small quantities of food in several (5 or 6) small meals to avoid nausea again. After 24 hours, you can go back to his normal amount of food.

Even if the diarrhea continues:
Your child can eat small amounts of food that are part of his regular diet.

Some tips

- Avoid any medication sold at the pharmacy unless it has been recommended by your doctor.
- When your child has gastroenteritis, don't give him liquids like apple juice (even if it's been diluted) or soft drinks like 7 Up™ (even flat). They may make the diarrhea worse and unbalance the mineral salts in his body. Only electrolyte solutions (Pedialyte™, Pediatric Electrolyte™, Gastrolyte™) can help your child get better.

- Despite the bland taste of electrolyte solutions, a dehydrated child will drink them eagerly because dehydration causes extreme thirst. If he refuses to drink the solution, it's because he's not dehydrated or thirsty. Don't add anything to improve the taste as it will change the sugar-salt balance that's needed for the treatment to be successful.
- Changing your child's milk while he has moderate gastroenteritis is not recommended; nor is giving him soy-based formula, unless recommended by a doctor. Avoid lactose-free formulas; they don't help heal moderate gastroenteritis.
- Returning to normal food within 4 to 12 hours helps get rid of diarrhea. A totally liquid diet, with no milk or solid food, may be given for 6 to 12 hours but never for more than 18 hours.

When to see a doctor

Regardless of your baby's age, you should quickly see a doctor if your baby shows any of the following symptoms:

- He is urinating very little.
- He has a dry mouth.
- His fontanel (soft spot on the head) is sunken.
- He cries without tears.
- He seems weak and drowsy.
- There is blood in his stools.
- His stools are black.
- The diarrhea has lasted longer than 5 days.

The doctor may request a stool culture to determine the bacteria, parasite or, in some cases, virus responsible for the illness.

Photo: Nicolas Delaitre

Prevention

Car safety seats

!

The law protects children by requiring that you use a car safety seat.

In a moving vehicle, your child must use a seat adapted to her size and weight until she has reached a height of 63 cm (25 inches) when seated. This measurement is taken from the seat to the top of the head.

A car safety seat must be used as soon as you leave the hospital. Check with your CLSC if you want to rent a car seat before you leave the hospital.

There are 3 types of seats: infant seats, child seats and booster seats. You will need to change the seat as your child grows. Carefully read the manufacturer's instructions before using the car seat.

Since September 2002, all new vehicles made in Canada are equipped with a Universal Anchorage System (UAS) (ISOFIX or LATCH). All car seats made in Canada are equipped with a belt that attaches to the vehicle's UAS, which makes installation easier.

For information about infant car seats, see pages 160 to 162.

Child seat

Installing a car seat in a vehicle – Place the car seat on the back seat. The seat should face the front ONLY when the baby is able to maintain an upright position, around the age of 12 months.

Before this age, if the seat allows, the baby will be safest if the seat is facing backward.

When the car seat is installed facing forward, the car seat must be attached to the bench using the car's seat belt or the UAS belt. You can buy a UAS belt separately if your car seat didn't come equipped with one. Attach the tether strap to the vehicle anchor point to prevent the top of the car seat from tilting. The manufacturer of the vehicle locates the anchor bolt there.

! Never place a car seat on the front seat if your vehicle is equipped with a passenger-side airbag. If the airbag goes off, it could seriously injure or kill your child.

For more information about installing car seats, read your vehicle owner's manual and the car seat manufacturer's instructions. You can also contact CAA-Québec.

You can ask at your CLSC for contact information for organizations that provide demonstrations on safely installing car seats. The police department in your area may also be able to help. Generally speaking, hospital staff are very helpful in this area.

★ In a vehicle, a properly installed child seat is the safest way to transport children weighing between 9 and 18 kg (20 to 40 lb.).

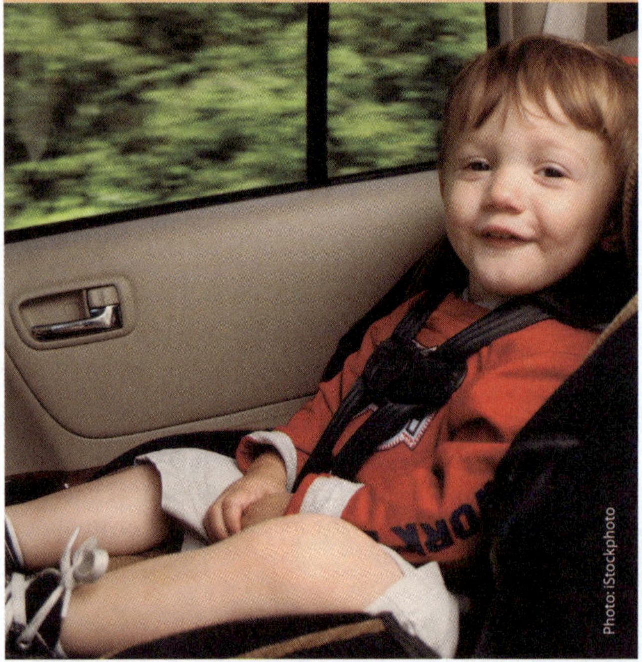

Photo: iStockphoto

If you do the installation yourself, we recommend it be checked before using the seat with your child, even if you think you have done it properly.

Adjusting the harness before use – Put the harness in the seat slots that are a little higher than your child's shoulders. Make sure the harness is snug (no more than 1 finger width between the harness and your child's collarbone) and the chest clip is up to your child's armpits (under the arm and in the middle of the chest). If your vehicle seat belts lock only on impact, the seat belt used to attach the car seat should have a locking clip on it (see the manufacturer's instructions).

Booster seat

Read the booster seat manufacturer's instructions carefully.

This restraint system helps place the car's shoulder belt in the middle of your child's shoulder (on the collarbone) and the lap belt on her hips (and not on the stomach). Put the booster seat on the back seat of the vehicle.

In a vehicle, a properly used booster seat is the safest way to transport children over 18 kg (40 lb.).

Photo: BSIP

Use a booster seat with a high back when:

- The vehicle seat back is low. The child's head must be well supported.
- The vehicle's back seat is equipped with shoulder belts. Never place the shoulder belt under your child's arm or behind her back.

Before you stop using the booster seat, make sure the seatbelt is properly positioned on your child's shoulder and hips. Booster seats must be used as long as necessary. Keeping in mind the weight limit recommended by manufacturers, some children are still safer in a booster seat even if they measure over 63 cm when seated.

When your child is big enough to ride in a car without a booster seat, have her sit in the back seat until she is at least 12 years old. Make sure she buckles up her seat belt.

Flying

If you travel by airplane with your child, you can sit her in her car seat if it meets the NSVAC 213, 213.1 or 213.2 standard.

Taxis

Unless there is a safety seat in the taxi, your child must wear a seat belt unless she is too small to maintain an upright position.

Children under the age of 12 should be seated in the back seat and use a seat belt; the back seat is the safest part of a vehicle.

The only car seat you'll ever need!

Alpha Omega® Elite

is the only 3-in-1 car seat designed to grow with your child from 2.3-45 kg (5-100 lbs). It starts as a rear-facing seat for infants, later faces forward for children, and eventually becomes a belt-positioning booster for older kids. This advanced car seat features a no-rethread 5-point harness that simply and conveniently adjusts from the front of the seat to accommodate your growing child. Kids ride in complete comfort with three-position recline, and adjustable headrest and padded pivoting armrests. Designed to grow with your child, the Alpha Omega® Elite is the only car seat you'll ever need!

Safety 1st®

Your baby's room

Bedrooms should be bright and well ventilated, with a window if possible. The room temperature should be about 20°C (68°F). If your child sweats, she is too heavily dressed or covered.

Humidity should be kept between 30% and 45%. Using a humidifier is no longer recommended. A humidity level that is too high, or poor upkeep of the humidifier promotes harmful moulds. If you need to use a humidifier, it is very important to clean it and change the filters according to the manufacturer's instructions. The water needs to be changed everyday. Every 3rd day, the humidifier needs to be washed with soapy water and disinfected with a solution of 1 part bleach to 9 parts water. If condensation appears on the windows, humidity is too high. Avoid rugs since they absorb humidity and trap dust.

Wood and vinyl-covered floors are best. They are also easier to maintain. Children like to play in their rooms so it's important to make sure bedrooms are safe.

Blinds

The pull cords of blinds must be kept out of children's reach because they can strangle themselves playing with the cords. Keep blind and drapery pull cords very high, out of children's reach, everywhere in the house. Be sure as well that there are no pieces of furniture or other objects close to the window that could allow your child to climb and reach the blinds.

Inexpensive PVC mini-blinds can cause lead poisoning and neurological problems in children. Health Canada recommends getting rid of these blinds. Check the packaging when buying blinds to make sure they don't contain lead.

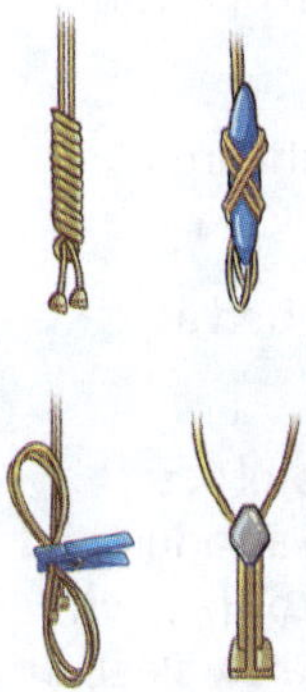

Illustration: Maurice Gervais

Crib

Your baby's safety in bed is very important. If the crib is not new, make sure it's safe. Check that your baby can't hurt herself on screws or parts that are not properly attached. The sides of the crib must be raised and locked into position when your baby is lying down.

Cribs manufactured before 1986 no longer comply with Health Canada product safety regulations and cannot be sold. Manufacturers and retailers are well aware of this regulation. Consumers can be confident that the new cribs being sold are safe. Be wary of cribs that are being given away and those sold in used furniture stores, flea markets and garage sales.

Check the crib regularly to make sure it's in good condition. The mattress should be firm and fit snugly in the bed, with no more than 3 cm (1 1/8 inches) of space around it. Movable hooks that support the mattress are not allowed. Check that the springs are solidly attached. They should not move. The space between the bars of the crib should be 6 cm or less (2 3/8 inches).

The baby's crib may be kept in your room.

If you tie toys to the crib, the cord should not be longer than 15 cm (6 inches). Never leave a young baby in an adult bed unsupervised by an adult.

You can use a cradle or baby basket during the first month of your baby's life. After that, it's too dangerous to do so.

If you find it easier, bring your baby into your bed to breast-feed. However, the Canadian Paediatric Society recommends putting your baby back in her own bed to sleep once she's finished nursing.

!

- If you're more tired than usual, or you've consumed alcohol, taken medication or other substances that could make you drowsy, don't bring your baby into bed with you, even to nurse.
- Don't sleep with your baby on a couch or on any other stuffed furniture.
- Waterbeds are dangerous for young children. A baby lying on her stomach can suffocate.
- Animals should not sleep in the same bed as a baby.
- When you're visiting or staying in a hotel, it's dangerous to have your baby sleep in an adult bed and even more so if she's surrounded by pillows, which can suffocate her. A baby can safely sleep on a floor covered with a big, thick blanket. Portable playpens can also be safe, but don't add a mattress, cushions, pillows or anything else for use as a mattress.

Bedding

The only bedding you need is a fitted sheet for the mattress and a blanket. Wash and rinse them thoroughly before use. Avoid using cushions or decorative fabric for bumper pads, pillows, roll-guard cushions, comforters and stuffed animals, since your baby could suffocate against these objects. You should continue to avoid these objects later when your baby starts moving around in her crib because she might use them to climb out of bed and injure herself in a fall.

Check blankets regularly for dangling threads.

If your family has allergies, the following tips might help:

- Wash sheets often in very hot water to destroy dust mites that feed off dead skin and live in warm, damp beds.
- Put a zippered plastic cover over the mattress and cover the zipper with tape.
- Avoid feather duvets and pillows, and fleece sheets.
- Avoid carpets, fabric-covered furniture, stuffed animals and knick-knacks that collect dust.
- Use a damp cloth to dust your baby's room.

Toys

Toys are stimulating for your child. Choose attractive toys that are right for your child's age and needs.

She can then repeat what she learned and play more independently.

Your baby will like having her parents or a big brother or sister help her discover her toys and learn how to use them.

Photo: Jean-François Gosselin

Be sure to choose toys that are:

- washable;
- non-toxic (read the label);
- unbreakable;
- non-flammable;
- big enough to stop your child from swallowing or putting them in her mouth;
- made according to Canadian government safety standards (www.hc-sc.gc.ca/iyh-vsv/prod/toys-jouets_e.html).

Avoid soft vinyl (PVC) toys and rattles. Some products used to soften the vinyl are toxic. Your child may absorb these products when she chews on the toy. Avoid rubber bath and wading pool toys that hold water because they promote germs.

Toy guns from the store or that children make are fairly popular. Supervise children when they're playing with these guns so they don't get hurt. The important rule is that your children must not "really" hurt a person. The pretend nature of these games gives children the opportunity to express their emotions. It also teaches them the important difference between make-believe and reality.

Tips before buying a toy

- Read the label for the recommended age.
- Check whether the toy is easy to handle.
- Make sure there are no sharp edges or pointed ends.
- Make sure that the eyes and nose of stuffed animals are properly sewn on. Big toys must not have parts that come off easily.
- Beware of small objects and parts. A child could put them in her nose or mouth and suffocate.
- Any rattle that can pass vertically through a 50 mm x 35 mm (2 inch x 1½ in.) oval is too small and dangerous.
- Musical toys are fine. They stimulate your baby's hearing and eyesight, but check the gears and make sure that any small pieces won't come off.
- Be careful of noisy toys! They can damage a child's hearing and irritate parents. Try them before buying them.
- Read the list of best toys on *Protégez-Vous* magazine's Web site (www.protegez-vous.qc.ca) (in French only); but remember that a toy recommended for a 3 year old may be dangerous for a baby under the age of 1.

You can buy used toys, furniture and other baby items at low prices. Over the past few years, stricter rules have been adopted to ensure your child's safety. Before buying a used product, contact Health Canada at 1 800 561-3350.

A few recommendations after you buy a toy

- Read the instructions.
- Throw out plastic, cellophane and polystyrene (styrofoam) packaging.
- Be careful with used batteries; the liquid that can leak from them is corrosive. Don't allow the liquid to touch your baby's skin or get into her mouth.

Always

- Remove battery-operated toys from your baby's crib when she's sleeping.
- Check toys carefully and get rid of any that are broken.
- Throw out deflated balloons; a child can choke on them if she puts them in her mouth. Only an adult should inflate balloons.
- Always keep an eye on a playing child.

Putting toys away

Even when she's very young, you can get your child used to putting away her toys in a basket, box without a lid or on a low shelf.

Once she's older, she can put them in a toy box with air vents. Make sure the lid is fastened in a way that keeps it from falling on her head or fingers.

Risk of injury

Your baby grows very quickly up to the age of 2 years. She explores her world without realizing its dangers. Be on the lookout! Be extra careful if you have an active baby. She can easily escape your attention.

Falls, burns, drowning, poisoning and choking are major causes of death among children. You can protect your child by making your surroundings safe. It's a good idea to check out all the rooms in your house from a child's eye level. You need to block the staircase. Lock drawers and the gate to the swimming pool. Electrical outlets should be covered with solidly installed socket covers. Toxic products should be locked away in a safe place.

★ Accidents happen quickly. You can reduce the danger by adapting your surroundings to your baby.

Photo: Chantal Jolicoeur

Kitchen

The highchair should be placed far away from kitchen counters and the table. Your baby could push on them with her feet and tip over. Strap her into the chair to keep her from slipping or from climbing over the tray or back.

Keep an eye on her at all times: some babies manage to get out of their highchairs even when they're strapped in!

If you use a portable chair (booster), make sure she's also strapped in. Don't put the booster on the table; put it on the floor instead to avoid falls.

You need to watch your baby at all times when she starts crawling. It's best not to use a tablecloth since your baby can pull it down, with all its contents. Kitchenware handles should be turned toward the centre of the table, buffet or counter. Don't leave utensils lying around.

Turn the handles of pots away from the edge of the stove. When you're frying foods, keep your child well away to prevent her from being spattered with fat or oil. Keep your baby away from a hot oven; she could put her hands against it.

Be careful with some foods that can be a choking hazard for young children (see How to prevent choking, p. 396).

Stairs

A gate needs to be placed at the top of each staircase. Solidly attach it to the door frame or hallway walls. If it's not new, make sure that it meets current Health Canada safety standards by visiting the following Web site: www.hc-sc.gc.ca/cps-spc/child-enfant/equip/gate-barr/index_e.html.

Outdoors

Here are a few instructions to stay aware of everything that could be dangerous for your child:

- A fence that is at least 1.2 m (48 inches) high and that has a gate that closes and locks should be installed to prevent access to any in-ground or above-ground pool. The filtration system should be installed more than 2 m (72½ inches) away from the pool to prevent children from using it to climb on. The water heater needs to be out of children's reach. A standard electrical ground must be installed to reduce the risk of electrocution. When no one is swimming in an above-ground pool, the ladder must be raised.
- Be careful around shallow bodies of water, like water gardens. A baby can drown in 2.5 to 5 cm (1 to 2 inches) of water.
- Never go in a boat with your child without first putting life preservers (PFDs) on yourself and your child, and properly fastening them. If the boat capsizes, this could save both her life and yours.

Keep a constant watch on your child around lakes and rivers. Your baby can go out of sight and hearing very quickly.

Photo: iStockphoto

- Swings and other playground equipment should be installed on a layer of sand or wood chips 15 to 30 cm (6 to 12 inches) deep. If your child falls, she'll be less seriously hurt than if she were to fall on gravel or grass. Don't let your child play on this equipment when the ground is frozen. Your child should not wear clothing with drawstrings or a bicycle helmet when playing on swings or playground equipment. Sandboxes should be covered to prevent animals from defecating in them. Trampolines require the same close watch as pools, and should be used by one child at a time.

Free advice and friendly inspections on the safe installation of residential pools are available by contacting the Lifesaving Society at 1 800 265-3093 / 514 252-3100 or by visiting its Web site: www.sauvetage.qc.ca/English/media_room.asp. Drowning prevention courses are also offered to help you learn how to react in emergency situations.

Young children often choke on small objects.

Photo: Nathalie Gignac

Caution...

Small objects

The following items should be kept well out of children's reach: buttons, thimbles, needles, marbles, matches, peanuts, safety pins, coins, jewellery, cigarette butts, bits of paper, paper clips, beads, popcorn, deflated balloons, and thumbtacks.

Razor blades, scissors and knives should also be kept away from children. Plastic bags can suffocate a child. Make a knot in used plastic bags and throw them in the garbage out of children's reach. Store other plastic bags out of their reach as well.

Dogs

> **!** Because of their small size and unpredictability, children are at risk of being bitten by a dog – even your own dog or a neighbour's. Children are UNABLE to recognize signs of aggression.

Never leave a child alone with a dog, even if the animal knows the child and doesn't seem dangerous. A dog that is gentle with your child can be aggressive with others. Don't take any signs of aggression lightly. Consult a veterinarian or dog trainer if the dog bares its teeth, growls or looks like it's going to bite. When visiting, be extra careful if your host's dog is not familiar with your child.

Dogs don't automatically have their owner's love of children. What should you do with Rover? Prepare it for your baby's arrival. Before her birth, gradually reduce the amount of time you spend with your dog. Push the stroller around or rock a doll to get your dog used to your future routine. Play baby sounds for it. Don't allow your dog to climb on chairs or take food off the table. As soon as your baby is born, let the dog sniff her clothes. Speak kindly to your dog when the baby is there and ignore it when the baby is sleeping. The dog will associate your baby with a source of pleasure.

Falls

Falls often happen when:

- Your baby's seat is on the table, she moves and the seat slides and falls to the floor.
- An adult is changing the baby's diaper on a changing table and moves away to get something.
- A child climbs onto a piece of furniture next to a window and falls out.
- A child is left alone in her highchair, gets out and falls or makes the highchair tip over.

If your baby moves a lot, change her on the floor.

Don't leave footstools or furniture close to a window. A baby who has started crawling may climb onto them. Make sure that no furniture or objects could fall on your baby's head.

Never leave a portable baby seat on a table; put it on the floor instead.

! Never leave your baby alone on the table when changing her diaper, even for a few seconds.

Electrical cords

Electrical cords that run across rugs or under furniture, such as floor lamps, can be covered up to avoid injury. Do not let your baby chew on them. Cords that are within your child's reach can be unplugged. Childproof socket covers should be placed solidly over wall outlets.

The cords of electrical appliances such as irons and kettles can be dangerous if left dangling. Put your baby in her playpen or another safe place while you're ironing.

Hot water

Hot tap water can give a child a 2nd or even 3rd degree burn. If the water temperature is 60°C (140°F) it only takes 1 second to get a burn. And children love playing with taps…

Keep your water no hotter than 49°C (120°F). Temperature control devices are available that can be installed on bathtub and sink taps to prevent burns. If you have a gas or oil water heater, you should set the thermostat at 49°C. However, if you have an electric water heater, set the temperature at 60°C to prevent bacteria that cause legionellosis, a severe type of pneumonia.

Run both the hot and cold water when you're preparing a bath. Always check the water temperature before putting your child in the tub.

Fires and burns

It's essential that you install a smoke detector on each floor of your home and that you replace the batteries once a year. If needed, the municipal fire department can give you information. You should also have a fire extinguisher. Don't leave matches lying around and make sure that your lighters have a safety lock. If you use candles, put them in a metal candleholder and keep the wicks short. Be careful of hot wax.

Children's clothing should be made of fabric that will not easily catch fire. Loose-fitting pyjamas catch fire more easily. Choose polyester or nylon fabrics that don't burn as easily as cotton.

Children have thinner skin than adults so they are at greater risk of being burned by hot liquids. Avoid eating soup or drinking coffee while holding your baby. Beware of steam and hot electrical appliances.

Put your baby in the shade, for example under a parasol.

Photo: Dominique Belley

Sun

Sunlight is essential for good health. But babies should not be exposed to the sun without proper protection. Their skin is very thin and burns easily. They need to be protected against the sun's strong rays, which can cause dehydration and allergic reactions. PABA-free sunscreen (PABA can cause allergic reactions), a hat and a parasol are good protection against the sun. Avoid the strong sunlight of mid-day, between 10 a.m. and 2 p.m.

Before the age of 6 months – The skin is very delicate at this age. Applying sunscreen could cause an allergic reaction.

After 6 months – When your baby plays outside, make sure she wears a hat and clothing made with tightly woven fibres; it should also cover her arms and legs.

! Apply sunscreen 30 minutes before she goes outside. Apply it again every 2 hours or after swimming.

Up to 85% of UV rays can pass through the clouds. Always apply sunscreen, even when it's cloudy. Choose one with a high sun protection factor (SPF of at least 15). Your pharmacist can advise you. Baby oil doesn't protect against the sun; it increases the risk of sunburn.

If your child is taking medication, talk to your doctor or pharmacist. Some medication may cause your child to develop photosensitivity; her skin may become more sensitive to the sun, or some sunscreens may cause irritation, redness or swelling.

Children should never go to a tanning salon.

Eyes and the sun

The sun's UV rays are dangerous to the eyes; this means both the sun's direct rays and rays that reflect off the sand, water or snow. The intensity of the rays can be decreased by:

- The natural closing of the eye's pupil;
- Wearing a wide-brimmed hat or cap;
- Wearing good-quality protective sunglasses with a scratch-proof surface that blocks UV rays (UV 400).

Practical advice about the sun

- Never seat your child facing the sun. A baby under the age of 1 must always be in the shade or in indirect sunlight.
- Never let your child look directly at the sun, even during an eclipse.
- Don't let your child play with magnifying glasses or mirrors that could reflect the sun's rays.
- See a professional (optometrist or ophthalmologist) if your child cannot tolerate sunlight, even if it is indirect, or if her eyes water when she goes outside.

Quality of sun protection

Choose sunglass lenses and frames carefully.

The lenses must block all of the sun's harmful rays, especially the UV rays. UV 400 should be indicated on the sunglasses. An indication of UV 100 or UV protection is not good enough.

Lens colour is important. Green and grey lenses don't change how colours are seen. Avoid other coloured lenses that change the way things look.

Most sunglasses sold in department and grocery stores have moulded lenses that may have defects. This can cause headaches and distort the way objects are seen.

! Poor quality sunglasses are worse for your child's eyes than no sunglasses. Your optometrist can offer you helpful advice.

Tobacco smoke

> **!** Cigarettes, cigars and pipes produce very dangerous smoke that is especially harmful to babies.

The children of smokers are more likely than those of non-smokers to get asthma, earaches, bronchitis, pneumonia and upper respiratory infections. Exposure to smoke also increases the risk of Sudden Infant Death Syndrome, regardless of the number of cigarettes smoked in the presence of the child. Children are more fragile than adults because their organs are still developing.

Good reasons to smoke outside

Smoking in the house threatens the health of your family and yourself. Hazardous products found in smoke spread through the air and stay there for several months, even if you open the windows, run the stove fan or smoke only in one room. Even a very powerful ventilation system, like those sometimes found in public buildings, can not completely eliminate tobacco smoke! That's why you should not smoke in the house even if your children aren't home. For the sake of your child's health, smoke outside your home or car.

Quit smoking

The only way to protect your child from the harmful effects of tobacco is to stop smoking. Make this a gift to yourself! Your baby will be grateful, both now and later. More children of smokers take up smoking as teenagers.

Many community resources offer support. Don't be shy to ask for help… Find out more at your CLSC. The telephone help line J'Arrête offers information and support to people who want to quit smoking: 1 866 527-7383. There are about 160 quit-smoking centres that offer free individual consultation and group programs for smokers that want to quit. To find out where stop-smoking centres are located, call 1 866 jarrête or visit www.jarrete.qc.ca

> A health professional can explain various ways to help you quit smoking.

Dangerous products: medication, cleaning products and others

Every year, several thousand children between the ages of 1 and 5 are poisoned in Québec. They've either swallowed a toxic product, got it in their eyes or on their skin, or breathed in toxic fumes. These products are found everywhere: in the home, at school and in the park.

Many common products are toxic for children, including vitamins and flu medication, cleaning products, fuel, plants, fungus and pesticides, nail polish remover, car-care products and hair colour. They're found in your kitchen cupboards, bathroom, bedroom, garage and even your purse.

Prevent poisoning

- Keep toxic products out of children's sight and reach.
- Keep them in cupboards or drawers that have safety latches or in places where they can't be reached.
- Never leave medicine on the changing table or near your baby's crib.
- Keep the telephone number handy for the Centre antipoison du Québec: 1 800 463-5060.

Other simple things that can help prevent poisoning in children:

- When buying medicine or hazardous products, choose containers with safety caps, even though the caps are not 100% effective.
- Keep products in their original containers.
- Don't transfer hazardous products into food containers, like gas in a soft drink bottle.
- Keep ashtrays and alcohol out of reach.
- To avoid overdoses, carefully read instructions on medication before giving it to your child, or talk to your pharmacist.
- Keep diaper bags and purses out of your baby's reach.
- When visiting, do a quick look around to make sure your child will be safe.

The Centre antipoison du Québec has published several pamphlets on how to prevent poisoning. For more information, visit the Web site at www.csssvc.qc.ca/services/capq.php.

When a chemical gets splashed in the eyes

If a chemical gets in your child's eye, rinse right away with warm water for 10 to 15 minutes while the eye is kept open.

Then call the Centre antipoison du Québec at 1 800 463-5060. They will be able to advise you on what to do next and tell you whether your child needs to see a doctor.

Plants

The leaves and fruit of many indoor and outdoor plants are toxic and can cause any of the following problems: skin irritation, swelling, difficulty swallowing, dry mouth, diarrhea, vomiting or hallucinations. As soon as your baby begins to crawl or walk, put your plants out of reach.

You can get a list of toxic plants from the Centre antipoison du Québec: www.csssvc.qc.ca/services/capq.php.

Health

Photo: iStockphoto

First aid

Prevention is better than cure. But if your child has an accident, the following first aid advice should be helpful. Start by washing your hands with soap and water before doing any first aid. And above all, stay calm.

A deep cut that bleeds a lot – Don't waste time cleaning the wound. Put a clean bandage on it and apply pressure to stop the bleeding. Call Info-Santé.

Photo: Société de sauvetage

Cuts

A small cut or scratch – Wash your hands with soapy water. Rinse the wound with running water. Clean it with soap and water, carefully removing dirt and pebbles, if necessary. Put an adhesive bandage on a small wound. On a larger wound, use a pressure bandage.

Call Info-Santé to find out if you should see a doctor for an examination or for stitches, butterfly bandages or tissue adhesive to heal the wound.

Bites

If your child has been bitten by an animal or another child, wash the wound under running water, and soap for several minutes. Rinse and cover the wound with a dry bandage if it's bleeding; otherwise leave it uncovered. Most bites don't break the skin. Teeth marks and bruises aren't considered broken skin.

Nosebleeds

If your child has a nosebleed:

- Reassure him;
- Have him sit up with his head tilted slightly forward;
- Make sure he's breathing through his mouth;
- Use your thumb and index finger to pinch his nose, just below the bony part;
- Maintain constant pressure for 5 to 10 minutes, until the blood clots.
- Your child may gently blow his nose after a few hours.

Babies rarely have nosebleeds, but it is a common problem among children. Bleeding often occurs when the nose is irritated after a cold or when your child puts his finger or another object in his nostril. Nosebleeds are generally not serious.

Photo: Société de sauvetage

The following are preventive steps to take after a nosebleed:

- Avoid using aspirin (ASA), antihistamine (cold or cough syrup, Benadryl™, Claritin™, Reactine™, Aerius™, etc.) and anti-inflammatories (Advil™, Motrin™, etc.). These medications thin the blood.
- Acetaminophen (Tempra™, Tylenol™, Abenol™) does not increase the risk of nosebleeds and can be used without any problem.
- Keep the humidity in your child's room between 30% and 45%.

Falls or blows

Did your child tumble down the stairs or hit his head? Is he conscious, crying, shouting or screaming? He isn't bleeding but already has a big bump on his head? You should put a wet washcloth rinsed in cold water on the bump. Watch him over the next few hours to make sure he's behaving normally.

After a fall or a blow:

- If your child is less than 1 year old, see a doctor, since it's harder to assess his condition.
- Regardless of his age, go to the emergency room if he loses consciousness at any time.
- If he stays unconscious, place him on his side and call an ambulance.

It's important to see a doctor in the following situations:

- The child is half asleep;
- He vomits several times in a row;
- He has trouble moving an arm or leg;
- He has convulsions, is very agitated, is shaking;
- Bruising appears behind his ear or under his eyes.

Mouth and teeth injuries

If your child bites his tongue or lip

Gently wipe off the blood with a clean, dry cloth. Apply direct pressure to stop the bleeding. A wet washcloth soaked in very cold water will prevent swelling. If the wound seems deep or continues bleeding, see a health professional to find out whether stitches are needed.

If a baby tooth is knocked out

Don't put the tooth back into the gum.

Put it in cold milk and avoid touching the root.

Go immediately to the dentist if possible; otherwise go to the emergency room.

Broken or shifted tooth

See a dentist as soon as possible.

Salinex®

Nasal hygiene - Application instructions

Child under 2 years or unable to blow its nose properly

1. Lay the child on its back, head straight.
2. Apply the contents of 1 full dropper of Salinex to each nostril.
3. Clean the inside of the nostrils with a cotton swab.
4. Repeat application of 1 full dropper to each nostril.
5. Children over 2 years: seat the child with its head bent slightly forward and help the child to blow its nose, one nostril at a time.
6. These instructions may be used for daily nasal hygiene. For children suffering from colds, earaches, rhinitis and sinusitis, use as recommended by a physician.

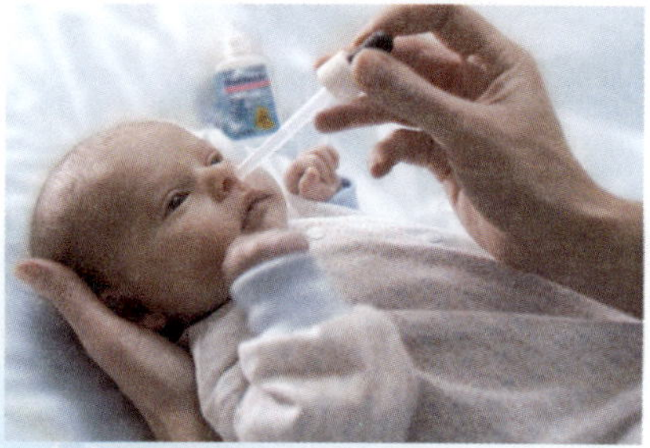

Child able to blow its nose properly

1. Seat the child on a chair, head facing forward and ask the child to look you in the eyes (to avoid wrinkling the nose).
2. Spray each nostril with Salinex according to recommended dosage, ask the child to tilt its head forward slightly and blow its nose, one nostril at a time.
3. In the case of nasal secretions, repeat the cycle of sprays in each nostril until the secretions stop (air flow).
4. Clean the inside of the nostrils with a cotton swab as needed, and ask the child to blow its nose again, one nostril at a time.
5. These instructions may be used for daily nasal hygiene. For children suffering from colds, earaches, rhinitis and sinusitis, use as recommended by a physician.

Salinex® : an aqueous solution containing 9 mg/mL of sodium chloride

SANDOZ QC, Canada J4B 7K8 1-800-361-3062 www.sandoz.ca

Salinex®

Breathe Freely!

RECOMMENDED BY PHARMACISTS, ENT* SPECIALISTS AND PEDIATRICIANS

A saline solution for soothing effective relief from a dry irritated nose.

SANDOZ

*ear, nose and throat specialists

January 2009

A hit to the teeth

If your baby falls or is struck on a tooth, the tooth may become greyish several months after the accident. See your dentist.

Burns

Scalds from hot liquid

If a boiling liquid touched a part of your child's body covered by clothing, don't remove the clothing before getting the burn into cold water. If you can't get the burn under water, put a clean, wet cloth soaked in cold water on it; don't rub the burn.

Never put baby oil, vinegar, butter, toothpaste or oily ointment on the burn, as these things will make it worse.

! Go to the emergency room if the clothing is stuck to the skin or the burn is widespread.

★ As quickly as possible, immerse the burn in cold water or hold it under running water for at least 10 minutes.

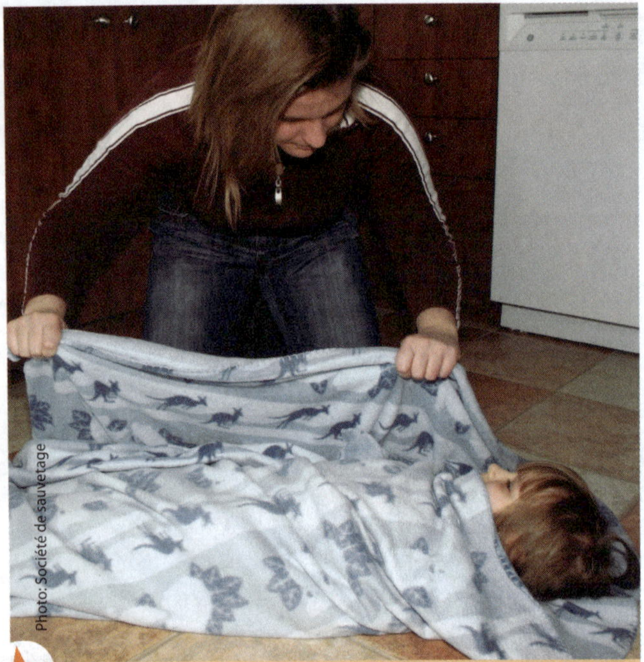

If your child's clothing is on fire, lay him down and put out the flames by quickly rolling him in a blanket (keep his head uncovered).

Scalds from fire

Don't remove the child's clothing. Immerse the burn in water or hold it under cold running water for 10 minutes.

If you can't get the burn under water, put a clean, wet cloth soaked in cold water on it; don't rub it.

Call 9-1-1.

Scalds from electric shock

If your child gets a shock, turn off the current before getting your child away from the outlet.

Call 9-1-1 if your child is unconscious.

If he's stopped breathing, start cardiopulmonary resuscitation (CPR) if you know how to perform it.

! Electricity can cause serious internal burns even when no burns are visible on the skin. Always take your child to the emergency room. He needs to be examined.

★ Your child can get a shock from a power cord or an electrical outlet without a socket cover.

Photo: Julie Ward

A small object in the nose

Even though your baby is being carefully watched, he can put all kinds of objects in his nose, such as buttons, rocks, pieces of foam, dried peas and peanuts.

> **!** If your baby is less than 18 months old, don't try to remove the object; you may push it further into his nose. Take him to the emergency room.
>
> If your baby is more than 18 months old, you can try to remove the object if it's visible, if you can grasp it with your fingers and if you're able to keep your child's head completely still. If not, take him to the emergency room.

Sand in the eye

To remove sand, rinse the eye gently with warm water. If you see a grain of sand in the corner of your child's eye, try to remove it with the corner of a damp tissue.

If you can't remove the sand:

- Don't keep trying;
- Stop your child from rubbing his eye, and apply a towel soaked in cold water for relief;
- See a doctor.

Insect bites

To protect children under the age of 2 from insect bites:

- Use mosquito netting on the stroller;
- Dress your child in long-sleeved shirts and pants;
- Avoid outings when mosquitoes are most active: at sunrise and sunset.

Insect repellents or products that keep bugs away should be used with caution. Soy-oil- or DEET-based products can be used on children between the ages of 6 months and 2 years when the risk of complications from insect bites is high. This could be the case when there are allergies or due to a risk of transmitted diseases when travelling abroad. You can use a product that contains less than 10% DEET. Apply only a small amount, once a day, to parts of the body exposed to the air. Don't put any on the face or hands. Citronella, lavender or citronella-scented eucalyptus-derived products are not recommended for children under the age of 2.

If your child gets an insect bite, wash it with soap and water. A cold compress will relieve itching and reduce swelling.

> ! If the swelling extends to other parts of the body or your child has difficulty breathing, he may be having a severe allergic reaction. Call 9-1-1.

Choking

> ! Call 9-1-1 if your child is choking, cannot cough and is having trouble breathing.

Choking can start like this: your baby puts an object like a candy, seed or piece of grape in his mouth and starts choking. He coughs, squirms and cries. Don't do anything as long as he can cough forcefully. He is trying to dislodge the object himself.

What should I do?

Children 1 year old or younger: If your baby is crying weakly, makes a high-pitched sound when breathing or is turning blue:

- Quickly lay him on his stomach on your forearm, which is resting on your thigh. The baby's head should be lower than his body and he should be facing downward (see illustration).
- With the palm of your hand, give him 5 quick hits to the back, between his shoulder blades, with the palm sliding towards his head.

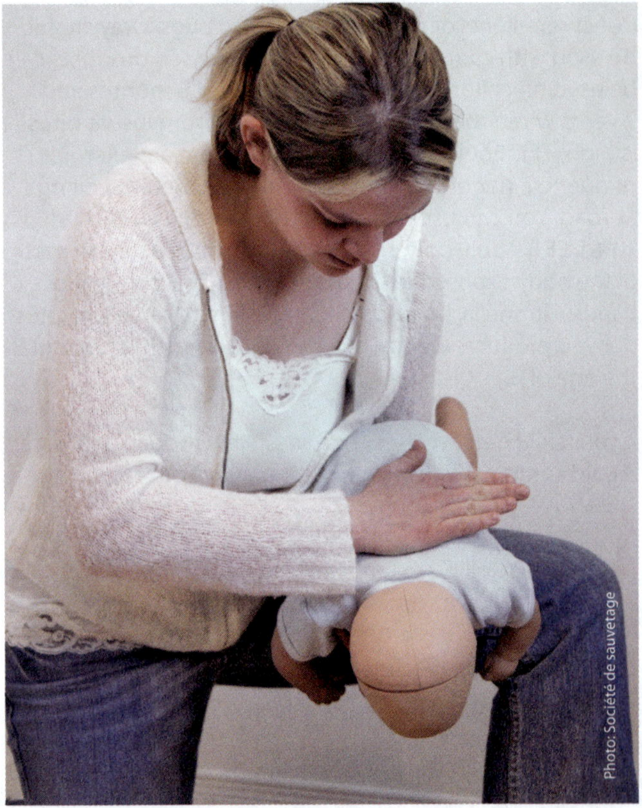
Photo: Société de sauvetage

If this doesn't work:

- Lay your baby on his back with his head lower than his body;
- Place 2 fingers on his sternum (between the breasts), keep your fingers straight and quickly press your fingers onto his sternum, then release. Repeat 5 times in a row without moving your fingers.

Make sure that you don't touch the tip of the sternum.

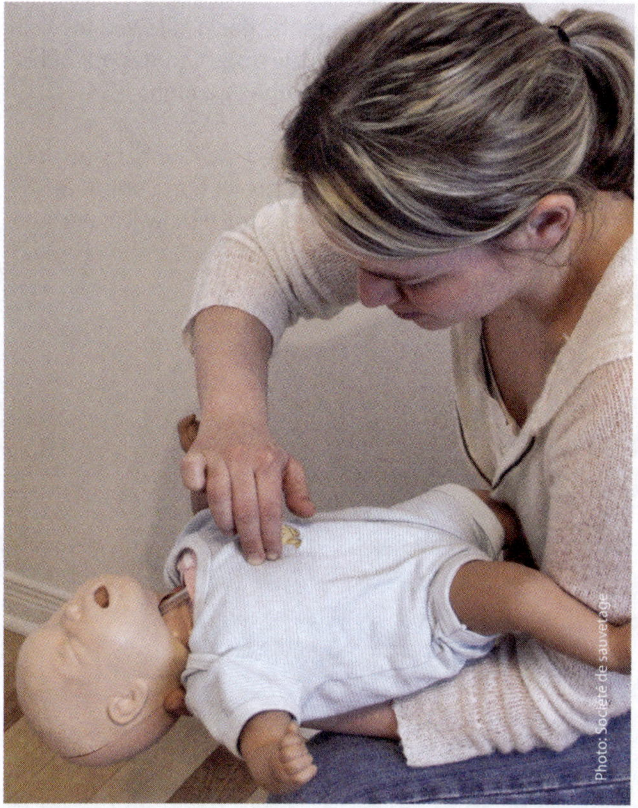

Photo: Société de sauvetage

Continue to give 5 quick hits to the back, followed by 5 presses to the sternum, until the object comes out of his mouth or the baby starts to breathe or cough.

Once the object has been dislodged, sit your baby on your knee to calm and reassure him. Only let him drink if he is breathing well. Take him to the doctor, who will make sure there are no complications.

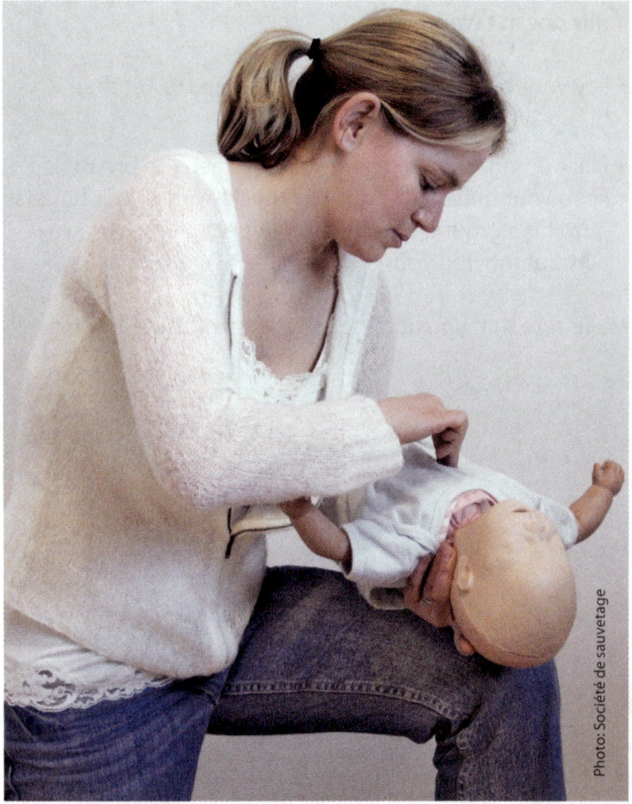

Photo: Société de sauvetage

This can also be done standing up.

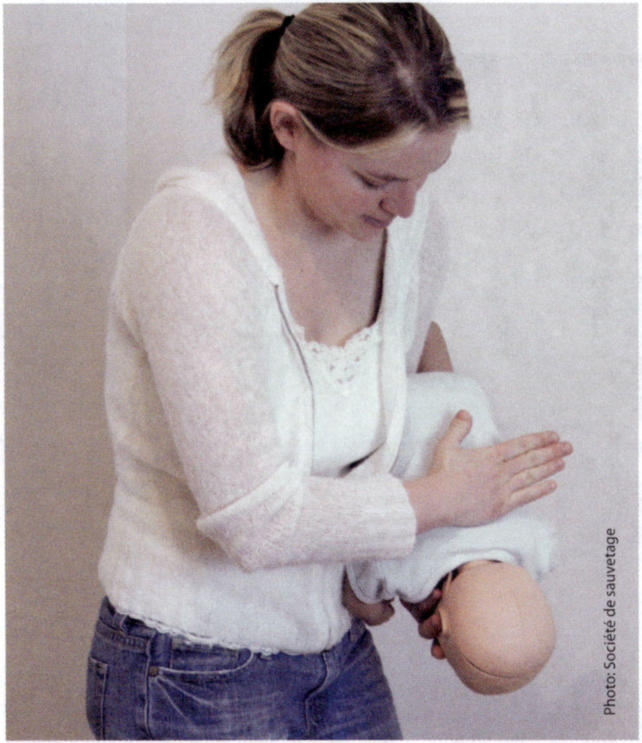

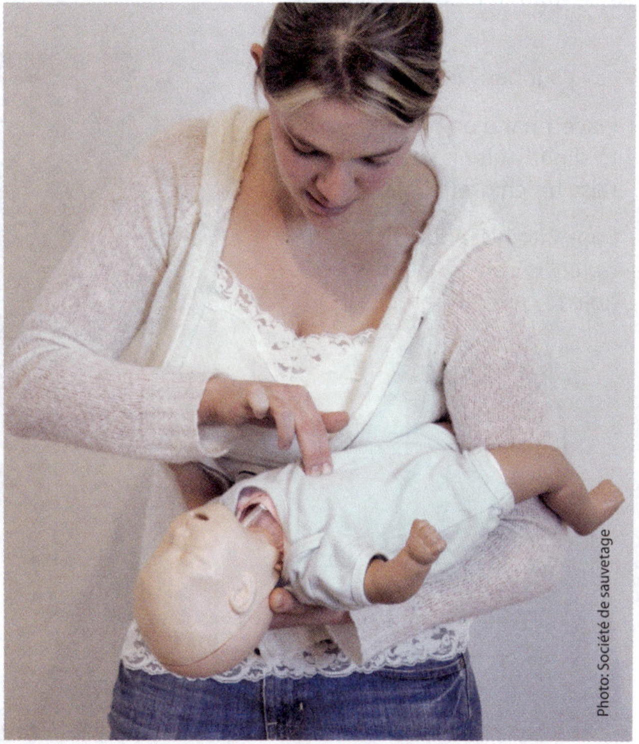

If the object is still stuck and your baby becomes unconscious, call 9-1-1 right away and perform the following steps while waiting for the ambulance:

- Lay your baby on his back.
- Place 1 hand on his forehead to slightly tilt his head back and raise his chin with 2 fingers;
- Look into his mouth. If the object is visible, you may be able to carefully remove it.

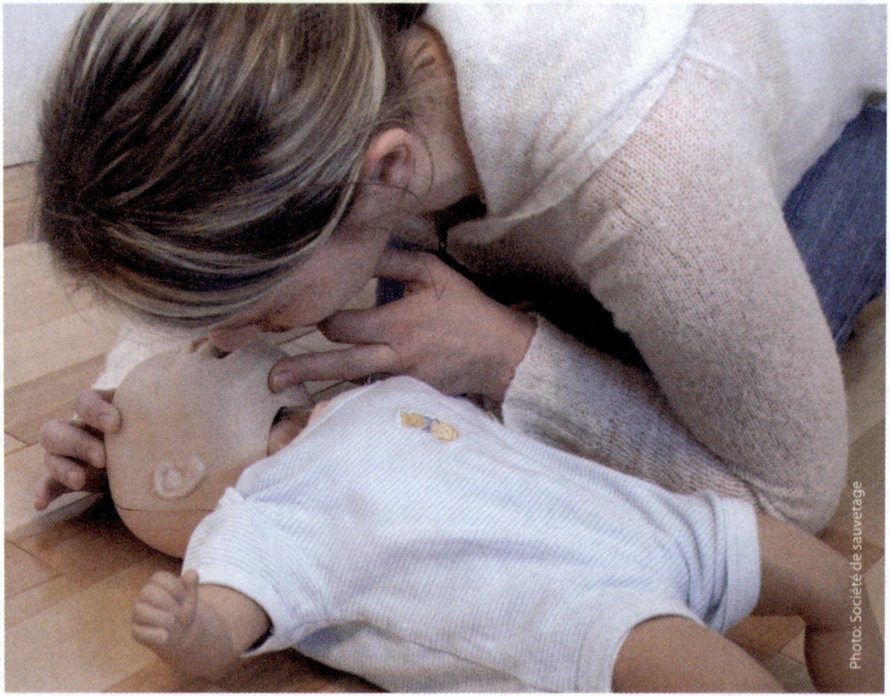

Photo: Société de sauvetage

If your baby is not breathing:

- Cover his nose and mouth with your mouth and blow twice;

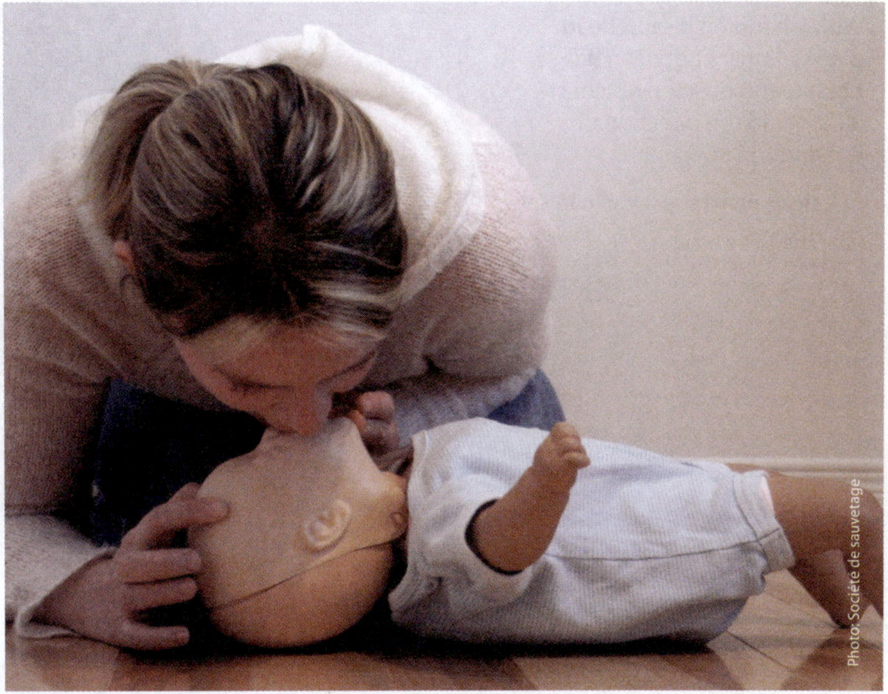
Photo: Société de sauvetage

- With 1 hand on his forehead, place 2 fingers between his breasts and push on his chest 30 times in the direction of the floor;
- Check again to see if you can see the object;

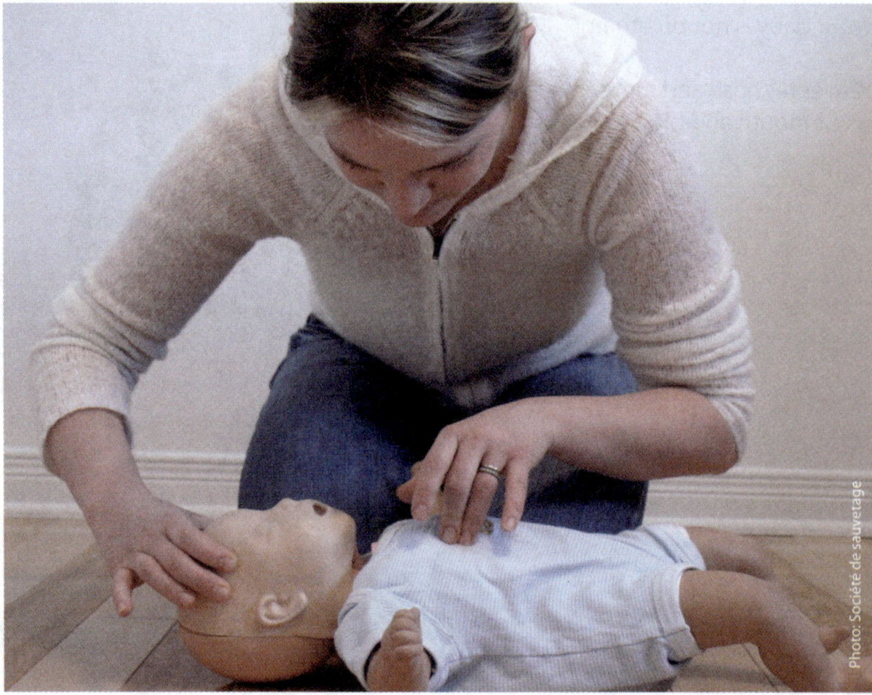

- Repeat these steps until the ambulance arrives or your baby starts breathing.

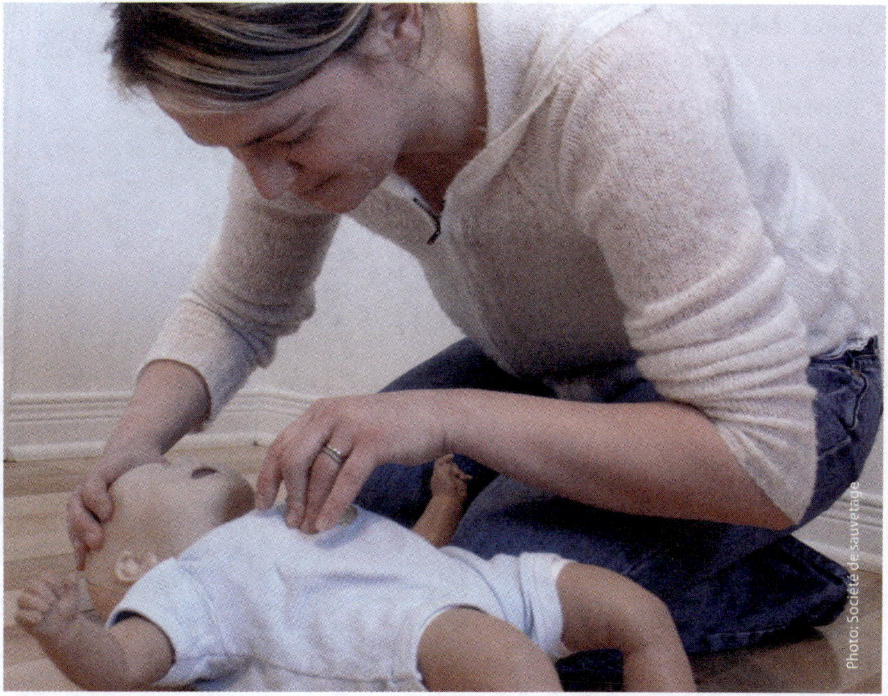

Children over the age of 1: Try the Heimlich manoeuvre:

- Stand behind your child and place your arms around his waist;
- Make a fist with 1 hand, cover it with the other hand, place it just above the navel;
- Exert quick and short blows inward and upward;
- Repeat until the object comes out.

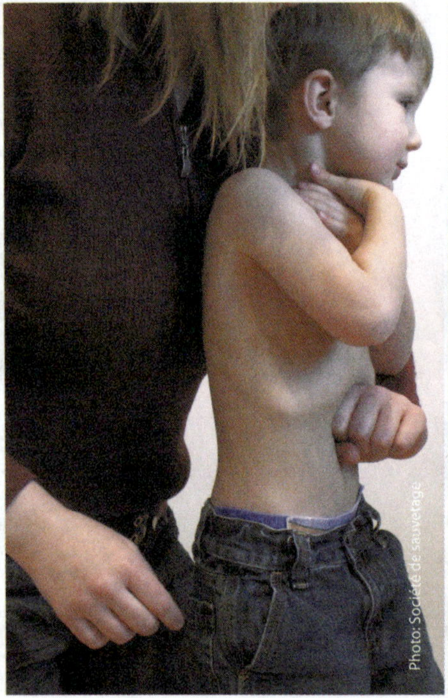

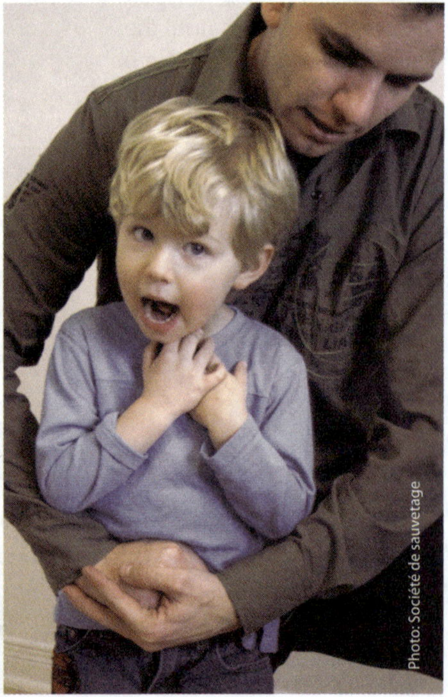

Poisoning

If you think your child has become poisoned or intoxicated, do the following:

!

- If he's not breathing or is unconscious, call 9-1-1;
- If he's swallowed a hazardous product, call the Centre antipoison du Québec: 1 800 463-5060.

Poisoning is the 2nd most common cause of hospitalization among children up to the age of 4. It often happens at home. Babies are often poisoned by medication (vitamins, antibiotics, fever medication) or household products (cleaning products, fuel, cosmetics, plants, etc.).

What should I do?

- Don't make your child vomit.
- Don't give any treatment (activated charcoal or an agent that induces vomiting) unless a nurse from the Centre antipoison du Québec or a health professional recommends it.
- Don't try to stop the product's effect.

Keep the product close by so you can read the label to the Centre antipoison du Québec nurse, if needed.

- If the toxic product got into your baby's eyes or onto his skin, rinse several times with clear water then call the Centre antipoison du Québec.
- Milk is not a cure. It doesn't help to give your child milk if he swallowed a toxic product.

The Centre antipoison du Québec is an emergency service available 24 hours a day. Staff will tell you what to do depending on your child's condition, the product in question and how the poisoning occurred (through the mouth, skin or eyes).

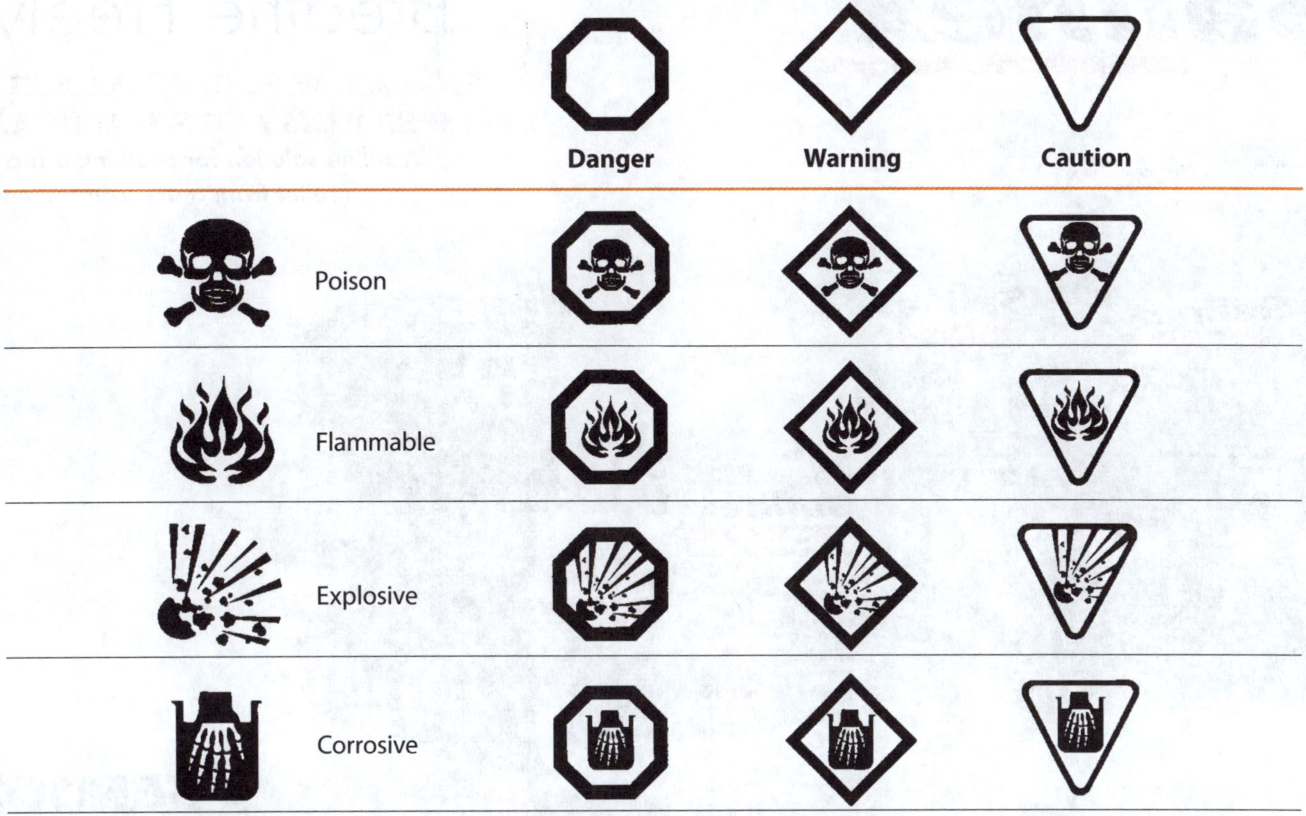
Danger
Warning
Caution
Poison
Flammable
Explosive
Corrosive

Salinex®
Breathe Freely!
RECOMMENDED BY PHARMACISTS, ENT* SPECIALISTS AND PEDIATRICIANS
A saline solution for soothing effective relief from a dry irritated nose.
30 mL
DIN 00489530
Code 7660
Salinex
INFANTS/CHILDREN
NASAL DROPS
BREATHE FREELY!
RECOMMENDED BY PHARMACISTS ENT* SPECIALISTS AND PEDIATRICIANS
Soothing effective relief from a dry irritated nose
SAFE for INFANTS and CHILDREN
SANDOZ
30 mL
DIN 00489530
Code 7640
Salinex
CHILDREN
NASAL SPRAY
BREATHE FREELY!
RECOMMENDED BY PHARMACISTS, ENT* SPECIALISTS AND PEDIATRICIANS
Soothing effective relief from a dry irritated nose
Safe for CHILDREN
30 mL
DIN 00489530
Code 7660
Salinex®
INFANTS-CHILDREN/BÉBÉS - ENFANTS
NASAL DROPS/GOUTTES NASALES
BREATHE FREELY!
RESPIREZ LIBREMENT!
SANDOZ
30 mL
Salinex
SANDOZ
SANDOZ
*ear, nose and throat specialists
January 2009

Photo: iStockphoto

Photo: iStockphoto

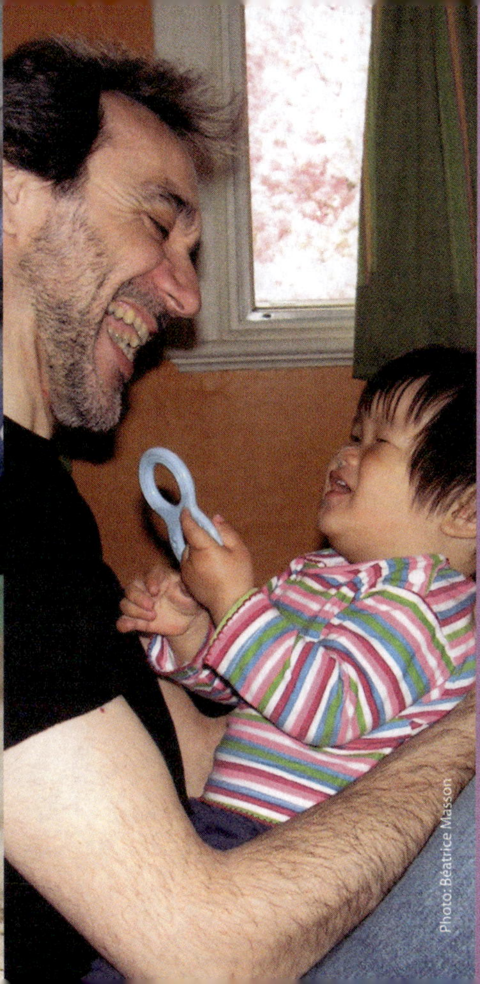
Photo: Béatrice Masson

Useful information

Becoming a parent

Foreword

Services Québec is delighted to present *From Tiny Tot to Toddler, Practical guide for parents from pregnancy to age two,* a guide designed to give parents the most comprehensive information on the important stage of family life marked by the arrival of a child. The "Becoming a parent" section of this guide provides general information on the government programs and services available to parents.

If after reading the "Becoming a parent" section, you have questions regarding the programs and services mentioned, go to www.servicesquebec.gouv.qc.ca, or feel free to call Services Québec at 418 644-4545 (Québec City area), 514 644-4545 (Montréal area) or 1 877 644-4545 (elsewhere in Québec), or visit a Services Québec office near you.

For information on Government of Canada programs, call Service Canada at 1 800 622-6232.

Services Québec wishes to thank all those involved for their assistance in updating the "Becoming a parent" section.

Happy reading!

Parental leave

Leave granted under the *Act respecting labour standards*

Unionized employees should check the clauses in their collective agreements dealing with leave. You should also refer to the section on the Québec Parental Insurance Plan because some unpaid leave specified by the *Act respecting labour standards* is now paid under the provisions of this plan.

Leave granted for medical examinations related to pregnancy

An employee may be absent from work, without pay, for medical examinations related to her pregnancy. She must notify her employer as soon as possible of the time she will be away.

Maternity leave

Generally speaking, Québec employees are entitled to the maternity leave provided for under the *Act respecting labour standards.*

"To take my parental leave, what do I need to do?"
"To terminate my lease, what do I need to know?"
"How do I obtain my child's birth certificate?"
Services Québec
is THE gateway to your government services.
Information on over 3,000 topics
www.servicesquebec.gouv.qc.ca
514-644-4545 • 418-644-4545 • 1-877-644-4545
You're at the right place!
Services Québec

Leave period

- Maternity leave may last no more than 18 consecutive weeks without pay.
- If the employee requests it, the employer can grant longer maternity leave.
- Maternity leave may not start before the beginning of the 16th week before the anticipated date of delivery.

Provisions also stipulate that the employee may be absent in certain cases, for example:

- When there is a danger of interruption of the pregnancy or a danger to the health of the mother or the unborn child because of the pregnancy
- When the pregnancy is interrupted before the start of the 20th week preceding the anticipated date of delivery
- When the pregnancy is interrupted as of the 20th week
- When the mother's or the child's state of health requires it

Three weeks before her departure, or less if her state of health forces her to leave sooner, the worker must provide her employer with a written notice indicating the date on which her maternity leave will begin and the anticipated date of her return to work.

The notice must be accompanied by a medical certificate attesting to the pregnancy and the anticipated date of delivery. A written report signed by a midwife may be substituted for the medical certificate.

At the end of the maternity leave, the employer must reinstate the employee to her usual position and give her the salary and benefits to which she would have been entitled had she remained at work.

Spousal leave upon the birth or adoption of a child

An employee may be absent from work for five days upon the birth or adoption of a child, or when the pregnancy is interrupted as of the 20th week. The first two days of absence are paid if the employee has accumulated at least 60 days of service. The employee must notify the employer of their absence as soon as possible. Since January 1, 2006, a person who adopts the child of his or her spouse has also been entitled to this leave.

This leave may be taken one day at a time if the employee so requests, but it may be taken no later than 15 days after the child's arrival at the residence of the father or mother, or the interruption of the pregnancy.

Paternity leave

When the Québec Parental Insurance Plan came into effect on January 1, 2006, so too did a provision of the *Act respecting labour standards*: employees are entitled to five consecutive weeks of unpaid paternity leave. They may also receive the allowance provided by the Québec Parental Insurance Plan. Paternity leave may not be transferred to the mother or divided between the father and mother. It is in addition to the five days of leave (two paid) mentioned in the section above. It may be taken at any time but may not begin before the week the child is born and must end no later than 52 weeks after birth.

For example, Paul's spouse gives birth on Wednesday, February 11, 2009. Paul is entitled to five days of leave (two paid) starting on February 11, 2009, although he is not required to take the three days of unpaid leave. Then Paul's spouse, who took an 18 week maternity leave ending on Wednesday, June 3, 2009, takes 32 consecutive weeks of parental leave (she is entitled to 52 weeks, as is Paul, but under the Québec Parental Insurance Plan, the allowance is paid for a maximum of 32 weeks, to be divided between the spouses). They agreed that Paul would take the five-week paternity leave to which he is entitled starting on June 3, 2009. This leave, for which he is entitled to an allowance equal to 70% of his average gross weekly salary under the Québec Parental Insurance Plan, will end on July 8, 2009, or within the timeframe specified by the *Act respecting labour standards* (paternity leave must end no later than 52 weeks after the birth of the child).

Parental leave

The mother and father of a newborn child as well as anyone who adopts a child are entitled to parental leave without pay for up to 52 consecutive weeks. This is in addition to maternity leave, which lasts a maximum of 18 weeks or, in the case of the father, to the five-week paternity leave that came into effect on January 1, 2006. Parental leave may be paid according to the terms of the Québec Parental Insurance Plan and, according to the terms of this plan, divided between the father and mother.

Since January 1, 2006, anyone who adopts the child of his or her spouse has been entitled to parental leave and to the allowance provided.

Parental leave may not begin prior to the week in which the child is born or the week the child is entrusted to the employee's care in the case of adoption. It can also begin the week that the employee leaves work in order to travel outside Québec to pick up the child. Parental leave ends no later than 70 weeks after the birth of the child or 70 weeks after the child is entrusted to the employee's care in the case of adoption.

To take parental leave, employees must give their employer at least three weeks notice, indicating the date on which the leave will begin and the date on which they will return to work. Notice may be shorter in certain cases.

At the end of parental leave, the employer must allow employees to return to their usual positions at the same salary and with the same benefits to which they would have been entitled had they remained at work. If the position has been eliminated, the employee retains the same rights and privileges as if he or she had not taken leave.

However, these provisions must not give the employee an advantage he or she would not have had if he or she had not taken leave. Furthermore, the employee's participation in group insurance and retirement plans must not be affected by his or her absence, provided he or she regularly makes the contributions required under the plans and the employer pays its share.

Unexpected events

If an unexpected event (e.g., a child becomes ill or is hospitalized, or an employee becomes ill or is injured in an accident) occurs during maternity leave, parental leave or (since January 1, 2006) paternity leave, the leave may be split up or suspended, with some restrictions. If such an event happens, contact Commission des normes du travail for information on your rights.

For more information, contact Commission des normes du travail (CNT):

- www.cnt.gouv.qc.ca
- Montréal area: 514 873-7061
- Elsewhere in Québec: 1 800 265-1414
- Teletypewriter (see page 622)

Financial assistance

Tax credit for infertility treatment

Individuals may apply for a refundable tax credit for artificial insemination or in vitro fertilization fees. The credit is equal to 50% of all fees eligible for the credit and may not exceed $10,000 per year. To apply for the tax credit, you must attach the duly completed form and supporting documents to your tax return.

For more information, contact the Revenu Québec office in your area or visit the Revenu Québec website at www.revenu.gouv.qc.ca.

Québec Parental Insurance Plan

A concrete way to strike a better balance between work and family

The Québec Parental Insurance Plan (QPIP) issues benefits to all eligible salaried or self-employed workers who take maternity, paternity, parental or adoption leave. As of January 1, 2006, it replaced the maternity, parental and adoption benefits available to new parents in Québec under the federal employment insurance plan.

The QPIP is an income replacement plan, which means you must have earned employment or business income in order to be eligible.

Advantages of the QPIP

With the QPIP, Québec families enjoy a more generous, more flexible and more accessible plan — in short, a plan that's better adapted to their actual needs.

More generous

The maximum insurable income taken into account when calculating the amount of benefits was $62,000 in 2009. This income is indexed every year on January 1 based on the rate set by the Commission de la santé et de la sécurité du travail. Benefits may cover as much as 75% of the recipient's average weekly income.

More flexible

The QPIP offers a choice of two options — the basic or special plan — that differ in terms of the duration of leave and the percentage of income replaced. This makes it possible to receive lower benefits for a longer period of time or higher benefits for a shorter period. Benefits are payable starting on the first day of eligibility.

More accessible

Both salaried and self-employed workers may be eligible.

Farmers with a salaried job on or off the farm who hold shares in a farming outfit may be eligible.

The minimum insurable income taken into account when calculating the amount of benefits is $2,000, regardless of the number of hours worked.

In addition, paternity benefits are available exclusively for new fathers.

Eligibility

To be eligible for the Québec Parental Insurance Plan, you must:

- Be the parent of a child born or adopted on or after January 1, 2006

and

- Contribute to the QPIP.

If you are a salaried worker, you must also:

- Reside in Québec at the start of the benefit period
- Have an insurable income of at least $2,000 in the reference period, regardless of the number of hours worked
- Have stopped working or seen a drop of at least 40% in your usual weekly earnings

If you are a self-employed worker, you must also

- Reside in Québec at the start of the benefit period and have resided in Québec on December 31 of the year prior to the benefit period start date
- Have had an insurable income of at least $2,000 in the reference period
- Have stopped your business activities or reduced the time spent on business activities by at least 40%

If you are both a salaried and self-employed worker, you must also

- Reside in Québec at the start of the benefit period and have resided in Québec on December 31 of the year prior to the benefit period start date
- Have had an insurable income of at least $2,000 in the reference period
- Have stopped your business activities or reduced the time spent on business activities by at least 40% and stopped working or seen a drop of at least 40% in your usual weekly earnings

Benefits

Four types of benefits are available under the QPIP: maternity benefits for the mother only, paternity benefits for the father only, parental benefits both parents can share, and adoption benefits both parents can share.

Parents must choose between two options: the basic plan or the special plan. They must then decide on the length of leave and their income replacement rate.

The first parent to receive benefits determines the choice of plan. This choice cannot be changed. Consequently, one parent's choice affects the other, even in the case of shared custody.

The following table indicates the maximum number of benefit weeks and the percentage of average weekly income for each type of benefit under each plan.

How to apply

The Québec government now offers the option of completing an application for benefits online at www.rqap.gouv.qc.ca.

Applications can also be made by telephone with the help of a customer service agent by calling toll-free 1 888 610-7727 (QPIP).

Type of benefits	Basic plan		Special plan	
	Maximum number of benefit weeks	Percentage of average weekly income	Maximum number of benefit weeks	Percentage of average weekly income
Maternity	18	70%	15	75%
Paternity	5	70%	3	75%
Parental	7 ▶ 25 (7+25=32) ▶	70% 55%	25	75%
Adoption	12 ▶ 25 (12+25=37) ▶	70% 55%	28	75%

Special pregnancy benefit

If an expectant mother is a beneficiary of the employment assistance (social aid) program, the Ministère de l'Emploi et de la Solidarité sociale may grant her an additional $55 a month as a special pregnancy benefit, in addition to her monthly benefit. This benefit may also be paid to the parent beneficiary of a dependent child who is pregnant.

This assistance, which is paid during each month of pregnancy until delivery, will enable the expectant mother to buy the foods required for a proper diet during this period.

To obtain this benefit, the expectant mother must provide her local employment centre case officer with a certificate signed by a physician or midwife confirming her pregnancy and setting out the number of weeks pregnant and expected delivery date.

For more information, contact your local employment centre.

The address is listed in the blue pages of the telephone book in the Gouvernement du Québec section, under the heading "Aide financière."

Child benefits

Québec families may be eligible for various benefits, such as the Canada Child Tax Benefit (CCTB), the National Child Benefit Supplement (NCBS), the Child Disability Benefit (CDB) for children under 18 years of age, and the Universal Child Care Benefit (UCCB).

To receive these benefits, both the eligible individual and his or her spouse must file income tax returns every year, even if they have no income to declare.

Canada Child Tax Benefit

The federal government's Canada Child Tax Benefit varies according to family income, the number and age of the children, the family situation and the deduction for daycare expenses.

The non-taxable benefit is paid every month. It is revised if any change occurs in the family situation, such as the birth or death of a child, a change in beneficiary, a separation or a divorce.

Eligibility for this benefit is reviewed every year in July based on the data provided on the income tax return for the previous year.

National Child Benefit Supplement (NCBS)

Low-income families with children are also eligible for the National Child Benefit Supplement (NCBS), which is included in the payment of the Canada Child Tax Benefit. The NCBS is the Canadian government's contribution to the National Child Benefit Program (NCBP), a joint initiative of the federal, provincial and territorial governments.

Child Disability Benefit (CDB)

The Child Disability Benefit (CDB) is a non-taxable supplement to the CCTB and can be as high as $2,394.96 per child. Only children with a severe and prolonged impairment, as stipulated in form T2201 (Disability Tax Credit Certificate) are eligible for the CDB. Form T2201 must be completed and sent to the Canada Revenue Agency to register a child if this has not already been done.

Universal Child Care Benefit (UCCB)

The Universal Child Care Benefit (UCCB) is paid monthly to eligible families in order to help them meet their childcare needs for children under six years of age. With the UCCB, families can receive $100 per month for each child under six years of age. The UCCB is paid separately from the Canada Child Tax Benefit (CCTB) and is taxable. The Canada Revenue Agency (CRA) issues payments on behalf of Human Resources and Social Development Canada.

For more information, visit the CRA's website at www.cra-arc.gc.ca/uccb.

ACCIDENT INSURANCE

Free for 12 months

Mail this pre-stamped reply card today!

| | | | | | | | | |

For Head Office use only

Yes, I would like to take advantage of the **Peek-a-Boo Plan** that provides **free accident insurance for 12 months.** I understand that this offer does not entail any further obligation on my part. Please send me the accident insurance policy and the nursery night light to which I am entitled.

Please print.

Your last name ______________________

Your first name ______________________

Adress ______________________ App. ______

City ______________________ Province ______________________

Postal code ______________________ Tel. ______ ______________

Child's date of birth ___/___/______ (D M Y) Expected date of birth ___/___/______ (D M Y)

Child's last name ______________________

Child's first name ______________________

Sex ☐ **M** ☐ **F**

Please allow 4 to 6 weeks for delivery of the accident insurance policy and the night light.

Detach and mail - No stamp required

peek a boo plan™

Gift

Special limited-time offer!

IA INDUSTRIAL ALLIANCE
INSURANCE AND FINANCIAL SERVICES INC.

Agent code | | | | | | |

Agency code | | | |

MV 08

F13-309A(1) (08-09)

Procedure

To apply for the Canada Child Tax Benefit, fill out Form RC66 (Application for Canada Child Tax Benefit) and send it at your earliest convenience to the address indicated on the envelope. If you already receive the CCTB, you do not need to file a new application to receive the UCCB. Your Canada Child Tax Benefit may be paid by direct deposit; simply fill out Form T1-DD (Direct Deposit Request – Individuals).

These forms are usually included with the information documents given to the mother during her stay in hospital. They can also be obtained by contacting the Canada Revenue Agency at one of the numbers below or by downloading them at www.cra-arc.gc.ca/forms:

- To order forms and publications: 1 800 959-2221
- Teletypewriter (see page 622)
- Service for the visually impaired: 1 800 267-1267

For more information on child benefits, please contact the CRA's information centre at 1 800 387-1193 or visit its website at www.cra-arc.gc.ca/benefits.

Child assistance

Régie des rentes du Québec administers the Child Assistance Payment, which provides financial assistance to all families with dependent children under 18 years of age.

The Child Assistance Payment has two components: child assistance payments and the supplement for handicapped children.

Our gift for your child's birth: **simplicity**

You don't need to file an application for child assistance with the Régie des rentes du Québec for your newborn.

By declaring your child's birth to the Registrar of Civil Status, you are automatically signed up for the program.

www.rrq.gouv.qc.ca /enfants

Régie des rentes Québec

Who is eligible?

You are eligible for child assistance payments if:

- You or your spouse are responsible for the care and education of a dependent child under 18 years of age
- The child resides with you
- You reside in Québec
- You or your spouse are one of the following:
  - A Canadian citizen
  - A permanent resident
  - A temporary resident living in Canada for at least 18 months
  - A protected person (refugee)

How to receive child assistance payments

To receive child assistance payments in the case of a **birth**, the parent need not submit an application. The Directeur de l'état civil will automatically notify the Régie of the child's birth.

However, with an **adoption**, you should apply to the Régie. To do so, use the online service or download the "Child Assistance Payment" form on the Régie's website at www.rrq.gouv.qc.ca/en/enfants.

How are benefits calculated?

The Régie calculates child assistance benefits every year based on the following four criteria:

- Conjugal status (with or without spouse)
- The number of dependent children under 18 years of age living with the recipient
- The number of children in shared custody
- Household income

This amount is indexed in January of each year.

To receive child assistance payments, both spouses must file a Québec income tax return form every year, even if one or both spouses have no income to declare. Revenu Québec will send the Régie information regarding household income. New Québec residents who have not filed a Québec income tax return must provide a federal statement of income outside Canada or notice of assessment.

You can use the Calcul@ide tool on the Régie's website to calculate the amount you may receive based on your family situation.

Supplement for Handicapped Children

The Supplement for Handicapped Children is paid to parents of a child with a physical or mental disability that significantly limits him or her in his or her daily activities for an expected period of at least one year. The supplement is paid until the child reaches 18 years of age or until his or her health improves and Régie des rentes du Québec no longer considers him or her handicapped.

The supplement for handicapped children is $171 per month per child in 2009. This amount is the same for everyone, regardless of the child's handicap and household income. The supplement is indexed each year and is non-taxable. It is paid to the person who receives child assistance payments.

To apply for the Supplement for Handicapped Children, you must complete Régie des rentes du Québec's Application for the Supplement for Handicapped Children. It is available on the Régie's website and at Régie client services centres, Services Québec offices, Office des personnes handicapées du Québec, CLSCs, and specialized children's hospitals. The application includes a section that must be completed by the healthcare professional who knows the child's health condition best.

Child assistance payments

Child assistance payments are made to only one person in a family. For a birth, payments are generally made to the mother. However, if the spouse is already receiving payments for other children, he or she will also receive them for the newborn. The spouses can also decide which of them will receive payments for all children in the family.

Child assistance payments are made in advance, four times a year, on the first working day of each quarter, that is, in January, April, July, and October. However, it is possible to apply online or by phone to receive monthly payments.

You can sign up for direct deposit on the Régie's website. This is a reliable, secure and environmentally friendly way to receive child assistance payments.

For more on child assistance payments:

Online:
www.rrq.gouv.qc.ca/en/enfants

By phone:
Québec City area: 418 643-3381
Montréal area: 514 864-3873
Elsewhere in Québec (toll-free): 1 800 667-9625

Teletypewriter:
1 800 603-3540

Sickness benefits

Sickness benefits are granted to people who stop working due to illness, injury or quarantine. To receive these benefits, you must submit medical proof. Sickness benefits may be paid for a maximum of 15 weeks. You must have accumulated 600 insurable working hours in the year prior to filing an application (or since the start of the last benefit period).

The number of hours you must work in order to be entitled to sickness benefits may be higher if you received benefits in the past and were informed in writing that you had produced a false return.

For more information on sickness benefits or to apply for sickness benefits, contact a Service Canada centre.

Service Canada centre addresses are listed in the blue pages of the telephone book in the Government of Canada section under the heading "Employment Insurance," or under the "Keyword Headings" section in the new blue pages.

You will also find contact information for the Service Canada centre nearest you by visiting www.servicecanada.gc.ca. The "Employment Insurance" section of this site provides access to online services and forms.

You can also contact Service Canada at 1 800 206-7218 (everywhere in Québec).

Assistance granted to parents of triplets or quadruplets

The Ministère de la Santé et des Services sociaux grants financial assistance to families in which the mother has given birth to triplets or quadruplets. This non-recurrent amount helps parents cope with the sudden and substantial increase in expenses.

The Minister issues, in the mother's name, a cheque for $6,000 for live triplets or $8,000 for live quadruplets when the children are discharged from the hospital.

The hospital is in charge of notifying the Ministère de la Santé et des Services sociaux and providing all necessary information following the births. The parents have no special steps to take and will receive their financial assistance approximately two months later. In the event of problems, the parents must check with the hospital to find out if their application was duly sent to the ministry.

In all cases, the hospital must fax the application to 418 266-5995 or forward it to the following address:

Ministère de la Santé et des Services sociaux du Québec
Direction générale de la coordination, du financement, de l'immobilisation et du budget
Direction des opérations budgétaires – réseau
1005 chemin Sainte-Foy, 2nd Floor
Québec City, QC G1S 4N4

Special breastfeeding benefit

The Ministère de l'Emploi et de la Solidarité sociale du Québec provides a special breastfeeding benefit of $55 a month to mothers who breastfeed their children, until the children reach the age of one. The mother must breastfeed her baby throughout this period.

To be entitled to the benefit, the mother must provide the local employment centre case officer with proof of the baby's birth, along with a signed declaration indicating the anticipated breastfeeding period. A second written declaration will be required once the baby is six months old.

Support for the purchase of infant formula

A parent receiving last-resort financial assistance may obtain regular, soy-based, or lactose-free formula for a baby less than nine months old without providing a certificate from a physician.

If the baby is nine months to a year old and suffers from intolerance to cow's milk or other particular disorders, the parent must present a medical certificate or a certificate from a physician indicating the need for support for the purchase of soy-based or lactose-free formula.

Note that it is not possible to receive the breastfeeding benefit and support for the purchase of formula at the same time, except during the month when the feeding method changes. Infant formula may be purchased only in drugstores.

As soon as the baby is born, the parent must get in touch with his/her case officer. The baby's birth certificate must be submitted promptly in order to benefit from this support.

For additional information, contact your local employment centre.

The address is listed in the blue pages of the phone book in the Gouvernement du Québec section under "Aide financière."

Work premium

The work premium is a refundable tax credit that may be requested on income tax returns (Appendix P). It is determined based on the income and personal and family status of the worker. Under certain conditions, Revenu Québec may pay the work premium in advance.

To be eligible, you must

- Reside in Québec on December 31 of this year
- Be either a Canadian citizen, aboriginal, permanent resident, or person who has been granted asylum in Canada
- Have a yearly employment income over $2,400 (for a single person or single-parent family) or over $3,600 (for a couple with or without children)
- Have an annual family income under those listed in the following chart:

Family status	Annual income
Single person	$14,973.20
Couple without children	$23,054.80
Single-parent family	$31,984.00
Couple with at least one child	$43,654.00

The following are the maximum work premium amounts:

Family status	Work premium yearly maximum
Single person	$517.72
Couple without children	$801.08
Single-parent family	$2,218.84
Couple with at least one child	$2,861.00

Starting at a certain income threshold, premiums progressively decrease until they reach zero.

You may choose to have Revenu Québec pay half of your work premium in advance rather than wait until you file your income tax return.

To receive advance payment of your premium, you must apply to Revenu Québec and meet certain conditions.

At the time of application, you must:

- Reside in Québec
- Be either a Canadian citizen, aboriginal, permanent resident, or person who has been granted asylum in Canada
- Be the father or mother of a dependent child
- Have a job
- Expect to be eligible for an annual work premium of over $500
- Be enrolled in direct deposit with Revenu Québec

Advance payments are quarterly and are made in equal installments on about the 15th of January, April, July and October.

Measures related to the work premium as of the 2008 tax year

If you are entitled to the work premium for the 2008 tax year, you may also be entitled to **a supplement to the work premium** granted on an individual basis for a maximum of 12 consecutive months. It may be paid for each month in which you earn at least $200.

Support tailored to your needs

Because each family has its own story!

To learn more about the government assistance intended for families

www.mfa.gouv.qc.ca

Famille et Aînés

Québec

In addition, if you or your spouse has a severely limited capacity for employment, it may be more advantageous to apply for the **adapted work premium**. The adapted work premium is determined on the basis of the income and family situation of the worker whose household includes an adult with a severely limited capacity for employment.

For more information, go to the Revenu Québec office in your area or consult Revenu Québec's website at www.revenu.gouv.qc.ca.

Shelter allowance program

Low-income families with at least one dependent child who devote a large part of their income to housing may, under certain conditions, be entitled to the shelter allowance. Financial assistance can be as much as $80 a month and is available to renters, owners, and households that share housing.

The shelter allowance takes the following factors into account:

- The number of persons in the household
- Total household income
- The monthly rent

For more information or to obtain an application form, contact the Revenu Québec office in your area.

The telephone numbers are listed in the blue pages of the phone book in the Gouvernement du Québec section under "Logement – Revenu Québec – Allocation-logement."

Advance payment of the refundable Childcare Tax Credit

The childcare expenses parents incur can be partially refunded through the Childcare Tax Credit. To receive this tax credit, you must file an income tax return. Certain expenses do not qualify, such as $7 a day subsidized childcare at daycare facilities or schools.

Parents may receive their estimated Childcare Tax Credit in advance under certain conditions from Revenu Québec in the form of a cheque or direct deposit. Payments are quarterly and made on about the 15th of January, April, July, and October.

To be entitled to advance payments, you must:

- Be the biological or adoptive parent (father or mother), either legally or in fact, of the child with whom you reside at the time of application, or be the spouse of this parent
- Comply with the tax credit eligibility requirements
- Have confirmation from the daycare worker regarding the rate and number of days of care provided during the year
- Reside in Québec at the time of the application
- Be enrolled in direct deposit with Revenu Québec
- Expect to be eligible for a daycare tax credit of over $1,000. This condition does not apply if in the same year you are also entitled to a work premium of over $500 (the work premium is another family assistance measure)

For more information, go to the nearest Revenu Québec office or consult Revenu Québec's website at www.revenu.gouv.qc.ca.

Filiation and parental obligations

Filiation

Filiation is the relationship that exists between a child and the child's parents, whether the parents are of the same or the opposite sex. The relationship can be established by blood, by law in certain cases, or by a judgment of adoption. Once filiation has been established, it creates rights and obligations for both the child and the parents, regardless of the circumstances of the child's birth.

Parents usually establish filiation by filling out and signing the form entitled Declaration of Birth, on which their names and that of their newborn child are entered. All the family names and usual given names of the mother and the father must be entered and spelled correctly. It is important to complete the declaration carefully, providing all the information requested.

If the parents are married or are in a civil union, only one parent needs to complete and sign the declaration before a witness in order to establish filiation. The date of marriage or of the civil union must be indicated.

If the parents are not married to one another or in a civil union with one another, they must both sign the Declaration of Birth before a witness in order to establish their individual filiation with the child.

A parent who anticipates being absent during the period when the birth must be registered with the Directeur de l'état civil can draw up a power of attorney authorizing another person to act for him or her. This form may be obtained from the Directeur de l'état civil. If this is not done and the deadline has passed, that parent may file a tardy declaration of filiation, circumstances permitting, or apply to the court to have his paternity or her maternity recognized.

All births in Québec must be declared to the Directeur de l'état civil in order to be entered in the register of civil status. Whether they are married or in a civil union, and whether or not they are living together, parents have the rights and duties inherent in the custody, supervision, and upbringing of their child, and they must feed and look after him or her.

All children are equal

The law makes no distinction based on the type of union of the parents, whether the child is related to his or her parents by blood or by adoption, or whether he or she was conceived naturally or by a medically assisted reproductive technique. By law, all children are born equal and are the legal heirs of their parents.

To contact the Directeur de l'état civil:

In Québec City
Directeur de l'état civil
2535 boulevard Laurier
Québec City, QC G1V 5C5
418 643-3900

In Montréal
Directeur de l'état civil
2050 rue De Bleury
Montréal, QC H3A 2J5
(Place-des-Arts Metro station)
514 864-3900

Elsewhere in Québec
1 800 567-3900

etatcivil@dec.gouv.qc.ca
www.etatcivil.gouv.qc.ca

The Directeur de l'état civil also provides services in a number of Services Québec offices. For a full list of these offices, visit the "Contact Us" section of www.servicesquebec.gouv.qc.ca.

Parental obligations

Parents must care for their minor children, feed them, clothe them, house them etc., and when they administer money or other assets in their name, they must not mix their assets with those of their minors. Parents must not use one child's assets for other members of the family, such as brothers and sisters, and must avoid situations where there may be a conflict of interest.

The fact that your children have assets or income of their own does not release you from your duty to support them with your own money. Parents have obligations to support and care for their children.

Child support

Parents—both father and mother—are required to provide for the basic needs of their children, such as providing food, clothing, housing, education, personal care, transportation and recreation.

Childcare

You also have the obligation to care for your children, which means you must look after them, supervise them and raise them.

Your obligation as a legal guardian

Except in certain cases, your minor children cannot exercise their rights themselves. They must be cared for and represented by an adult. In Québec, under the Civil Code their parents are their legal tutors and as a result have certain obligations, including the administration of assets.

As a legal guardian, you act as the administrator of the assets of your minors. That means you must ensure that your children's assets (inheritance, life insurance benefit, allowance received or any other tangible asset) are preserved so that they can be transferred to them when they are of full age. At that time, you must account for your administration of their assets.

Curateur public du Québec

The Curateur public du Québec informs parents and assists the tutors of minor children. It also monitors administration of the assets of children by:

- The parents when the total value is more than $25,000
- A tutor other than the parents (dative tutor) regardless of the value of the assets

To ensure it is able to monitor cases and intervene as needed, the Curateur public must be informed in advance by any natural or legal person—parents, members of a professional corporation, public or private agencies or institutions—of any compensation paid to a minor, even if the value is less than $25,000, and of any donation or bequeathment worth more than $25,000.

Financial management of the assets of minors therefore involves many different people: family and friends, legal officers, counselors, insurers and any other person with ties to a minor as well as the Curateur public.

For more information, visit the Curateur public du Québec Web site or:

Curateur public du Québec
600 boul. René-Lévesque Ouest
Montréal, QC H3B 4W9
514 873-4074 or 1 800 363-9020
information@curateur.gouv.qc.ca
www.curateur.gouv.qc.ca

Registering a child

Registering a child 's birth with the Directeur de l'état civil

Under the Civil Code of Québec, all parents must declare the birth of their child to the Directeur de l'état civil, whether or not a baptism or other religious ceremony is planned. To this end, they must fill out the Declaration of Birth form and **send it to the Directeur de l'état civil within 30 days following the birth.**

Attestation of birth

The Declaration of Birth is filled out and signed by the physician, nurse, midwife or any other person who assists the mother during delivery. It indicates the date, time and place of birth, the sex of the child, and the name and address of the mother. The hospital or birthing centre staff gives the parents a copy of the Attestation of Birth as well as the Declaration of Birth, which is to be filled out.

Declaration of Birth

The information gathered using the Declaration of Birth will be used to register the newborn in the Québec Register of Civil Status and establish his or her legal identity and filiation. The parents must copy the information from the Attestation of Birth onto the Declaration of Birth and indicate the child's given and family names, the type of union of the parents and the parents' addresses.

The Declaration of Birth is available in French and English. It should be obtained in the desired language, as the certificate of birth will be subsequently issued in this language. It must also be filled out in block letters while avoiding as much as possible any erasures or changes that may lead to confusion. If changes must be made to the Declaration of Birth, the declarant or declarants should enter their initials beside each correction. **The Declaration of Birth may not and must not be altered with liquid paper or otherwise.**

The declarant or declarants must fill out and sign the Declaration of Birth in the presence of a witness, who must also sign the document.

A witness is a person aged 18 or older who attests to the signature of the parents. The witness must indicate his or her identity by filling in the appropriate sections (in block letters) and must then sign and date the form.

It is important that the spelling of the child's family name and given names be correct and that the whole declaration be reread before adding the necessary signatures, in order to ensure that the information is entirely in keeping with the parents' wishes.

When should the Declaration of Birth be filled out?

It is recommended that the Declaration of Birth be filled out at the hospital or birthing centre and immediately given to the staff, who will see that it is sent to the Directeur de l'état civil.

If it is impossible to see to these formalities on site, the Declaration of Birth should be sent to the Directeur de l'état civil no later than 30 days after the birth of the child. Be sure to leave several days for mailing and to send in the documents as soon as possible.

Once the Act of Birth is drawn up, it is entered in the Québec Register of Civil Status. Concurrently, the Directeur de l'état civil forwards to the Régie de l'assurance maladie du Québec and to the Régie des rentes du Québec the information needed for the newborn to be eligible for the various plans. This is done confidentially.

! Delay in registering a birth in the Québec Register of Civil Status or failure to do so may result in problems for the child. The Act of Birth establishes the child's identity, sex and filiation, in short, his or her legal existence. Without this Act, it will be difficult, if not impossible, for the child to obtain certain documents (health insurance card, social insurance card, passport, etc.) or to prove entitlement to government programs or social benefits.

In addition, a $50 fee must be paid when the birth is declared after the prescribed 30 day deadline. If the birth is declared more than a year later, the fee is $100.

Obtaining a birth certificate

A birth certificate is accepted as proof of birth by many organizations. You can obtain one by filling in the form entitled Request for Certificate or Copy of Act for Birth. This form is available at Directeur de l'état civil counters in Québec City and Montréal, and at CLSCs, Desjardins branches, court houses and Services Québec offices. Also available online at www.etatcivil.gouv.qc.ca, it can be transmitted electronically or printed, signed, dated, and mailed.

It is preferable to apply for a full-sized birth certificate for a minor child since it shows the names of the parents. Note that there is no expiry date for a birth certificate.

You can submit the form to the Directeur de l'état civil electronically, by mail or by taking it to a service centre.

In Québec City
Directeur de l'état civil
2535 boulevard Laurier
Québec City, QC G1V 5C5
418 643-3900

In Montréal
Directeur de l'état civil
2050 rue De Bleury
Montréal, QC H3A 2J5
(Place-des-Arts Metro station)
514 864-3900

Elsewhere in Québec
1 800 567-3900

etatcivil@dec.gouv.qc.ca
www.etatcivil.gouv.qc.ca

The Directeur de l'état civil also provides services in a number of Services Québec offices. For a full list of these offices, visit the "Contact Us" section of www.servicesquebec.gouv.qc.ca.

Choosing a given name and a family name

A child's parents may choose for him or her one or more given names and a single or composite family name consisting of no more than two parts of the parents' family names.

It is recommended that the child have no more than four given names and that **the usual given name (the name to be used regularly) be entered in the appropriate box on the Declaration of Birth.** In the case of a composite given name, the two parts must be joined by a hyphen.

The given name of one of the parents may never be used as the child's family name. It may, however, be one of his or her other given names. In addition, the family name of one of the parents that is not used for the child's family name may be used as one of his or her given names.

In regard to the child's family name, the parents can choose from among the following options:

1. If both parents have family names that are not composites, such as Gardiner for one parent and Patton for the other, the child may be given the following as a family name:

   - Gardiner, the first parent's family name
   - Patton, the second parent's family name
   - Or a composite name made up of the two family names linked by a hyphen, Gardiner-Patton or Patton-Gardiner

2. If both parents have composite family names, such as Talbot-Gardiner for one parent and Smith-Patton for the other, they may, if they wish, give their child a single family name composed of one of the parts of their family names:

   - Talbot only
   - Gardiner only
   - Smith only
   - or Patton only

3. However, if the parents wish to give their child a composite name, a choice must be made, since the family name of the child cannot have more than two parts:

   - Talbot-Gardiner, one parent's family name
   - Smith-Patton, the other parent's family name

- Or a name made up of part of one of the parent's family name and part of the other parent's family name. Ten combinations are possible:
  - Talbot-Smith
  - Talbot-Patton
  - Gardiner-Smith
  - Gardiner-Patton
  - Smith-Talbot
  - Patton-Talbot
  - Smith-Gardiner
  - Patton-Gardiner
  - Gardiner-Talbot
  - Patton-Smith

A child whose maternal filiation or paternal filiation alone has been established bears the family name, in whole or in part, of the parent whose filiation with the child has been established in the Act of Birth.

Additional information

When the family name given to the child is composed of two parts joined by a hyphen, this is the name that will become, along with his or her given name, the child's legal name. It will then have to be used as registered, with no change in the order of the parts. Also note that the parents may not combine the initial of the family name of one parent with the family name of the other parent to form the child's surname. However, they may include the initial in the child's given names.

Since the baby's name must appear on the Declaration of Birth, the parents must make their choice as early as possible.

The full name of our child will be

Family name: ______________________________,

Usual given names: ______________________________,
usual (name used regularly)

______________________________,
second

______________________________,
third

______________________________,
fourth

To contact the Directeur de l'état civil:

In Québec City
Directeur de l'état civil
2535 boulevard Laurier
Québec City, QC G1V 5C5
418 643-3900

In Montréal
Directeur de l'état civil
2050 rue De Bleury
Montréal, QC H3A 2J5
(Place-des-Arts Metro station)
514 864-3900

Elsewhere in Québec
1 800 567-3900

etatcivil@dec.gouv.qc.ca
www.etatcivil.gouv.qc.ca

The Directeur de l'état civil also provides services in a number of Services Québec offices. For a full list of these offices, visit the "Contact Us" section of www.servicesquebec.gouv.qc.ca.

Health insurance card

In order to receive a health insurance card, the child must be registered with the Régie de l'assurance maladie du Québec (RAMQ). When the birth occurs in Québec, it is sufficient to register the newborn in the Québec Register of Civil Status to initiate the registration process at the RAMQ.

One of the parents must fill out, as carefully as possible, and sign the Declaration of Birth provided by the hospital where the child was born or by the midwife. Parents have no further forms to complete.

The hospital staff or one of the parents must send the duly completed document to the Directeur de l'état civil within 30 days of the child's birth. Subsequently, the Directeur de l'état civil will notify the parents of the registration of their child in the Québec Register of Civil Status. The Directeur de l'état civil will send the information to the RAMQ confidentially. After checking the eligibility of the child, the RAMQ will issue the health insurance card. Only one card will be issued for the child.

Children under one year of age who have not yet received their health insurance cards are still entitled to healthcare services covered by the plan. However, the physician may ask to see a parent's health card.

For a birth outside Québec, contact the RAMQ to register the newborn child:

- Québec City area: 418 646-4636
- Montréal area: 514 864-3411
- Elsewhere in Québec: 1 800 561-9749
- Teletypewriter (see page 622)

Prescription drug insurance

Once eligibility for health insurance is confirmed, the parents must ensure their newborn is covered by a prescription drug insurance plan.

Parents registered with a group insurance plan comprising drug coverage are obliged to include their newborn in their plan.

However, if the parents are covered by the public prescription drug insurance plan administered by the Régie de l'assurance maladie du Québec, the newborn will be automatically registered under this plan.

If your baby suffers from milk intolerance, the physician can prescribe certain special preparations that may be reimbursed in some cases. If your baby is registered under the public prescription drug insurance plan, the physician generally applies to the Régie for authorization for reimbursement. Otherwise, contact your insurance company for information.

Passport

Traveling with a child

Since December 2001, children need their own passports to travel abroad. One of the parents must complete the form entitled Passport Application for Canadians Under 16 Years of Age, but **both parents** must give their approval and sign the form. In cases of separation or divorce, only the parent with legal custody of the child may apply for a passport for the child.

The cost of a passport for a child under 3 years of age is $22, and the document is valid for a maximum of three years. For children 3 to 16 inclusively, a passport costs $37 and is valid for a maximum of five years.

A word of advice though: carefully read the application form instructions and do not wait until you are just about to depart before applying, because processing a passport application takes 10 working days if you submit your application at a regional office and 20 working days if you mail your application.

Procedure

Forms for children under 16 are available at the five regional offices of Passport Canada (Montréal, Laval, Saint-Laurent, Québec City and Jonquière) and at Canada Post outlets.

On October 1, 2007, a new passport application form was introduced both for children under 16 and adults. For children, the applicant is the parent. The sponsor can be a holder of a valid or non-expired Canadian passport for over a year who has known the applicant for the past two years.

For more information, call Passport Canada toll-free at 1 800 567-6868.

"Mon arbre à moi" campaign

In the "Mon arbre à moi" campaign of the Ministère des Ressources naturelles et de la Faune, any child born or adopted in the year in progress can receive a small seedling tree that will grow along with him or her. Each seedling given to a child is accompanied by a growth chart and a souvenir certificate to be kept in the child's scrapbook. Seedlings are distributed every year in May in the various regions of Québec for Tree and Forest Month.

The seedlings given by the ministry are only about 30 cm to 45 cm high. However, since they are tree species, they will grow a lot. At maturity, i.e., in 75 to 100 years, most of the trees will be 20 m to 30 m tall.

To receive a seedling, new parents must register directly online at www.mrnf.gouv.qc.ca/maf/mon-arbre. Subsequently, parents will be notified by mail just prior to May of the procedure to follow to receive the seedling. Please note that the reply card should reach the ministry no later than April 15.

For additional information on the campaign, contact:

Ministère des Ressources naturelles
et de la Faune du Québec
Direction des services à la clientèle
Service de l'accueil et des renseignements ministériels
880 chemin Sainte-Foy
Québec City, QC G1S 4X4
Phone: 418 627-8600 or 1 866 248-6936
Fax: 418 644-6513
mon-arbre@mrnf.gouv.qc.ca
www.mrnf.gouv.qc.ca/mfa/mon-arbre

Health, prevention and family safety

Prenatal meetings

All CLSCs offer prenatal information services. Mothers-to-be should contact their CLSC to find out about the services available.

Perinatal services

Perinatal services include group and individual prenatal meetings, parental education meetings (age 0–4), integrated perinatal and early childhood services for families in vulnerable situations, information on promoting breastfeeding and postnatal visits. These services are designed to better prepare parents for pregnancy, delivery and the arrival of the child. Meetings are available in most institutions in the various Québec regions.

To find out where to register, contact the CLSC in your area.

Nutrition

Good nutrition during pregnancy is vital to the health of the unborn child. As part of the integrated perinatal and early childhood services for families in vulnerable situations offered through CLSCs in Québec, Fondation OLO helps ensure healthy babies at birth by providing essential foods (eggs, milk, orange juice) and vitamin and mineral supplements to needy pregnant women.

In addition to helping prevent malnutrition in pregnant women and improving the health of newborns, Fondation OLO helps connect young families with other key resources through the CLSC network and its teams of perinatal professionals.

For more information on Fondation OLO or other nutritional assistance programs, contact the CLSC in your area.

The address is listed in the white pages of the telephone book under "CLSC."

For a safe maternity program

A worker who is pregnant or breastfeeding enjoys special protection under the *Act respecting occupational health and safety*. If her working conditions are dangerous to her health or to her unborn child or the child she is nursing, she is entitled to be reassigned to other duties that are not dangerous and that she is able to perform.

If her workstation cannot be modified or if no other assignment is possible, she may temporarily stop working and receive compensation from the Commission de la santé et de la sécurité du travail (CSST). This is not maternity leave, but rather a preventive-type program whose main objective is to allow the worker to stay at work in a safe environment.

The measures that employers have at their disposal to meet this objective are the following:

- Elimination of danger at source
- Change in the worker's duties
- Workstation modification
- Reassignment to another duty or job

To avail herself of the For a Safe Maternity Program, the worker must ask a physician to fill out the form entitled Preventive Withdrawal and Reassignment Certificate for a Pregnant or Breastfeeding Worker.

That physician must consult the physician in charge of health services at the establishment where the worker is employed. If there is no physician at the establishment, the physician designated by the head of the public health ministry in the area where the establishment is located must be consulted. The certificate is valid only if such a consultation is carried out. There is no charge to the worker for the certificate.

A worker must proceed in the same way if she wishes to avail herself of the program in regard to breastfeeding. Even if she obtained a reassignment or preventive withdrawal because of pregnancy, she must get a new certificate for breastfeeding. In such cases, however, only conditions that put the breastfed child's health at risk can be taken into consideration.

For more information, contact one of the regional divisions of the CSST.

The address is listed in the blue pages of the telephone book in the Gouvernement du Québec section under "Santé et sécurité du travail" or under the "Keyword Heading" in the new blue pages.

Adoption

For a growing number of people, adoption is the answer to having children in the family. International adoption has contributed greatly to this phenomenon, and there has been an increase in recent years in the adoption of children domiciled in Québec. This section of the guide briefly discusses the main steps to take in the process of adopting a child in or outside Québec.

Adoption in Québec

Adoption has changed in Québec over the last few years. The number of adoptions has increased and more and more children are being placed in permanent families. The age of the children is generally from birth to three years, but they may be older and are, in some cases, siblings.

Although for the most part native-born Quebecers, the children may also be of different ethnic origins. Some are entrusted to families by their parents, who consent to the adoption. But most often they are under the protection of the Directeur de la protection de la jeunesse, who must apply to the Youth Division of the Court of Québec for a judgment of eligibility for adoption.

These children are often from families that cannot provide everything that a child needs to develop harmoniously. The biological parents were unable to improve the situation that led to the decision to remove the child from their environment. Most of the children are oriented toward adoption as part of the Foster-to-Adopt Program.

Québec youth centres are responsible for carrying out the adoption procedures for children domiciled in Québec. The first step in the adoption process is a request in writing or by phone by the future parents to the youth centre in their area. This pre-registration is followed by an evening information session during which the parents can receive answers to their questions. The registration procedure can then officially begin. People interested in pursuing the adoption process must undergo a psychosocial assessment at that time.

Once these steps have been completed, two types of adoption are possible: regular adoption and the Foster-to-Adopt Program.

Regular adoption

Some biological parents give the Directeur de la protection de la jeunesse their consent to the adoption of their child. After the expiry of a 30-day time period during which the consent can be withdrawn, the Youth Division issues a placement order that grants the adopter the exercise of parental authority. This order is followed by an adoption judgment.

Note that regular adoption has become very rare in Québec and requires a waiting period of several years for adopting parents.

Foster-to-Adopt Program

The Foster-to-Adopt Program was set up in 1988. Its objective is to enable children at high risk of being abandoned to be placed as soon as possible in a stable family that is prepared to provide foster care with a view to adoption. The stability thereby ensured encourages the child's development in terms of security, as well as confidence and self-esteem.

The biological parents of children placed under the Foster-to-Adopt Program are grappling with personal problems that prevent them from assuming responsibility for the care and upbringing of their children.

People who register for the Foster-to-Adopt Program want to adopt the child entrusted to them where possible, but they agree to take the child in initially as a foster family. They must first undergo a psychosocial assessment. Once accepted, they are available to be matched with a child whose needs correspond to the conclusions of the assessment. Following the assessment, the waiting time before they can take in a child 0 to 2 years of age varies from several weeks to several months. The waiting time is shorter for parents who want to take in a child who is 2 years of age or older and has special characteristics, such as ethnic origin or state of health.

To find out more about the adoption of a child domiciled in Québec, contact the youth centre in your area.

The address is in the white pages of the telephone book under "Centre jeunesse."

International adoption

Under the Youth Protection Act, the Ministère de la Santé et des Services sociaux du Québec, through the Secrétariat à l'adoption internationale (SAI), oversees the adoption of children domiciled outside Québec by persons domiciled in Québec. More specifically, SAI has the following responsibilities:

- Coordinate international adoption activities in Québec in the best interests of the children and in keeping with their fundamental rights
- Assist and advise the people and families that plan to adopt a child domiciled outside Québec, and ensure the adoption proceeds in accordance with all regulations
- Provide administrative follow-up with regard to the Convention on Protection of Children and Co-operation in Respect of Intercountry Adoption (the Hague Convention)

Photo: Marc Sinotte

- Recommend to the Ministère de la Santé et des Services sociaux the certification of international adoption organizations
- Advise and support certified organizations and monitor their activities as prescribed by law
- See that the legislation is applied and that Québec's policy directions and ethical rules for international adoption are respected
- Ensure that adoption-related requirements are met in each case
- Advise the authorities of the Ministère de la Santé et des Services sociaux regarding international adoption
- Establish, with the competent authorities of foreign countries, working relations and agreements on international adoption that are in keeping with the countries' legislation and culture

As regards international adoption, the Civil Code of Québec and the Code of Civil Procedure (R.S.Q., c. C-25) establish the ground rules. The *Youth Protection Act* then clarifies these rules. Next come specific orders, the Convention on the Protection of Children and Co-operation in Respect of Intercountry Adoption, and the *Act to implement the Convention on the Protection of Children and Co-operation in Respect of Intercountry Adoption and to amend various legislative provisions in relation to adoption* (R.S.Q., c. M-35. 1.3).

In Québec, adoption confers a filiation on adoptees that replaces their filiation of origin. Adoptees cease to belong to their families of origin. Adoption also engenders the same rights and obligations as filiation by blood. The rules governing child consent and adoptability are those of the country of origin.

The Civil Code of Québec requires that adoption procedures be carried out by a certified organization responsible for assisting, supporting and advising adoptive parents who use its services.

Exceptions to this general rule can be made if the criteria and conditions in the *Order respecting the adoption without a certified body of a child domiciled outside Québec by a person domiciled in Québec* are met (R.Q., c. P-34.1, r. 0.02). Only persons who meet the criteria and conditions set out in the Order may make arrangements for the adoption of a child domiciled outside Québec without the assistance of a certified agency. This type of adoption plan must first be submitted to and approved by SAI.

Steps in an international adoption

Information request

A person wishing to adopt a child domiciled outside Québec can request information from SAI, which provides general information on international adoption, eligibility requirements, adoption criteria and related procedures. If adopters have questions about one country in particular, they can also contact that country's certified international adoption organizations directly. Some provide information sessions and pre-adoption consultation services.

Signing of a contract with a certified agency

A contract between the adopter and the certified agency must be signed before adoption procedures begin.

Opening of a file with SAI

The certified agency has the potential adoptive parent fill out a form, which is then sent to SAI with the required documents. SAI then evaluates the adoption plan and, if it is found to be eligible, sends the adopter a letter confirming that a file has been opened with SAI. This letter is required for the adoption process to continue.

Psychosocial assessment

The psychosocial assessment looks at the adopter's ability to meet the physical, mental and social needs of a child adopted from abroad. It allows the competent authorities in Québec and in the child's country of origin to ensure that the potential adoptive parent is able to meet the child's specific needs.

In accordance with Québec's legal framework and the requirements of the child's country of origin, the psychosocial assessment is performed, under the supervision of the Directeur de la protection de la jeunesse, by a social worker or a psychologist in private practice who is a member of his or her professional order. If the Hague Convention of May 29, 1993, is in force in the child's country of origin, the psychosocial assessment must, without exception, be performed under the supervision of the Directeur de la protection de la jeunesse. A positive recommendation is required for the adoption process to continue.

Assembly and transmission of the adoption file in the child's country of origin

The potential adoptive parent assembles the adoption file in cooperation with the certified agency, which provides advice and guidance with respect to data collection and document translation and authentication.

The adoption file is then sent to the authorities in the child's country of origin, with the certified agency ensuring follow-up.

Choice of citizenship or immigration process, or start of immigration process, if required

Canadian citizens may apply for Canadian citizenship for a child adopted abroad without first having to apply for permanent residence or follow the immigration process starting with a sponsorship application. However, some adopters have no choice but to follow the immigration process for example, when adoption is finalized abroad or will not be finalized until after the adoptive child arrives in Canada. The potential adoptive parent can obtain all information in this regard from the certified agency.

Waiting period

The waiting period for a child to be proposed depends on the country of origin and the profile recommended in the psychosocial assessment. International adoptions are also subject to the vagaries of national or international events that disrupt the adoption process.

During this time, the adoptive parent informs the certified body of any material change in his or her personal or family situation (e.g., pregnancy, job loss, separation, divorce, death, new cohabitation, illness). Depending on the change's potential significance or impact with regard to the proposed adoption, the psychosocial assessment may have to be updated.

Proposal of a child

Authorities in the country of origin generally determine which children will be proposed for international adoption and to whom. According to the procedure agreed upon between the certified agency and the foreign authorities, the agency submits the proposal to the potential adoptive parent, who must indicate his or her agreement to the foreign authorities within a certain period of time.

Authorization to proceed with the adoption (letter of no objection)

At this step, SAI verifies the documents demonstrating the child's adoptability and the consents to his or her adoption, and ensures that the proposal is consistent with the recommendations of the psychosocial assessment. Then, SAI issues a statement declaring that it has no grounds to oppose the child's adoption (letter of no objection). The adopter need not request this letter but will receive it in due time, i.e., when the certified agency sends the required documents to SAI.

The adoptive parent then proceeds with the required steps for the citizenship or immigration process, as the case may be.

Administrative and legal formalities in the child's country of origin

Administrative and legal formalities may vary depending on the child's country of origin and whether the country is a party to the Hague Convention of May 29, 1993. In all cases, the adoptive parent must obtain a decree entrusting the child to him or her. This may consist of an adoption decree issued by an administrative or legal authority, or a placement order. The certified agency informs the adoptive parent of the procedure to follow and the steps to take.

If the Hague Convention of May 29, 1993, is in force in the child's country of origin, the adoptive parent must obtain the certificate of compliance issued by the central authority in the child's country of origin, since he or she must then submit it to SAI.

The adoptive parent must also complete all the required steps in the citizenship or immigration process, as the case may be.

Depending on the country of origin, the adoptive parent may travel alone, as part of a couple or with a group of adoptive parents. Some certified agencies offer on-site guide and interpretation services. The length of the stay may vary. In some countries, a person designated by the certified agency or the country of origin escorts the child to Québec. In such cases, the adoptive parent picks the child up at the airport.

Arrival of the child in Québec

The adoptive parent must notify the certified agency of the date the child is entrusted to him or her and the date of the child's arrival in Canada. The certified agency forwards the information to SAI.

The adoptive parent can contact his or her local CLSC to schedule a visit with a health professional. This is part of the basket of services offered by the CLSC in the 14 days following the child's arrival in Québec. Its purpose is to establish a first contact with the adopted child and provide appropriate advice and care. The adoptive parent is encouraged to make an appointment as quickly as possible after the child's arrival in order to benefit from this service.

Administrative and legal formalities in Québec

The steps in the adoption process must continue in Québec for the adoption to have effect here. They vary depending on the type of adoption decree issued by the child's country of origin, e.g., notification of a certificate of compliance or of a document in lieu of one (the country of origin is a state that is a party to the Hague Convention of May 29, 1993, and issues a certificate of compliance or a document in lieu of one), recognition of a foreign adoption decree (the country of origin issues an adoption decree), or a placement order and adoption judgment in Québec (the country of origin issues the child's placement order).

In the first case, the decree does not have to be recognized by the Youth Division of the Court of Québec. However, the adoptive parent must submit the documents pertaining to said decree to SAI within 60 days of their issuance.

In the two other cases, the adoptive parent must apply to the Court to obtain an adoption judgment from the Youth Division of the Court of Québec. In the case of a placement order, the adoptive parent must obtain a final adoption judgment after the placement period ends. The adoptive parent can call on an attorney to provide assistance and represent him or her during this process.

An adoptive parent following the immigration process for his or her child must take the required steps to obtain Canadian citizenship for the child.

Preparing the child's progress reports and submitting them in the child's country of origin

In all adoption files concerning a child domiciled outside Québec, upon signing the contract with the certified agency, the adoptive parent undertakes to submit progress reports on the adopted child to the authorities in the country of origin, in accordance with the requirements of that country. The form, frequency and number of reports, as well as the duration of this commitment, may vary considerably from one country to another. The reports are prepared at the adoptive parent's expense by a psychologist or a social worker appointed by the Directeur de la protection de la jeunesse, by a social worker or psychologist in private practice, or by the adoptive parent, depending on the requirements of the country of origin. The certified agency sends these reports and their translations, as required, to the country of origin.

Progress reports may also have to be submitted to the Youth Division of the Court of Québec when the Court issues a placement order and an adoption judgment. The same reports can be submitted to the Court of Québec and the country of origin.

Closing the adoption file

SAI keeps all files pertaining to the adoption of children domiciled outside Québec. Certified agencies have the legal obligation to remit their files to SAI two years after the child's arrival in Québec, when the proposed adoption has been abandoned, or when the agency is no longer certified.

Under Québec legislation, files pertaining to a child's adoption are confidential, and the information they contain can only be disclosed where permitted by law. Once the adoption procedure is complete, SAI closes the adoption files, which are then archived and digitized. They may eventually be used to prepare a report on a child's history in the event SAI receives a request for a sociobiological history or for a reunion.

Secrétariat à l'adoption internationale
201 boulevard Crémazie Est, Suite 1.01
Montréal, QC H2M 1L2
Phone: 514 873-5226 or 1 800 561-0246
Fax: 514 873-1709
adoption.quebec@msss.gouv.qc.ca
www.adoption.gouv.qc.ca

Educational childcare services

Educational childcare services play a key role in a child's development. Children in childcare interact with other children and acquire abilities that prepare them for kindergarten and help them adapt and succeed in school. Childcare services have also become a necessity for many parents who must balance family and work responsibilities.

Before choosing a childcare service, you must identify your needs and those of your child. What are your preferences? Would you prefer a family or group environment? Are you seeking a childcare service located near your home or workplace? Do you have an unusual work schedule? Would you like a space at the reduced contribution rate? Your educational values will also influence your choice. To ensure you can choose from among a number of childcare services, you should begin your search immediately.

Childcare services in Québec

Québec has an educational childcare service network with more than 200,000 seven-dollar-a-day reduced contribution spaces located in childcare centres, daycare facilities and home childcare services. These childcare services are designed for children from birth up to the start of kindergarten.

In addition, free continuous educational childcare services, up to a maximum of two and a half days or five half days per week, are available to children under five years of age whose parents are beneficiaries of the social assistance or social solidarity program.

Childcare providers follow an educational program designed to foster harmonious overall development of the child and promote optimum emotional, physical and motor, social and moral, and cognitive and language skills.

Childcare providers ensure the health and safety of toddlers by providing healthy food, good hygiene and an environment that protects them from infections, diseases and injury.

Anyone who offers or provides childcare services to more than six children is governed by the Educational Childcare Act and as such must hold a childcare centre or daycare centre permit issued by the Ministère de la Famille et des Aînés du Québec. Caregivers who look after more than six children in a private residence must be recognized as a home childcare provider by a home childcare coordinating office.

The 165 ministry-certified coordinating offices throughout Québec are responsible for coordinating the educational childcare services offered by recognized home childcare providers in a given area. In particular, they must ensure compliance with regulatory standards and provide an information service for parents.

Site visit recommended

Before entrusting your child to childcare, meet with the centre manager as well as the staff who will be caring for your child. Ask questions about the age of the children who go to the centre, the educational program and the quality of meals. Make sure the permit is posted in the case of a childcare or daycare center, observe the environment your child will be living in and find out about the activities offered as well as how your child's health and safety will be protected.

To facilitate your child's integration, visit the childcare centre with him or her. This will allow you to observe the teacher's approach and your child's response. Following this visit, have your child experience routine activities in the childcare environment. Snacks, meals and nap time are good opportunities for your child to adjust to a new person. Avoid leaving your child for too long a period in the first few days in order to help him or her adapt gradually. By taking these steps, you will help your child see that you trust these new people, and your child will accept them more readily.

Childcare available for children with disabilities

Integrating a child with a disability into a childcare establishment gives him or her a chance to be with peers and develop through daily activities. It also helps him or her become increasingly independent, just like other children.

The Ministère de la Famille et des Aînés du Québec provides childcare establishments with extra financial assistance to allow them to welcome children with a disability. Usually, this involves adapting the premises, equipment, and activities to promote each child's participation.

The role of parents and childcare staff is crucial to the success of this process. The support of health and social service professionals is another success factor.

Definitions

Childcare centre

A childcare centre is either a nonprofit organization whose board of directors is at least two-thirds composed of parent users, or a cooperative. In its facilities it provides spaces at the reduced contribution rate ($7 a day).

Daycare centre

A daycare centre is generally a for-profit organization that furnishes childcare in a facility. It is obligated to form a parents' committee. Most daycare centres, having signed an agreement with the Ministère de la Famille et des Aînés du Québec, offer space at the reduced contribution rate ($7 a day).

Other daycare centres are not subsidized and can set their own contribution rate.

Home childcare

Home childcare is a remunerated service provided by a person in a private residence.

If providers are recognized by a coordinating office, they provide educational childcare to a maximum of six children, of whom no more than two may be younger than 18 months. If another adult assists them, they may accept up to nine children (of whom no more than four may be younger than 18 months).

If providers are not recognized by a coordinating office, they may not accept more than six children.

For more information, contact the Ministère de la Famille et des Aînés du Québec. You can also check the childcare locator on the ministry's website at www.mfa.gouv.qc.ca. This tool will help you find daycare centers located close to your home or workplace.

Ministère de la Famille et des Aînés du Québec
425 rue Saint-Amable
Québec City, QC G1R 4Z1
or
600 rue Fullum
Montréal, QC H2K 4S7
Québec City area: 418 643-4721
Elsewhere in Québec: 1 888 643-4721

www.mfa.gouv.qc.ca

Services for the deaf or hard-of-hearing who have a teletypewriter

The following numbers are for the exclusive use of the deaf or hard-of-hearing who have a teletypewriter.

Canada Revenue Agency
Throughout Québec: 1 800 665-0354

Commission des normes du travail
Throughout Québec: 514 864-3920

Government of Canada
Service Canada: 1 800 926-9105 and 1 800 465-7735

Office des personnes handicapées du Québec
Montréal area: 514 873-9880
Elsewhere in Québec: 1 800 567-1477

Régie de l'assurance maladie du Québec
Québec City area: 418 682-3939
Elsewhere in Québec: 1 800 361-3939

Régie des rentes du Québec
Throughout Québec: 1 800 603-3540

Revenu Québec
Montréal area: 514 873-4455
Elsewhere in Québec: 1 800 361-3795

Services Québec
Montréal area: 514 873-4626
Elsewhere in Québec: 1 800 361-9596

Société de l'assurance automobile du Québec
Montréal area: 514 954-7763
Elsewhere in Québec: 1 800 565-7763

Québec government portal

For any information on the programs and services of the Québec government, simply visit the Québec government portal at www.servicesquebec.gouv.qc.ca. You can also call one of the following numbers:
418 644-4545 (Québec City area),
514 644-4545 (Montréal area) or
1 877 644-4545 (Elsewhere in Québec).

Teletypewriter
The deaf or hard-of-hearing can reach Services Québec using a teletypewriter.

Montréal area: 514 873-4626
Elsewhere in Québec: 1 800 361-9596

Useful information

Resources for parents

Emergency resources

Centre antipoison du Québec
1 800 463-5060
www.csssvc.qc.ca/services/capq.php
Information on what to do in the event of poisoning, downloadable brochures.

Éducation coup-de-fil
514 525-2573 / 1 866 329-4223
www.education-coup-de-fil.com
Parents can consult professionals through this bilingual telephone service.

Info-Santé
Across Quebec, except for one region: 8-1-1
The far north (Terres-Cries-de-la-Baie-James and Nunavik): Look in the phone book under the heading "Centre de santé et de services sociaux."
A nurse provides health advice 24 hours a day, seven days a week.

La ligne parents
514 288-5555 / 1 800 361-5085
www.ligneparents.com
Bilingual telephone support for parents of children up to the age of 18 years.

S.O.S Grossesse
www.sosgrossesse.ca
1 877 662-9666
Telephone help line, referral and information for any questions about pregnancy, contraception and sexuality (in French only).

SOS Violence conjugale
514 728-0023 or 514 728-2353 / 1 800 363-9010
www.sosviolenceconjugale.ca/ligne.html
Bilingual telephone service accessible 24 hours a day, seven days a week.

Professional associations

Association des Allergologues et Immunologues du Québec *(allergists and immunologists)*
514 350-5101
www.allerg.qc.ca

Association des Obstétriciens et Gynécologues du Québec *(obstetricians and gynecologists)*
514 849-4969
www.gynecoquebec.com

Association des Omnipraticiens en périnatalité du Québec *(general practitioners working in perinatal care)*
www.aopq.org

Association des Optométristes du Québec *(optometrists)*
514 288-6272 / 1 888 767-6786
www.aoqnet.qc.ca

Association des Orthopédagogues du Québec *(special education teachers)*
514 374-5883 / 1 888 444-0222
www.adoq.ca

Association des Pédiatres du Québec *(pediatricians)*
514 350-5127
www.pediatres.ca

Société des Ostéopathes du Québec *(osteopaths)*
514 524-6560
www.soc-osteopathes.qc.ca

Professional orders

Ordre des Chiropraticiens du Québec *(chiropractors)*
514 355-8540
www.ordredeschiropraticiens.qc.ca

Ordre des Dentistes du Québec *(dentists)*
514 875-8511 / 1 800 361-4887
www.ordredesdentistesduquebec.qc.ca

Ordre des Ergothérapeutes du Québec
(occupational therapists)
514 844-5778 / 1 800 265-5778
www.oeq.org

Ordre des Hygiénistes dentaires du Québec
(dental hygienists)
514 284-7639 / 1 800 361-2996
www.ohdq.com

Ordre des Infirmières et Infirmiers du Québec
(nurses)
514 935-2501 / 1 800 363-6048
www.oiiq.org

Ordre des Optométristes du Québec *(optometrists)*
514 499-0524
www.ooq.org

Ordre des Orthophonistes et Audiologistes du Québec
(speech-language pathologists and audiologists)
514 282-9123 / 1 888 232-9123
www.ooaq.qc.ca

Ordre des Psychologues du Québec *(psychologists)*
514 738-1881 / 1 800 363-2644
www.ordrepsy.qc.ca

Ordre des Sages-Femmes du Québec *(midwives)*
514 286-1313 / 1 877 711-1313
www.osfq.org

Ordre professionnel des Diététistes du Québec
(dietitians)
514 393-3733 / 1 888 393-8528
www.opdq.org

Ordre professionnel de la physiothérapie du Québec
(physiotherapists)
514 351-2770 / 1 800 361-2001
www.oppq.qc.ca

Ordre professionnel des Travailleurs sociaux du Québec *(social workers)*
514 731-3925 / 1 888 731-9420
www.optsq.org

Government agencies

Association québécoise d'établissements de santé et de services sociaux
514 842-4861
www.aqesss.qc.ca

Government of Canada – Health Canada
www.hc-sc.gc.ca
Provides information on various topics related to children's health and safety.

Government of Canada – Transport Canada – Car Time
www.tc.gc.ca/roadsafety/childsafety/menu.htm
This federal government site offers extensive advice on installing children's car seats and explanations concerning the seats.

Gouvernement du Québec – Directeur de l'état civil
514 864-3900 / 418 643-3900 / 1 800 567-3900
www.etatcivil.gouv.qc.ca
Contact the Directeur de l'état civil to obtain birth certificates.

Gouvernement du Québec – Ministère du Développement durable, de l'Environnement et des Parcs du Québec
1 800 561-1616
www.ceaeq.gouv.qc.ca/accreditation/palae/lla03.htm
Lists laboratories accredited to check the quality of water from private wells.

Gouvernement du Québec – Ministère de la Santé et des Services sociaux du Québec
www.msss.gouv.qc.ca
Information on the services and publications available from the ministère de la Santé et des Services sociaux.

Gouvernement du Québec – Office de la protection du consommateur
1 888 672-2556
www.opc.gouv.qc.ca

Gouvernement du Québec –
Régie de l'assurance-maladie du Québec
514 864-3411 / 418 646-4636 / 1 800 561-9749
www.ramq.gouv.qc.ca

Gouvernement du Québec –
Régie des rentes du Québec
www.rrq.gouv.qc.ca/en/enfants
Information on the family allowance program.

Gouvernement du Québec – Société de l'assurance automobile du Québec – Secure them for Life
www.saaq.gouv.qc.ca/publications/prevention/siege_an.pdf
Complete information on the installation of children's car seats and includes a link to the children's car seat verification network.

Programme québécois de dépistage néonatal urinaire – Centre hospitalier universitaire de Sherbrooke, Hôpital Fleurimont
819 564-5253
www.formulaire.gouv.qc.ca/cgi/affiche_doc.cgi?dossier=3594&table=0
This bilingual service provides information on the hereditary metabolic diseases screening program available to all newborns.

Public Health Agency of Canada
www.phac-aspc.gc.ca
Informations on a broad range of topics about health issues.

Secrétariat à l'adoption internationale
514 873-5226 / 1 800 561-0246
www.adoption.gouv.qc.ca

Associations, agencies and support groups

Allergy Asthma Information Association
514 694-0679 / 1 866 694-0679
www.aaia.ca
Support and information on allergies.

Anaphylaxis Canada
416 785-5666
www.anaphylaxis.ca
Support and information for families living with anaphylaxis.

Association de parents de jumeaux et plus de la région de Québec
418 653-9607
www.apjq.net
Organization that helps families in the Quebec City region who have experienced a multiple birth (in French only).

Association de parents de jumeaux et de triplés de la région de Montréal (APJTM)
514 990-6165
www.apjtm.com
The Association helps families in Montréal who have experienced a multiple birth (in French only).

Association de parents pour l'adoption québécoise
514 990-9144
www.quebecadoption.net
Promotes the adoption of children born in Quebec. Support, seminars and family activities.

Association québécoise des allergies alimentaires (AQAA)
514 990-2575
www.aqaa.qc.ca
Support, sharing and information on food allergies.

Association québécoise des consultantes en lactation diplômées de l'IBLCE
514 990-0262
www.ibclc.qc.ca
To obtain the list of breast-feeding consultants.

CAA Québec – Child car seats
www.caaquebec.com/Automobile/SecuriteRoutiere/SiegesEnfants/Sieges-Auto-Enfants.htm?lang=en
Web site that offers advice on the safe installation of child car seats as well as addresses of garages that will check to ensure that child car seats are properly installed.

Canadian Child Care Federation
613 729-5289 / 1 800 858-1412
www.cccf-fcsge.ca
Ideas on a broad range of topics of interest to families, including outings, activities, care, and tips.

Canadian Coalition for Immunization Awareness & Promotion
613 725-3769 ext. 122
www.immunize.ca
Information on vaccines and the vaccination schedule, answers common questions and lists resources.

Canadian Institute of Child Health
613 230-8838
www.cich.ca
Devoted to child and family health and offers parents numerous publications and resources.

Canadian Paediatric Society – Caring for kids
613 526-9397
www.caringforkids.cps.ca
Information on children's health.

Canadian Red Cross
613 740-1900
www.redcross.ca
Information on Red Cross prevention and first aid courses for the parents of young children and on the course for babysitters.

Centre de soutien au deuil périnatal
1 866 990-2730
www.csdeuilperinatal.ca
Support offered to parents and workers affected by perinatal loss.

Centre québécois de ressources à la petite enfance
514 369-0234
www.cqrpe.qc.ca
A variety of information on support groups, health organizations, suggested reading for parents, Web sites on parenting, etc.

Child Health Information Center – Hôpital Sainte-Justine
www.chu-sainte-justine.org/en/famille/cise
Indexed information bank with cards available for consultation or order. Also offers a variety of training programs for parents of children aged 0 to 6.

Éditions de l'Hôpital Sainte-Justine
www.chu-sainte-justine.org/editions/index.asp
The hospital's publications dealing with childhood and families listed on this site can be ordered online (in French only).

Extenso
www.extenso.org
Reference centre on human nutrition (in French only).

Family Resources Center of Quebec
514 593-6997/1 800 361-8453
www.crfq.org
Organization offering a wide range of services including a telephone help line, professional legal advice, a database of more than 2000 community resources and information sessions.

Family Service Canada
613 722-9006
www.familyservicecanada.org
The organization promotes families as the primary source of nurture and development of individuals. English and French.

Fédération des associations de familles monoparentales et recomposées du Québec
514 729-6666
www.fafmrq.org
The federation defends the rights and interests of single-parent and blended families in Quebec. Bilingual service is available in Montréal and some regions of Quebec.

Fédération du Québec pour le planning des naissances
514 866-3721
www.fqpn.qc.ca
This bilingual service provides information on contraception and women's sexual health.

Fédération québécoise des organismes communautaires Famille
450 466-2538
www.fqocf.org
Gathers together and supports family-oriented community organizations and helps ensure that the family has a place in Quebec society (in French only).

Info-circumcision
www.infocirc.org/index-e.htm
Documentation and professional references concerning circumcision.

Invest in Kids Foundation
1 877 583-5437
www.investinkids.ca
Promotes the healthy development of children up to the age of 5 years.

La Leche League
1 866 255-2483
www.lllc.ca
Telephone support by recognized leaders. Books and breast-feeding accessories for sale.

Ligne J'ARRÊTE
1 888 853-6666
www.jarrete.qc.ca
Information and support to individuals who wish to stop smoking (bilingual service).

Lifesaving Society
514 252-3100 / 1 800 265-3093
www.sauvetage.qc.ca/english/contenu-splash.asp?id=86
The Lifesaving Society (Société de sauvetage) is a provincial association dedicated to preventing drowning and water-related injuries through free advice on how to safely install a residential pool. The Society also offers a complete range of first-aid, lifesaving, resuscitation, and pleasure-craft courses.

Magazine Enfants Québec
www.enfantsquebec.com
Summaries of many articles about early childhood (in French only).

Nourri-Source
514 948-9877 or 1 866 948-5160
www.nourri-source.org
Telephone support, breast-feeding support meetings, prenatal information sessions, training and information, rental and sale of breast-feeding accessories (in French only).

Petit monde
www.petitmonde.com
Web site focusing on childhood and families (in French only).

Préma-Québec
1 888 651-4909
www.premaquebec.ca
Quebec association for premature children (in French only).

Regroupement Naissance-Renaissance
514 392-0308
www.naissance-renaissance.qc.ca
Breast-feeding support, post-natal assistance and other services (in French only).

Relevailles de Montréal
514 640-6741
www.relevailles.com/relevailles
Telephone support, courses, meetings, assistance at home, videotape lending and referrals (in French only).

RePère
514 381-3511
www.repere.org
Assistance and support program for fathers. Service in French and English.

Réseau des centres de ressources périnatales
418 603-3762
Network to learn about the perinatal resource centre in your area (in French only).

Réseau québécois d'accompagnantes à la naissance
1 866 NAISSANCE
www.naissance.ca
Information and referral centre to inform the public of services offered by members (doulas). In French only.

Safe Kids
www.sickkids.on.ca/safekidscanada/default.asp
Safe Kids Canada ensures the promotion of effective injury prevention strategies.

Serena
514 273-7531 / 1 866 273-7362
www.serena.ca
Promotes natural family planning methods. Service in French and English.

Service d'information en contraception et sexualité du Québec
Quebec City 418 624-6808
Toll free 1 877 624-6808
www.sicsq.org
In French only.

Today's Parent
www.todaysparent.com
Parenting magazine Web site.

The authors have chosen the organizations and references mentioned in this section because of their relevance to the users of this guide. However, the list is by no means exhaustive and neither the authors of the Institut national de santé publique du Québec are in any way responsible fot the contents of the references indicated.

Photo: iStockphoto

Index

Index

C

D

E

F

G

H

M

N

O

P

Q

R

S

T

U

V

W

X

Y

Conversion table

OUNCES (oz)	GRAMS (g)	POUNDS (lbs)	GRAMS (g)	POUNDS (lbs)	GRAMS (g)
1 oz	28 g	1 lb	454 g	17 lbs	7,711 g
2 oz	57 g	2 lbs	907 g	18 lbs	8,165 g
3 oz	85 g	3 lbs	1,361 g	19 lbs	8,618 g
4 oz	113 g	4 lbs	1,814 g	20 lbs	9,072 g
5 oz	142 g	5 lbs	2,268 g	21 lbs	9,525 g
6 oz	170 g	6 lbs	2,722 g	22 lbs	9,979 g
7 oz	198 g	7 lbs	3,175 g	23 lbs	10,433 g
8 oz	227 g	8 lbs	3,629 g	24 lbs	10,886 g
9 oz	255 g	9 lbs	4,082 g	25 lbs	11,340 g
10 oz	283 g	10 lbs	4,536 g	26 lbs	11,793 g
11 oz	312 g	11 lbs	4,990 g	27 lbs	12,247 g
12 oz	340 g	12 lbs	5,443 g	28 lbs	12,701 g
13 oz	369 g	13 lbs	5,897 g	29 lbs	13,154 g
14 oz	397 g	14 lbs	6,350 g	30 lbs	13,608 g
15 oz	425 g	15 lbs	6,804 g	31 lbs	14,061 g
16 oz	454 g	16 lbs	7,257 g	32 lbs	14,515 g

KEY

1 once (oz) = 28 g
1 livre (lb) = 454 g
1 kilogramme (kg) = 1,000 g
1 kilogramme (kg) = 2.205 lbs

EXEMPLE

6 lb et 10 oz = 3,005 g
or 3.005 kg

LIQUID MEASURES

1 oz = 30 ml
1 tasse = 240 ml
1 teaspoon = 5 ml
1 tablespoon = 15 ml

To convert Fahrenheit degrees into Celsius degrees:

$$°C = \frac{(°F - 32) \times 5}{9}$$

To maintain a tradition of scientific rigour and ensure ease of use, we ask you, the users of *From Tiny Tot to Toddler*, to share with us your comments and your expectations concerning the future edition of the guide.

Please fill out the evaluationform below and send it to:

Institut national de santé publique du Québec
From Tiny Tot to Toddler

945, ave Wolfe, 5e étage
Québec (Québec) G1V 5B3

pascale.turcotte@inspq.qc.ca

Please feel free to share additional comments in a separate letter and return it with this form. Thank you!

Tell us what you think

1. Has this guide been useful to you? In what way?

____

2. Who around baby use the guide and at which **frequency**?
   - ◯ Father: ______________________________
   - ◯ Mother: ______________________________
   - ◯ Grand-parents or other family: ______________________________
   - ◯ Babysitters, friends: ______________________________
   - ◯ Other peoples: ______________________________
3. Which topics are the most helpful to you?

____

4. Which subjects seem most important for you for the future edition of the Guide?

____

5. What do you think of the new sections *Pregnancy* and *Delivery*?

____

6. Are you replying as (please check the appropriate answer):
   - ◯ a parent?
   - ◯ someone who works in the health and social services or daycare services networks?
   - ◯ other?

We would like to thank our advertising partners for their valuable contribution making the distribution of this 2009 edition possible.

Our Advertising Representative:
Catherine Brochu, 418 694-2363
or catherinebrochu@sympatico.ca